LINKED

LABOR

HISTORIES

AMERICAN ENCOUNTERS/GLOBAL INTERACTIONS
A series edited by Gilbert M. Joseph and Emily S. Rosenberg

This series aims to stimulate critical perspectives and fresh interpretive frameworks for scholarship on the history of the imposing global presence of the United States. Its primary concerns include the deployment and contestation of power, the construction and deconstruction of cultural and political borders, the fluid meanings of intercultural encounters, and the complex interplay between the global and the local. American Encounters seeks to strengthen dialogue and collaboration between historians of U.S. international relations and area studies specialists.

The series encourages scholarship based on multiarchival historical research. At the same time, it supports a recognition of the representational character of all stories about the past and promotes critical inquiry into issues of subjectivity and narrative. In the process, American Encounters strives to understand the context in which meanings related to nations, cultures, and political economy are continually produced, challenged, and reshaped.

LINKED

New England, Colombia,

LABOR

and the Making of a

HISTORIES

Global Working Class

Aviva Chomsky

Duke University Press

Durham and London 2008

© 2008 Duke University Press

All rights reserved

Printed in the United States of America on acid-free paper ∞

Designed by Heather Hensley

Typeset in Warnock and Meta Plus by Keystone Typesetting, Inc.

Library of Congress Cataloging-in-Publication Data appear
on the last printed page of this book.

CONTENTS

ACKNOWLEDGMENTS

Because this is a book intertwined with many projects, I would like to thank the people I have worked with on the different aspects of these projects: Jeff Barz-Snell, Greg Bates, Hope Benne, Matt Buchanan, Heather Cahill, Carlos Camelo, Claudia Chuber, Lucy Corchado, Michael Collins, Jim and Maggi Dalton, Remedios Fajardo, Gray Fitzsimons, Ellen Gabin, Alan Hanscom, Dan Kovalik, Garry Leech, Dan Malloy, Eric Martin, Lois Martin, Lisa Matthews, Patrick McDermott, Caroline Nye, Lynn Nadeau, Donna Neff, Deb Pacini, José Julio Pérez, Armando Pérez Araújo, Francisco Ramírez Cuellar, Dave Ramsey, Francisco Ruiz, Ray Rogers, Richard Solly, Steve Striffler, Bill Thomas, Rosario Ubiera-Minaya, Kat Wright, and Cecila Zarate. Special thanks also to Louise Lamphere for sharing the transcripts of her interviews with Colombian textile workers in Central Falls; to the Interlibrary Loan staff at Salem State College, whose patience with my endless requests was inexhaustible; and to Barry Carr and David Watters for their useful comments on the manuscript. The Academic Affairs Office and the Graduate School at Salem State College generously provided funding at several crucial moments.

Nancy Schultz and Dane Morrison offered me the first opportunity to explore the ideas that led, eventually, to this book when they encouraged me to write a chapter on "Salem as a Global City" for their anthology *Salem: Place, Myth and Memory*. The New England American Studies Association, the Latin American Studies Association Labor History Group, the New England Council of Latin American Studies, the Berkshire Conference on the History of Women, and the Greater Boston Latino Studies Consortium provided opportunities for me to present portions of this work as it progressed and receive valuable feedback from colleagues too numerous to mention.

Working with Duke University Press has been a great pleasure. I feel especially privileged to have found in Valerie Millholland a friend and intellectual comrade as well as an editor. Thanks also to Miriam Angress and Mark Mastromarino at Duke, copyeditor Judith Hoover, and indexer Nancy Zibman.

There are a few friends, compañeros, and colleagues whose ideas and support have contributed invaluably to the concept of this book. Jeff Crosby, Guillermo Fernández Ampié, Eileen Findlay, Cindy Forster, Jim Haskell, Aldo Lauria-Santiago, Victor Silverman, and Amanda Warnock helped me to uncover and trust the logic behind "linked labor histories" over the course of many years and many conversations. Un gran abrazo a todos.

ACTWU	Amalgamated Clothing and Textile Workers Union (formed in 1976 through the merger of the Amalgamated Clothing Workers and the TWUA)
AFL	American Federation of Labor
AFL-CIO	American Federation of Labor-Congress of Industrial Organizations
AFSCME	American Federation of State, County and Municipal Employees
AFT	American Federation of Teachers
AIFLD	American Institute for Free Labor Development
AMTAC	American Manufacturing Trade Action Coalition
ANUC	Asociación Nacional de Usuarios Campesinos / National Peasant Association
ATMI	American Textile Manufacturers Institute
ATPA	Andean Trade Preference Act (1991)
ATPDEA	Andean Trade Promotion and Drug Eradication Act (2002)
AUC	Autodefensas Unidas de Colombia/United Self-Defense Forces of Colombia (right-wing paramilitary organization founded in 1997 by ranchers Carlos and Fidel Castaño)
Augura	Association of Banana Growers of Urabá
Banadex	Colombian subsidiary of the United Fruit Company
CAFTA	Central America Free Trade Agreement
CAFTA-DR	Central America-Dominican Republic Free Trade Agreement (the Dominican Republic was added in 2004)
Carbocol	Carbones de Colombia (state-owned coal company)

CBI	Caribbean Basin Initiative
CCI	Cotton Council International
CIO	Congress of Industrial Organizations (founded in 1935, this U.S. federation of industrial unions merged with the AFL in 1955)
CLASC	Confederación Latinoamericana de Sindicatos Cristianos / Latin American Confederation of Christian Unions
CLC	Canadian Labour Congress
CLU	Central Labor Union
Coldesa	Colombian Agricultural Development Company (African palm grower in Urabá)
Colsiba	Coordinadora Latinoamericana de Sindicatos Bananeros / Latin American Coordinating Committee of Banana Workers Unions (a regional confederation of Central and South American unions formed in 1993)
Comandos Populares	"Self-defense" paramilitary organization formed by demobilized EPL members in the early 1990s
COSATU	Congress of South African Trade Unions
CSTC	Confederación Sindical de Trabajadores de Colombia / Trade Union Confederation of Colombian Workers (Colombian union federation affiliated with the Communist Party)
CTAL	Confederación de Trabajadores de América Latina/Confederation of Workers of Latin America
CTC	Confederación de Trabajadores de Colombia (Colombian union federation founded in 1936 and close to the Liberal Party)
CTM	Confederación de Trabajadores de México (official Mexican union federation)
CTV	Confederación de Trabajadores de Venezuela / Confederation of Venezuelan Workers (union federation opposed to many of President Hugo Chávez's radical reforms)
CUT (Brazil)	Central Unica dos Trabalhadores (Brazil's main national union confederation)
CUT (Colombia)	Central Unitaria de Trabajadores de Colombia/Colombian Federation of Workers (Colombia's main national union confederation, founded in 1986)

CWA	Communications Workers of America
DAS	Departamento Administrativo de Seguridad / Administrative Security Department (Colombian state security agency similar to the FBI)
Ecopetrol	Empresa Colombiana de Petróleos / Colombian Petroleum Company (state oil company created in 1948)
ELN	Ejército de Liberación Nacional/National Liberation Army (Colombian guerrilla organization)
EPL	Ejército Popular de Liberación/Popular Liberation Army (Maoist Colombian guerrilla organization founded in 1967)
Esperanza	Esperanza, Paz y Libertad / Hope, Peace and Freedom (political party founded by demobilized EPL members in 1991)
FARC	Fuerzas Armadas Revolucionarias de Colombia / Revolutionary Armed Forces of Colombia (Colombian guerrilla organization founded in 1964 with close ties to the Communist Party)
FAT	Frente Auténtico del Trabajo (Mexican independent union)
FECODE	Federación Colombiana de Educadores / Colombian Federation of Teachers
Fedepetrol	Federation of Petroleum Workers (Colombian union federation)
Fedeta	Federación de Trabajadores de Antioquia (regional Colombian labor federation affiliated with the Communist Party/CSTC)
FLT	Federación Libre de Trabajadores (Puerto Rican labor federation affiliated with the AFL)
Funtraenergética	Federación de Trabajadores Minero-Energéticos / Federation of Mining and Energy Sector Workers
IBEW	International Brotherhood of Electrical Workers
ICEM	International Federation of Chemical, Energy, Mine and General Workers' Unions (an international trade secretariat)
ICFTU	International Confederation of Free Trade Unions
IFPCW	International Federation of Petroleum and Chemical Workers (an international trade secretariat)
ILGWU	International Ladies Garment Workers Union (founded in 1900 and affiliated with the AFL)
ILRF	International Labor Rights Fund

IMF	International Monetary Fund
Intercor	International Colombia Resource Corporation (Exxon subsidiary in Colombia)
ISWA	Independent Sheeting Workers of America
ITS	International Trade Secretariat (international federations of unions in related industries)
IUE-CWA	International Union of Electronic, Electrical, Salaried, Machine and Furniture Workers-Communications Workers of America
IUF	International Union of Food and Beverage Workers (an international trade secretariat)
IWW	Industrial Workers of the World
L.U.	Local Union
NAFTA	North American Free Trade Agreement
NEA	National Education Association
NLRB	National Labor Relations Board
NTWU	National Textile Workers Union (Communist)
NSCC	Naumkeag Steam Cotton Company
ORIT	Organización Regional Interamericana de Trabajadores / Interamerican Regional Organization of Workers (part of the ICFTU)
PC	Partido Comunista / Communist Party
PRD	Partido de la Revolución Democrática (Mexican leftist political party)
PRIDCO	Puerto Rico Industrial Development Company
PTTI	Postal, Telegraph, and Telephone International (an international trade secretariat)
SEIU	Service Employees International Union
SICO	Sindicato Nacional de Trabajadores de la Industria de las Bebidas / National Union of Workers in the Beverage Industry
Sinaltrainal	Sindicato Nacional de Trabajadores de la Industria de Alimentos (leftist union at Colombia's Coca-Cola bottling plants)
Sintagro	Agricultural workers union established in Urabá in 1972
Sintercor	Sindicato de Trabajadores de Intercor / Union of Intercor Workers
Sintrabanano	Banana workers union established in Urabá in 1964

Sintrainagro	Sindicato Nacional de Trabajadores de la Industria Agropecuaria / National Agricultural Workers Union (Sintagro and Sintrabanano united in Sintrainagro in 1988)
Sittelecom	Sindicato de Trabajadores de Telecom
TWUA	Textile Workers Union of America (founded in 1939 and affiliated with the CIO)
UE	United Electrical Workers (a progressive, independent union in the United States)
UFCO	United Fruit Company
UFCW	United Food and Commercial Workers
UMWA	United Mineworkers of America
UNITE	Union of Needletrades, Industrial and Textile Employees (formed in 1995 through a merger of ACTWU and the ILGWU)
UNITE-HERE	Union of Needletrades, Industrial and Textile Employees-Hotel Employees and Restaurant Employees International Union (formed in 2004 through a merger of UNITE and HERE)
UP	Unión Patriótica / Patriotic Union (leftist Colombian political party founded by demobilized FARC members in 1985)
UPIU	United Paperworkers International Union
US/LEAP	U.S. Labor Education in the Americas Project
USAID	U.S. Agency for International Development
USIA	U.S. Information Agency
USO	Unión Sindical Obrera (Colombian oil workers union)
USWA	United Steelworkers of America
UTC	Unión de Trabajadores de Colombia (Colombian union federation founded in 1946 and close to the Catholic church and the Conservative Party)
UTW	United Textile Workers (founded in 1901 and affiliated with the AFL)
WEPZA	World Economic Processing Zones Association
WFTU	World Federation of Trade Unions
WTO	World Trade Organization

INTRODUCTION

They complained in the East,
They are paying too high.
They say that your ore ain't worth digging.
That it's much cheaper down
In the South American towns
Where the miners work almost for nothing.

—BOB DYLAN, "NORTH COUNTRY BLUES" (*THE TIMES THEY ARE A-CHANGING*, 1964)

The depictions we did have of Latin America in movies and novels and occasional news articles had prepared me to recognize President Estrada Cabrera [of Guatemala in the 1920s] right away. He was a familiar figure: the tropical dictator—exotic, brutal and absurd. It was a stereotype that helped us explain the backwardness of countries like Guatemala as the result of unenlightened leadership. . . . What . . . surprised me was finding out that the great dictator had himself been, in large part, a creature of globalization.

—DANIEL WILKINSON, *SILENCE ON THE MOUNTAIN*, 2003

The regions where new commercial crops and export products have developed over the past 40 years are the most violent places in Colombia today.

—CATHERINE LEGRAND, "THE COLOMBIAN CRISIS IN HISTORICAL PERSPECTIVE,"
2003

The Conventional Wisdom

This study grows out of a frustration with conventional wisdom about globalization. During fourteen years teaching Latin American and world history, I have become accustomed to some of the unexamined ideas and preconceptions that students bring into the classroom. One reason for writing this book is to challenge a worldview that is overwhelmingly prevalent among my students, but that not only is fundamentally flawed and historically inaccurate, but also fails utterly to explain the world we live in today.

The prevailing, generally unarticulated understanding goes something like this: For mysterious reasons, inexplicable by history, the world is divided into wealthy and poor regions. Wealthy regions have industrialized and become "developed," and therefore their populations have access to a high degree of security, material comfort, and consumer goods. Poor regions have failed to do so (yet), probably because their populations lack the initiative, and have allowed themselves to be governed by corrupt leaders. Although wealthy regions have tried in the past to help poor regions, this aid is misguided, because there are problems at home in the wealthy regions that should be resolved first and because, given the inherent characteristics of the poor regions, it will be misused anyway.

Globalization, according to this perspective, is something new, something inevitable, and something generally positive for all concerned. Industrialization created the technology that is now bringing regions closer together, which will thus extend the benefits of industrialization to all. The definition provided by the International Monetary Fund is as benign as they come: globalization refers to "the increasing integration of economies around the world, particularly through trade and financial flows." The only problem with globalization, according to the IMF, is that not all regions are equally prepared to benefit from it—poor countries have remained less integrated in the process. The solution, then, is to help poor countries integrate more fully.[1]

When critiques of globalization emerge in the mainstream, they often take a protectionist and/or xenophobic cast. Some may note that because the world lacks the resources to sustain 6 billion people living an "American way of life," it's probably better to concentrate on maintaining that way of life at home, not exporting it. Others may claim that immigration is undermining the U.S. economy, as immigrants gain access to precious jobs and resources. Still others blame cheap imports for undermining U.S. industries.[2]

The debate, then, is framed on one hand by the IMF perspective, which argues that globalization should be celebrated because integration will gradually extend its benefits to everybody, and on the other by what we might call the nativist perspective, that globalization will dissipate or undermine the advantages that the United States has attained so it should be reined in to protect these advantages.

An Alternative Perspective

This book suggests a different perspective on globalization, one that requires that we question some of the basic premises that have informed the debate.[3] First, it assumes that economic integration among regions is in fact the *cause* of the regional inequalities that characterize the world today. Unequal exchange allowed some regions to industrialize while others did not. It focuses, however, on the process of industrialization from the mid-nineteenth century on. From its inception, the factory system has depended on, and re-created, regional inequalities in order to strengthen its control over labor. Producers have used two basic methods to do this: bringing workers from poor regions to the site of production, and moving the site of production to where poorer workers are available. That is, immigration and capital flight.

Employers stand to benefit when there is a surplus of labor. When there are more workers than jobs, employers can simply dispense with workers who protest, strike, or seek better conditions and replace them with others whose desperation for a job will lead them to accept inferior conditions. The very threat of surplus labor serves as a disincentive to workers organizing or protesting. Both immigration and capital flight serve the purpose of creating a surplus of labor, because they enlarge the labor pool beyond regional boundaries. They increase what some analysts currently term "flexibility" for employers. (Critics would argue that "flexibility" is a euphemism for employer power over workers.)

Immigration and capital flight serve the interests of employers in another important way. Both strategies relieve employers of paying for the *reproduction* of their workforce. In theory, through wages that go directly to workers, benefits that go to institutions that provide services (such as medical insurance), and taxes that go to governments that provide social services, industries contribute to the sustenance and education of new generations of workers. In fact, throughout much of history, this has not been the case. By relying on immigration and capital mobility, factories rely on others to support the sustenance and education of their workers. If a worker is born and raised in Mexico, Mexican institutions provide for the worker until he or she begins to work for a U.S. company (whether through immigration or through capital flight). Like the plantation owner who found it cheaper to purchase a new slave of prime working age rather than to encourage reproduction and be encumbered with the costs associated with raising a child, a factory owner can use immigration and capital flight to benefit from a seemingly endless supply of workers, with little or no social investment.

From the beginnings of the factory system, workers and their organizations have been faced with the tension between their need for a job and their desire to improve their working conditions and pay. When employers can point to a ready supply of surplus labor—through immigration or through capital flight—workers' ability to struggle collectively to improve their conditions is severely hampered. When employers can create an environment in which workers *blame* immigrants, or workers in other countries or regions, for being used by employers in this fashion, employers further benefit by deflecting awareness of their own role in the system.

For workers, and unions, the question of how to confront immigration and capital flight (deindustrialization) has been a central one over the entire twentieth century. This book encourages readers to consider the intertwined historical processes—which I call "linked labor histories"—that have led to cycles of deindustrialization and immigration in the United States. If, as I argue, labor history is at the heart of understanding globalization, then the New England textile industry is the place to start examining globalization. The textile industry was one of the first to recruit large numbers of immigrant workers, and it was the first to use its ability to move to cheaper areas as a way to control its workers and to play regions and governments against each other in its search for optimum conditions of production.

From a labor history perspective, globalization has less to do with countries, cultural contact, and speed and more to do with capital's search for cheap labor. A fundamental contradiction between democracy and capitalism emerges from this approach. Democracy demands government by, for, and of the people. Capital seeks governments that will control the people in its interest. Democracy thrives on social equality; capitalism thrives on social inequality.

Can democratic labor movements challenge the ability of capitalism to foster the social inequality it thrives on? Examples abound to suggest that they can. Lack of political democracy, however, can help tip the balance in favor of capital. Where companies can mobilize violence and where workers have few rights, their movements can be crushed. The U.S. government mobilized violence at home, and to a much greater extent it has mobilized violence abroad, to cater to capital's pursuit of profits.

Some analysts have suggested that the power of national governments is diminishing in the age of globalization. The labor history approach suggests a somewhat different perspective. From a labor history perspective, national governments have frequently been tugged between the demands of capital and the challenges of popular movements. When pressed by popular movements, they have been at their most democratic. When pressed by capital, they have gone to extraordinary lengths to repress, undermine, and evade popular aspirations.

The results of this tug of war can often be seen in policies that structure the distribution of resources. Democratic movements tend to pursue economic policies that distribute society's resources downward and broadly. Capital seeks policies that allow resources to be concentrated at the top. When New England governments broadened the democratic rights of labor and began to protect workers' rights, textile companies fled south, where local governments wooed them with promises and gifts (and inequality). In the 1930s and 1940s, the New Deal implemented redistributive policies, which included granting rights and voice to labor. Capital got something in the bargain too: guaranteed markets in military production and an aggressive foreign policy that set the stage for a massive transfer of investments abroad by crushing workers' movements and democracy itself.

As the twentieth century drew to an end, former industrial cities in the United States were turning themselves into enterprise zones, mimicking the third world's free trade zones, which in turn replicated the way southern communities marketed themselves to northern firms in the early part of the century. Connecticut advertises its "business-friendly environment," including high worker productivity ("at an all-time high, with output per worker more than 33% above the national average"), and low corporate taxes. "We've developed creative incentives to Connecticut businesses including financial assistance, tax abatements and credits, labor training and flexible utility rates," the state's Department of Economic and Community Development brags.[4]

The Structure of the Book

This study approaches the large themes in global labor history through a detailed examination of several specific, interrelated cases. The first part of the book (four chapters) focuses on the New England textile industry and its workers; the second part (three chapters) looks at labor and violence in Colombia. Workers in New England's textile industry were among the first to face the challenges of globalization that confronted almost all U.S. workers and unions in the late twentieth century, as textile factories began seeking more favorable investment conditions in the U.S. South starting in the late nineteenth century. Colombia at the turn of the twenty-first century has been called the cutting edge of neoliberalism and privatization, as much of Latin America, led by Colombia's neighbor Venezuela, has shifted to the left. U.S. foreign aid and investment are flooding Colombia, and workers and unions struggle against the combined threats of disinvestment, job loss, and paramilitary terror. In both cases, control of labor forged a favorable climate that made these regions magnets for investment, and workers struggled to preserve their jobs while imagining that another world was possible.

The two parts of the book are connected not only conceptually, but in immediate terms, as Colombian workers and products produced by Colombian workers flow into New England, and as the products of the U.S. defense industry (many produced by what used to be textile factories) flow into Colombia. The AFL-CIO's long history in Colombia also provides a link, as its involvement there has shifted from cold war policies to grappling with new forms of cross-border solidarity in the 1990s. These concrete connections are developed in each of the chapters.

The book approaches the topic of global labor history by exploring three main conceptual areas through its case studies in New England and Colombia: migration, labor-management collaboration, and the mobility of capital. Each of these themes is woven into each of the chapters. Each chapter suggests a different way that the issue can be approached historically. Together, they offer an intricate, interwoven tapestry of two regions, their industries, and their workers and the myriad links between them over the long twentieth century, as well as a new way to conceptualize globalization as a long-term process.

Themes

The first major theme is migration. Chapter 1 looks at radical immigrant workers in the early twentieth century in the Draper loom factory. Draper was a Massachusetts company that also exported looms to Latin America. The company was active in anti-immigrant politics at the same time that it employed immigrant workers, and both company and workers tried to appropriate the concept of "Americanism." The global use of Draper looms contributed to the restructuring of the textile industry, and to late twentieth-century Colombian immigration to old New England textile centers. Chapter 2, on the Naumkeag Steam Cotton Company, looks at another group of early twentieth-century immigrants, and how more recent immigrant radicalism challenged older immigrant conservatism in their union. Chapter 3 addresses the relationship of outsourcing and the global assembly line to immigration, and chapter 4 looks at Latin American migration to old New England textile towns. Chapters 5, 6, and 7 shift to Colombia, looking at how foreign investment and U.S. foreign policy contribute to domestic conditions spurring out-migration. Chapter 5 looks at contemporary domestic migration and labor patterns in Colombia in the context of U.S. investment in the Urabá banana zone. Chapter 6 discusses how the AFL-CIO has dealt with the issue of immigrant workers over its history. Chapters 5 and 7 depict displacement and violence associated with foreign investment as a spur to out-migration.

The second theme is labor-management collaboration. Chapters 1, 2, and 3 look at how New England factory owners used the threat of plant closure to try to domesticate their labor force starting in the late nineteenth century, the development of a strategy of labor-management collaboration on the part of some U.S. unions, and how this related to concepts of patriotism and Americanism. Chapter 6, on the AFL-CIO, looks at how the organization's business unionism related to its international policies in the post–World War II period, focusing on the activities of the American Institute for Free Labor Development (AIFLD) in Colombia. Chapter 5 relates how extraordinary violence combined with threats of disinvestment domesticated a radical union in Colombia's banana zone. Chapter 7 examines how unions in Colombia's foreign-owned coal mines have negotiated paramilitary violence and their rather privileged position in the country's labor force and how U.S. unions have dealt with the closure of U.S. mines that have moved to Colombia.

The third theme is global economic restructuring. In New England, this has meant deindustrialization; in Colombia, it has meant privatization and neoliberalism. Chapters 1, 2, and 3 locate the phenomenon in New England in the early twentieth century rather than the end of the century, where it has traditionally been imagined to occur. These chapters also look at how unions and workers have struggled with this issue and show that despite management threats, labor militancy alone rarely led to plant closure. In the case of New England's textile industry, federal immigration restrictions in the 1920s played a key role in limiting access to cheap labor, but, in part because of outsourcing, textile unions remained weak. These chapters also examine how the textile factories under study ended up shifting into defense production and the role of defense production in the new global economy. Chapter 4 looks at how recent immigration into postindustrial communities is structurally related to global shifts in production, how workers fit into the new economies, and how U.S. unions are slowly coming to grapple with the new challenges. Chapters 5 and 7 look at two Colombian export industries, bananas and coal, that have grown dramatically under conditions that one analyst termed "the cutting edge of neo-liberalism in Latin America," and how workers and communities have continued to struggle for their rights under the most adverse conditions.[5] Chapter 6 discusses how the AFL-CIO created its niche in the postwar economic order, how its actions to preserve that order ended up contributing to transformation rather than preservation, and how it is coming to terms with the new forms of corporate globalization that have emerged.

Case Studies: Part I

Part I of this book consists of four chapters that place New England's labor history in global context. The first focuses on the Draper Loom Company (after 1916, Draper Loom Corporation) of Hopedale, Massachusetts. Draper designed automatic looms that transformed the global textile industry in the twentieth century. Rather than refurbish antiquated New England mills, many investors took advantage of the new technology to shift operations to the U.S. South. Starting in 1917, Draper looms also supplied textile factories throughout Latin America. Draper's Hopedale workers were mostly immigrant Italians, many of whom joined the Industrial Workers of the World (IWW) in the second decade of the twentieth century. Although benefiting from immigrant labor, Draper's owners were also active in anti-immigrant politics, promoting organizations like the Pioneer Fund, the sponsor of racist research throughout the twentieth century. Draper's looms outlived the company and the industry they helped to build and destroy, and in the 1960s some of the last remaining New England textile mills began recruiting Colombian workers trained on Draper looms in Medellín to staff their factories, creating Colombian enclaves in Central Falls, Rhode Island, and Lowell, Massachusetts.

The second chapter examines the Naumkeag Steam Cotton Company of Salem, Massachusetts, focusing especially on the issue of labor-management collaboration. Naumkeag manufactured Pequot brand sheets from the mid-nineteenth to the mid-twentieth century. In the 1920s, the mill became a national paragon of labor-management collaboration as the United Textile Workers (UTW) local convinced workers to participate in an innovative joint research plan to raise productivity. The union believed that this approach would keep the mill in Salem while so many New England factories were closing, but by 1933 the mill's workers rebelled and began a wildcat strike against the research plan. With help from the communist National Textile Workers Union (NTWU), immigrant French Canadian and Polish workers won their demands after an eleven-week strike, and the mill stayed in Salem. In the early 1950s, however, it followed so many others and moved to Spartanburg County, South Carolina. After passing through several owners, the assets of the bankrupt mill were turned over to the GE Capital Corporation in 2001.

The third chapter takes a long historical view of the issue of speculation, outsourcing, and deindustrialization, following the textile industry from New England to the U.S. South, to Puerto Rico, Japan, Mexico, Central America and the Caribbean, and Colombia. It follows the trail of the Textron company from its New England roots into global reach over the course of the twentieth century. It focuses in particular on U.S. federal and local government policies aimed at creating business-friendly environments, company investments strategies and the factors guiding them, the relationship of the textile industry with the military and the system of "military Keynesianism" that developed after World War II, the growth of export-processing zones, how the mobility of capital has affected workers, and what unions have tried to do about it. The chapter ends by looking at Colombia's textile industry and the various free trade agreements that have encouraged U.S. manufacturers to invest and outsource there.

Chapter 4 examines the question first raised by the sociologist Michael Piore in the 1970s of the apparent paradox that even as working conditions have improved for some workers in industrialized countries, industrialization seems to continue to create low-wage employment and to seek immigrant workers to fill substandard jobs. "How is it," Piore asks, "that industrial economies seem not only able to absorb, but in fact are actively seeking out uneducated, illiterate workers from the very types of societies to which they are, in the conventional view of what industrialization is all about, generally contrasted?"[6] In the post-1970 period, as deindustrialization took hold in New England, even larger numbers of immigrants flowed into the region to fill low-paid jobs in the service sector.

Throughout New England, old textile towns have become home to a new generation of Latino immigrants as deindustrialization deepened. Chapter 4 looks at Central Falls, Rhode Island, and Lowell, Massachusetts, two former textile centers that began to import Colombian workers just as their last textile factories were struggling to survive. In some cases, like the Colombian textile workers, migrant streams began with workers directly recruited in their homelands. In others, manufacturers transferred or sought workers from larger immigrant centers such as New York. Most ended up, however, in the vast, unregulated lower end of the service economy, cleaning houses, offices, hospitals, and yards, caring for elders, or washing dishes. They worked to maintain the lifestyles of the wealthy and of stressed two-income families in what was formerly the middle class in a society and economy that were shifting from a globe-shape to an hourglass as the industry that had turned an earlier generation of working-class people into a middle class lurched away in search of a more exploitable proletariat.

Case Studies: Part II

If New England's textile industry and its workers were among the first to confront the challenges of globalization, Colombia's workers today are seen by many as being at the forefront of the struggle to rein in the race to the bottom. As by far the largest recipient of U.S. military aid in the hemisphere, Colombia is the centerpiece of current U.S. strategies for a neoliberal model of labor control. Colombia's organized working class has also been on the front lines of resistance to this strategy, and thousands of union members and organizers have been killed since the 1980s.

Chapter 5 looks at a part of Colombia where violence against organized labor has been particularly acute, the Urabá banana zone in the north. When the Boston-founded United Fruit Company (UFCO) entered the Urabá zone in the early 1960s, it recapitulated systems and patterns that it had developed almost a century earlier in its operations in Central America and in Santa Marta, Colombia, in lightly populated areas, isolated from the centers of government and power, with little state presence. As in its earlier operations, it was able to ally with sectors of the local and national elite and convince the state to offer it economic, fiscal, police, and military support for its project. The United Fruit Company had invented its own race to the bottom long before late twentieth-century activists gave it a name: from the very beginning of the century it hedged its bets and spread its risks by maintaining production in numerous countries at once and playing national governments off against each other to achieve optimal conditions, always with the threat of pulling out if its wishes were not granted.

Labor unions in Urabá were weak until the 1980s, when a strong guerrilla presence in the region contributed to the growth of leftist unions. In the 1990s, paramilitary forces took over the region and decimated the left, leaving a union open to good relations with management in the project of maintaining the conditions to keep the industry strong. International union federations have responded in complex and sometimes contradictory ways to the divisions between left and right in Colombia's union movement.

Chapter 6 takes up the thorny question of U.S. union involvement in foreign policy and in creating and maintaining optimum conditions for U.S. corporations operating abroad, focusing on the AFL-CIO's involvement in Colombia. In the 1960s, Colombia became a laboratory for U.S. counter-insurgency doctrine. The AFL-CIO collaborated with the U.S. government to undermine the left in the trade union movement there, as elsewhere in the continent and the world. By the 1990s, Colombia had become the most dangerous country in the world for unionists, and the AFL-CIO was revamping both its programs and its image, replacing the discredited AIFLD with the new Solidarity Center. The Colombia program was one of the centerpieces of the Solidarity Center, bringing unionists whose lives were under threat to the United States for nine months of refuge, training, and activism. While some Colombians have argued that the Solidarity Center programs have continued to work against the left in Colombia, others believe that it represented a clear break from the AFL-CIO's conciliatory past.

The final chapter looks at the coal mining industry, another example of U.S. industry and labor involvement in Colombia. If the globalization of the textile industry is more visible, the globalization of the energy industry is no less crucial. In the 1980s two U.S. coal mining companies, Drummond and Exxon, began to close their U.S. operations to move to Colombia, where they opened two of the largest open-pit coal mines in the world. In the

1990s, the World Bank and International Monetary Fund (IMF) began to impose a neoliberal agenda on Colombia, mandating the privatization of the mining sector, lower taxes, and deregulation. Paramilitary forces also stepped up their activity in the mining zone. This chapter looks at how the different social actors, especially labor unions in both countries, have been affected by and been actors in this process. It also looks at how the consumers of coal, in particular power plants and their customers along the East Coast of the United States and Canada, have become involved.

My conclusion locates globalization as a phenomenon of the entire twentieth century, with labor history as its center. It looks at parallels, continuities, and connections between the labor history of the New England textile industry, the first example of deindustrialization and the race to the bottom, and that of Colombia, the site of the most vicious repression of organized labor in the late twentieth century. Attempts by capital to control labor, and attempts by labor to resist that control, characterize much of this linked labor history. There are parallels in workers' struggles and unions' attempts to grapple with runaway industries in different times and places, and in capital's use of threats of disinvestment, manipulation of racial and ethnic divisions, and promotion of collaborationist unions to control workers. There are continuities in capital's search for optimal investment conditions in a shifting global environment. There are connections created by the products, from looms to fabrics to bananas to coal, that travel across borders and create links among people, and organizations from the IWW and the Communist Party in the early twentieth century to the unions and other cross-border solidarity movements that have tried to construct their own globalization from below as the century ended.

PART I *New England*

CHAPTER 1

THE DRAPER COMPANY
From Hopedale to Medellín and Back

Let me tell you what has happened in Fall River; it was told to me by one of the spinners there. "Twenty-five years ago," this man said, "we had 2,000 men in our union, spinners, and there has never been a time since then that a spinner working in that city did not belong to our union," and he felt proud of his union. He was asked "how many power mules have you here now?" and he answered "About 350." Now, this is what has happened: In these twenty-five years the number of mules had decreased from 2,000 to 350. What has become of them? They have been carried to the scrap heap, and their places have been taken by the spinning frame, and the father is out on the street looking for a job at whatever he can get, and the child is in the mill working at spinning. I want to tell you about the loom, the Draper loom. No one would have been more surprised at this than the textile worker of twenty five years ago. To-day in the town of Waterville a cotton weaver is running forty looms. Do you know what that means? Well, that means ten times as many looms as the weaver in India ran ten or twelve years ago. That means four times the number of looms that the most expert cotton weaver ran in the city of Fall River ten years ago, and is nearly four times as many as they are running there to-day, but that loom has not come there as yet. . . . I doubt very much if there is cotton enough grown in the world to supply the production which is made possible through the introduction of this loom.

—THOMAS POWERS, PROVIDENCE, RHODE ISLAND, AT THE FOUNDING CONVENTION OF THE IWW IN CHICAGO, JULY 7, 1905

The troops, the older people that were in the mill, came to me and said, "Hey, I don't want any more students. I'm through teaching." So I got 'em together. I sat 'em down in the back room and said, "How come? What's the matter?" They're thoroughly disgusted that people don't want to learn. They're wasting their time; and they're wasting my money; and they don't want to have any part of it. O.K. Then comes the time when my first Colombian came in here.

Oh, Christ, it must have been 1970. Can't remember, somewhere in there. He was legal. His name was Mario. I'll never forget the guy as long as I live. He drove up in a car, he spoke English, he asked me if I needed a Draper loom fixer. And I said, "Buddy, I'll give you a kiss if you know how to fix a Draper loom." He says, "Let me show you." He . . . puts on a set of coveralls, takes his tool box out, walks out in the mill, and shows me that this man knows what he's doing. I said, "Jesus Christ, you've got a job." He said, "Would you like some more Colombian people?" I said, "I sure as hell would."

—TED LARTER, PRESIDENT OF WANNALANCIT TEXTILE COMPANY, LOWELL, MASSACHUSETTS, 1979, QUOTED IN ELEANOR E. GLAESSEL-BROWN, "A TIME OF TRANSITION: COLOMBIAN TEXTILE WORKERS IN LOWELL IN THE 1970S"

I f Mario was an expert at fixing Draper looms, he came by this knowledge, and brought it to Lowell, as part of a long historical process that intertwines the labor and industrial histories of New England and Latin America. The capital that initiated New England's industry had its origins in the slave trade between Africa and Latin America, and its new pattern of industrial investment quickly spread beyond New England. The Hopedale, Massachusetts, Draper Loom Corporation—the largest in the world—supplied looms to Latin America's burgeoning textile industry in the early twentieth century. New England capitalists invested in mills in the U.S. South and in Latin America; they exported their products to Latin America, they built mill equipment to sell there, and, when they closed their New England mills, they shipped the machines, obsolete or not, to these locales. The Colombian textile workers who migrated to New England in the 1970s were the heirs to decades of the intermeshing of capital, machinery, education, ideology, and labor management techniques that shaped a global textile industry. And if unions in the United States at the end of the twentieth century were facing the so-called race to the bottom as industries challenged regions and countries to offer them the most lucrative deals and the lowest wages, they were only the latest players in a drama that textile workers and unions have been facing for many decades.[1]

Many of the paradoxes inherent in the process of industrialization, deindustrialization, and the waves of immigration that have accompanied both processes can be seen played out in the history of the Draper Corporation, producers of textile machinery for the global textile industry. Owned by a family with many members prominent in Massachusetts politics, Draper was built over the remnants of the nineteenth-century utopian community of Hopedale. The mills employed immigrant workers—including Italian anarchist Nicola Sacco—and when the IWW organized a bitter four-month strike at the Hopedale plant in 1913, the Drapers were not loathe to use scabs and violence to break it. The Drapers were major players in the creation of the southern U.S. textile industry and Latin America's textile industry. Like Salem's Pequot Mills, Draper opened a plant in, and eventually moved to, one of the largest textile-producing regions in the South, Spartanburg, South Carolina. Draper fortunes supported anti-immigrant legislation in the 1920s and right-wing racist and eugenicist causes throughout the century, even as the Draper plant brought immigrants to the United States. The looms that the Drapers sent to Latin America were a key factor in bringing Latin American workers to New England in the 1960s and 1970s.

The drive to lower costs is an inherent aspect of the capitalist system of production, and technological development and automation are inherent aspects of industrialization. Few companies, however, embody the system as overtly and as enthusiastically as Draper.[2] The power loom that the company perfected in the early 1900s allowed textile companies to dramatically increase production while decreasing the hours of work. Draper's advertising relentlessly pursued this theme: to compete successfully, textile factories must reduce the cost of labor, and Draper's Northrop loom was the way to do it.

Over the course of the early twentieth century, as state and federal legislation began to restrict hours of work and establish minimum wages, Draper explicitly offered companies a way to avoid suffering any decrease in profits. "High cost labor with shorter working hours makes a large increase in manufacturing costs," a company newsletter warned in 1919. "Should the mills adopt a 48 hour week, this reduction in hours will largely increase the overhead expense as the product per loom, or other textile machine, per hour will be the same whether the working hours are more or less per week. THE NORTHROP LOOM under such conditions **has a greater advantage than ever before**."[3] "With the trend towards less hours per annum the advantages of automatic machinery in general and Northrop Looms in particular need no argument. The capacity of the Northrop Loom to be operated during the noon hour and a corresponding time night or morning without any weavers at all is a great advantage both to stockholders in the mills and to the weavers. Looms under such conditions increase the amount of cloth 15 to 25 per cent per loom compared with common looms on the same goods running mill hours only," the Draper newsletter enthused a year later. Best of all, "Looms under such conditions VIOLATE NO LABOR LAWS. The shorter the working day the greater the proportional advantage of the Northrop Loom in product both per loom and per weaver."[4]

The Drapers and Their Corporation: Profits and Perfection

The capitalists who invested in New England's early industries brought to their operations a curious ideological heritage. They were the elites in a society that was founded on principles of racial inequality, yet they considered themselves the purveyors of an unprecedented egalitarianism. They trembled at the social ills they saw in England's nascent industries, yet believed that they could avoid those ills in their own industrial experiments. Their capital had its origins in international commerce and in the slave economy, yet they fought for protective tariffs and against slavery (sometimes). They prided themselves on their American independence, yet clung to their Anglo-Saxon identity. They invested their money to make a profit, yet were fervently committed to using their wealth for the betterment of society. They were at once radical, imagining themselves capable of creating an entirely new world, and conservative, bent on maintaining their privilege and containing movements from below that threatened the social order.

Robert Dalzell's study of the Boston Associates who founded the Waltham-Lowell mill system illuminates many of these paradoxes and provides a useful counterpoint for analyzing the beliefs and actions of the Draper family and the goals of their company. Dalzell argues that for Francis Lowell, Nathan Appleton, and other members of the Boston elite, investing in textiles was a means to an end that went beyond simple profit. They held a particular vision of the role of elites in society based on civic engagement, public service, and philanthropy. "Money alone was never enough; it had to be paired with an appropriate measure of public service."[5] Investment in textile production was a way of amassing the resources and security that would allow these men to fulfill their proper social functions in government and to create and sustain private institutions like colleges and hospitals that would both maintain the class structure and uplift the overall level of society.

The dual goals of class privilege and general uplift also underlay the Associates' decision to establish their mills in rural areas and seek a workforce of young women from "respectable" farming families whose moral character would be overseen by the boarding house system. The industrial revolution in England had brought about "dirty towns, corrupt and debased lower classes, beggars and thieves."[6] Not only was this an undesirable social order, but without the instruments of repression that the English upper classes could rely on, it was downright threatening to American elites. The Boston Associates brought a strong dose of utopian engineering to their industrial experiments.

Other New England utopians engaged in their own forms of social engineering in the nineteenth century, establishing intentional communities such as Brook Farm (founded in 1841 in West Roxbury) and Fruitlands (founded in 1843 in Harvard) in which intellectuals from Nathaniel Hawthorne to Ralph Waldo Emerson to Bronson Alcott (father of Louisa May) participated. Among these was Hope Dale, established in Milford, Massachusetts, by the minister Adin Ballou in 1841 to embody his philosophy of Practical Christianity, incorporating "Christian socialism, abolitionism, temperance, nonviolence, and racial and sexual equality."[7] One of the founding members was Ebenezer Draper, the son of Ira Draper, who had invented and patented the rotary temple, an early predecessor of the automatic loom. Unlike some of the other utopian communities, Hope Dale intended to produce for profit at the same time it sought moral perfection, by manufacturing and selling textile machinery. Members purchased stock in the enterprise, combining collective management with individual profit.[8]

In 1856 Ebenezer's brother George Draper joined the community, and the two carried out what historians have referred to as a "coup," violating the voluntary bylaws by withdrawing all of their stock—which amounted to three quarters of the total shares—thus essentially destroying the community. "The Drapers took . . . the land, mill, streets, shops, houses, and other buildings; in 1873 they even took possession of the cemetery."[9]

George and his sons William, who became president after his father's death in 1887, Eben Sumner, who took over from William and ran the company until he died in 1914, and George Albert, who took over until his own death in 1923, had little interest in Practical Christianity. Nevertheless, they inherited their own form of utopian thinking, which shaped the way they ran and invested in their business and what was, essentially, their town, Hopedale.[10] In George Albert's son Wickliffe Draper, born in 1891, utopianism emerged as obsession with eugenics.

Like the Boston Associates, the Drapers were committed to a paternalistic view of social betterment and urban uplift, and they committed their company's resources to their town. Hopedale was a company town, "not a tenement-ridden slum associated with many of the era's factories and sweatshops but a rural textile community totally under the paternalistic control of the Draper company, which offered job security, medical aid, and low rent in company houses for its employees in an effort to promote unity of interest between labor and capital. . . . To preserve the town's rural character, the Draper Company prohibited fences, street signs, and mailboxes and created an extensive system of parks and gardens" and even a pond.[11] The design of their worker duplexes received awards at international expositions from St. Louis to Paris to Milan.[12]

Wickliffe Draper inherited both his father's fortune and his "ardent desire . . . to use his wealth for some loftier purpose." Like the Boston Associates, he believed that his wealth should be used to have a "larger impact on the well-being of the society."[13] He found his cause in eugenics, the pseudoscience of the era dedicated to proving the superiority of the white race and enforcing policies toward the Nordicization of the U.S. population, including the repatriation of blacks to Africa, selective sterilization, and immigration restrictions.

Draper was not unique in his infatuation with racial thought and racial betterment. New England's cultural and intellectual elite and its institutions were permeated with these ideas in the early twentieth century. Harvard University, so generously funded by the Boston Associates in earlier years, and Wickliffe Draper's alma mater, was one of the centers of racist scholarship.[14] Draper went beyond many of his contemporaries, however, in choosing racist research specifically as the beneficiary of his philanthropic largesse and in continuing to be faithful to his passion until his death in 1972, long after it had been marginalized from the academic mainstream.

His interest in eugenics put Draper in close contact with men like Harry H. Laughlin and Charles Davenport of the Eugenics Record Office, which conducted the research that helped convince Congress to pass the 1924 immigration restrictions drastically limiting immigration from southern and eastern Europe. Draper served as vice president of the Boston-based Immigration Restriction League, whose best known member was the racist researcher Madison Grant, an important influence on Adolf Hitler in later years.

Draper's financial backing of eugenics began in the mid-1920s with several small grants to Davenport and the Eugenics Research Association. In the 1930s he began to fund Earnest Sevier Cox, who was working assiduously to convince Congress to legislate the repatriation of blacks to Africa. In 1937 Draper founded the Pioneer Fund, appointing his old colleague Harry Laughlin president, as a conduit for distributing his money to racist causes. While the fund was nominally governed by a board of directors, Draper "clearly exercised final authority on whether to fund a proposal because the money came out of his private coffers, and Pioneer had no other resources."[15]

Over the course of the twentieth century Pioneer became a key source of research to prove racial inequality, aimed at public policy to maintain racial segregation, and Draper's money continued to be its bastion. Draper contributed to the movement against civil rights and racial integration in the 1950s and 1960s and kept alive the flames of neo-Nazism. According to his biographer, Draper's fortune was "the most important single financial resource for the struggle to maintain American apartheid." After Draper's death, Pioneer continued the tradition that his private donations had established during his lifetime, subsidizing research, policy initiatives, and public relations campaigns by proponents of white racial superiority the likes of Wilmot Robertson (*The Dispossessed Majority*), William Shockley, and Arthur Jensen. After the immigration reform of 1965, Pioneer revived Draper's earlier interest in decrying the malevolent influence of immigrants considered nonwhite on the country's racial well-being. The Federation for American Immigration Reform and the American Immigration Control Foundation, both of which fought to enhance the whiteness of the United States by restricting the immigration and citizenship of nonwhites, were major Pioneer recipients.[16]

The tradition of public engagement and philanthropy among U.S. industrial magnates could take different forms. Dalzell's most generous account suggests that a genuine commitment to social uplift, combined with an unquestioned sense of noblesse oblige and commitment to maintaining a class society, underlay the Boston Associates' philanthropy. Wickliffe Draper's passionate commitment to eugenics and racial inequality could be interpreted as mere eccentricity, as could the textile magnate Roger Milliken's devotion of time and resources to economic nationalism in the 1980s, in an era in which most textile producers were discovering the profitable potential of free trade (see chapter 3). Eccentric though they may have been personally, their ideas and the movements they funded were far from marginal to the development of the U.S. economy and the place of workers in it.

At first glance, it would appear that anti-immigrant agitation would run counter to the interests of an industry that depended so heavily on immigrant labor. In fact, the Draper loom company was a major employer of the very southern and eastern European workers whose suitability as citizens was being challenged by institutions close to the Draper family and members of the family themselves. But an examination of the company's relationship with its mostly Italian employees, using the most bitter strike in Draper's history in 1913 as a case study, reveals how and why anti-immigrant attitudes and policies were in fact quite congruent with the use of immigrant workers. Anti-immigrant racism underlay a social order that naturalized and justified exploitive working conditions and violent repression of worker activism.

Anti-immigrant racism, like economic nationalism, also created a space for employers to appeal to the mainstream union movement, epitomized in the early years of the century by the American Federation of Labor (AFL), based on a shared conception of "Americanism." Americanism divided native from immigrant workers, but it also provided a route for immigrant workers to "assimilate" by distancing themselves from their radical pasts. Racism and the exclusion of blacks from the workforce helped the textile industry to avoid and crush unions for many generations in the U.S. South.[17] Milliken's program of economic nationalism created new opportunities for labor-management collaboration in the 1980s, as unions struggled to redefine international solidarity in the context of the anti–corporate globalization movement. In both cases, a form of exclusivist, white-identified nationalism encouraged white workers to join their employers in promoting an economic system that granted certain privileges to the white working class.

Radical Immigrants in Hopedale and Milford

Like New England's textile mills, Draper employed primarily immigrant workers in the early twentieth century. Unlike the textile mills, however, Draper's workforce was overwhelmingly male: out of 2,200 workers in 1913, the company stated that only eight to ten were women.[18] Most of the workers lived not in the company's award-winning duplexes in the bucolic company town of Hopedale but in tenements in neighboring Milford. While Draper was the largest employer in the area, Milford was also home to a number of other industries, including granite cutting, foundries, and shoe factories.

Between the 1880s and the second decade of the twentieth century, Milford, like many U.S. industrial cities, experienced a large influx of immigration from southern and eastern Europe. William Draper was ambassador to Italy from 1898 to 1902, and perhaps did some recruiting for the factory while he was there.[19] In a pattern of chain migration, villages and regions were re-created in the United States as friends, kin, and acquaintances followed each other to the same location. Milford's "little Italy" was "a veritable 'Little Foggia,'" as hundreds of immigrants from a few neighboring towns in the Italian province of Foggia settled there.[20] One immigrant who arrived in 1916 explained, "Foggiani had been emigrating to Milford for a long time. Most left for economic reasons. It was a poor province with a history of strikes and peasant disturbances."[21]

The first mass by an Italian priest was held in Milford in 1894, and in 1905 the bishop of Springfield sent Reverend Rocco Petrarca to minister to Milford's Italian population. One of his first goals was to establish a new church, what was known as a "national parish" specifically for the Italian workers, which was accomplished with the founding of the Sacred Heart Parish later that year.[22] One elderly Italian in Milford recalled that Sacred Heart "was the Italian Catholic church in town. There was another Catholic church attended by the Irish and a Congregational church for the Yankees. They didn't like the Italians—the Irish or the Yankees."[23]

When Ferdinando (later Nicola) Sacco left Italy in 1908 at age 17, he sailed with his brother from Naples to Boston. They continued directly on to Milford, where they stayed with a friend of their father's who had settled there, "amid a colony of Foggian immigrants, including a barber, a baker and an undertaker, in addition to shoe workers, laborers, and mill hands."[24] He first found work as a water boy working for a Draper contractor, then in the Draper foundry itself. Sacco left Draper after a year to train in a small shoe factory in Milford, and after a brief hiatus when he worked in a shoe factory in Webster, he returned to Milford to the Milford Shoe Company, where he worked from 1910 to 1917.[25]

As in many Italian and other immigrant communities, radical newspapers, ideas, and organizations formed a strong component of working-class life in Milford. Two radical Italian newspapers, *Il Proletario*, edited by the IWW activist Arturo Giovannitti, and *Cronaca Sovversiva*, edited in Lynn, Massachusetts, by the anarchist Luigi Galleani, circulated in the community. Many workers joined or attended events sponsored by the anarchist Circolo di Studi Sociali or the Milford Socialist Club, founded by the Rhode Island Socialist Party activist Joseph M. Coldwell.[26] A Milford resident recalled, "The radicals—mostly socialists and IWWs—had a club on East Main street, directly across from our house. All the radicals met there and called themselves socialists."[27] A member of an anarchist group in nearby Franklin, Massachusetts, explained, "We went to Milford quite often—it is not far from Franklin—for picnics and plays."[28]

The 1912 textile strike in Lawrence, Massachusetts, aroused significant interest in Milford's immigrant community. The Milford socialists enthusiastically supported Lawrence's Bread and Roses strikers (Coldwell later said that his first visit to Hopedale was to raise funds for the Lawrence strikers), and the IWW organizers Joseph Ettor and Arturo Giovannitti spoke twice at mass meetings in the Milford Town Hall.[29] The "fiery Joe Ettor, one of the Wobblies' most gifted speakers," later played an important role in the Hopedale strike.[30]

At the Hopedale meetings, "Coldwell didn't attempt to veil his references to the Hopedale plant, and these brought forth cheers that showed there is a strong undercurrent of feeling, particularly among the Italians employed there, against the practices that have reduced wages to a minimum in the big works."[31] In particular, the piecework system at the plant made it extremely difficult for workers to earn even a minimal subsistence wage. A three-week strike at Milford's Archer Rubber Company, where fifty to sixty workers were IWW members, in February 1913 further set the stage for Draper's workers.[32]

On March 20, 1913, three hundred Draper workers attended an IWW meeting—conducted in Italian—in Milford's Oliveri Hall after being refused a permit by the board of selectmen to use the town hall or an outdoor square. As enthusiasm for a strike built, another IWW meeting on March 23 also attracted three hundred, and on March 28 a crowd of five hundred at the Charles River Hall listened to speeches in English, Italian, and Armenian, and "cheered the utterances lustily, the same being plentifully punctuated with references to the Draper Co. and the Hopedale plant, where most of the men are employed." According to the newspaper, some five hundred

Figure 1. Draper strikers demonstrate in front of the company's main office on Hopedale Street in 1913. Courtesy of the American Textile History Museum, Lowell, Massachusetts.

Draper employees were dues-paying ıww members, and many others were sympathizers. "Scattered through the crowd were many English-speaking men, and a small sprinkling of other races, besides the Italians, who, of course, predominated."[33]

Three days later, on Monday, March 31, workers at another mass meeting at the Charles River Hall voted to strike. Organizers quickly printed up leaflets in Italian and English which were distributed through the town, and the following day some one thousand workers struck, with hundreds rallying around the factory gates to urge workers to stay out.[34]

Ethnic and Class Identities

Anita Cardillo Danker, author of the lone published study of the strike, emphasizes the ethnic division in the workforce, "with the immigrants walking and the natives, for the most part, remaining loyal to the company." The company insisted that "it was only the immigrant workers, easily excitable and unfamiliar with the give and take of the system, who deserted the company." Danker partially agreed: "As outsiders largely unaware of the utopian tradition and the Draper history of benevolent paternalism, [immigrants] were quicker to ignite and to erupt into defiant protest at perceived injustices than were the long-established, more loyal, native operatives."[35] The company's "benevolent paternalism," however, was directed toward its more established, and better paid, English-speaking employees.

The strike immediately attracted attention from activists and organizers outside Milford. The IWW organizer John Morris was a "forceful orator" at the March 28 meeting, describing the 1909 strike of Slavic workers against the Pressed Steel Car Company in McKees Rocks, Pennsylvania. On the first day of the strike Morris (this time identified as Frank Morris—the same person?) again spoke, along with Italian and Armenian speakers, this time "deploring the fact that not more of the English-speaking employees were with them."[36] Morris, along with an Italian organizer from Boston, Flavio Albizzati, continued to address the crowds and coordinate actions during the first days of the strike.[37] Joseph Coldwell also returned to Milford (from Worcester) in the first days of the strike and took a leading role. On April 2, he addressed a meeting of Armenian workers at the Armenian Club. The strike committee, formed at a mass meeting of workers on April 2 to present workers' demands to the company, consisted of four workers carefully chosen to represent the four nationalities of the strikers: Italian, American, Lithuanian, and Armenian.[38]

The IWW as an organization, and IWW leaders, including "Big Bill" Haywood, who came to Hopedale to assist with the strike, were nourished by the experience of the Lawrence strike a year earlier.[39] In Lawrence, neighborhood and ethnic and national organizations formed the backbone to the strike. While earlier studies credited the IWW with a definitive role in leading the strike, Ardis Cameron sees more of a give-and-take between outside organizers and local activists: "The genius of the Wobblies who came to Lawrence lay in their ability to assimilate local leadership into the decision-making process and to build upon the scattered bases of local power that already existed in the community."[40]

In particular, IWW organizers in Lawrence had to reconcile strikers' ethnic solidarity with their organization's commitment to internationalism. "Rooted in the traditions of revolutionary syndicalism, Wobblies were understandably suspicious of the nationality form of organization, which they saw as an explosive barrier to cooperation and united action. . . . Strikers, however, had already established patterns of authority that crisscrossed ethnic communities, and [the iww organizer Joseph] Ettor wisely adhered to the decentralized format that had been established . . . Locally organized and attuned to the ear of the neighborhoods, the language federations allowed for the widest possible participation among a population comprised of over forty national groups."[41]

In Hopedale, the company clearly promoted the idea that the strikers were outsiders, in all possible ways: not workers, not from Hopedale or Milford, and not Americans. On the first day of the strike the company's statement to the press emphasized all three aspects, describing the strikers variously as "a number of men, largely not employees of the Draper Co"; "principally Italians and Armenians"; and "so-called iww leaders, and it is believed that organization is responsible for the trouble." A few days later another company statement reiterated the point: "Of the several hundred men who are out there are not more than 36 who are American citizens, and they are substantially all of Italian or Armenian extraction."[42] In the company newsletter, the editors reiterated this: "None of the strikers are Americans by birth; most of them are Italians and Armenians; few of them are able to speak English; hardly any are citizens by naturalization."[43]

Joseph Coldwell responded with a biting statement of his own: "It is too late for the Draper Co. to raise the question of American citizenship, as they have been notorious in displacing American with foreign labor for the simple reason that they could hire these poor foreigners cheaper than the American citizen." Besides, Coldwell argued, it "is not a question of citizenship or nationality. It is a question of humanity." Finally, he insisted that the company's attack on the iww was missing the point: "The strikers have presented their demands as employees of the Draper Co. and not as members of the iww. They have not requested, neither do they expect recognition of that organization by the company, therefore the company cannot hide behind the cloud which they have raised of iww-ism, as that is not embodied in the demands."[44]

When the workers formulated their demands, respect was high among them, indicating that the derogatory racial and national atmosphere in the Draper plant was a long-standing grievance. "Conditions at the mill are not as they should be," the strikers' statement noted. Whether for tactical or other reasons, strikers blamed individual foremen, rather than the company, for the treatment they received in the plant. "The foremen were haughty and insolent to us. They looked after their own personal interests, and not after the interests of the Company. Therefore we respectfully and earnestly desire that the Company shall come to an agreement with us." In addition to specifying an end to the piecework system and a call for a nine-hour work-day, the strikers' petition began with a demand for the recognition of a shop committee of workers to resolve everyday problems at the plant.[45] In a statement later in the strike, the committee reiterated that "for a long time the bosses were abusing and ill treating us, and with words they would also hurt our feelings."[46]

Posters that strikers carried during one of their early days of picketing clearly showed the divisions between immigrant and "white" workers: "One carried by an Armenian said: 'Armenian wants white man to help him.' One small boy displayed a sign, 'My papa is on strike, is yours?' Still another read, 'Don't be afraid of my papa. He won't hurt you.' 'Mr. Whiteman, don't be yellow,'" ran the legend on one pasteboard, and "'Please, Mr. Whiteman, don't scab,'" ran another inscription.[47] The next day as picketers marched they sang "the 'Marseillaise' and Italian songs." The strike leader Joseph Coldwell called it "the battle of his class" and added that sometimes "I've been ashamed of the fact that I have Anglo-Saxon blood in my veins, when I see the men behind me [i.e., strikers] and then look at the cowardly, cringing chaps entering the mills, who ought to be with these others in their fight."[48]

Patriotism

In addition to economic and workplace issues, competing conceptions of Americanism were at stake in the Draper strike. Coldwell appealed to a moral, rather than ethnic, definition of "American" when he urged State Representative Charles H. Morrill to launch an investigation of conditions at the Draper plant. "It will show where the wages paid to the workmen employed by them are insufficient to give them a decent living; it will show that the conditions under which these strikers work, with a stopwatch placed over them, timing them and grinding their lives out, is un-American and inhumane; it will show to the public, who are unaware of the conditions in that plant, conditions which will be the talk of the entire state and the entire country."[49] (The House Committee on Rules refused, advising that any such investigation would have to be carried out by the State Board of Conciliation and Arbitration.)[50]

The Boston-based anarchist and anti-imperialist Morrison Swift suggested that extreme class divisions themselves contradicted American values: "The IWW is trying to peacefully persuade Mr. Draper to think less of himself and his luxury, and more of an uplifted humanity about him and in the country. Is this unpatriotic or un-American? Mr. Draper uses both of these bad names for the IWW. Is Mr. Draper patriotic when he absorbs the cream of wealth produced by his workers, and gives the skim-milk, diluted with water, to them? Is it Americanism to pay work-men less than $2 a day? If so, no one can have any pride in America. But I think that Mr. Draper is unpatriotic and un-American, for we cannot have a decent country while the working people are kept down for the great enrichment of a few."[51]

Swift referred to Draper as a "czar" and the mills as his "feudal posses-sions." This theme was echoed by Ettor, who compared Hopedale to "a city in the Middle Ages" where one man owned everything. Swift also suggested that "Eben Draper is 75 years behind the times, and in his mental and moral attitude is in the same position as the holder of slaves before the war. He has the ideas of the slave owner." Nor did Ettor hesitate to accuse the Drapers of godlessness. "The capitalists," he argued, have "exchanged the God of their fathers for the yardstick and the scales, making money their guiding star. 'You can't appeal to their hearts,' he said, 'because the heart has been re-placed with a pocketbook.' "[52]

Competing definitions of patriotism were evoked over the use of the American flag. When the Milford Foundry dismissed thirty-five foreign workers whom they suspected of supporting the IWW and the Draper strike, the company emphasized its position by erecting a huge flagpole over the plant to fly the American flag. Coldwell accused the company of "a disposi-tion to discriminate against the foreign-born workers" and threatened to call a general strike of all foreign workers in Milford, "Italians, Armenians, Polanders and others," unless the foundry problem was resolved. Young women at two Milford factories, "where many of the sisters and daughters of the strikers are employed," did join the strike, and an American flag quickly appeared over the doors of one of these factories as well. As Patriot's Day ap-proached, strikers asked the Milford selectmen for permission to carry their own national flags in a demonstration planned for that day. When permis-sion was refused, they prominently displayed a large number of American flags, with the placard "These flags were not bought by the Draper Com-pany," among others.[53]

In the speeches that followed the funeral of Emilio Bacchiocchi, a worker shot by police, the concept of what it meant to be American was raised again and again. Coldwell acknowledged that the strikers had offered to pay for his court costs (related to his arrest for picketing), but he refused their contributions: "I told them to save their money to buy bread with. I've been put in jail by Americans, and if they don't let me out, I'll rot in an American prison before I'll use money collected for you to be used to secure my liberty." Morrison Swift derided those who accused the IWW of anti-Americanism, "calling it the ideal American organization, with its motto, 'perfect justice to men of all classes.' "[54]

Swift continued on the same theme in a statement the following day. "This strike is also going to do away with the undemocratic, un-American Draper paternalism," he announced.

> The present strike will notably help to break up this autocratic claim of the large employer to the right to rule or ruin. . . . It is demonstrated by this that when the "American" element is ready to assert its rights by strike, it can absolutely shut up the place. It is a discovery which liberates Milford from the sense of a master standing over it in Hopedale, by proving that the great capitalist's power is fictitious, since the workers in his mills hold the situation in their own hands. To the Milford citizens I therefore suggest: Since this industrial battle by the Italians and Armenians will so greatly help you and your town, help them. . . .
>
> And to the English-speaking "loyal" workers I say, you have never had such a chance as this before. The hard work has already been done. By joining the strike you will greatly increase the already certain gains of the struggle. The victory will be for yourselves and the community. And the final results will be better for the Drapers themselves. Though the profits they obtain from your toil will be a little less the Drapers will become more human by finding that their autocracy does not pay.[55]

While the Drapers relied on an ethnic definition of Americanism, radical organizers and the workers themselves proposed a moral definition based on social justice. The men who carried out the Draper strike may have had revolutionary ideas, as the activism of radical movements in Milford suggests, but their goals in this strike were more modest. They called for a just reward for their work and used the language of Americanism, rather than that of anarchism or socialism, to challenge the Drapers' absolute control.

Milford's Catholic Church

Milford's Catholic church, under Father Rocco Petrarca, took an outspoken stand in favor of Draper's Italian workers, placing itself in contrast to the stance of the Catholic church in other textile disputes. Petrarca echoed the language of social justice proposed by the strikers, and insisted on the legitimacy of their demands.[56]

"They are my people," Petrarca said.

They have told me that they cannot live unless they receive more money. They are not bad men. They want work to support their families and I hope that something can be done to bring about a settlement as soon as may be.

The present question is not one of religion, of patriotism or nationality, or less than all of an organization. It is whether these men can receive for their labor what they must have to provide for themselves and those dependent upon them.

Petrarca also castigated the city for refusing to grant permission for workers' gatherings to "explain these things to the English-speaking people."[57]

At his sermon the next day, Petrarca spoke in English and Italian in support of the strikers. He blamed low wages and "intolerable conditions" for the strike. "Wages paid to some of the employees," he said, "are insufficient to provide for their families the barest necessities, since the increase in the cost of everything that they consume has been matched with a lessening rather than any raise in pay." And he again criticized the town of Milford for refusing workers a permit to meet "to state their grievances and win the sympathy of the English-speaking people." The *Daily News* quoted Petrarca to the effect that "the Draper Co., when the men were at work, praised them highly as good and desirable citizens, but now that they are on strike they are called anarchists, socialists and worse." When Coldwell visited Petrarca the following day to thank him for his support of the strikers, Petrarca replied "that he did not need any thanks for what he conceived to be his duty." The priest also appeared in court in Coldwell's defense when the latter was arrested for breaking the new Hopedale antipicketing legislation.[58]

When the Italian foundry worker Emilio Bacchiocchi was shot and killed by police on the picket line on April 24, socialist leaders joined Father Petrarca in leading "the biggest funeral the community of Milford had ever witnessed."[59] Milford's Italian residents spontaneously stayed home from work and closed their businesses in mourning. "Mourning for Emilio Bacchiocchi today caused the complete suspension of business by the Italian residents of Milford. Since noon yesterday all the stores in the Plains district are closed and many of them bear crepe. Even the barber shops of the countrymen of the deceased are closed until after the funeral, and no Italian workmen are at their places in any factory, quarry, cutting shed or other place of employment in town."[60]

The funeral was part cultural celebration, part mourning, and part political event. The newspaper called it "a spectacle unlike anything that Milford has witnessed in all its history." Over two thousand marched in the funeral cortege, and thousands more gathered along the streets to watch. Coldwell and several other union activists led, followed by the Italian Boys Band playing a funeral march, members of Italian social organizations, family, friends, and other mourners.[61]

Taking a Hard Line

Striking workers faced a formidable opponent: as governor of Massachusetts from 1909 to 1911, the company's president Eben Draper had been a staunch advocate of business interests, vetoing the eight-hour day for public employees. At the Draper plant, according to the local newspaper, the company employed "detectives" to carry out "espionage" among the workers in the different departments. Coldwell explained that the strike had originally been planned for May 1 but had been pushed earlier because "the men were being weeded out."[62]

Utterly refusing to meet with the strike committee or discuss workers' demands, the company immediately began to bring in replacement workers. Rumors quickly swirled that striking workers were being evicted from company housing, and while the company denied this, by the third day of the strike the newspaper was reporting that "the desertion of Milford by large numbers of Italians and Armenians continues, full a dozen men taking the first M. A. & W. car this morning, all carrying large bags and soft cases, containing their belongings."[63]

Meanwhile the company announced that any workers not back on the job by Wednesday, April 9, would be fired, and declared that the workers they were bringing in "are to be permanently employed by the company and are not strike breakers in the sense of coming merely to fill in while the trouble is on." The company also began renovating an empty company boardinghouse to lodge the newcomers while striking "Italian employees" departed with their families and vacated the company tenements. By April 7, furnishings had arrived and were being installed in the Park House for the replacement workers. The extra police agents who were brought in to Hopedale were also lodged in this company house, as were workers who chose not to strike and did not want to face picket lines coming in and out of Hopedale every day.[64]

By April 13, Draper was taking out advertisements for replacement workers in the Boston papers, explaining that about one third of their workers, "largely Italians and Armenians" and led by the IWW, had struck. "Only those desiring permanent employment need apply," the advertisement ended ominously. On April 30, they began evicting striking workers from their company-owned housing in Milford.[65]

The first large contingent of replacement workers came not from Boston but from Waterville, Maine, where the Draper foreman Bill Austin's brother ran a barber shop. Austin did some informal recruiting, avoiding any reference to the ongoing strike. On the evening of April 13 the company's assistant superintendent William McCaslin welcomed the first contingent of thirty-five French Canadian replacement workers who arrived by rail from Waterville and were taken directly to Park House. Several quickly became aware of the strike and sought out strike leaders to confer with them. The following day six of the newcomers took strikers up on their offer of free passage home if they would agree not to break the strike. Another twenty arrived from Maine a few days later, along with fifty from Lawrence. Two weeks later another twenty Mainers joined them. Strikers continued their efforts to dissuade the new arrivals from working. A week after the Lawrence workers arrived, fifteen decided to leave, saying that "they didn't know there was trouble when they were induced to come."[66]

On April 15 company representatives finally agreed to meet with a committee of strikers. The statement they issued after the meeting reiterated that they would not consider compromise on any of the issues raised by the strikers: wages, working conditions, and piecework. Further, they stated categorically, "We refuse, absolutely, to have anything to do with the so-called IWW as an organization. We do not consider that it is an ordinary labor union, but that it is a society which is un-American and anarchistic, and if its principles were carried out it would result in the destruction of our American government."[67]

A Company Town

Strikers continually faced the problem of finding a space where they could legally convene and rally. The Milford Central Labor Council, while issuing a statement supporting the strikers and criticizing the town for denying them the use of the town hall for a meeting, also refused to make the request itself. When the Granite Cutters Association, which also came out in support of the strikers, did make a formal request for the use of the hall, it was denied. The Draper Company's attorney appeared before the Milford City Council (despite protests that Draper, located in neighboring Hopedale, had no right to a voice in Milford town policy) and argued that the Granite Cutters had made the request on behalf of the iww, and that the iww should be refused any forum. He "said the opposition of the iww to trade unions is as great as it is to capitalists, and he then read many of the principles of the organization, bearing upon the point he was making.... He said the Draper Co. ... is not willing to treat with any organization which recognizes no God and no country, and which seems to be in control of this strike."[68] Draper representatives also succeeded, in mid-April, in having the Hopedale town meeting ban all mass picketing at its facility.[69] This led to a continuing series of arrests of strikers, strike leaders, and picketers, and effectively undermined strikers' attempts to convince more new replacement workers to join them.

Shortly after the new antipicketing bylaws were passed, Hopedale police arrested Coldwell and twenty-two others for peaceful picketing. The very existence of the strikers, Morrison protested, was being criminalized:

> The Draper company has thus opened a war on all the people of Massachusetts. If it wins, some of the oldest, dearest, most sacred rights of the citizens of this commonwealth will be lost.
>
> Free speech and the right to peaceably parade are as nearly as possible annulled. ... The crowning act comes in the design to destroy the state-wide right to peaceably picket. This is a body blow at all Massachusetts labor.
>
> The Drapers committed the incredible blunder or raising their strike into a national issue. They have affronted not only all labor, but all citizens who still revere New England liberties and national traditions. Through this vast blunder the power of the Drapers will disintegrate. Through it they have lost the strike. For by it they have made enemies of all classes. The strikers need now but quietly sit and wait, committing no violence, in order to win. Public admiration of the strikers' self-control and disgust with the anti-American Draper policy will do the rest.[70]

But the Drapers, and the Hopedale authorities, continued to increase the pressure. With all types of picketing or presence banned, strikers organized an early-morning march of schoolchildren from Milford to Hopedale on April 30 and May 1. They too were dispersed by police, escorted back to the Milford town line, and told not to return. "Arrived within the Milford town limits the boys and girls, who had been quiet while outside their home town, sang songs lustily and kept this up through Main street to their homes."[71] "A young woman, Palmira Mirolini, who lived across the street from us, was called 'the lady in red,' a firebrand who led the children (including me) up the street singing 'La Bandiera Rossa,'" recalled one participant.[72]

The following day, some four hundred strikers and one hundred children, accompanied by the Lawrence IWW leader Arturo Giovannitti as well as Coldwell and Albizzati, were blocked by "a big squad of Boston and Metropolitan park police, Hopedale specials and state officers" as they approached the Hopedale line from Milford. The leaders were once again arrested.[73]

With picketing effectively banned and replacement workers pouring in, the plant was able to maintain production virtually unscathed. When the strike committee met again with management at the end of June, the company's stance was adamant. As far as it was concerned, the strike was over. Company General Superintendent C. E. Nutting wrote a public reply:

> In the first place, I desire to state to you that I should not have had the pleasure of seeing you when I did had I known that you were members of a "strike committee." . . . The time for discussion between "committees" in regard to returning to work . . . has passed. The men who went on strike at the Draper Company, now more than three months ago, gave up their jobs at that time. . . . Any claim that they may have had for certain jobs at which they were at work expired long since. . . . We regret extremely that, because many hundreds of good and faithful men who had formerly worked for us, have been led astray by labor agitators of bad principles and bad judgment, the opportunity of very many of them to work for the Draper Company has gone.[74]

Draper Looms and the Race to the Bottom

Draper's first markets were in the New England textile industry; in fact, they created the market themselves. In 1893, in the context of a decline in the local lumber industry, city officials from Burlington, Vermont, invited Draper's owners to visit the city and consider investing in a mill there. "The Drapers were attracted to Burlington because of the favorable business climate generally, and low cost of labor, power and freight specifically," and in 1894 they formed the Queen City Cotton Company, opening their new mill with two hundred workers (primarily French Canadian, but also Jewish and Irish immigrants), and 792 new automatic Draper looms—the company's first sale—in 1895.[75]

It was only a matter of months before Draper had another customer, the Gaffney Manufacturing Company founded in 1892 in Gaffney, Spartanburg County, South Carolina, which began to purchase Draper looms in 1895.[76] In 1908, father William and son Arthur Draper were major investors in Chadwick-Hoskins, helping it "in a single stroke" to become "the largest textile corporation in all of North Carolina, operating 98,000 spindles," and also contributing to the trend of consolidation of the South's textile industry under a few, mostly northern-controlled, giants. Arthur moved to Charlotte, North Carolina, to become president of the new firm. (In 1946, the Chadwick-Hoskins mills were acquired by Textron; they then went through a succession of owners, and were closed by the 1980s.)[77] By 1909, Draper was shipping over twenty thousand looms a year to U.S. mills, primarily in New England and the U.S. South.

In 1910 Draper opened a loom manufacturing shop in Atlanta, in 1929 a warehouse in Spartanburg, South Carolina, and, in 1936 a parts manufacturing plant in Spartanburg. "From the outset, this sprawling factory had a large foundry operation—one of the largest in the Southeast—and from those castings, Draper manufactured more than 2,000 different parts used on looms."[78] In constructing the warehouse about two miles from the center of Spartanburg, Draper noted, "We are to proceed at once with the construction of four dwelling houses and garages for those who are to have charge of the plant. We are also planning a small village for the colored employees of the warehouse. This will be located at a point easily accessible."[79]

In New England, the new automatic looms tended to replace the old common looms in existing factories. In the South most went to supply new mills.[80] By 1912, the company boasted that 88,163 of its Northrop automatic looms were operating in New England textile factories, and 121,292 in the factories of the South, 65,974 of these in South Carolina and the others scattered between Georgia (19,608), North Carolina (18,003), Alabama (8,803), Virginia (4,845), and Tennessee (2,818).[81] By 1915 there were 110,994 in New England and 146,338 in the South. By 1924 there were 162,453 in New England and 223,898 in the South.[82]

Figure 2. In 1929 Draper proudly announced its new warehouse in Spartanburg, South Carolina. Draper Corporation, *Cotton Chats* 294, April 1929. Reprinted by permission of the Bancroft Library, Hopedale, Massachusetts.

Salem's Naumkeag Steam Cotton Company was in some ways an anomaly when it rebuilt after a fire and installed 2,644 new Northrop looms in 1915. Few mills were building new facilities in New England any more, but Naumkeag decided to rebuild an entirely new and modern facility on the site.[83] As early as 1902 a consultant recommended to the Boott Mills in Lowell that they demolish their entire factory and start anew.[84] Few New England mills were prepared to take that course.

By producing more cloth more quickly and with less labor, the automatic looms contributed to the recurrent problem of overproduction, low wages, and underemployment in the textile industry. In a downward spiral, workers lost buying power, consumption declined, and overproduction was exacerbated, leading to further layoffs and competition among companies to lower prices by lowering wages, further depleting buying power. This cycle underlay the Great Depression that started in 1929. In the textile industry, in part because of the effectiveness of the Draper loom, the Depression started after World War I and only worsened in the 1920s.

In the midst of the textile depression, Draper urged textile companies to increase their commitment to the very approaches that had caused the problem, in the same kind of beggar-thy-neighbor attitude that underlies the modern "race to the bottom." "How Many Northrop Looms Does Your Weaver Run?" read the headline to an editorial in the company newsletter in 1924. While acknowledging that tariffs and legislation regulating wages, hours, and working conditions could ameliorate the problem of competition

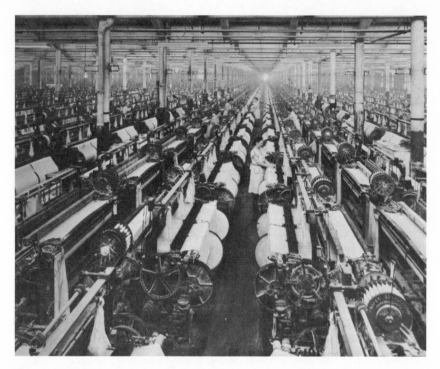

Figure 3. The Naumkeag Steam Cotton Company's new weave shed filled with Draper looms, 1949. *The Pequot Story* (Salem, Mass.: Naumkeag Steam Cotton Company, 1949).

from lower-wage regions (outside and inside the country), the essay dismissed these options: "All of these are jobs for collective effort. The solution of some of them may take years. Meanwhile, what can the individual manufacturer do on his own account?" The individual solution, the company urged, was to produce more at a lower cost by switching to the automatic loom, if a factory did not already employ it, and by increasing the number of looms tended by each worker, if the factory was already automated. This would allow companies to surmount "the handicap of high wages by increased production per unit of labor."[85]

"The South, with new mills, new methods and new help, proved some of the possibilities of the Northrop loom in its early days while Northern manufacturers were skeptical and Northern labor antagonistic. The North as a whole has never quite caught up," the editorial concluded ominously.[86]

Draper also offered concrete advice on how to implement the speed-up using its looms. "Keep a score card," another essay recommended cheerfully.

Where would the baseball manager be without his carefully kept score card? If you would have your weavers run more looms, find out how much work they are doing; how often the looms fail to do the work automatically. Get the batting average of the looms. . . . Note how many times the looms stop, cause of each stop, time lost before the loom is started. . . . If you need a coach, we have them. They are at your service without charge. They are well-trained, have helped others and can work with you.

With complete figures before you, with or without a coach to assist, proceed to reduce the loom stops at the source. . . . When the scorer's sheet shows less work for the weaver, increase the number of her looms. Take one step at a time, but keep stepping until you know what can be done. . . .

And don't be satisfied too easily. Study the possibilities of using unskilled help to relieve the skilled worker. . . . Make the change with the scorer still on the job—and don't stop short of real achievement.[87]

It was precisely this kind of pressure that caused the 1933 Naumkeag strike, symbolized in the protest of one speeded-up Naumkeag worker: "I guess it's me, I'm just not quite automatic!"[88]

Finally, Draper advised its customers on how to apportion the savings they achieved from increased production. Most important, "you must meet present economic conditions—which call for decreased prices on the finished product to bring business to keep your mill running." In other words, use your lowered costs to undersell others and contribute to the race to the bottom. Second, of course, "you must have a profit on the decreased prices." Finally, "your skilled weavers . . . are entitled to some increase." However, since speeded-up factories will need far fewer weavers, a slight wage raise should not impinge on the bottom line. In addition, "to give them their just share will insure co-operation."[89] In other words, they will be encouraged to adopt the same beggar-thy-neighbor stance and enjoy their position as an aristocracy of labor, separating their interests from those of the unskilled and the laid-off.

While Naumkeag's and other factories' workers were protesting forcefully against "research" aimed at speeding up the work pace, Draper was promoting precisely that course. "If you don't have somebody on the job of studying the job all the time, you will soon be a back number," the Draper newsletter urged. "Are you getting a day's work for a day's pay?" Weavers' workloads must be increased, Draper insisted. "Why not get the full value of your investment in improved looms and let them supervise enough machines to earn their wages? It is fair to them, for otherwise you cannot meet modern competition and soon you will have no jobs for them." In addition to "stretching out" skilled weavers, many of them could be eliminated entirely and replaced by unskilled, young "bobbin girls." Weavers spend too much time changing bobbins, Draper argued. "This work requires no brains and only such skill as young and nimble fingers can easily acquire. Use bobbin girls at the pay of unskilled help," they recommended. "Studying the job has been the keynote of Draper service to the textile industry for more than a century. It brought every advance we have made in improved machinery. We are still on the job of studying the job. Our service men are at the call of those who want to study the job in their own particular mill and under their own special conditions."[90]

Two years later, Draper invented a new warper and urged its customers to employ the scorecard method to the warp room as well. "Your warper-tenders," they explained "probably think they are doing a day's work. . . . What does the scorecard show? Try the scorecard on your warping." It will tell you "what changes in methods or equipment you should have for an increased production per unit of labor." "Studying the job with the scorecard will enable your warper-tenders to run more machines. . . . The scorecard did it on looms. Why not give it a chance on your warping?"[91]

Even in 1929, when the textile industry was struggling under years of overproduction and depressed conditions and a major depression was only months away from striking the entire country, Draper relentlessly pressed the cause of increased production. "Any weaver can run more Northrop looms of the type built today than they ran of the models of 20 years ago. This is one of the reasons for shorter hours and better pay," they wrote, a bit disingenuously. "The textile industry cannot come back unless it uses every means it can devise to reduce costs. . . . High wages are dependent upon the prosperity of the industry. Prosperity and high wages cannot be maintained if the industry does not keep step with the modern trend to increased production per unit of labor. There can be no high wages unless operatives give a fair day's work. . . . **The more-looms-per-weaver movement seeks only a fair day's work for a fair day's pay.**"[92]

Looms to Latin America and the World

While bringing in immigrant workers, Draper was also exporting its machinery. When "at the turn of the century, gangs of men and mules hauled

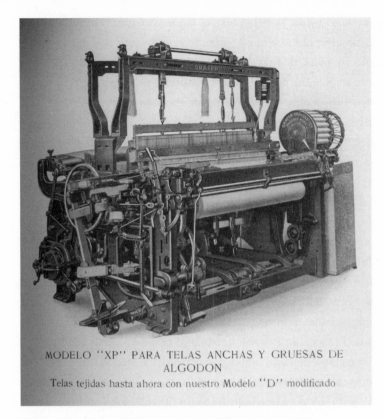

MODELO "XP" PARA TELAS ANCHAS Y GRUESAS DE
ALGODON
Telas tejidas hasta ahora con nuestro Modelo "D" modificado

Figure 4. Draper's Spanish-language version of its company newsletter advertised looms for Latin American mills. Draper Corporation, *Cotton Chats* 331, May 1939. Reprinted by permission of the Bancroft Library, Hopedale, Massachusetts.

textile machinery over the mist-shrouded trails" to build Medellín, Colombia's first textile factories, or during the Depression, when these same factories "did well by buying discarded looms cheaply from the United States" (still brought up the mountains by mule), they almost certainly included the same Draper looms that men like Mario were trained on in later generations.[93] The damage that the looms suffered in transportation meant that Colombians soon became expert at repairing them; this training was one of the factors that led New England textile factories to turn to Medellín to recruit workers in the 1960s (see chapter 4).[94]

During its first decades, Draper saw little potential in exporting looms to low-wage countries. "We had one overarching goal at Draper: to reduce the cost of labor," a company publication explained. The price of cotton was the same worldwide, but the cost of labor varied enormously by region, and was higher in the United States than anywhere else in the world. If U.S. textile factories had to compete with the rest of the world, they would have to reduce the cost of labor per pound of cotton manufactured. Draper solved this problem with its automatic loom. "If, back then, our Latin American friends had asked our opinion about the use of automatic looms in their factories, we would have told them frankly that we could not in good conscience advise it, due to the low cost of labor in their countries."[95]

Prior to World War I, British textile machinery dominated world markets. The war, however, cut deeply into European exports of both textile machinery and textiles. The U.S.-based W. R. Grace & Co., with mills in Peru and Chile, the El Prado cotton mill in Ecuador, and the Obregón mill in Colombia all began to order Draper looms in 1917. It was in Colombia that their use first became widespread, and it was the Colombian experience that "made [Draper] see our error, and convinced us that Draper looms could not only find a good market in Latin America, but could be very profitable for their users."[96] As New England mills closed during the Depression, they sold their old looms to Colombian factories like Coltejer.[97] By the 1930s, Draper was publishing its *Cotton Chats* newsletter in Spanish for Latin American distribution.[98] By 1946 three Medellín factories, Fabricato, Coltejer, and Tejidos El Cóndor, had converted to Draper looms and "their modern factories were not surpassed by any in America."[99]

A Draper Latin American publicity pamphlet quoted "one of the best-trained South American textile industrialists," who explained the advantages of the automatic loom in terms of labor:

> Where labor is cheap, it's impossible to expect a quick return on investment in automatic looms. In the long run, though, the investment is justified and the automatic loom is more profitable than the ordinary loom. . . . Many of the workers formerly needed can be eliminated. It is only necessary to retain the best, training them to run the automatic looms. As they become more expert, they can attend a larger number of looms, and earn higher salaries. This way, the worker improves his status, raises his standard of living, feels proud, takes more interest in his work, and takes better care of the looms. This translates into higher production and better quality cloth, which increases weaving efficiency. Thus profits can exceed original expectations.[100]

A Victim of Its Own Success

As the textile industry moved south, Draper gradually shifted most of its operations to its Spartanburg, South Carolina, plant. However, it faced competition in the post–World War II period from two European textile machine companies that also established plants in Spartanburg. Like the U.S.-based maquiladoras, these companies spread out the manufacturing process, placing sales and assembly in Spartanburg and keeping the better-paying high-tech jobs at home. "In time their machinery, and that of other European producers, would largely displace American equipment and would drive the technological revolution that would sweep through the industry in later years."[101]

In the late 1960s, the Rockwell Standard Company (later North American Rockwell; Rockwell International, 1973; and Rockwell Automation, 2001) succeeded, after several tries, in taking over Draper. Rockwell had a fine history of military and government contracts ranging from the B-1 bomber to the *Apollo* spacecraft. In some ways, Rockwell itself embodied the contradictions inherent in the postwar U.S. economy. On one hand, it was accustomed to feeding at the public trough and taking on projects in which a "success at all costs" philosophy prevailed. "The former Chief Engineer of the Apollo Project headed a textile study directly budgeted at over $500,000, with extensive indirect support, that yielded little impact on product development at Draper. . . . The Rockwell engineers were inexperienced in dealing with . . . cost conscious technical problems, given that their crowning achievement was the 'success at all costs' direction of the Apollo moon shot."[102]

Even while it enjoyed hefty government funding for its own operations, Rockwell Automation, as its new name implies, continued Draper's long tradition of management consulting to improve efficiency. In the textile industry, firms like Barnes and Associates and Lockwood Greene specialized in everything from mill design to time management studies to increase productivity in their global textile customers (see chapter 3). Draper's automatic looms served the same purpose and were often part of the process. Rockwell's consulting teams continued to help global industries cut their labor costs as the twentieth century drew to a close.[103]

Government largesse and the quest for efficiency underlay the larger shift of industrial production out of the United States, and loom production was no exception. Rockwell closed the Hopedale plant in 1980 and sold the company in 1983, and in 1996 it was bought by the Indonesian firm Texmaco.[104] Although factories like Wannalancit in Lowell, Massachusetts, still used the old Draper looms, it was becoming more and more difficult to find workers in the United States willing and able to operate them. As Draper's former owners poured money into organizations trying to halt immigration from Latin America, it was the owners of factories relying on their own looms that were just as desperately seeking Colombian immigrant workers.

NICOLA SACCO

Ferdinando Sacco was one of many thousands of Italians who left their homes near the turn of the century to come to America. Like so many others, he formed a link in a "chain migration," moving to a place where friends, *paisanos*, and relatives had already established a community. In Sacco's case, this community was in Milford, Massachusetts, a town of some fifteen thousand about thirty miles southwest of Boston. The Plains section of Milford was home to dozens of families from several towns in the north of the Italian province of Foggia, including Casalvecchio, and Torremaggiore, where Sacco was born. His father's friend Antonio Calzone, who worked at the Draper Loom Company, had urged the elder Sacco to send his sons to America, and when Ferdinando and his older brother arrived in April 1908, they were taken in by Calzone.

Ferdinando worked as a manual laborer in several different jobs during his first months in Milford before Calzone helped him obtain employment at Draper, where he worked for a year. Then another Casalvecchio neighbor helped the young man enter a training program to learn edge trimming, a skilled craft in the shoemaking process. Sacco's first job as an edge trimmer was in the town of Webster, but he soon returned to Milford, where he obtained steady employment at the Milford Shoe Company (where he had trained). He remained at this job from 1910 until 1917, when he left the United States for a period of exile in Mexico. "To this day, Sacco is remembered with affection by the older residents of the town, for whom he was a hardworking young man and a credit to the community, incapable of committing the crimes with which he was charged," writes his biographer.[105]

In Milford, Sacco was exposed to a vibrant radical community of Italian anarchists and socialists. He began to read *Il Proletario*, an IWW weekly edited by Arturo Giovannitti, and he soon subscribed to *Cronaca Sovversiva*, an "Anarchist Weekly of Revolutionary Propaganda" published by Luigi Galleani in Lynn. When the textile workers of Lawrence went on strike in 1912, Sacco was among their Milford supporters who worked to collect money both for the strikers and for the defense fund of Giovannitti and Joseph Ettor when they were arrested in connection with their activities in the strike.[106]

In 1913 Sacco began attending meetings of the Milford anarchist group Circolo di Studi Sociali, joining a number of his neighbors who were also immigrants from Foggia. "Sacco found these men, all of them about his own age, more sympathetic than other radicals he had met: more militant, more eager to learn, more willing to dedicate their energies to the cause of their fellow workers." He soon "threw himself body and soul into the anarchist cause."[107]

When Draper's workers went on strike in the spring of 1913, Sacco and the other anarchists of the Circolo were quick to come to their support. "He was not an orator," the strike leader Joseph Coldwell later said of Sacco, "or even a fluent speaker, but he was a mighty good worker in detail matters and never hesitated to do his share of the appointed work. . . . Never in the limelight during the strike . . . he was one of the silent, active, sincere workers, giving of his time and money to help his fellow men."[108]

Sacco's first contribution to the *Cronaca Sovversiva* was in August 1913, when the journal published a brief account that he wrote of the Draper strike and the campaign to raise money for the defense of strikers who had been jailed. Over the next few years Sacco became a frequent contributor to the journal, documenting the fabric of anarchist social and political life in Milford. His contributions described "attending picnics and conferences, acting in social dramas, continually raising money to aid political prisoners and jailed strikers, always collecting money for 'the propaganda.' "[109] He later told a biographer that while in Milford, he and his wife, Rosina, "used to arrange for dramatic performances and to raise money for all sorts of causes."[110]

A friend and fellow Foggian immigrant anarchist described some of these activities: "We put on plays in Milford, like *Rasputin* and *Tempeste Sociali*, and organized picnics to raise money for the movement. . . . There were two radical circles in Milford, an IWW group on East Main

Street and an anarchist group on Plains Street. Each had about twenty-five members, all Italians. . . . Some of its members had been involved in the 1913 strike in Hopedale, when the IWW tried to organize the workers and a striker . . . was killed. Sacco also took part in it. In 1916 Sacco, my brother Saverio, and Luigi Paradiso were speaking at a meeting and were arrested by the Milford police chief."[111]

Sacco's 1916 arrest occurred when Milford's anarchists mobilized in support of striking IWW iron workers in the Mesabi Range in Minnesota. They faced the usual obstacle: in December the Milford police banned all open-air meetings. When the group defied the order and met on December 3, Ferdinando Sacco was one of three arrested and sentenced to three months in jail. (The charges were later dismissed.)[112]

When the U.S. Congress passed its military conscription act in May 1917, shortly after the U.S. entrance into World War I, the *Cronaca Sovversiva* urged its readers to refuse to register. (The act required non-citizens to register even though in theory they were not liable for military service.) Many of its readers went underground or fled the country. Sacco, along with Bartolomeo Vanzetti and some sixty others from around the country, decided to leave for Mexico.[113]

When Sacco returned to the United States several months later, his family had moved to Cambridge, and he joined them there. He obtained a job in Stoughton through a former superintendent from the Milford Shoe Company, Michael Kelley, who had since opened his own business there, and remained there until his arrest in May 1920.[114]

Kelley's grandson later recalled, "Grandmother was extremely fond of him. She always stood up for him and couldn't believe that he could do those nefarious things. . . . They were aware of his radicalism but didn't know what to make of it. They saw him as a good worker, a family man, a kind person. Grandmother asked him to kill a chicken now and then, and he was very squeamish about it. He didn't like killing chickens. It was an odd relationship between an Irish business family and an Italian worker. 'Give up the radical crap. Be an American,' Grandfather would tell him. Dad said that, apart from everything else that was said against them, Italian immigrants were regarded as bomb-throwers."[115]

The end of the story of Ferdinando Sacco's life (he took the name Nicola when he returned from exile in Mexico, to avoid being discovered as a draft registration evader) is far better known than the story of his

Milford years. He was arrested along with Vanzetti, with whom he had shared his Mexico exile, for a robbery and murder in South Braintree, Massachusetts, in the spring of 1920; the two were convicted on flimsy evidence and sentenced to death. The case became a national and international cause célèbre, and the two were executed in the electric chair in August 1927. (See the discussion of Robert Bakeman, the socialist mayor of Peabody, Massachusetts, in chapter 2 for a description of the activities in one Massachusetts city on the eve of their execution.) On the fiftieth anniversary of their deaths, Massachusetts Governor Michael Dukakis proclaimed August 23, 1977, "Nicola Sacco and Bartolomeo Vanzetti Day."

THE NAUMKEAG STEAM COTTON COMPANY
Labor-Management Collaboration and Its Discontents

The history of Salem, Massachusetts's Naumkeag Steam Cotton Company provides a window through which to explore the dynamic of militant versus accommodationist unionism and a company's long-term flirtation with, and eventual decision to open, a southern location. Chapters 1 and 3 of this book touch on some of the larger, structural issues involved in the deindustrialization of New England. This chapter focuses on a single textile factory, one of the largest in New England, and explores the complex dynamic among the workers, management, the union, and the city as they struggled, variously, to maintain profits, productivity, and decent working conditions and resist the relentless race to the bottom.

Although management did not hesitate to claim that unions were driving them to cheaper lands, other factors were often the decisive ones. Even as popular opinion came to accept the equation of labor militancy and plant closure, plants often left just as unions were making huge concessions to induce them to stay.

Naumkeag explored a move south in the 1920s, a period of labor quiescence but increasing federal immigration restrictions which began to limit the mills' labor supply. In the decade when many New England mills closed, Naumkeag's union participated in what became a national paragon of "labor-management collaboration." As union leaders worked with management on research to implement labor speed-ups, rank-and-file workers became more and more uneasy with the arrangement. In 1933 workers finally rebelled, engaging in a two-month wildcat strike against research, the speed-up, and their own union leadership. In 1935 they struck again for a union shop (for their new, independent union). Both times, against the grim warnings of national union leaders, local civic officials, and the mill management, workers won their demands, and the mill stayed in Salem.

In the 1950s, during the second major wave of New England mill closings, Naumkeag succumbed. Following the trend of so many other companies, Naumkeag bought a plant in Whitney, South Carolina, in 1949 and closed its Salem operation in 1953. It soon sold the Whitney factory as well, which went through a rapid succession of owners, including the inveterate speculator Textron, before finally closing in 2001.

Spectacular labor actions like the two 1930s Salem strikes could be successful even when opposed, as they often were, by official union bodies. The Naumkeag story shows how union leaders lost the faith of factory workers; how workers united across gender, ethnic, and language barriers; how a lively local context of variegated radicalism nourished and supported their strike; and how workers, unions, and governments (local and national) confronted the challenges of productivity, profitability, and social justice in the first major wave of deindustrialization in the United States.

Establishing a Labor System at Naumkeag

The Naumkeag Steam Cotton Company was incorporated in 1839, two years before Adin Ballou established his utopian community of Hope Dale and just sixty miles to its northeast. It went into production in the 1840s, manufacturing sheets under the Pequot label. Fragmentary evidence exists of strikes at the mill as early as the 1850s, just as the workforce was beginning to shift from New England–born to, first Irish, then French Canadian and Polish immigrant workers.[1] By the second decade of the twentieth century Naumkeag followed a strategy of collaborating with Lowell's and Lawrence's mills in setting pay scales. Mills in the three cities coordinated wage increases of 10 percent on October 8, 1917, April 1, 1918, and June 17, 1918. In June 1918 the Salem mill's doffers, roving boys and oilers—almost exclusively young male workers in a mostly female workforce—challenged the increase, demanding instead a raise of 17.5 percent. The mill refused—based on the argument that Salem had to maintain parity with Lawrence and Lowell—and the doffers struck the following morning. By nine o'clock workers in the carding department joined in, asking for a 25 percent raise, and by the lunch break, most of the mill's other workers had also left the job.[2]

The mill agent reported to the board of directors several days later, "The strikers refused to start work pending an investigation and adjustment of wages, consistently demanding the advance asked for. Wednesday evening the strikers held a mass meeting and were addressed by labor men from New Bedford and Manchester N.H., and members of the Central Labor Union. They signified a wish to join the Union and asked for a charter." The following day a committee of strikers and two union organizers met with mill officials and declared their intention to remain on strike pending a decision by either the National War Board or the State Board of Conciliation and Arbitration regarding the wage scale.[3]

The government official who arrived in Salem early the following week was Henry J. Skeffington, the U.S. immigration commissioner in Boston. Mill officials hoped to reopen the mill on the strength of his impending arrival, "however after careful consideration of the attitude of the strikers it was decided inadvisable to take any action of the sort until after the arrival of the Commissioner." In their meeting with Skeffington, also attended by Salem's mayor and John O'Connell of the Central Labor Union (CLU), mill officials agreed to turn the wage question over to the State Board of Conciliation and Arbitration and abide by its decision.

Meanwhile, "a mass meeting of the strikers was in session at the CLU Hall with a very large attendance." When Skeffington, the mayor, and mill officials presented their proposal to the mass meeting, workers agreed "after much discussion . . . but the sentiment of the meeting was that there would be no return to work until the award was definitely made." The "Austrian Poles" were particularly adamant about not returning to work, "and it was only after Mr. Skeffington had declared it a patriotic duty, and fairly threatened them, that they reluctantly agreed to go to work." Almost all of the workers did indeed return to work the following day, although "the Polish operatives seemed unsettled." (This is the first documentation, but certainly not the last, of the radicalism of Naumkeag's Polish workers. In general, Polish workers tended to be more recent immigrants, and received lower pay, than French Canadians.)[4]

After hearing from representatives of the mill and the workers, as well as union representatives like Horace Riviere, a UTW organizer from Manchester, New Hampshire, the board ordered an investigation of working conditions and wages at mills in Lowell, Lawrence, Holyoke, New Bedford, and Fall River. On August 9, it handed down a decision on a new wage scale, granting the 17 percent increase to most workers, retroactive to June 25.

"The decision of the State Board of Conciliation and Arbitration was in effect the granting of the demands of the striking operatives," the mill's board of directors noted drily.[5]

The following fall saw another long strike, from September 22 through November 12, once again over the issue of wages. On August 20, UTW Local 33 (representing workers at the mill and bleachery) called for a 25 percent across-the-board wage increase. Between August 20 and September 22 the company and the union remained deadlocked, and on Monday, September 22, both union and nonunion workers walked out. The management once again pegged its position on other New England mills: "The attitude of the Management consistently maintained was, that a general increase in wages could not be granted inasmuch as a careful inquiry failed to reveal a similar demand in any of the textile centers in New England and the rate of wages paid was fully as high as in any mill working on the same class of goods, but should there be a general increase in wages in textile centers the employees of the Mill and Bleachery should participate in it and to the fullest extent." This time, the mill refused the participation of the State Board of Conciliation and Arbitration.

After attempts at mediation by the War Labor Board and the Salem Chamber of Commerce Industrial Relations Committee, workers voted on November 11 to return to work, with only those earning less than the minimum wage being raised. However, a few days later the mill's board of directors voted "that the Agent be authorized to increase wages approximately five per cent beyond any increase granted in New England." This victory came with a price, however: at the same meeting, the board instructed the agent "to investigate the matter of increasing production 25% to 33−1/3% and report in detail at the December meeting."[6]

The early history of labor-management relations at the mill raises many issues that would continue to play a major role in this mill, in the textile industry in general, and in the question of industrial restructuring that would later become a global issue. The geographic dispersal and competitive nature of the textile industry led its owners to develop a strategy of collaboration in setting wage rates even prior to the expansion of unionization of the industry. Mill managers used the agreements they had made with others in the industry to bolster their refusal to negotiate wages with their own workers. Together, they established a prevailing wage rate and then argued that they could not exceed it because it would render their factory uncompetitive. This strategy encouraged workers too to see their fates as inextricably tied to those of workers in other New England mill centers.

The central question addressed by this chapter, however, is that of labor-management collaboration. Confronted with the constant threat of factory relocation, the UTW explored ways that the union itself could help companies to increase their productivity and competitiveness. The company's 1919 decision to concede a wage increase, but accompany it by a study on how to raise productivity, illustrates one of the key issues that would repeatedly confront textile and other unions. A tension between protecting the interests of individual companies to preserve individual jobs and a more class-oriented strategy that saw the drive for increased productivity as a way of increasing the exploitation of labor frequently drove a wedge between workers and their own unions. "If we lose this strike, all textile workers will be affected," wrote the leaders of the wildcat strike at Naumkeag in 1933 that sought to put a brake on a joint company-union program to speed up the labor process.[7] The question of how to negotiate the pressure for concessionary bargaining in the interests of maintaining competitiveness was at the heart of the challenges facing the U.S. and global labor movements in the context of corporate globalization at the end of the twentieth century.

Looking South

New England textile investors and entrepreneurs began to look south from the very first days of their volatile industry. Not only were labor costs lower in the South, but southern governments offered investors significant incentives. Because start-up costs were comparatively low and because textile machinery technology advanced rapidly, the incentive to establish new mills was high, and newer mills with newer machinery could produce more, and higher quality, goods at lower cost. The ease of entry into the industry meant that markets could quickly be saturated, creating even greater incentives to cut costs.

The textile depression of the early 1920s, following the World War I boom, led to a veritable hemorrhage of the industry to the South. The Naumkeag mill's directors considered two opportunities for expansion in 1926. One was a New Bedford mill placed up for sale. Although the mill agent reported that the property was "in splendid shape and quite in accord with 'Naumkeag' standards," the board showed little interest in pursuing a purchase in New England. However, at the same meeting, the board voted that the president appoint a committee to investigate the possibility of opening a new mill in a southern location.[8]

The committee sent Mr. Seamans to a number of southern locations, and he was especially taken with Alabama. Cost saving was high on the agenda, and southern cities were experimenting with a prototype for what would later become the free trade zones of Puerto Rico, Mexico, and the rest of Latin America, soliciting industrial investment by offering tax cuts, state-provided infrastructure, subsidies, and cheap labor. In the twin cities of Albany-Decatur, for example, "to show the spirit of co-operation that the South extends to northern manufacturers, the local people have raised $600,000.00 to buy the site and build the building" for the Connecticut Mills of Danielson, Connecticut. The Alabama Power Company had provided electrification in advance, agreeing to be reimbursed out of profits.[9]

There was plenty of low-cost labor available, and in general, southern workers were "a contented, happy, American lot." Seamans also noted approvingly that many mills operated around the clock. Visiting the Anniston Manufacturing Company's mill at 10 P.M., he was pleased to report that "there again I saw the same happy, eager employees." Seamans did have one reservation, in Albany-Decatur: the presence of the railroad in the city. "My chief objection to the location is that the railroads all over the country have always been strongly unionized, and it seems to me that the wives of union operatives would be more than likely to inherit the tendencies of organized labor."[10]

Seamans was also intrigued by the "mill village" arrangement common in the South. "Much can be said pro and con as to the advisability of maintaining a village, the particular advantage being that you can form your own environment and when an objectionable worker settles down it is very easy to remove him. Moreover, being outside of the city limits you can escape the city tax, which may run to $10.00 a thousand." While anxious to avoid paying city taxes, Seamans was not at all reluctant to make use of city services: "I would locate on the very edge of the city limits," he wrote, "so as to have their schools, hospitals, stores, and churches accessible to our employees." Seamans included a chart that compared city, county, state, and income taxes in Massachusetts and Alabama, noting that in Massachusetts Naumkeag's tax bill amounted to $35,625 a year, while in Alabama it would be only $14,000 a year.[11]

"I prepared a map of the South and located the various mills thereon with pins to see the distribution, and found that, while North and South Carolina had a great abundance of mills, Alabama had comparatively few. Our competitors, as well as other cotton mills, have apparently formed the same conclusion, as, during the course of our travels, we found the following northern mills either located there and running, or with sites secured for future development . . . : the Merrimack, Indian Head, Dwight, Otis, Pepperell, Everett, and Utica Steam Cotton."[12]

Nevertheless, the mill's directors declined to pursue a move south in the 1920s. One reason may have been that Naumkeag was one of the most technically advanced of the New England mills, having thoroughly upgraded its facility and installed new Draper looms after a major fire in 1914. Another was that the mill was pursuing a different route to cost saving: taking full advantage of its new machinery to speed up the work pace and involving the union in the process, taking labor-management collaboration to its extreme.

"Research"

Over its first decade, the Naumkeag union had gradually gained a voice in the plant management, with contracts governing areas like working conditions, job classifications, and seniority. As conditions in the textile industry tightened in the 1920s and options for relocation were aired, the mill management began to implement speed-ups in different departments in the mill, and the union, cozy in its relationship with management, went along. Workers—especially the Polish workers—began to question the union's ability to represent them effectively. A move by Polish workers to replace Local 33's business agent John O'Connell with a Polish agent was blocked by Irish and French Canadian workers. In early 1927, the directors applauded the increased production pace that they had achieved in the mill but cautioned that the "congested situation at the Bleachery" would only worsen as mill output increased. Pressure on union leaders grew from both sides.[13]

O'Connell was spurred by the shifting terrain to pursue an entirely new course—"unique in cotton manufacturing"—to establish a system of labor-management collaboration.[14] The agreement, signed in April 1927, was predicated on the idea that labor and management shared an interest in the company's sales and profitability. Management recognized the union as "desirable . . . inasmuch as the cooperation of their members is essential to the continued and successful function of the Mills." The union committed its members to promoting the distribution of Pequot products and "pledges its support in a constructive and responsible way to the end that quantity and quality production may be maintained and further pledges its cooperation in effecting such economies in manufacturing as may be brought about by the introduction of new machinery." The union further agreed to allow a period of sixty days to resolve any dispute before a strike could be called and to "use every effort at its command" to maintain production in the event of a wildcat strike. For its part, the company agreed to "use every effort to maintain good working conditions, fair wages and continuity of employment." The parties agreed to meet monthly to maintain a dialogue about all work-related issues.[15]

Over the course of 1928 the mill management used this agreement to develop a plan to drastically increase job assignments. Weavers were asked to jump from tending thirteen looms to tending twenty-four, and other workers were to increase their workloads accordingly. In addition, a significant number of workers would be laid off. Mill officials submitted the plan to the union in December 1928, and union officials spent several weeks debating with management before agreeing to present it to the workers.[16]

When the union presented the plan at a mass meeting at the Now and Then Hall, workers predictably objected. Union officials found themselves in the increasingly familiar position of being "able to see both sides but . . . influence neither."[17] Rather than representing the workers, union leaders had come to serve as intermediaries between management and labor.

O'Connell then proposed another innovative plan to manage the work process: the union would collaborate with management in a "joint research" plan to hire an industrial engineer, study the work process, and come up with a mutually acceptable plan for any speed-ups.[18] The collaboration, the union argued, would allow the company to increase productivity and remain competitive—thus remain in Salem—while protecting acceptable working conditions. The original management plan for the speed-up had been made by overseers and supervisors on the shop floor. Now the union itself was calling for an outside expert in scientific management to recommend the contours of a speed-up. Where workers and unions elsewhere were challenging, protesting, and resisting scientific management and the stretch-out by all means possible, Salem's union was actually inviting it.

The technician chosen to oversee the process brought in a textile engineering firm to conduct a four-month study of every aspect of the mill's operations. They chose the weave room as the pilot site for time-motion studies to recommend specific ways to speed up the work pace. "The consulting engineers had assured [the technician] that although the weaving department would probably be the 'hardest place in the mill to sell labor extensions,' 'stretch outs' there would be likely to yield larger savings than he would expect to obtain in any of the other departments." In addition, "because of the prestige of the weavers, who were among the more highly skilled and better paid workers of the mill," the precedent there could make the process more acceptable in other departments.[19]

Two-thirds of the weave room's 550 workers were women, evenly divided between Polish and French Canadians. "On the whole they were older, of longer service, and more highly paid than the workers in the other parts of the mill." Most were between 21 and 45, a third were married, and many had dependents to support. They had worked at the mill for an average of ten years.[20]

Union and management finally agreed to a compromise stretch-out for the weavers in early 1930, increasing from thirteen to twenty the number of looms tended, and causing 100 to 150 workers to be laid off. Although the 1930 stretch-out and the attendant layoffs and demotions provoked little organized resistance, the process highlighted what was to become a major bone of contention a few years later: How would layoffs be determined?

Conflicting interpretations of seniority brought to the fore a number of different problems regarding gender, as well as the purviews of management, union, and the collective bargaining agreement. The establishment of a seniority system had been an early and important gain of the Naumkeag union. One provision, however, particularly rankled married women, who comprised approximately half of the mill's 1,800 workers: absence from work due to childbirth led to automatic loss of seniority.[21] The weave room stretch-out required layoffs of a significant number of skilled positions, but not so the unskilled positions in the weave room. Workers voted clearly that "straight" seniority—length of service—should govern any layoffs, rather than a system that separated workers by job category. Skilled workers with seniority should be offered the positions of unskilled workers with less seniority, rather than being laid off.

The mill management, however, insisted that length of time *on the job*, rather than at the mill, be the basis for calculating seniority. This system would allow the mill to lay off more married women. The company apparently hoped to receive local government and community support for this plan, with the rationale that married women would be able to rely on their husbands' earnings when laid off, in contrast to men or single women who might need to seek public assistance. The mill agent insisted that the purpose of this change was to preserve the jobs of those who needed them the most: men and unmarried women. Workers, however, suspected that this was simply further discrimination against married women, a failure to recognize married women's role as breadwinners, and an attack against "a large and particularly independent group of workers."[22] Nevertheless, the union agreed to the time-on-the-job definition of seniority. One hundred and twenty-three weavers lost their jobs and were either laid off or ended up demoted to unskilled positions in the process.[23]

As this was going on in the Salem mill, the management was considering yet another southern property. Peerless Mills in Thomaston, Georgia, was for sale, and agents contacted Naumkeag's management regarding the possibility of their purchasing it. Although the issue was never brought up as a threat during the complex negotiations over the stretch-out, this time the board proved a bit more interested than it had on previous occasions when the possibility of a southern purchase had been discussed. The board authorized the treasurer to contract Lockwood Greene & Company, at a cost of $3,000, to carry out a detailed comparison of manufacturing costs at Peerless and at Naumkeag. When the board received the comparative analysis, however, it decided to abandon the prospect.[24]

After the successful stretch-out in the weave room, in the spring of 1931, the process was extended to the spinning department. Because worker turnover tended to be much higher in spinning, the issue of layoffs and seniority was less contentious. The company was pleased: managers reported that by the fall of 1931 payroll expenses had been reduced by over $300,000 a year, and the cost of the entire joint research project was being recouped every seven months. Naumkeag began to receive national attention from business, labor, academic, and media organizations. The Taylor Society and the American Federation of Labor, faculty from Harvard and Yale, and representatives of other mills and unions proposed Naumkeag as a model for labor-management collaboration, while national media from the *New York Times* to the *New Republic* to *Cosmopolitan* reported favorably on the Naumkeag experience.[25]

Workers, however, continued restive about union-ordered speed-ups, especially as they became accompanied, by late 1931, first by a shortened work week, and then by across-the-board wage cuts spurred by the growing Depression.[26] In particular, the large number of skilled married women who found themselves in unskilled jobs at a much lower wage rate (in the weave room, those demoted suffered a drop in wages from $27.55 a week to $16.55 a week), created a focus of dissatisfaction. Worker attendance at union meetings, which had fallen during the apparently successful cooperation period, rose, and workers did not hesitate to express their feelings: "Union meetings had more and more been taken over by the workers for the purpose of making known their dissatisfaction. Increasingly the union officials had become the object of acrimonious remarks and disparagement."[27] In mid-1932 a worried union leader, under pressure from management to agree to reinstate research *and* accept another wage cut, polled the workers and found that while 520 were willing to accept a further cut in wages (and 635 opposed), 980 out of 1,190 were prepared to go on strike rather than accept any further "research on their jobs."[28] Joint research was quietly put on the back burner.

Nevertheless, relations between workers and their union leaders were fast deteriorating. "The workers became increasingly bitter in their disparagement of the Union and contemptuous of the ability of its officials to represent them and protect their interests. Many of the workers now openly accused the union officials of 'selling out' to the management. . . . Still others claimed that the union officials had maintained control only by reporting workers who had been critical of them to the management for discharge as 'reds' and undesirables." The union leaders did not help matters when they amended the constitution to allow future amendments to be passed by a two-thirds vote of those present at any meeting, quickly followed by an amendment reelecting themselves for another two-year term.[29]

At the beginning of 1933, management convinced the union to revive joint research. Throughout March and April 1933, the local union leadership tried in vain to convince Naumkeag workers to accept the new company plan for the next stretch-out, the renewal of joint research, and the layoff of married women first. Of the local's elected officials, only Vice President Wilfred Levesque challenged the union's stance.[30]

In increasingly raucous union meetings and through a series of votes, workers reiterated their position: no stretch-out, no research, and maintaining the seniority rule for layoffs. On May 8, against the explicit orders of their elected leaders, workers voted to strike. "The members have flayed their officers at all the meetings held recently. Pres. Fecteau and John P. O'Connell, union agent, have admitted that their supposed control of the union was only a myth and have agreed that just now the situation is out of hand."[31]

A Tale of Two Strikes: Naumkeag and Draper

The 1933 Naumkeag strike had much in common with the 1913 Draper strike, but there were also major differences. Most revealing, in 1933 as in 1913, the existence of strong and dynamic radical organizations of various political perspectives nourished and sustained the strikers in both practical and ideological terms. Salem's workers encountered the same problems finding public and private spaces that would allow their meetings. And they faced a company that was practically synonymous with local politics and institutions, creating a united front against striking workers.

Most of the workers at Draper were recent immigrants, while in Salem, the strike took place ten years after immigration had been slowed to a trickle. Salem's workers had a union; Draper's did not. Ethnic identities were strong in Salem, however, and most immigrant workers felt that their union did not effectively represent them. Many of Salem's workers spoke only French or Polish. As in Hopedale, organizing and strike meetings were carried out in a variety of languages. Local institutions did not hesitate to dismiss striking workers as undesirable foreigners. The *Salem Evening News* cited approvingly a column in the stockbrokerage house Orvis Brothers & Co.'s newsletter that called the strike "particularly regrettable" because of the mill's well-known good treatment of its workers. "Many of the employees cannot speak English and presumably such words as appreciation or gratitude are not in their native vocabularies."[32]

Nevertheless, the issue of "Americanism" played a much smaller role in Salem than it had in Hopedale. Instead, the question of "radicalism" dominated the debate, as the city and the newspapers launched a relentless attack against the "radicals" who had supposedly taken over the workers' struggle, while strikers insisted that their commitment was based on the justice of their demands, not on manipulation by outsiders.

In Salem, the fact that many of the strikers were women added to authorities' unease with the strike's threat to the established social order. The importance of the issue of seniority—one that affected overwhelmingly the jobs of women—and the role women took as leaders also unnerved local authorities. The Salem city marshal announced in early June, "There seems to be a number of women who are inciting the violence on the part of the mill strikers. They seem to have forgotten how to act like ladies. If that continues we shall cease to treat them as ladies."[33]

Another major difference was that Naumkeag was one of many textile mills in an industry that had already demonstrated a strong propensity for plant closures. The fear that the plant would close or relocate permeated the debate throughout the strike. Yet strikers refused to be cowed by this threat. At Draper, the largest and most important loom factory in the world, there was no question of relocation. But the company quickly resorted to exceedingly aggressive tactics against the strike, employing antipicketing injunctions and violence and almost immediately hiring permanent replacement workers. Naumkeag, for all its refusal to compromise on the basic issues of the strike, did not resort to these tactics. One reason, of course, was the Depression: Naumkeag had little need to keep up production levels, and in fact probably saw some benefit in temporarily closing the factory.

During the course of the eleven-week strike the mill management, as well as local authorities and mediators, attempted several times and through various means to bring the workers back through concessions on wages and hours. Strikers, however, made it clear by overwhelming majorities that wages and hours were not the issue: the issues were research and seniority. At a huge outdoor rally in mid-July, Wilfred Levesque reiterated the point: " 'The reason we are out on strike,' he told the crowd, 'is because of research.' This opinion was also voiced by several members of the strike committee . . . all of whom said it was impossible for them to handle more work."[34] "The wages are not a prime issue, he said: retention of workers is the main demand."[35] An undated flyer by the strike committee referred to it as "the strike against the Research plan of the Naumkeag Steam Cotton Company."[36]

The mill's management, for its part, was just as committed to "research" as the workers were to abolishing it: "Any check or limitation placed upon research, or improved efficiency, will stop progress and halt the march of civilization itself," an NSCC statement announced in early July, as the strike entered its tenth week.[37]

Against the Strike: A United Front

When the workers walked out, the UTW International office in New York immediately telegrammed them to return to work. When that failed, the International rushed the union president Thomas McMahon to Salem, where he spent a week trying vainly to achieve the same goal. The International also froze the local's funds—some $10,000—leaving the strikers with no support.[38]

Local institutions closed ranks against the workers. Salem city officials, led by the mayor, insisted that the workers abandon their two central demands, return to their union, and sever any links with "outsiders." Town officials were not hesitant to dangle the threat of flight south over the heads of striking workers. "Predictions were made late today that if the Pequot mills close for a number of months, the Salem and Peabody plants will never be opened again by the Pequot management," the *Salem Evening News* warned. "It is generally known that southern states would welcome with open arms the local mill which has been in operation for 90 years and is considered the outstanding organization of its kind in the country."[39]

The paper greeted the strike with the gloomy announcement, "It is admitted that the Pequot mills are slowly being strangled by competition from mills where wages are much lower than those paid local workers and sanitary and work conditions cannot be compared to those found here. It is further stated that the mill has been operating on a loss for the past several years and that unless something is done to lighten their burden, the mill is doomed to join the list of plants throughout New England that have gone out of existence."[40] The *News* further editorialized that "in these days of such wide-spread unemployment, persons with a Job are mighty lucky and should appreciate that fact"; the paper urged social service agencies and businesses to refuse to lend any aid to the strikers.[41] A few weeks later the paper continued in the same vein, telling workers to "be thankful you have a job and stick to it, not letting any radicals stir you up to quitting it."[42]

Radicals

In the face of a wall of opposition from the mill, the city, and their own union, some workers contacted the communist National Textile Workers Union, to the dismay of the UTW leaders. When NTWU organizers met with Salem workers a few weeks before the strike, Local 33 business agent O'Connell accused the organization of being "an out and out red outfit" that "may be all right for Lawrence and other cities, but has no place in Salem and Peabody." He conceded that some of Naumkeag's workers "might be classed as reds, but they are very few."[43]

Once the strike began, the UTW was quick to blame it on these "radicals":

"Union officers assert that a radical element has stirred up the workers to the point of ignoring the national organization. Local officials went to the point last night of saying that some of the members of the union were in the pay of radical elements. The so-called radical wing met in Ward One, Saturday." For the UTW national president Thomas McMahon, "The radical leanings of the local textile workers, a new complex for them, was as astonishing as it was perplexing"[44]

The *Salem Evening News* suggested on several occasions during the 1933 strike that Polish workers—whom the paper sometimes referred to as the "Ward One group" because that was the Polish neighborhood—were the source of the radicalism. At an early union meeting, "a Polish-American worker demanded if the French workers were going to stick and this aroused the ire of the latter workers who thought 'she had a nerve to ask that question.' "[45] (The rumor persisted, however.)

Just how radical were the workers? Who were the outsiders, how much did they contribute to the radicalism of the strike, and what exactly did this radicalism consist of? How did the various political factions and interests intersect in shaping the workers' demands and the course of the strike?

Two fundamental issues—research and seniority—provoked the strike and remained the workers' central demands, and the company's central absolute negative, until federal arbitrators achieved a company concession on both over two months later. When their union refused to back them up on these issues, workers formed their own strike committee and reached out to a variety of social actors and institutions to support their cause. The NTWU, and in particular the young organizer it sent to Salem, Anne Burlak, proved to be a steadfast, though contested, ally. Workers also called on the ex-mayor of Peabody, a socialist, who lent his support to strikers as a negotiator and advisor. Other local unions, particularly those outside of the AFL, sent support and funds.

While Naumkeag's strikers were eager for outside aid, they also made it clear that they were in charge of their own strike. They quickly established their own leadership, organizing picketing, meetings, and relief efforts and maintaining a united front around their central demands. Given the factors arrayed against them, they were surprisingly successful. They not only won the strike, but they maintained what all sides agreed to be an extraordinary spirit and momentum over the long and hungry weeks of the strike. Union meetings and social events regularly attracted hundreds of workers; songs, cheering, and spirited picket lines remained characteristic of the strike week after week, and workers speaking different languages and adhering to different political beliefs, sometimes even attending competing rallies, continued to collaborate and concentrate on their concrete demands, despite the untiring efforts of local officials to sever those they identified as "radicals" from the rest of the movement.

The UTW International president Thomas McMahon was greeted with "boos and hisses" when he repeatedly urged strikers to return to their jobs in a mass meeting during the first days of the strike.[46] "You no have children and you no care about strikers. You speak of God, but you're cut throat," one striker shouted at him.[47]

The NSCC worker Phileas Peltier, who headed the first hastily formed organizing committee, found himself immediately confronting the city marshal, who banned the strikers' first mass meeting for being "red." "Peltier . . . rapped those responsible for spreading rumors about the meeting being 'Red' in its character. 'We are not here to fight and this is not a "Red" meeting. We are here to work for our own good,'" he insisted. With this assurance, city officials decided to permit the meeting. It was the first of many large, long, and enthusiastic gatherings, attracting some one thousand workers and lasting over three hours.[48]

According to the *Salem Evening News*, which covered union meetings in great detail, "The crowd was particularly enthusiastic, and cheers and stamping of feet greeted speakers who . . . urged the crowd to stick together and warned 'scabs' to keep away." Speaker after speaker reiterated a common set of themes: their union had betrayed their interests; research had led to unbearable workloads; seniority must be maintained; and while outside help was welcome, striking workers would make their own decisions.

Striker A. Dumas outlined the themes in the first speech of the evening:

> You and I know that the present officials have worked contrary to our votes. We want them to represent us as we are, and to fulfill the demands of the members. We wanted them to go to the mill office and express our views. I firmly believe that the present officials of our organization are not entirely in favor of the members. You would not know by their vote that we voted nine to one against the plan. Why do they oppose our demands? We cannot accept the mill proposal. It is too much for us; we cannot do it.
>
> In an article today [the UTW International] Pres. McMahon has stated

that the meeting was illegal. I want to say right here and now that we workers have a right to meet at any time. We have a right to express our opinion. We have a right to fight for our own good when our livelihood is at stake. Many large families are suffering today, but we have no support from the officers to whom we have paid high salaries, or the International union, which we have supported for years.

Who is illegal, he or we? The majority say we cannot accept the work along those lines. I want to say that I am an American and not a red. I am just a worker, and working for the interest of the employes of the Pequot mills. . . .

We have no officers to go to. Let us take this matter into our hands.[49]

Bleachery worker Margaret McGuinness emphasized the harsh conditions of work: "She said that in certain departments the work was to be doubled and more than doubled and that the workers had reached the limit. She told about workers going home nights with their fingers and hands cut, blistered and burned and that the only relief given them was in the form of gloves. 'You speak about this "Buy American" stuff,' she continued, 'those gloves were made in Germany. I know because I've looked them over.'" She charged that "workers getting $10 for four days had been cut to $8, because [supervisor] Shackleford had said they were getting too much." Her comments were greeted by laughter and applause.[50]

"I want to go back, but when I do I want to go with a smile on my face and not with my head hanging in shame," another speaker urged. "We have no hard feelings against the officials of Naumkeag, but we have got to get to the point where the stretching is a little too much. . . . Stick together. You are out and don't go back under conditions which impair you physically."[51]

A few days later strikers once again were called upon to deny being under the control of outside agitators: "The leaders . . . discredited reports of 'Reds' taking a part in the strike and definitely stated that [local socialist leader Joseph] Massidda, an important figure in the recent leather controversy, had nothing to do with the mill situation." Again in late May, "In regards to the rumor that Ann Burlak has been agitating the strikers to prolong their struggle with the Pequot Mills, Edward O'Leary secretary of the striker's committee said 'The rumor about Ann Burlak and other reds talking to the strikers and stirring up trouble is not true.'"[52]

By just over a week into the strike, the split between the strike committee and the union had become definitive. When union leaders mailed ballots to all strikers, urging them to vote to return to work, the strike committee was outraged. "We consider this ballot against our interests because it is an underhanded trick to get us back to work with no victory," a strike committee flyer protested. "Every ballot is numbered, so that every striker who votes will be exposed. Do not vote on it!"[53]

Workers' insistence that their demands were simple justice, not the machinations of outside radicals, characterized the strike until the end. A newspaper account of a huge open-air meeting in mid-July summarized the strikers' speeches as explaining "that girls lose weight because of research demands; many are injured by machines, the mill disregards the human side and thinks only of statistics and that no 'Red' element was assisting them in the battle."[54]

These denials represent a partial truth. It appears quite clear that strikers set their own agenda and were not about to be manipulated by anybody from any side, but their repeated denials of any *involvement* by outsiders were belied by the active presence of these very outside actors. While their advice and collaboration were welcomed, strike leaders also found themselves repeatedly caught between the need for outside support, their clear understanding of who was willing to provide this outside support, and the adamant prohibition by local authorities, including the mayor, the police, and the local newspaper, of any person or organization considered "radical." If activists like Anne Burlak or Robert Bakeman planned to speak or even be present at a meeting, the city quickly prohibited all venues.[55] So strikers trod a delicate line between officially disavowing their relationship with these "radicals," while in fact working closely with them in pursuit of their goals.

The "radicals" represented different ideologies and different organizations. Robert Bakeman (the former mayor of Peabody), Joseph Massidda, and William Mullins (of New Bedford) were socialists; Anne Burlak, June Croll, and Ned Sparks were communists. Although Bakeman and Burlak were the only two who devoted themselves full time to the Salem strike, all of those named spoke at meetings and rallies and met with workers.

When June Croll spoke at the Polish Falcon Hall to a crowd of 150, mostly women, she compared their situation to "the treachery of the UTW officialdom" in the 1931 Amoskeag and Lawrence strikes.[56] "All mill centers, she added, were watching the Salem strike and were hopeful that the strikers would win in order that demands for better wages and conditions could be made in their respective communities." When another speaker (Representative Felix Irzyk) brought up the "red" issue, Croll "reminded him that it made no difference whether they were 'red, blues or greens' as long as they were working in the interest of the workers."[57] "Loud cheering followed her promise to help raise funds for the strikers through mill gate collections in Lawrence next Friday night, when it is pay day."[58]

Anne Burlak's presence was first reported in Salem in late May, about two weeks after the strike began.[59] The *News* reported that, "with the red flame of communism threatening to cause further dissension in the ranks of Pequot mill strikers," an "insurgent group" had emerged among the strikers and that "a small minority of workers will open a drive to have the strikers seceded from the union." However, the *News* assured its readers, "the movement to have the strikers join a communistic union has already met with strong opposition from certain members of the strike committee who have been anxious to settle the strike without 'outsiders' stepping in."[60]

Salem's mayor George Bates worked diligently to counter the "radicals" and restore Naumkeag's workers to their union. On May 19, eleven days into the strike, he called the strike committee to meet with the International president Thomas McMahon in a marathon nine-hour session in City Hall, to "have issues which have divided the union discussed in a friendly way, eliminate any misunderstandings and finally to unite all members of the local into one solid group," he explained. A week later, Bates issued another statement to the effect that "the first step in the settlement of the strike should be to heal the breach existing in the union itself. . . . There can be no settlement of the strike unless the strikers put their own house in order and stop fighting among themselves."[61] What this statement ignores, of course, is that the workers were in fact not fighting among themselves; they were quite united in rejecting the stance of their union and its leaders.

Whether in gratitude for Bates's stance or in order to exert pressure on him, the mill, in the very midst of the strike, quietly negotiated a $100,000 loan to the City of Salem. The item was buried inconspicuously in the *Salem Evening News* but picked up by the Communist *Daily Worker*, which commented bitingly, "This shows clearly that the company is not so hard up as it pretends to be when it declares that it must increase the speed-up to compete with other mills. Furthermore it also shows up the real purpose of the mayor's interest in the strike. He has been posing as an 'impartial' mediator."[62] Two days after the loan was announced, Bates bluntly informed strikers that "the mill management found it absolutely necessary to carry out its program for additional work. Unless it did so, it would be forced to go out of business."[63]

While insisting on his own right to mediate the strike, Bates just as adamantly rejected the participation of any outsider he considered radical. When strike leader Wilfred Levesque attempted to arrange a meeting at which Bates and Bakeman would both participate, Bates bluntly informed him that "he would not stand for Bakeman crashing in."[64] He further announced that "oratory and mass meetings" were counterproductive, and he made it utterly clear that he would "not tolerate any interference by Ann Burlak or any other red agitators."[65]

But the strike committee was determined not to be overwhelmed by the mayor's insistence. After spending the day in conference with the mayor, strike committee chair Wilfred Levesque and other members organized an evening meeting with Anne Burlak, where the discussion continued, much to the mayor's dismay:

> The mayor made it clear that he was disgusted with the tactics of a few members, who had called the special meeting at which Anne Burlak, "Red Flame," had presided and had assailed him without having any one member of the committee present to take his defense. . . . Commenting upon the interference by Communists, the mayor this morning said, "If Anne Burlak is looking for trouble, she will get plenty of it from now on. I have instructed the city marshal to watch her closely, and every meeting from now on, will be covered by the police. We have had too much trouble from this source, and the people of Salem, I am certain, are sick and tired of this."
>
> His Honor was embittered particularly by the fact that the few members of the strike committee had gone to Anne Burlak after spending the entire day at City hall in conference with him, and then permitting the "Red Flame" to break up all progress. "Remember this," the mayor added, "you can't have both of us."[66]

Some 250 strikers "and radical friends" attended the meeting, in the Ancient Order of Hibernians Hall, where Burlak was the main speaker. Levesque explained to the press afterward, "Miss Burlak had spoken on the relief program and had emphasized the necessity of winning the local fight, because it meant so much to workers in other industrial centers."[67]

The local paper took the opposite position. Rather than raising standards industrywide, the strike would merely drive the mill from Salem. The *News* decried "the actions of Red leaders and others whose sole purpose is to stir up trouble. The leadership of these agitators has misled the strikers. From the public standpoint there is more involved than the strike itself. There is the need to foster an industry that furnishes a backbone payroll for Salem and Peabody."[68]

In mid-June, the strike committee finally agreed to present to the strikers the mayor's plan, which essentially asked workers to return to the job without any concessions on the issues of research and seniority. The NTWU distributed a leaflet that described the proposal as "Make more money by killing yourself with more work" and urged workers to refuse it. "We stand ready to help you gain a 100 per cent victory," the leaflet proclaimed.[69] A four-hour meeting at the Now and Then Hall, attended by 1,400 workers, ended with a decision not to vote, despite the mayor's insistent pleas. Although the *Salem Evening News* acknowledged that "expressions by some of the strikers last night indicated that they were absolutely opposed to research and additional work," it claimed that its failure to pass was due to "an organized group of 300 strikers with Communistic tendencies [who] blocked every attempt" at calling a vote.[70]

This recalcitrant group, the paper insinuated, was made up of Polish workers who were under the control of the ever-powerful Anne Burlak: "Rumors were current last night that the Franco-American group contemplated removing itself from the Polish-American section and would likely meet and vote in favor of returning to their jobs. There is a feeling that many of the Ward One group has been taken over by Anne Burlak and it is felt that progress toward a strike settlement under her leadership will be impossible," the paper explained. The paper concluded that "practically everyone" had supported the mill's proposal, but that the vote had been blocked by "a group with communistic ideas."[71] The NTWU countered with another leaflet, challenging the mayor directly: "If Mayor Bates wants to settle the strike, let him help you win your demands of *no research*. He is trying to make the presence of Ann Burlak the main issue in this strike. This is not an issue. The main issue is to defeat the vicious research plan, which constantly reduces your wages, piles more work upon you and then throws you out on the street."[72]

A week later, when the vote finally occurred, strikers resoundingly rejected the mill's plan urged by the mayor, by a margin of 813 to 462. The *Salem Evening News* complained that workers' rejection of the proposal was due in large part to "the work of Anne Burlak, 'Red' agitator, who, with a number of strikers, was reported as holding a 'victory' meeting last night."[73] The *Daily Worker* described the events in some detail: "Before the voting took place, Ann Burlak, secretary of the NTWU, addressed a meeting of over 1900 strikers and sympathizers on Derby Square. She exposed the Pequot plan of 'company-worker co-operation.' She pointed out that the company claims it is losing money, but it has raised its dividend payments from 75 cents a share to 80 cents a share. The Pequot Company also loaned the city $100,000 and has on hand $3,000,000 in cash." The paper then described the mood of the vote:

> Hundreds of striking Pequot workers gathered on the Common here and in front of the Mill, and then marched in a body to the Union Hall to vote against the Pequot Company's plan of a research system to lower wages. The strikers waved their "No" ballots high in the air. . . . Hundreds of strikers massed around the Union Hall at 8 o'clock to get the returns of the voting. When they received the news of the rejection of the company's proposal the strikers broke out into loud cheering and singing.
>
> Spontaneously over 600 strikers massed into parade formation and marched through the main streets of Salem, singing their strike songs and chanting "We want no research."[74]

A week later, in early July, police granted permission for a rally at the Salem Common, provided that Anne Burlak not be allowed to speak. She was not listed on the program, and Levesque, in the name of the strike committee, formally refused her permission. However, when Robert Bakeman, the last official speaker, finished, Burlak simply took the platform (the *Daily Worker* said that "workers called for her"), introduced herself, and made her speech, ending with a rousing call to "fight them to the end."[75]

> Exposing the vicious stretch out system at the mill, Burlak said: "It is like the old wheel used during the days of the Spanish inquisition to tear the limbs from the criminals. It stretches you and stretches you until it breaks you and then you are thrown on the scrap heap."
>
> She exposed the treachery of the AF of L and the local politicians, and called for mass picket lines as the only effective answer to the company's latest move. She stressed the necessity for mass action against evictions of strikers from the company houses. She again called upon the strikers to rely only on their own organized strength for settling

the strike. "All strikers and sympathizers to mass on the Monday morning picket line," was her final call.[76]

Relief

The mill management, local government officials, and the established union were unified around the project of returning the workers to the job as quickly as possible, with no concession on their demands. They shared the profound belief that workers' demands regarding research and seniority were inimical to the well-being of the mill. Although the mill management itself did not raise the specter of relocation, city officials and the union did, and the mill did not deny the possibility. The rationale of the city officials and the union was essentially the same as the rationale of the southern cities that advertised their subsidies and their cheap labor: industry must be coddled and attracted. It was a profoundly localistic view, in which cities and workers competed to offer industries the most profitable conditions.

The NTWU and the other "radicals" took the opposite view, arguing that a victory in one mill would improve conditions for workers everywhere. If Salem workers lost, lowered productions costs at Naumkeag would exert a downward pressure on costs and working conditions at other mills. Statements by the so-called radicals repeatedly urged the workers to hold out for their demands and reminded them of the importance their victory would hold for textile workers everywhere.

This difference in basic approach was manifested in the two sides' attitudes toward relief efforts. The union leadership, and the city, made every attempt to block workers' access to relief funds, in the belief that economic necessity would force them to give up the strike and return to work. The "radicals," in contrast, placed great emphasis on providing the relief that would allow workers to continue their strike and hold out for victory.

While local officials and the UTW International were blocking strikers' access to funds, the NTWU and the *Daily Worker* focused on collecting strike relief funds.[77] By the middle of May, strikers had set up shop for relief distribution in the Father Matthews building on Essex Street; and Anne Burlak "made her office" there, holding meetings and, according to police, conducting her strike campaign.[78] In a flyer that seems to combine the voices of the strikers and Burlak, the strike committee begged, "Our International President Thomas McMahon declared our strike 'illegal' and took over the entire Local Treasury. He refuses to give one cent to relieve the

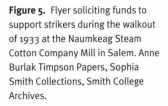

Help Us Win Our Strike!

The strike against the Research plan of the Naumkeag Steam Cotton Co. began on May 8th. Our International President Thomas McMahon declared our strike "illegal" and took over the entire Local Treasury. He refuses to give one cent to relieve the suffering of strikers' families.

If our children starve, it will be hard to continue this strike. If we lose this strike, all textile workers will be effected.

HELP US WIN!
Give As Much As You Can!

NAME	ADDRESS	AMOUNT
1.		
2.		
3.		
4.		
5.		
6.		
7.		
8.		
9.		
10.		
	TOTAL	

List No. _4 / 8_   Collected by_____

Address _____

Figure 5. Flyer soliciting funds to support strikers during the walkout of 1933 at the Naumkeag Steam Cotton Company Mill in Salem. Anne Burlak Timpson Papers, Sophia Smith Collections, Smith College Archives.

suffering of strikers' families. If our children starve, it will be hard to continue this strike. If we lose this strike, all textile workers will be effected."[79]

Many of the events that the relief committee organized took on the air of community celebrations. Salem residents recall the community spirit during the strike, with neighbors preparing food and strikers sharing with local children.[80] The committee held a tag sale in mid-May in Peabody, Salem, and Beverly. About two hundred people attended a May 31 "benefit show" featured boxing and wrestling, "with local boys as performers" and Wilfred Levesque presiding. Another benefit event was a baseball match between two local teams, the Falcons and the Canadiens. The independent National Shoe Workers Union, formed in the local leather shops, voted in early June to donate $100 a week to the Naumkeag strikers.[81] (The *Daily Worker* credited Anne Burlak with making the appeal to the shoe and leather workers.)[82] After the strike ended in mid-July, the committee continued to distribute food from its "relief stores" in Salem and Peabody, with "Saturday chicken" on the list, until workers' received their first paychecks.[83]

Late in the strike, the relief committee organized a huge Sunday picnic at the Old Thomas Farm on Highland Avenue (today the site of the Campfire children's summer camp). The picnic featured "games, sports, music and entertainment" for a dime's admission. The *Salem Evening News* described quite a cheerful scene, despite the more than ten hard weeks of no paychecks in the midst of the Depression:

> Between 600 and 700 were on hand to enjoy a program which included games, races, music, tug-of-war and speaking. The crowd shifted throughout the day and the total number present for the entire day probably amounted to more than the number estimated, but all seemed to be having a good time, men, women and children alike.
>
> All of the strike leaders were present, as well as several visitors. Music provided entertainment. Refreshments were served in good measure. An electrical arrangement permitted both music and voice broadcasting so that all could hear what was going on. It was an orderly, friendly outing group and while the purpose of the picnic was to help the relief committee and to keep up the morale of the strikers, the latter seemed to have the same confidence in the outcome of the strike as they have had right along.[84]

The *News* claimed that Burlak was silenced again at this event: "Ann Burlak was present but did not speak. She wanted to, but Chairman Levesque had a 'showdown.' The crowd voiced its approval of Mr. Levesque's stand, so the 'Red Flame' took a back seat."[85] Others, however, have a different recollection of the event. One Salem resident, who was 15 at the time of the strike, recalled going with her older sister, a striking worker, to this same picnic and listening to Burlak's speech there: "Boy, she was really the 'red flame.' She was fire, she was like a ball of fire, honest to god. You just stood there, people would just stand there, and she would mmmhh, talk talk talk. People were excited, I was excited, to meet this woman who was so active, so . . . fire and brimstone. She really was something else."[86]

The End of the Strike

After eleven weeks, culminating in lengthy meetings with two U.S. labor commissioners who came to Salem to mediate talks between the mill and the strikers, the mill's management conceded to almost all of the workers' demands, in particular the oft-shouted cry of "No more research!," the return to straight seniority rules, and recognition of their new, independent union. Within days of the victory workers, except for the loom fixers, had fled the UTW and formed the Independent Sheeting Workers of America (ISWA), Local One. The company agreed to recognize the new union, while maintaining an open shop.

Several factors converged to bring about the mill's concession on the two major issues of research and seniority. First, the longevity and success of the strike surely challenged the company's desire to simply wait it out. Second, although no record remains of the meetings with the two federal concilia- tors, Anna Weinstock and E. H. Dunnigan, who arrived in Salem on June 20, it was out of these negotiations that the company's concessions emerged.[87] Third, the passage of the Cotton Textile Act in July placed legal limitations on research and the stretch-out, enshrining some of the workers' demands in law.

The *Boston Globe* described the agreement as "an almost complete vic- tory" for the strikers.[88] The *Daily Worker* called it a "smashing victory" for the workers, "of outstanding importance not only to the textile workers of Salem, who go back to the mills with substantial gains, but to the textile workers of the whole country. In the victory of the Salem workers, the textile workers have the example of the courageous and militant strike action taken over the heads of the A F of L fakers, who were determined to force a speed- up system on the workers."[89]

Contemporary and subsequent accounts are unanimous regarding the jubilation of the strikers. While the strike committee met with the mill management and the conciliators in the Hawthorne Hotel for over seven hours, striking workers gathered at the Saltonstall School. By midevening, when the committee arrived to make its report, "the hall was jammed to the doors." Anne Burlak was escorted from the hall as workers greeted the committee with a standing ovation. Wilfred Levesque read the proposed agreement, ending with the provision "There will be no further research requiring an extension of work during the next two years."[90]

"The announcement of 'no research for two years,'" the *Salem Evening News* recounted, "a real victory for the strikers, brought forth round after round of applause and Mr. Levesque had to wait before he could continue, so deafening was the demonstration." This time no ballot was necessary; a unanimous show of hands the hundreds of workers enthusiastically ap- proved the proposal.[91]

Strikers cheered for the strike committee, the federal conciliators, and Robert Bakeman, then "formed a parade outside the Saltonstall school and marched down Lafayette street to the center of the city, cheering and shouting, and then went here and there in high spirits to let as many know as possible their pleasure in the strike being broken." Anne Burlak led the group through Salem, pausing for a rally in Derby Square where she spoke, along with the NTWU's June Croll. "A rousing vote of thanks was given Ann Burlak for her guidance and active leadership in the strike. The parade then passed through the streets of Salem, with the strikers shouting slogans, waving banners and handkerchiefs and singing loudly."[92]

A few days later, back at the Saltonstall School, workers again filled the hall as they met to secede from the United Textile Workers and the AFL. There was no dissent on the question of separating from the UTW and forming an independent union, but a clash developed when Wilfred Levesque, who was chairing the meeting, ordered the NTWU's Anne Burlak to leave. According to the *News*—no supporter of Burlak by a long shot—the majority of workers opposed him and insisted that she be allowed to stay. After "some stormy minutes" it was agreed that she would be allowed to speak, and then retire. "The reason why she was going out was to permit them to get together to organize their own union," she explained.[93]

Although a large number of workers had enthusiastically supported Burlak's contributions to the strike, they also voted that no "outsiders" could hold office in their new union, the ISWA. Workers elected Levesque as business agent, with other leaders of the strike taking the other leadership positions.[94]

Two Years Later

When the first contract signed with the ISWA ran out in August 1935, the mill and the new union found themselves once again at loggerheads. Under the newly passed Wagner Act, their employer was obligated to recognize any union chosen by the majority of the workers as the exclusive bargaining agent, which Naumkeag had consistently refused to do. The two-year moratorium on research was drawing to a close, and workers wanted the conditions they had gained in 1933 preserved or even improved. "Recognition of the union, collection of dues on the inside, increase in wages of 25 per cent., no research and no stretchout, and a 40-hour week with an eight-hour day" comprised the union's initial proposal.[95]

This time, the mill did not hesitate to make a direct threat to close. Mill agent J. Foster Smith announced:

In some New England cotton textile communities, mill managements have found it necessary to sell machinery and make permanent cuts in employment. In others, entire mills have been closed and the machinery either sold or scrapped. Nearly 10,000 New England mill workers have lost their jobs so far this year because mills have gone out of business. This is a gloomy situation and not one on which it is pleasant to dwell.

The Pequot mills have survived all of the difficulties with which New England cotton mills have been faced, despite the fact that the mill products must face the competition of low wage mills.[95]

A few days into the strike, the management sent a letter to every employee, enclosing a copy of a recent speech by New Hampshire governor H. Styles Bridges warning of the imminent closure of the Amoskeag mill in Manchester. "This letter is not intended as a threat that the Pequot mills or the Danvers bleachery will go out of business," they insisted. "We merely wish to show that the cotton mills of New England are fast losing ground. Since 1923 more than 300 New England cotton mills have closed forever or moved south. Today more than two-thirds of the cotton mills of the country are located in the southern states. Some years ago most of the cotton mills were in the north." In statement after statement, the mill owners reiterated the point: 316 mills had left New England since 1923. "You may reasonably ask why prosperity has left these mills. The answer is simple—the extreme depressed condition of the cotton textile industry and competition, particularly the increasingly strong competition from the low wage mills of our southern states."[97]

The *American Wool and Cotton Reporter* weighed in with a statement entitled "Will Labor Ruin Pequot?" "The recent history of cotton manufacturing in New England," the editorial explained, "has proven by the liquidation of scores of properties that New England cannot compete with wages and other costs that are wholly out of line. The Pequot workers, instead of wage advances, must accept lower wages. Instead of a week's made easier they must accept jobs of greater productivity and lower costs. Pequot is not at the parting of the ways. It is definitely a very considerable distance down the wrong road."[98]

Workers, however, were unimpressed by this argument. Levesque reported that strikers were quite ready to call the mill's bluff. "We'll help them move out," workers declared, "we will be glad to see them go if they do not give us a living wage."[99]

Once again, the workers saw the issues at stake extending well beyond their individual situation. "The union wishes to further point out that this is a fore-runner of a general reduction in wages which is bound to affect every other industry, and even go to the point of affecting government employes," a union statement explained. "If the mill, representing as it does organized big business in this community, is allowed to get away with this shameful procedure, then practically every man, woman and child in the community will eventually be affected, and the storekeepers and small business men will run into debt and will be out of business in a very short while."[100]

The UTW was quick to remind observers of the advantages of a concilia-tory union. When textile mill executives argued that unions in New England made it impossible for them to remain competitive, citing the Naumkeag strike as an example, the UTW International president Thomas F. McMahon retorted, "In the case of the Pequot mills, when the United Textile Workers had the agreement . . . we lived up to every part of it. Had the manage-ment gone along with us (the UTW), the present strike would not have occurred. International officers of the UTW agreed with the management, and not with the workers, in that instance," he boasted. "But the manage-ment broke away and subsequently dealt with an independent union, which is now on strike. There was no strike and no strike threat during the life of our agreement."[101]

Nevertheless, after nine weeks, the company proposed concession on every issue except wages, which it offered to submit to a state arbitrator. In a mass meeting strikers approved the proposal except for the wage provision. Two weeks later, in the midst of hearings regarding the mill's request for a court injunction preventing further picketing at the plant, workers met again and agreed to accept state arbitration on the wage issue. Once again, a strike against seemingly insurmountable odds had succeeded at a New En-gland mill.[102]

Responses to the Mobility of Capital in the 1930s

If the United Textile Workers' global analysis led the union to advise against militancy because it could lead to capital flight, the communist National Textile Workers Union took the opposite approach. Both socialist and communist organizers believed that a victory for one group of workers would contribute to improving conditions nationwide, and implicitly, perhaps, worldwide, and tended to advocate militancy. What the AFL unions saw as a threat, the NTWU saw as an opportunity. Anne Burlak emphasized that the Salem strike "meant so much to workers in other industrial centers."[103]

For Naumkeag workers, the communist NTWU was not, as critics implied, imposing an outside agenda. It strongly promoted what the workers had already set as their goals: no more research, no speed-up, and strict seniority.[104] In leaflets, articles, and speeches, NTWU representatives repeated that their goal was to support the demands as formulated by the workers. "No research in any department. Seniority rights for all workers. No discrimination and recognition of mill committee," one NTWU flyer reiterated.[105]

Yet like the UTW, the NTWU also clearly saw this local strike in a larger context. For the UTW, maintaining the legitimacy of their union and of the larger project of labor-management collaboration was paramount. Many of the aspects of the AFL that reformers critiqued throughout the century were visible in this strike. Maintaining legitimacy meant distancing the union from any stance that could be interpreted as "radical" or "red." The hierarchy of the union must be maintained: there was little room for internal democracy or worker participation in decision making. Jealous of their own positions, respectful of the rights of management, and utterly convinced that labor and management shared a project of increasing profits, the UTW's local and international leaders proposed only one solution to the problem of runaway plants: concessions.

The communists had a much more critical view of the race to the bottom. This strike needed to be won because a loss at one factory would lead others to impose similar concessions on their own workers. A victory, on the other hand, would raise the industry standard and allow workers elsewhere to claim the same gains.

Not all strikes that the communists and the NTWU were involved in were as successful as the Salem strike. Some, in fact, were unmitigated disasters. By the mid-1930s textile organizing had ceased to be a Communist Party priority, and the NTWU faded out of existence. Yet the issue of investment decisions, who got to make them and under what circumstances, and how workers, unions, citizens, and governments could shape both the circumstances and the decisions, only grew in importance over the course of the twentieth century.

Naumkeag Moves South

Local governments in the South had tried to entice other New England textile mills to relocate there since the late nineteenth century, beginning the shift of textile production away from New England. In fact, the first New England textile company to invest in Spartanburg County, South Carolina— a region that advertised itself as "the Lowell of the South"—was a Newburyport, Massachusetts, firm, Whitfield Mills, which helped to found Spartan Mills there in 1888 in the "first direct movement southward of New England capital." This movement became a flood in the first decades of the twentieth century, but a flood that Naumkeag resisted until 1949. In that year, Naumkeag purchased the Whitney mill in Spartanburg, renaming it Pequot and continuing production in the two locations.[106]

In 1952, Salem's Naumkeag workers agreed to increased work assignments to keep the mill in Salem. However, in mid-1953, company president Rudolph C. Dick announced that the Salem mill would close later that year when the company moved its entire operation to Spartanburg. The company claimed, rather perversely, "that the closing was not a case of moving south, since the company had been operating a mill in Whitney, South Carolina for two years." The eight hundred workers remaining at the Salem plant were left jobless.[107]

The Naumkeag buildings still stand, and now house the Shetland Office and Industrial Park. Naumkeag ran the Whitney mill only until 1955, when it merged with Indian Head Mills, which had recently spun off from Textron and was beginning a process of aggressive acquisitions along the lines of Textron itself. (In 1957 Indian Head also took over Textron's Ponce, Puerto Rico, operation, which it ran until 1961; see chapter 3.) Between 1973 and 1976 Indian Head—and Naumkeag along with it—was gradually bought by the Dutch industrial holding company Thyssen-Bornemisza NV.[108]

The Whitney plant, however, was purchased by Spartan Mills in 1964 and renamed Whitney. Several decades later, Whitney's workers also lost their jobs when Spartan closed it in 1996 as it began to shift production to Mexico. In 2001 Spartan itself was shut down, throwing another 1,200 workers out of work.[109] The GE Capital Corporation, Spartan Mills' largest creditor, seized its remaining assets.[110] Ironically, General Electric remains one of the few industrial employers left on Boston's North Shore.

In the decades following Naumkeag's closing, other Salem industries followed the same path. Parker Brothers, the game company that had operated in Salem since the late nineteenth century, and GTE Sylvania, producer of light bulbs and consumer electronics, both closed in the 1990s. The Parker Brothers facility was converted to luxury apartments, and the GTE plant was purchased by Salem State College. These industries' replacements have not brought the kind or the number of jobs that the city hoped for and needed. Salem provides a classic case of the deindustrialization of the United States that began with the textile industry and now afflicts so many of the country's communities.

Shortly after the mill closed, Puerto Rican and Dominican immigrants began to move into the old mill tenements, some of them working in the new small industries opened in the mill facility and some in Salem and Peabody's remaining leather shops. Increasingly, however, Latino immigrants in Salem, as elsewhere in the United States, have worked providing services to the mainly Anglo middle class, even as this middle class has shrunk in recent decades, many of its members being pushed into the working poor and a few of them reaping the profits of the new global economy.

ROBERT BAKEMAN

Robert Bakeman was well known in Salem and Peabody—where he twice served as mayor in the 1920s—as a socialist, a passionate advocate of free speech, and a supporter of workers' causes.

Bakeman was born in 1879 in Auburn, Maine, and educated at Colby College, Harvard, and the Newton Theological Seminary. He served as minister at a Baptist church in East Jaffrey, New Hampshire, and later in Schenectady and Little Falls, New York. On several occasions he preached and spoke in favor of workers' rights; in Little Falls he was arrested four times for speaking at public rallies in favor of striking workers.[111]

Later he received an MA in Education at Harvard, taught civics in Springfield, and became principal of a school in Adams, Massachusetts. He served in the U.S. Army in France during World War I and came to Peabody in 1919 to take a position as pastor in the Second Congregational Church in South Peabody, where he almost immediately became involved in support of striking leather workers.[112]

While in Peabody, Bakeman was also appointed by the State Board of Education to teach a citizenship class to immigrants. In late 1920

Figure 6. Peabody, Massachusetts, socialist Robert Bakeman. The George Peabody House Museum collection. Reprinted by permission.

Peabody's mayor accused him of "being a Socialist, and advocate of the Socialist-Labor party which preached revolution and the overthrow of the government," and asked the School Committee to remove him from his teaching position. (Bakeman identified himself, variously, as a "Christian Socialist" and an "Independent Republican.") The School Committee, however, voted in Bakeman's favor. The incident spurred Bakeman to run for the School Committee himself.[113]

Bakeman lost a bid for mayor of Peabody in 1922, but won in 1924 and again in 1926. His iconoclastic and populist style was evident in the ceremony as he took office in January 1925. Sixteen hundred people attended the standing-room-only affair in City Hall, during which, the newspaper noted bemusedly, he addressed the audience as "folks" and led them in a recital of a "pledge to the people": "Realizing that I am a partner in the life of this community—with malice toward none and with charity toward all, I promise to give my level best in word and deed to make our city a better place in which to live."[114]

In August 1927, as the execution of Sacco and Vanzetti approached, Massachusetts towns systematically denied permits to those attempting to organize public meetings protesting the execution. When Alfred Baker Lewis, the secretary of the state's Socialist Party, contacted the Peabody mayor's office requesting a permit, Bakeman informed him that no permit was necessary, since Peabody had no regulation restricting public or outdoor meetings. Bakeman thus placed himself on a collision course with acting chief of police Edward D. Callahan, who announced that he intended to give any demonstration "the bum's rush," despite the mayor's explicit instructions "to use the soft pedal and not to interfere with the gathering." "You know how I stand on this question," Callahan explained, "I am over here to keep the streets clear."[115]

As Lewis began to speak at the corner of Chestnut Street and Lowell Street in downtown Peabody on the evening of August 19, to a crowd of some three thousand to four thousand, "including quite a sprinkling of 'Reds' from Revere, Lawrence and Lynn," Callahan stepped in and placed him under arrest, thus breaking up the meeting. The mayor, who had been vacationing in New Hampshire, hurried back to the city, announcing his intention of appearing with Lewis in a hastily rescheduled meeting on Monday, August 22, the eve of the execution. He reprimanded Callahan, who "called Bakeman 'Red' and said that he would rather go down with the flag flying straight, than to stay with the Stars and Stripes upside down," and vowed to arrest the mayor himself if he participated in Monday's protest. This Bakeman precluded by quickly firing Callahan.[116]

That evening's meeting was "the biggest crowd ever gathered at a public meeting" in Peabody. Bakeman, who had previously openly expressed his support of Sacco and Vanzetti, used the occasion to speak about freedom of speech. The crowd was double that of a few nights before; the newspaper reported between seven thousand and eight thousand people.

In his speech Bakeman waxed eloquent about the history of freedom and democracy, from the *Mayflower* to World War I, "the background, the hallowed traditions, which reddens each stripe and whitens each star in the flag of the United States." Far from being un-American, he insisted, immigrant radicalism was the very essence of American identity.

You may call me what you will, any color, Red, if you choose, but I hope to be man enough to be as red as the Pilgrims, red as the Revolutionists of 1776; red as Abraham Lincoln; as red as the constitution of the United States and the Declaration of Independence.

This meeting is here tonight, because on last Friday night, contrary to my expressed wish, that the reality of freedom of speech in Peabody be maintained, the then chief of police arrested a man who had been informed through my office that no permit was needed in Peabody to speak. . . .

I am here tonight, not to discuss the Sacco and Vanzetti case, although I have my own opinion of that, but to defend with all my power the freedom insisted upon by our ancestors, which lies at the very heart of our government.[117]

The American Civil Liberties Union carried out a survey in 1928 entitled "Blue Coats and Reds" that investigated local town and police restrictions on public speech. "With a few notable exceptions practically every police official answering our questionnaire shows active hostility to radicals . . . and a strong determination to keep them out of his city if he can do it. Most of them lay stress on the essential 'Americanism' of their cities." In almost all of the cities surveyed, public and private spaces were denied to speakers identified as "reds" or radicals. In the textile town of Fall River, the chief of police openly explained, "Owners or lessees of halls notify this office when they are suspicious of any meeting to be held, the police investigate, and if they find it is to be a Red or radical meeting it is not allowed to be held." The ACLU was successful, however, in ending police raids on striking textile workers' meetings in a vacant lot christened "Liberty Lot."[118] (Two years later, Anne Burlak became one of the main users of the lot.)

During the 1933 shoe and leather strike in Peabody Bakeman helped to form a "citizens committee" (of which he was secretary) to try to negotiate an agreement.[119] From the very first day of the Naumkeag strike, he expressed his willingness to play a similar role, and though Salem's mayor George Bates angrily rejected Bakeman's participation, he played an active role in supporting the strikers and aiding the strike committee.[120]

Bakeman denounced the company's research plan in dramatic terms in a letter to the local newspaper in early June:

It is high time that the people were told in simple language that these textile workers are staying out in protest and revolt against an industrial plan which, under the fine-sounding name of "research," reduces the wages of the worker, makes a frenzied nightmare of this work, throws human beings at an early age upon the scrap-heap, and wipes out, as far as possible, the distinction between the man and woman and the machines upon which they work.

When girls whose hands are burned and blistered on hot machines, protest against being "speeded up," and are told that their hands will soon be calloused over; when a girl is told by her own business-agent that "a girl is only good for two years on this job"; when girls are constantly sent to the nurse with strained wrists due to the turning of heavy sheets (a job formerly done by men); when girls lose weight because the heat and speed required to get out their day's quota—isn't it about time that there should be a revolt somewhere? To hear the weavers and spinners tell the stories of the impossible standards of both quantity and quality put upon them for a day's work—is to believe them. They are dead in earnest.

The girl who said, when her foreman asked her whether the trouble was with her or her machine, "I guess it's me, I'm not quite automatic!" —told the story with pathetic eloquence. The workers at the Pequot Mills are fighting against being sucked in by the machine!

It is a righteous fight and these workers deserve the active support of everyone who believes that the machine was made to be the servant of man and not his despotic master![121]

In a July speech to a large crowd of workers on the Salem Common, Bakeman depicted the condition of the mill's workers as the product of a long history of exploitive labor relations. "Bakeman attacked 'the machine' which he said was making slaves out of the workers. The beautiful homes on Chestnut street, he said, had been built by men who had, during the days of Salem's supremacy on the seas, brought slaves into this country."[122]

"Bakeman scored residents of the Chestnut and Federal Streets sections and said that their ancestors were sea captains who left here with ships loaded with Medford rum, bibles and missionaries for Africa and returned with the hatches loaded with black men whom they sold to southerners as slaves and then turned around and fought to free the slaves. That was the beginning of slavery in America and they still are trying to continue it in the Pequot Mills and Danvers Bleachery."[123]

ANNE BURLAK

Anne Burlak was the twenty-two-year-old national secretary of the communist National Textile Workers Union when she came to Salem in 1933. Born in 1911 to radical working-class immigrant parents, she dropped out of high school when she was 14 to work in a silk mill near Bethlehem, Pennsylvania, where her father was employed at Bethlehem Steel. She quickly became involved in union organizing, and in the Communist Party. "My class struggle education developed rapidly," she wrote later. "Daily experience in the mill taught me that my boss and I had nothing in common. He was looking out for ever more profits, which he could only achieve at his workers' expense. We were anxious to increase our wages, which we could accomplish only if our boss would part with a bit of his profits."[124]

By the time she came to Salem in mid-May 1933 to offer her help to striking workers, Burlak had been blacklisted for union organizing in Bethlehem-area mills and arrested for reading the Bill of Rights at a Bethlehem protest. She went with the NTWU to South Carolina to participate in an organizing drive in the wake of the Gastonia strike at the Loray Mill (owned by the Rhode Island–based Manville-Jenckes Company, which had just closed two Rhode Island mills when the workers there went out on strike).[125]

The struggle between the AFL and the NTWU in Salem mirrored what developed in their respective southern campaigns in 1929. Burlak described the AFL campaign in the South in derisive terms:

> After the Gastonia experience, the AFL, and especially its President, William Green, became alarmed at the prospect of "red unionism" growing among Southern textile workers, and a decision was made . . . to start a campaign to organize the South. . . . William Green did not speak at any mill gates, or to meetings organized specially to reach textile workers. When he came to the southland, he addressed bankers, politicians and mill owners. He was wined and dined by Chambers of Commerce, who received him politely. Green talked of the "patriotism" of the AFL, of its dedication to the free enterprise system, its no strike policy, and advocated union-management cooperation in the mills. He also painted the horrors of "communist" organization as an alternative, if the AFL was not accepted. Green was also accompanied

by an efficiency engineer, who tried to demonstrate to the mill owners that the AFL could actually help in introducing efficiency methods (speed-up or stretch-out as the mill workers called it) into the mills.[126]

Although this was before Burlak's involvement with Naumkeag, the Salem mill was the case study that the AFL used in its southern campaign to tout the benefits of labor-management collaboration. As a contemporary account explained, a pillar of the campaign was "the advertisement of union-management cooperation through speeches and articles, and most important of all, through the field-work of the consulting engineer, Mr. Geoffrey Brown, who was retained to approach employers throughout the South with an explanation of the principles of union-management cooperation as they had been worked out at the Naumkeag Mills of Salem, and with an offer of his assistance in putting similar plans in operation in southern establishments." The three lone Georgia employers who took his bait signed an agreement "copied directly from one in effect at the Naumkeag mills."[127]

After a public protest in Atlanta in May 1930, at which, "as was our custom, Jim Crow rules were ignored," Burlak was arrested with five others and charged with "violation of the State Insurrection Law," a charge carrying the death penalty. After six weeks she was released on bail, but for the next seven years the trial was delayed and the charges against her remained open. After her release, she spent the summer and fall on a tour in support of the Atlanta Six, ending in Boston in October just in time to attend the AFL's fiftieth convention. There AFL president William Green argued against a national system of unemployment insurance. "It was hard for me to imagine a labor convention opposing federal unemployment insurance in the face of the mass misery and hunger in the land," she commented later.[128]

A hallmark of NTWU organizing in the 1930s was linking workplace issues to larger societal issues. In the South, this meant the call for racial justice; in New Bedford, where Burlak was sent as an organizer in late 1930, it meant the rights of the unemployed. "Our union helped to organize a couple of Unemployed Councils, offering our Union Hall as a place for the Councils to hold their meetings. This brought about close working relations between the employed and unemployed Union members. . . . Our Union considered it vitally necessary to maintain close relations between the workers in the mills, and the unemployed workers. So we

ANN BURLAK

Ann Burlak, long termed the "Red Flame" of the left wing of the Communist party in these parts, found only a small, impassive gathering facing her when she spoke on Boston Common last night on the evils of the textile situation in these parts. Here she is as she addressed the listless gathering. 9/14/34

Figure 7. Anne Burlak speaks on Boston Common, 1934. Anne Burlak Timpson Papers, Sophia Smith Collections, Smith College Archives.

organized regular mill gate rallies, to discuss the need for unity and joint action around such demands as 'adequate relief,' and for 'federal unemployment insurance for laid off workers.'" In neighboring Fall River, the NTWU, barred from public and private spaces, purchased a vacant lot for its events. "Liberty Lot earned quite a reputation as the one spot in Fall River where 'freedom of speech' for Unions existed."[129]

The NTWU shifted Burlak to Rhode Island in the spring of 1931, where the union was headquartered in the Right to Live Club in Olneyville. Along with NTWU staff in Rhode Island Jim Reid, Martin Russak, and Bill Murdock, Burlak took an active role in several strikes there. At General Fabrics in Central Falls, in a situation very comparable to Salem's, eight hundred workers struck against a stretch-out and its accompanying layoffs. The strike lasted for months, during which the NTWU helped to organize daily picket lines, a rank-and-file strike committee, a relief committee and strikers' kitchen, and daily mass meetings. "Entire families of the strikers were involved in the struggle, including the children. We organized special meetings of children to discuss why their parents or older siblings were on strike. We taught them Union songs which they sang on picket lines, and at the public strike meetings."[130]

Building community support in the face of a hostile establishment and media was an important element of the strike. "We dispatched strikers and their friends to surrounding towns to collect relief for the strikers. We visited local grocery stores and local farmers for food contributions. Fishermen on the docks in Providence and Boston were visited. The fishermen were most generous in contributing fresh fish for the strike kitchen. Bakeries donated day old bread and cakes."[131]

The strike lengthened, and workers at Weybosset mill in Pawtucket, owned by American Woolen, joined in.[132] Authorities began arresting "aliens" ("some of these workers had been living in the United States since the turn of the century, and had families of grown American sons and daughters") to thin the ranks of the strikers. In mid-July, Burlak herself was arrested as an alien and spent a week in the Boston Immigration Station, until her father was able to produce her baptismal certificate proving that she was born in Slatington, Pennsylvania. ("According to our Constitution," she noted wryly, "in a criminal case, one is considered innocent until proven guilty; in an immigration case the burden of proof is on the arrested person.")[133]

In the fall of 1931, she was sent to Lawrence when NTWU leaders there, including Edith Berkman, the original "red flame" (dubbed such by Rev. James McDonald) were arrested and deportation hearings begun against them. "A vicious red-baiting attack was made on the National Textile Workers Union. City Officials and the press urged the strikers to join an 'American Union.' "[134]

"It was after Edith Berkman was jailed," Burlak explained, "that the newspapers began calling me 'the Red Flame.' Though I was quite blond in my youth, the press embellished their description of me. They often wrote that I had red hair, and wore bright red clothes. This was not true. As a blond, my taste in clothes usually ran to pastels. My guess is that the press called me 'the Red Flame' because of the militant class struggle policy carried out by our Union."[135]

As in the Salem strike and many others, "the Lawrence mill owners carried on an intensive campaign trying to justify their proposed wage cut.

They argued that competition with the Southern mills made the wage cut necessary if they were to continue doing business in Lawrence. At the very time they were presenting this argument, they were preparing to move their mills South. What they did not tell the public, was that many directors of mills in the north and south, were one and the same."[136]

The Lawrence strike was broken after six weeks. Burlak attributes the loss to several factors: "The favorable treatment given to the (AFL) United Textile Workers Union, the permission for them to use the bandstand on the Common; the statements in the press calling on the strikers to join 'an American Union' if they wanted to be recognized by the mill owners, finally caused division among the strikers." However, she also blamed the NTWU: "It seemed to me that our Union did not carry on a sufficiently effective campaign for unity among the strikers, regardless of what union they were members of."[137] The positions that Burlak took during the Salem strike seemed shaped by this self-critique.

In the spring of 1932, Burlak's father answered a call from Soviet leaders for skilled workers to help build Soviet industry. He had been unemployed for over a year, lost his company house in Bethlehem, and brought his wife and three sons, ages 16, 12, and 7, to live in a small basement apartment in a New York City complex where he worked as a janitor. In the depths of the Depression, over one hundred thousand U.S. citizens and residents applied for six thousand spots; Anne Burlak's father got one of them.[138]

Despite the great detail in which Burlak described her experiences in the Lawrence and Central Falls strikes, as well as numerous other organizing campaigns, strikes, and political activities, she had virtually nothing to say in her (unpublished) autobiography about the ten weeks she spent in Salem. The entirety of her reference to the Naumkeag strike was as follows: "In the spring of 1933 I spent several months in Salem and Peabody, Mass., where a strike against speed up spontaneously took place in the Naumkeag Steam Cotton Mill and at the Danvers Bleachery. That strike was won in spite of great odds."[139]

JAMES LUTHER ADAMS

Salem's religious community did not take a particularly active role in the strike. On the day the strike was declared, Rev. Jean Baptiste Labossier of St. Joseph's Church asked his parishioners to pray for an early

Figure 8. James Luther Adams in an undated photo, circa 1930. Photo from collection of Eloise Adams. Reprinted by permission.

settlement. He and Rev. Joseph Czubek of St. John the Baptist Church met with Mayor Bates in early June to discuss the situation. They did not, however, seem to take an active role in urging a conciliatory position on the workers, as Catholic priests did in some other New England strikes.[140]

Toward the very end of the strike, the young James Luther Adams, minister at the Second Unitarian Church of Salem—attended by few workers, but several of the mill's management and board of directors—preached a lengthy sermon decrying the city establishment, especially the media, for privileging the mill's point of view over that of the workers. Adams went on to become a well-known progressive theologian, and in later life credited his experience with the Salem strike as being a foundational event in his political development.[141]

Because a lengthy excerpt from Adams's sermon was published in the *Salem Evening News* the following day, its content quickly became widely known. Because he went on to become one of the best-known American theologians, and because he viewed his experience in Salem as central to the formulation of his theology, his writings became the only place in which the 1933 Naumkeag strike entered the historical record.

"The depression and the early Roosevelt years," wrote Adams in a 1977 essay entitled "The Evolution of My Social Concern," "along with a markedly unideological interest in the writings of Marx, an increasing interest in the problems of unemployment and of the labor movement, participation as a minister in the activities incident to the great textile strike in Salem, Massachusetts—all these things conspired to develop a social concern, both theoretical and practical, which had previously been relatively peripheral."[142] In his autobiography, Adams devoted a chapter to his years in Salem and described the strike in greater detail. (It seems probable that the strike had a greater effect on him than he had on the strike; in his recollections he appears to play a larger role than the published sources from the time reflect.)

In his July 16 sermon, Adams chose as his text "To him that hath shall be given, and to him that hath not even that which he hath shall be taken away." The mill owners, he argued, enjoyed numerous advantages:

> They belong to a homogeneous racial and economic group. They are a small body of men. They are capable of arriving co-operatively at a well-thought-out point of view and policy. Their dissensions do not reach the public press. They can keep a solid front in their attitude towards us, the public in general, and towards the workers. They have the advantage of hiring skilled lawyers who can, in an efficient, professional manner, state their point of view, present it to the public and defend it against the workers. Furthermore, they have a solid political influence. They can, if they wish, effectively bring pressure to bear on important public officials who may, in turn, bring pressure to bear upon mill workers. And last of all, they have a distinct advantage in getting the attention of the public. Their facts can be presented to the newspapers in a cogent, persuasive manner and in some cities, mill owners can, if they wish, force the newspapers to give preference to their own point of view. With all of these advantages, we may readily see how public opinion may very efficiently and effectively be formed by this group.

The workers, in contrast, suffered a myriad of disadvantages:

> There are various religions, economic and racial groups. All of these men and women are constantly subjected to the varying winds of

doctrine which are set up by our chaotic social order. It is inevitable that there should be numerous factions and a constant shifting from one point of view to another.... A solid front either for influencing the mill owners or for influencing public opinion is impossible. Furthermore, the workers have been abandoned by the national union and the experienced, trained leaders familiar with the whole situation disappeared early on from the scene, and the previously subordinate officials have had to take charge and obtain experience in these past few weeks. Moreover, the funds of the workers have been tied up so they cannot be used. Hence, the workers cannot employ highly-paid, professionally trained lawyers and strike experts. With all these disadvantages, the workers have various inadequate means for influencing public opinion.

Adams insisted that he was not personally advocating the workers' position, only arguing that it had not received a fair public hearing and that the public deserved and needed to hear both sides of the issue. "These workers have, whenever allowed to vote on the proposals made by the management, overwhelmingly rejected them. At great sacrifice, because of disorganized conditions, resulting from the alienation of the local from the national union, with much real suffering and, in spite of varying attempts to force them, both on the part of radicals and of local citizens and politicians, the workers have persistently and with surprising consistency, maintained essentially the same attitude for 10 weeks. They must think they have a real grievance."[143]

On one issue, Adams agreed with many of the other actors: this strike, and its outcome, were of profound national importance: "The way in which this strike is settled and the policy of the mill and the workers in the next few weeks may in large measure determine the success of the national recovery act. We may almost say that the Salem case is a test case."[144]

Adams's recollection of the end of the strike, recounted years later in his autobiography, differs substantially from what was recorded at the time. Several newspapers covered the march and rally, but none of them described the events that Adams recalled. It is worth repeating, however, for its drama, and for its salutary reminder that eyewitnesses sometimes see very different versions of the same event: "At least a thousand workers," Adams wrote, with their wives and children, paraded through the streets of Salem and ended up on the lawn of our home. Some of their leaders came into the house and persuaded me to go and stand under a large tree to make a speech. I had to think fast about what I was going to say. In the course of my remarks, I was rudely interrupted by a ravishing, red-haired Communist. She seized me and started to pull me away from the tree, shouting at the people. "Don't listen to this bourgeois defender of the capitalists. You listen to ME!" Whereupon some of the workers picked her up and carried her off bodily, while I said a few more words to the crowd.[145]

CHAPTER 3

GUNS, BUTTER, AND THE NEW (OLD) INTERNATIONAL DIVISION OF LABOR

A great body of manufacturers have found the southern people willing to work for very low wages. Northern mills can't operate if this difference in wage rates becomes too great. If the textile workers think they can improve their position by striking, which is quite doubtful, the one policy that gives them any hope is to do their striking only in the low wage Southern mills that cause these conditions.

—EDITORIAL, *SALEM EVENING NEWS*, AUGUST 23, 1935

In seeking to meet the multiplying challenges to worker organization posed by an industry in the throes of dislocation, relocation and structural transformation, the Textile Workers Union of America [TWUA] unwittingly became the first major union in the United States to confront the specter of postindustrialism in actualized form.

—CLETE DANIEL, *CULTURE OF MISFORTUNE: AN INTERPRETIVE HISTORY OF TEXTILE UNIONISM IN THE UNITED STATES*

The lure of cheap labor, low taxes, and lax regulation elsewhere leeched resources from New England's textile industry starting in the late nineteenth century and accelerating in the twentieth. The first generations of "cheap" immigrant textile workers in New England, primarily from Ireland, French Canada, and southern and eastern Europe, became more expensive after immigration to the United States was severely curtailed after 1917, and the labor mobilizations and shifts in federal policy during the Depression and World War II upgraded the conditions for workers in the northern United States. The industry responded by accelerating its capital mobility, but also by importing a new generation of immigrants, already trained in U.S. machines and labor regimes in Latin America. The companies explored in this chapter show various faces of the pattern of disinvestment and speculation that began in the textile industry and seemed to have taken over the U.S. economy by the end of the twentieth century.

The stories also illustrate the intimate relationship of the textile industry with the U.S. military. While many textile producers benefited from wars and military contracts, Textron went further than most in abandoning textile production altogether by the 1960s and moving into heavy industry. By 2003, nearly 50 percent of the company's revenues came from its two aircraft divisions, Bell and Cessna, and the company was a major beneficiary of military contracting.[1]

U.S. military adventures abroad helped U.S. industries in various ways, and U.S. industry has often been an enthusiastic partner in U.S. military adventurism. At the end of the nineteenth century, foreign conquests were seen as ways of providing access to the raw materials (and the labor necessary to extract them) and the markets that industries needed to grow. As industrializing European countries engaged in the "scramble for Africa," the United States looked to its West and South, taking control of the northern half of Mexico in the 1850s, Cuba and Puerto Rico in 1898, Panama in 1903, and most of the other independent countries of Central America and the Caribbean between 1910 and 1930.[2]

Some sectors of the U.S. labor movement believed that labor should be a partner in this enterprise. Cheap raw materials and captive markets would help industry profit, and U.S. workers would benefit. Wars that served to maintain this global system of inequality also seemed to directly benefit both industry and workers in the United States.[3]

Beginning with the Mexican Revolution of 1910, Latin American countries began a shift away from a strategy of economic growth driven by the export of raw materials (which perfectly complemented what the United States saw as the correct global economic role for Latin America) to a policy of import substitution industrialization. Populist governments nationalized key resources, provided state support for the development of industry, and constructed a social safety network, especially in urban areas, that included protections for workers and public social services. (It looked a little bit like the New Deal in the United States.)[4]

Between the 1930s and 1954 the United States, having adopted a "good neighbor policy" toward Latin America and occupied with the Depression and World War II, was willing to accept these developments. In the postwar period, however, several factors coincided to reshape the terrain. The social welfare state created in the United States during the Depression and the war, and business's acceptance of (admittedly somewhat tamed) unions, limited opportunities for profits at home. Populist leaders in Latin America from Jacobo Arbenz and Fidel Castro in the 1950s to João Goulart and Juan Bosch in the 1960s, and popular and armed mass and guerrilla movements, threatened to take populist policies in Latin America to the next level.

At the same time, the U.S. government began experimenting with its own form of state-supported industrialization in Puerto Rico: the precursor to the Export Processing Zone, where instead of national governments sponsoring domestic industries aimed at a domestic market, the United States would collaborate with Latin American governments to sponsor foreign investment in industries aimed at an export market. Latin American organized labor and the social welfare state were increasingly seen as an obstacle to this project.

U.S. labor, however, proved to be an enthusiastic partner. Heady with the jobs created by wartime and cold war military contracts, disingenuously trusting of business's commitment to the high-wage, social welfare model of the 1940s, eager to maintain legitimacy by jumping on the anticommunist bandwagon, and imbued with a sense of nationalist and racial superiority intertwined with its craft identity, the American Federation of Labor needed little prodding. The Congress of Industrial Organizations was slower to join in, and the United Auto Workers broke with the consensus in the 1960s. But for the mainstream of the U.S. union movement, the cold war consensus seemed intuitively correct.

Thus began the drive, bolstered by anticommunism, to tame and diminish organized labor in Latin America, dismantle the welfare state, privatize the state-run enterprises which governments had incurred huge debts to subsidize and which were only beginning to show a return on these investments, and impose a neoliberal agenda that opened investment opportunities and granted maximum flexibility and profits to investors. The experiment began tentatively in Puerto Rico in the 1940s, expanded in Mexico in the 1960s, and peaked in Chile in the 1970s. As many South American governments began to challenge the model and shift leftward in the beginning of the twenty-first century the United States poured money into Colombia, its remaining bastion. The development model was bolstered by the American Institute for Free Labor Development, by structural adjustment loans from the World Bank and the International Monetary Fund, by huge influxes of U.S. military aid (much of it, of course, returned to the pockets of U.S. military contractors), and by U.S. industries primed to take advantage of the new opportunities.

Latin America had served as a source of investment and profit on the extraction or production of raw materials for U.S. businesses and speculators for decades. Now, with a heavy dose of U.S. government manipulation, it would serve as a source of investment and profit on the production of manufactured goods. Like the U.S. South at the beginning of the century, it offered cheap labor, tax breaks, lax regulations, and ready access to violence to enforce these conditions. It also offered a chance to elude a New Deal social pact that business had little commitment to maintaining.

Regional Differentials: Why They Exist, and Who Wants Them

When textile mill owners decided to close their New England plants and move south, they often emphasized the demands of labor and unions as the reason for their decisions. In fact, however, labor was one of an interlocking set of factors that created a regional differential between the northern and southern United States, and the correlation of unionization with the cost of labor was not automatic. Even before textile companies began to look to the South, some employed a strategy of maintaining multiple sites in New England, allowing them "to maintain production during periods of labor unrest by shifting work to other cities."[5]

Various historical and political factors, in particular the South's long dependence on slavery, contributed to the wage differential between the northern and southern United States. Stronger labor legislation in the North also contributed to increased costs, and decreased "flexibility" (as it is now euphemistically called), with respect to the South.[6]

The regional differential went beyond labor costs. Coming relatively late to textile production gave the South several advantages. By the turn of the century, the machinery and facilities in New England's mills were severely outdated. Southern mills, built closer to the end of the century, were designed to accommodate the latest technology. Some New England companies found it cheaper to upgrade in a new, low-wage location rather than refurbish existing facilities. Finally, southern towns offered tax incentives, subsidized transportation and energy, lax regulation, and other lures to potential investors, all adding to the cost differential.

The regional differential could be harmful to New England textile manufacturers. If southern plants could produce more cheaply, their low prices could make New England's goods uncompetitive. Thus in some ways, New England mill owners stood to gain from labor organizing in the South and from federal legislation to reduce the cost differential between the two regions: these changes would make New England textiles more competitive.[7]

However, there were some ways in which the differential worked to the advantage of New England producers. First, they themselves could invest in southern plants, taking advantage of the enhanced profits available there.[8] Second, they could use the existence of cheap southern competition to extract concessions from their own workers and local governments. The case of the Naumkeag Steam Cotton Company proves illustrative. The company told its workers, and the public, that it could not increase wages because it could not pay more than others and remain competitive, and it constantly dangled the possibility of plant closure and flight to the South when faced with workers' demands. In this respect, social inequality and regional inequality strengthened capital with respect to labor. Plants in higher-paying regions could use the existence of lower-wage regions to justify lowering their own wages. In the same way, management at a unionized plant could use the existence of nonunionized plants elsewhere as leverage over its workers.

The regional differential was exacerbated by federal government policies that facilitated the geographic mobility of capital, and hence its power at home.[9] One study argued that "the most salient incentive for moving south was the federal tax laws that made it possible for textile companies to deduct the losses of an acquired company against the purchasing firm's profits for at least two years." In this context, banks encouraged large corporations to acquire New England mills only to shut them down.[10]

During World War II, new price regulations controlled the price for staple "gray" goods, while leaving the price for finished goods flexible. It was thus in manufacturers' interest to finish their own goods, allowing them to sell at a higher price; finishers, in response, began to purchase mills in order to guarantee a supply of fabric. Commercial houses like J. P. Stevens, a cotton sales agency "with intimate ties to the Stevens family's New England woolen and worsted interests," followed suit. Federal tax laws that encouraged profitable firms to liquidate compounded the problem.[11] Soon, these plants were making the same decision to shift their investments to Latin America. Puerto Rico played a pivotal role in this process, for it was there that, in the 1940s, the U.S. government first experimented with incentives for offshore production that were to spread throughout the continent by the end of the twentieth century.

This process in the textile industry presaged the widespread phenomenon of deindustrialization in the United States at the end of the twentieth century.[12] "During the 1980s, an even more ruthless band of speculators and leveraged-buyout artists would lay waste to broad areas of the nation's manufacturing base, using variations on many of the same tactics that the TWUA had exposed three decades earlier." The phenomenon of capital flight put enormous pressures on workers and on unions to take a conciliatory stance toward management in hopes of keeping plants open. Capital flight was one of the main reasons the textile industry remained one of the least organized in the early to mid-twentieth century, and it was one of the main reasons for the decline of unions in all industries at the end of the century. By orchestrating global inequality and facilitating capital mobility, the U.S. government helped to increase businesses' leverage over labor.[13]

Investment Patterns of Northern Textile Companies

New England capital looked to the U.S. South at the same time that it established itself in the North, around the beginning of the nineteenth century. Depression in New England's textile industry when English imports resumed after the War of 1812 led textile investors to look south as a way of cutting costs. The first two mills in Spartanburg County, South Carolina—the ultimate home of both Draper and Naumkeag—were built in 1816 and 1819 by Rhode Islanders.[14] Textile producers also made their first venture into what would become characteristic of the industry throughout the nineteenth and twentieth centuries: turning to the federal government to impose protective tariffs on their products in 1816.[15]

New England capital underlay some of Spartanburg County's major endeavors after the Civil War. Several New England companies built branch plants in the South during the depression of the 1890s.[16] Boston investors owned a significant portion of the Clifton Manufacturing Company, organized in 1880, and northern firms like mill engineering firm Lockwood Greene and New York cotton broker Seth Milliken were major players in Spartanburg's industrial boom of the 1880s and 1890s.[17] New England mill machinery manufacturers like Draper also leapt at the opportunity for sales in the U.S. South. Both machinery manufacturers and cotton brokers had a

Figure 9. An 1899 flyer advertising Spartanburg County as "the Lowell of the South." The Regional Museum of History of Spartanburg County. Reprinted by permission.

vested interest in the growth of the southern textile industry to provide markets for themselves.[18] These types of firms also played an important role in the global spread of the industry in later decades.

Lockwood Greene, "America's pioneer of mill engineering," was originally based in Boston. The firm "selected factory sites, designed buildings and power plants, laid out machinery, supervised construction and organized management." One of its many southern mill projects "was considered by many to be the prototype mill for the Southern textile industry and helped to initiate a Southern textile boom that placed Lockwood as a leader in the field by 1880."[19]

Like Draper, Lockwood Greene moved its headquarters to Spartanburg in the 1970s.[20] By the 1990s the company had subsidiaries in Puerto Rico, Brazil, Mexico, and Argentina. In 2005, it had become a comprehensive industrial consulting firm, offering its clients "site selection" services to help reduce labor, tax, and environmental costs as well as "economic development" services to governments "to prepare and market communities and regions as locations for business investment and growth." The company also offered global "Lean and Agile Manufacturing" workshops.[21] In other words, it actively promoted the race to the bottom. Clearly, the lessons Lockwood Greene learned in the textile industry served it well.

Textile Unions Confront the Question
of a Favorable Investment Climate

From the very beginning of their struggle for more decent wages and working conditions, textile workers faced paradoxes created by the mobility of capital in the industry and the problem of convincing New England mills to remain in the region. Organizing for better conditions in the older, New England plants provoked owners to respond with wails that their mills were no longer competitive and threats to move to cheaper areas. Workers clearly had an interest in keeping the plants they worked at competitive—but at what cost to their working conditions?

Popular opinion has often blamed union demands for the flight of industry to cheaper, more flexible climates. But the history of the textile industry in fact shows that unions have more often made huge concessions, often futile, to keep industries in place.[22] On the other hand, beginning as early as the 1890s companies did not hesitate to use the existence of cheaper competition to pressure their workers for concessions.[23]

As one analysis explains, in the 1940s "textiles remained an extremely unstable industry, with more than its share of marginal producers. This presented TWUA officials with problems then unknown to labor leaders in industries like steel and autos. . . . In its efforts to come to grips with the dilemma, the TWUA urged companies to modernize their plants, even though such programs invariably eliminated jobs. . . . Union leaders not only had to induce mill owners to make needed investments. They also had to convince both workers and local union officials that facilitating economic modernization was in their best interests."[24]

The AFL and the more radical unions to its left often split over the issue of concessions. The UTW (AFL) was extremely wary of radical actions that could challenge its leadership, threaten privileges achieved by its members, or encourage the flight of industry. More radical unions (the IWW, the communist NTWU) were often more successful in appealing to the industry's immigrant workers. Many of the textile strikes of the early twentieth century were led not by the UTW but by anarchists, socialists, and communists outside of the official union structures. After 1939, the new CIO-affiliated TWUA took the lead in textile organizing.

If they often avoided militancy on the shop floor and at the bargaining table, textile unions were nevertheless among the first to pressure the government to address workers' needs in its industrial policies, suggesting paths that other unions were only beginning to open at the end of the twentieth century. William F. Hartford sees the TWUA as an innovative pioneer, an example to be followed by unions facing deindustrialization in the late twentieth century: "In its efforts to regulate capital mobility, for example, the union's various tax reform initiatives were supplemented by calls for an international labor code to govern foreign investment. Similarly, demands for area redevelopment legislation were often coupled with proposals for a tripartite federal textile agency that would develop a comprehensive plan for industry growth."[25]

For the labor historian Clete Daniel, the TWUA's resort to pleas for government intervention was more a sign of its weakness as a union than of a progressive vision. "'Less a union than a spectral lobby,'" he argues, the TWUA tried "to achieve through a relentless importuning of federal bureaucrats what it was unable to achieve through feeble threats hurled at heedless southern mill owners." "It was precisely because the TWUA had lost confidence in its independent agency that, from the early 1950s onward, it was forced to look to others for help in reversing a decline that it could not successfully reverse on its own."[26]

Although the New Deal and the postwar order created a strong role for government in promoting social welfare, the federal government was not inclined to take the kind of actions that the TWUA pressed for. As Hartford suggested, "This was the heyday of the American Century, and U.S. corporations ruled the world. Any legislative initiatives that either threatened their mobility or sought to interfere with their internal operations had small chance of enactment." Even the CIO leadership had little interest in the TWUA's continuing pleas and proposals for state, regional, and federal attention to the crisis in the textile industry, which seemed to hold little relevance for the booming mass manufacturing sectors.[27]

The textile industry, and thus the TWUA, had the misfortune to be the first to confront the new perils of the post industrial order. "It is a stark and inescapable fact," [the TWUA leader Wesley] Cook declared [in 1958], "that, because of the peculiar situation of the textile industry, the very existence of unionism is more closely related to legislative and political developments than is the case in any of the other basic American industries. . . . The textile industry is caught up in a worldwide depression which relates to the problems of international trade, international economic reconstruction, tariffs, quotas, and a host of other complex difficulties which even the strongest union cannot master without the aid of Congress and the Administration."[28]

Unfortunately for U.S. industrial workers, the explosion of the runaway plant phenomenon in the 1980s coincided with political shifts that made the U.S. government even less amenable to considering an industrial policy to protect workers and communities at the expense of profits.

Should Unions Support Mechanization?

The issue that sparked the 1933 Naumkeag strike, mechanization and the speed-up, was fundamental to the problem facing textile unions. The speed-up threatened working conditions and jobs, but if factories did not invest in modernization and impose the speed-up in the North, southern factories' competitive advantage would be augmented. And to the extent that unions succeeded in improving working conditions in the North, companies had a greater incentive to replace them with machines. "Skilled millhands were often at a loss to decide whether entrusting their imperiled futures to the UTW, or to any other union, would make things better or worse. . . . They often decided that activism would only hasten the pace of their displacement through further technological change."[29]

Mechanization and the stretch-out divided what Hartford characterizes as "persisters," manufacturers who were committed to maintaining production in New England, from "interregionalists," New Englanders who saw investment in southern mills as their hope for the future. The interregionalists saw the regional differential as a clear indication that the future lay in abandoning their northern factories. To the persisters, it showed the need to upgrade their northern plants and increase worker productivity. Naturally, it was the persisters who saw the greatest need to invest in modernizing their New England plants. But this meant that they were also the manufacturers with the greatest interest in maintaining their competitiveness by speeding up the work pace in line with their new machinery.[30]

Textile unions, therefore, faced different types of obstacles to maintaining or improving wages and conditions in the two different types of plants.

With the interregionalists, they had to confront the likelihood of the plant simply closing if faced with union demands.[31] With the persisters, they had to confront the company's urgent need to modernize in order to remain competitive.[32] Of course, persisters could always shift camps, like the Naumkeag Steam Cotton Company or the Guerin Mills in Woonsocket, which "persisted" and made peace with a radical union until the 1950s, when it "announced the impending shutdown of all Woonsocket operations unless its workers accepted a reduction in pay exceeding 25 percent" and, when workers struck, quickly made good on its promise.[33]

Yet the persisters also shared with the unions a desire to harmonize wages North and South.[34] Given the extraordinary weakness of textile unions in the South, companies too periodically turned to an ambivalent federal government to legislate improved wages, working conditions, and union rights there. Despite the boost to the northern industry during the 1930s and 1940s when federal legislation began to reduce the regional differential, manufacturers continued to invest far less in their northern than in their southern plants.[35] The trend was clearly toward interregionalism.

Textron: Leaving New England

The Textron company offers an excellent example of how interregionalism worked. Textron's origins were in two companies founded in the 1920s in New England by Royal Little: the Special Yarns Corporation of Boston and the Atlantic Rayon Company, one of the first synthetic fabric manufacturers, of Providence. In the 1940s, Little reorganized and renamed the company Textron, one of the first national conglomerates. With excellent connections to financial institutions and consulting firms throughout New England, Little was well positioned to take advantage of tax regulations that encouraged speculation. "Little began by buying failing New England mills with the intention of operating them at a loss to provide enough of a tax break into other, more profitable, industries."[36] Even profitable mills might not be profitable enough: "To maintain the cash flow needed to sustain his highly leveraged empire, Little set strict productivity and profit requirements for Textron mills. Those that did not measure up were singled out for liquidation."[37] Between 1943 and 1947 Little acquired "a growing interregional network that included seventeen textile mills and twelve sewing and cutting plants."[38]

The case of the Nashua Manufacturing Company, makers of Indian Head products, illuminates how the process of plant closure could occur and the limits of what a union could to do affect it. From the late nineteenth century, Nashua operated a mill in Nashua, New Hampshire, and one in Cordova, Alabama. In 1945, the company was acquired by Textron, which proceeded to engage in a series of dubious transfers of the company's assets from Nashua to Textron, including the sale of a significant amount of machinery to South America.[39]

Little then hired a management consulting firm to conduct a yearlong study on how to increase efficiency in the New Hampshire plant. The study recommended a $1 million investment in new machinery and laying off 1,500 workers, or 35 percent of the workforce. Textron's representatives, backed by their consultants, met in New York with the UTW president Emil Rieve. Rieve brought his own time-study expert and promised that if Textron actually made the investment, and if the union's research supported the need to lay off workers, it would agree. "We convinced Rieve that over 4,000 textile workers in Nashua would ultimately lose their jobs in that high-cost New England plant unless it was modernized and efficient. It would be better to help us save 2,500 jobs than to lose everything," Little explained. The union signed the pact in August 1947. Yet it could do nothing to prevent Textron from closing the Nashua plant a year later. What it could do, and did, was to shift to the political sphere, demanding a federal investigation of Textron's practices, hoping for a revision of the tax code to discourage frivolous liquidations.[40]

Not only was little amelioration forthcoming, but during the Korean War further loan and tax provisions were put into place that actually increased the incentives to companies moving south, especially if they were involved in defense production. Once again, Textron led the pack. "One program provided accelerated depreciation for new investment in defense-related plant and machinery, and the Reconstruction Finance Corporation furnished low-cost loans to participating companies." Textron was quick to take advantage of the opportunities provided to increase its southern holdings.[41]

The Alabama plant continued to produce the Indian Head label, while the Nashua, New Hampshire, Foundation purchased the Nashua buildings to try to attract small businesses and industries to the area.[42] In 1953 Textron sold Indian Head as well, in a complex deal which left the new company under the presidency of Textron's executive vice president—who promised "aggressive management" and quickly hired "a superb labor negotiator"—

and with a $5 million debt to its former parent.[43] (The new Indian Head purchased the Naumkeag Steam Cotton Company's South Carolina mill only two years later; see chapter 2. It was also the purchaser of Textron's Ponce, Puerto Rico, plant in 1957.)

Textron's Manchester, New Hampshire, experiment followed a similar path. Little describes the Manchester experiment as his final attempt to operate a plant in New England. In 1949, the company decided to use the Manchester facility to produce rayon lining fabrics. "The reason we chose this particular construction to test our ability to meet southern competition was that it had the lowest labor component of any synthetic fabric," which would compensate for the higher labor costs in the North. In addition, Textron invested in 960 new Draper looms to make production as efficient as possible and carried out studies to demonstrate that a weaver could tend a hundred of these new looms. The union at the plant, however, disagreed.

> We therefore built a beautiful new, single-story, windowless plant in Williamston, South Carolina, and equipped it with about a thousand identical automatic looms to make exactly the same fabric we were weaving in Manchester. When the mill announced that we were ready to accept applications for jobs, we had over five thousand young people off the farms in the countryside apply to get work. . . . We had no difficulty getting people to work three full shifts, and even to operate the plant on Saturdays. . . . The same was not true in New England.
>
> Within six months of starting up, the Williamston plant was running at a higher loom efficiency than New England. The weavers were tending one hundred looms each instead of forty-eight as in Manchester, wages and fringes were considerably lower, and power costs were half those in the North. It was a most successful operation. . . .
>
> Finally, after this sad experience, we gave up any further hope of operating textile mills in New England competitively with southern plants.[44]

Two years later, Little rewrote Textron's articles of incorporation to diversify out of the textile business: "I decided that there must be some better medium than the textile business in which to use the stockholders' capital to their advantage." Twelve years after that, in 1963, Textron sold its last remaining textile operations to the Spartanburg County textile empire Deering Milliken.[45]

Short of abandoning textiles altogether, northern textile factory owners followed several routes to self-preservation in the face of southern competition. They could make greater demands of their workforce, they could invest in improved technology, they could move south themselves, or they could seek government intervention to reduce the regional differential. Southern companies, confronted with foreign competition a generation later, used some of the same tactics: they made greater demands of their workforce, they invested in technology, and they moved abroad. Never, however, did they imagine trying to reduce the global differential. Instead, those that chose not to invest abroad sought a different kind of government intervention: tariffs and protectionist legislation. Those that chose to move abroad, in turn, looked to the government to protect their profits through free trade agreements and political influence and sometimes direct military intervention in support of the neoliberal model. The sections that follow trace the path from regional to global differentials and explain why and how the process of globalization has taken the contours that it has in the late twentieth century.

Puerto Rico Offers a Favorable Investment Climate

While textile workers and unions were acutely aware of the North-South differential in the early part of the century, they were less conscious of the links that the companies and the industry they worked for were forging with a new nonstate, Puerto Rico. Yet as early as the second decade of the twentieth century, some textile and garment manufacturers were contracting out work to Puerto Rico, especially fine handwork like embroidery and lace making. The process followed precisely the lines, and the logic, of today's offshore assembly plants.[46] U.S. manufacturers sent semifinished products to Puerto Rico, where they were finished either in small factories or at home, through a system of contracted labor. The finished products were then returned to the U.S. for sale.[47] "It is said that the manufacturer can ship his raw materials to the island, make them up, re-ship the finished product to New York—and cut his manufacturing costs by a full third," reported a journalist in 1923.[48] By 1930 needlework products accounted for 14.2 percent of Puerto Rico's exports to the United States, following sugar, molasses, and tobacco.[49]

In a multitude of ways, the system established between U.S. retailers and manufacturers, on one end, and Puerto Rican contractors and subcontractors, on the other, prefigured the process that overtook the global textile and apparel industry in the 1990s. From 1910 to 1920 the new department stores brought to a mass market fashions and styles formerly available only to the elites and sought cheaper sources to produce them. A Chicago department store developed a system of "stamped designs" to de-skill and standardize the needlework process. "Puerto Rican women's traditional needlework came to be defined by these conventional designs. . . . United States firms supplied garments, usually precut with designs already stamped onto them, to contractors to distribute."[50] A 1934 report noted that Puerto Rican–embroidered products were made for U.S. department stores, including Altmans, Lord & Taylor, Macy's, Sacks, and Marshall Field.[51]

Today discount retailers like Wal-Mart and branded apparel distributors like Liz Claiborne are following the same path, becoming the spearheads of globalized production. They are not involved in manufacturing at all; they are simply contractors who scour the globe for cheap suppliers. Like the retailers that outsourced needlework to Puerto Rico at the beginning of the century, today's outsourcers work through layers of contractors and subcontractors to evade regulation and accountability.[52]

Increasing regulation of labor conditions in the United States, union organizing in the textile and garment industries beginning in 1910, and the slowing of European immigration due to World War I and the legislative restrictions culminating in the quota system of 1921 and 1924 all led manufacturers and retailers to look to Puerto Rico as a potential source of labor.[53] U.S. government policies played an important role in facilitating the move. Most important, the colonial government's Departamento de Instrucción Pública worked with manufacturers and the Philadelphia Textile School to implement a needlework curriculum that trained over twenty-six thousand Puerto Rican girls and women between 1909 and 1926. In some cases, U.S. commercial houses like the New York–based D. E. Seicher actually contracted with public schools to have students embroider their products in their home economics classes.[54]

Needlework was divided between homework and small shops, with several layers of contractors and intermediaries distributing risk and accountability. By the 1930s some forty thousand women were contracted to do this work in their homes; over ten thousand worked in small factories.[55] The first attempt at imposing a minimum wage law in Puerto Rico in 1919 covered the women who worked at needlework in factories and small workshops, but excluded home workers. It resulted in 75 percent of needlework employers simply shutting their operations and contracting the work out to home workers.[56] It was precisely the conundrum facing New England textile workers at the time and that reemerged globally at the end of the century. Would improving conditions simply hasten the industry's departure for cheaper climes?

Some advocated keeping wages low to keep the industry from leaving. The needlework industry, one study explained, had no "foundation except misery. It could exist only on desperation wages. . . . Once employment opportunities improved, or minimum standards of employment conditions were imposed by legislation, the industry would pack up its carpet bags and move on" to Asia or elsewhere in the Caribbean, where workers would be willing to accept even lower wages. "This is the essence of the minimum wage problem."[57]

This debate came to a head in the mid-1930s, when the first of the New Deal legislation attempted to regulate conditions in the textile and apparel industries. The 1933 codes excluded Puerto Rico. U.S. manufacturers were divided among those who did not do business in Puerto Rico, who argued for a strong code to abolish the wage differential, and those who were involved in contracting there and urged that the differential be maintained. One noncontracting company urging for the code protested, "Unscrupulous American manufacturers are and have been exploiting cheap Puerto Rican labor in the needle trades to the detriment of our own American workers." In contrast, those with operations in Puerto Rico "argued that a minimum wage of even eight dollars a week [in Puerto Rico] would force them to China and other cheap labor markets, thus hurting mainland workers as well."[58] The debate presaged the discussions that textile and apparel manu- facturers would be having in the 1990s.

When the National Industrial Recovery Act was extended to Puerto Rico in 1934, needlework was one of the three industries that it covered, and it raised wages significantly and included home workers (though maintaining a wage differential). However, the provisions were "widely violated and with considerable impunity."[59] Needlework unions, based in the factories, strongly supported the provisions, understanding that low wages for home workers undermined factory wages as well. "The workers outside of the shop are working so cheap, we in the shops are without work," explained one needleworkers leader, explaining why she supported a wage raise for home workers.[60]

By 1934 the Federación Libre de Trabajadores (FLT), a Puerto Rican federation which had been affiliated with the AFL since 1901, claimed to have organized 75 percent of the needlework factory workers and three thousand home workers.[61] But with a government reluctant to enforce wage legislation, and an extensive system of subcontracting and a large unorganized contingent of home workers, the union's position was weak. A 1933 strike mobilized thousands of shop workers but failed to affect production because contractors simply shifted to home workers.[62] When eight thousand needleworkers struck in Mayagüez in 1939, demanding compliance with the minimum wage law, the contractors openly announced that they had no intention of complying. The government refused to uphold the legislation, "blatantly demonstrating the impotence of the Labor Department to enforce labor laws." After only a few days the workers gave up.[63]

In the meantime, the Puerto Rican government began to explore the possibility of attracting other low-wage industries to the island. As the implementation of the New Deal in the United States began to undermine the regional differentials inside the country and conditions for workers in U.S. industry improved significantly, both government and industry saw Puerto Rico as a site to re-create the low-wage, high-profit conditions that were shrinking inside the United States.

Operation Bootstrap and Textron in Puerto Rico

Puerto Rico's experiment in export-oriented industrialization had its origins in Boston, with the Arthur D. Little consulting firm that elaborated the first proposal for attracting industry to Puerto Rico. After receiving the firm's initial recommendations, which included building a textile mill, the Puerto Rican Industrial Development Company (PRIDCO) renewed the contract for Little to continue to advise the industrialization process.[64] By the mid-1940s, the foundations for Operation Bootstrap, which aimed to entice mainland U.S. firms to transfer production to the island, were being laid.[65] The development company offered investors a low-wage workforce, freedom from federal income taxes, and a government agency dedicated to preparing individual incentive packages, including some of the same things southern cities had offered northern textile factories in the 1920s: subsidized buildings, transportation, energy, workforce training, and other infrastructure.

Like the labor recruiters who had enticed workers from afar to New

England's textile factories, PRIDCO now sent recruiters to New England to entice textile manufacturers with tales of Puerto Rico's advantages.[66] Two of the first companies to take advantage of Operation Bootstrap's incentives were textile producers: Textron—whose owner Royal Little happened to be Arthur D. Little's nephew—and Newberry Textile Mills of South Carolina.[67]

The Newberry project ended before it even began. Newberry intended to transfer its machinery directly from its South Carolina plant to Puerto Rico. Puerto Rican authorities initially accepted this proposal, but when PRIDCO's appraisers reported that "the machinery had been substantially overvalued, that much of it was old, some obsolete, and some inappropriate for the type of mill proposed," the company decided to reject Newberry's proposed contract.[68]

Puerto Rico provided a number of attractions to Textron beyond the family relationship of its owner with the architect of the island's industrialization plan. First, it offered the low-wage, nonunion environment the company had enjoyed in its southern plants. (It was not until 1975 that the federal minimum wage was extended to Puerto Rico.) Second, the company only had to put up $500,000 in working capital, and the Puerto Rican government agreed to build a $4 million plant for it in Ponce, leasing it back at "a most attractive rent." "Since there was no duty on shipping either raw cotton into Puerto Rico or the fabrics back into the states, and since Puerto Rico had a ten-year income tax exemption on profits made on the island, this idea seemed most logical and attractive."[69] Puerto Rican officials were no less pleased: "It would be difficult to over-estimate the joy that was in San Juan when Textron signed—or the ease with which the Development Company officials agreed to terms more generous than they had granted or would grant to any other firm."[70]

Although Puerto Rico was not an independent country, Little clearly saw the move as a venture into Latin America: "Before going ahead with the project, we decided to study the operations in other countries of Latin American background to see how the efficiency of the workers compared to that of our low-cost southern mills in similar product lines. We visited a mill in Cuba, which was highly profitable, owned by an American named Hedges. We went to Medellín, Colombia, where we inspected five large textile plants, all of which were efficiently run, and earning close to 100 percent after taxes annually on their equity due to war created shortages and protective tariffs on the fabric at the time. In addition, we had the opportunity of inspecting many textile plants in Mexico, and again found highly successful operations."[71] Both Hedges's Cuban Ariguanabo mill and the Medellín mills produced their cloth with imported Draper looms.[72]

Textron's initial venture into Puerto Rico, however, was fraught with difficulty. Although the company soon began building a second plant, a tricot mill, by 1951 Textron's Ponce management team "prepared a 12-point indictment of Puerto Rico as a location for a textile plant, based on a comparison with their experience in the Southeastern U.S." In late 1954, a development program staff person reported, "Almost every day I get reports from my men in New England telling of one manufacturer or another who has heard very bad things about production conditions in Puerto Rico. As a rule these rumors originated with Textron, which seemed to complain to everybody in the textile field about how bad things are in Puerto Rico." The following year, "[Teodoro] Moscoso [director of PRIDCO] felt moved to appeal to the top Textron management to stop undermining the development program by spreading unfavorable reports on Puerto Rico among mainland manufacturers."[73]

Some of the problems went beyond location: in the two years it took to construct the plant, import the machinery, and put an administrative team in place, the price of cotton print cloth had fallen precipitously.[74] The end of the Korean War in 1953 had the usual effect of bringing a drop in demand. "At that price," wrote Little, "even our most efficient southern plants couldn't earn money."[75]

Other problems that Little declined to discuss also confronted his Puerto Rican operation. One was that the island's indeterminate political status meant that it was partially subject to U.S. wage regulation. While wages were far lower than in the continental United States, they were not as low as in the other countries Little had visited as models. By the mid-1950s opportunities for outsourcing had extended to even more lucrative areas. The fact that Textron was able to start operations in Puerto Rico with virtually no investment, since the government provided all of the infrastructure, also meant that it had little to lose by changing course midstream.[76]

By 1957 Textron had sold both the tricot mill and the Ponce plant. The Ponce plant was sold to Indian Head Mills, the former Textron subsidiary.[77] Indian Head, in turn, sold the Ponce plant in 1961, but it remained in operation.[78]

According to the former PRIDCO official David Ross, Textron's decision to sell Indian Head and its decision to leave Puerto Rico were part of the same process: "The company was responding to the textile crisis by getting out of textiles. . . . As far as it could, Textron was changing over its capital resources from investment in textile manufacture to a widely diversified investment in other branches of manufacture. The enthusiasm with which Royal Little had entered this new area of Puerto Rico was quickly transferred to the still new area of product diversification."[79]

The ILGWU and Puerto Rico

Textile workers unions remained focused on the situation in the continental United States during the 1950s and 1960s. The International Ladies Garment Workers Union (ILGWU), however, quickly became deeply involved in the apparel industry's move to the island. The union toyed with a push to raise Puerto Rico's wages to reduce the competition it offered New York garment workers, but by 1955 decided instead to support a policy of wage restraint for Puerto Rico.[80] Union leaders found ways that the union as an institution could benefit from the regional differential.

Puerto Rico's governor Luis Muñoz Marín negotiated between the desire to attract industries and the need to maintain the support of Puerto Rico's working class, his main pillar of electoral support.[81] In choosing to maintain a wage differential between Puerto Rico and the continental United States as an incentive to industry, he found a reliable ally in ILGWU president David Dubinsky.[82] The role of labor unions, Muñoz Marín explained, was to cooperate in "the economic development of the country" by maintaining a conciliatory stance toward industry. Wage issues would be determined through tripartite commissions made up of government, industry, and unions rather than in the workplace.[83]

"Elder statesman Muñoz Marín is credited (or discredited, depending on one's bias) with popularizing austerity among the wage-earning populace, who passively accepted the inevitability of relatively low wages on the strength of his oft-repeated dictum that 'the worst wage of all is no wage.'" And, as one study concluded, "The specter of the abrupt closing of a firm . . . is an ever-present threat at the bargaining table that cannot be ignored. Relatively few firms have made good their constantly reiterated threat to move elsewhere unless wage demands are restrained, but those who do shut down have a markedly inhibiting influence on labor militancy in an economy where alternative employment is severely limited."[84]

The ILGWU did establish a presence in the new industries in Puerto Rico, but its conciliatory attitude and policy of wage restraint led to a cozy relationship with management and government, including participation in the tripartite boards governing wages.[85] Richard Bolin, the A. D. Little consultant to Puerto Rico's government, recalled the pact warmly: "In the early days the climate with labor unions was very good. The International Ladies Garment Workers Union (ILGWU) was supportive of Puerto Rico's governor, Luis Muñoz Marín. One story went that Dave Dubinsky, head of the ILGWU, even went so far as to persuade two garment firms in New York to move to Mayagüez at the remote western end of the island when the very first two garment factories to be attracted there quit because of tough conditions there."[86]

Though this particular anecdote may be apocryphal, its contours are a reflection of the union's policies. And why would a union be so eager to encourage capital flight? Dana Frank explains that the ILGWU came to depend increasingly on a system of "liquidated damages" wherein companies that moved abroad had to pay a fine to the union: "The system cut the union's actual members out of the loop. A unionized firm could move work overseas, lay off or never hire domestic union members, and the union would still collect the money. The deal was cut between the leadership and the manufacturers."[87] Sweetheart deals also allowed the union to collect dues in shops where it did little to actually represent the workers.

> An observer who participated in the process at the time explained that . . . the Puerto Rican government facilitated agreements between the company and the union at the U.S. headquarters at the moment when the companies were establishing their Puerto Rican branches. Thus many Puerto Rican workers in the new factories found themselves automatically paying dues to a union they knew nothing about but which had already made a wage agreement with the company. This kind of arrangement was made principally with the International Ladies Garment Workers Union which was already well-known in the United States for its extremely cordial relationship with management.[88]

It was not until the retirement of both AFL-CIO president George Meany and Dubinsky in the 1960s that Puerto Rican unions began to challenge the low-wage consensus. (Muñoz Marín's party's electoral loss in 1968 contributed to the realignment of forces.) Underlying the shift lay the recognition that the low-wage model had not resolved Puerto Rico's high unemployment rate. "The impression grew that it was futile, as well as inequitable, to expect employed workers to perpetually subsidize employment creation efforts, which never seemed to bear dividends anyway—other than dividends on capital investment."[89] Even an ILGWU spokesperson conceded that "substantial increases in minimum wages in prior years have in no way hurt economic development in Puerto Rico. Present levels of unemployment are not the result of past minimum wage action and the proposed increases will not curtail employment opportunities."[90] Finally, at the end of the 1970s, the Fair Labor Standards Act gradually increased the Puerto Rican minimum wage to eventual parity with the mainland.

Despite Textron's departure, textiles and clothing production remained an important segment of Operation Bootstrap. Textile employment grew, slowly, during the period: from 2,862 in 1952 to 4,358 in 1956.[91] Textiles accounted for 13.7 percent of Puerto Rico's manufacturing firms in 1949, 19.5 percent in 1954, and 19.9 percent in 1967.[92] In 1969 Puerto Rico supplied more clothing to the U.S. market than any other country, though the island lost this position in the 1970s. Still, as late as 1978, Puerto Rico accounted for 34.1 percent of direct U.S. investment in Latin America and 42.4 percent of the profits that U.S. corporations made in Latin America.[93]

In 2005 PRIDCO's website boasted, "Puerto Rico offers a business climate second to none. Companies benefit from the Island's wealth of facilities, favorable, pro-business environment, and a well-educated, bilingual workforce that is loyal and capable of maintaining demandingly high-quality standards. The government of the Commonwealth of Puerto Rico supports this pro-business view by offering a wealth of incentives and favorable tax laws combined with cash grants, tax credits, and venture capital initiatives, making Puerto Rico the ideal place for your operation."[94]

In 2005, Sara Lee Corporation was still operating a Hanes menswear plant in Ponce, employing over a thousand people.[95] Most of Sara Lee's Puerto Rican operations, however, had already been closed to move to the Dominican Republic: 2,200 Sara Lee Puerto Rican employees lost their jobs in 2001; by 2003 the number had risen to 3,900 and the company was preparing to cut 1,200 more.[96] Just as at the beginning of the twentieth century other countries, even more desperate, offered even more than Puerto Rico's "wealth of incentives" for garment producers.

From Puerto Rico to Asia: The Promotion of Outsourcing

U.S. government efforts to promote textile production outside of the United States went far beyond Puerto Rico. After World War II, the United States invested heavily in reconstructing Japan's textile production capacity for strategic reasons: "to contain communism and promote the political and economic ties that would link Japan to Western democracies." This meant that the United States proffered loans to Japan to enable it to buy U.S. cotton and textile machinery and worked to reduce tariffs to facilitate U.S. purchase of Japanese-produced textiles. General William H. Draper Jr. of the Draper Loom Company clan was appointed by U.S. Secretary of State George F. Kennan to head the Textile Mission to promote Japan's industry.[97]

Cotton producers and textile machinery manufacturers directly benefited from the U.S. government's promotion of Japan. When the United States lowered its quota requirements for Japanese textile imports in 1955, however, "all hell broke loose in South Carolina. . . . Local journalists immediately likened the trade concessions to Pearl Harbor. In March 1956 the South Carolina legislature passed a law requiring that any business that sold textiles originating in Japan had to post a sign in its window proclaiming 'JAPANESE TEXTILES SOLD HERE.' Lobbyists sped to Washington; discreet and not-so-discreet pressures were applied. . . . In 1956 the Japanese government itself ended the crisis by volunteering to restore the quota on Japanese textiles."[98]

Although they initially opposed these programs that created competition with U.S. industries, U.S. textile manufacturers were not slow to jump on the bandwagon. By the mid-1950s they began to find ways to themselves take advantage of reduced tariffs by setting up their own operations at low-wage, underregulated sites abroad. The creation of free trade zones further spurred the process.[99]

Truman's Point IV program, established in 1948, provided another element in the export-oriented industrialization of poor regions. Based in part on the Puerto Rican experience, Point IV offered technical and financial development assistance to third world countries, who responded, " 'Do for us what you did for Puerto Rico.' . . . Thus began a steady stream of Africans, Asians, and South Americans to Puerto Rico, to study her program . . . and the results of her industrialization effort." It is no mystery why other countries looked to the Puerto Rican model: "The U.S. State Department saw to it that news of the impressive strides being taken was disseminated all over the world. . . . The advertising programs reached millions." "A constant stream of students and experts from underdeveloped countries all over the world comes to Puerto Rico to study the program or particular aspects of it, sometimes on their own initiative, sometimes under the guidance of the U.S. State Department."[100]

The Mexico Connection

The complex web linking colonialism, corporate profits, and the cold war as steps toward late twentieth-century globalization can be traced from the U.S. South to Puerto Rico to Asia and back to Mexico, where the 1965 Border Industrialization Program built on the Puerto Rican and Asian experiences and responded to the long colonial and neocolonial relationship between the United States and Mexico, as well as to a new phase in the colonial/cold war complex: the Cuban Revolution. Mexico laid the groundwork for a cascade of offshore processing agreements and free trade zones in the 1970s, 1980s, and 1990s.

Mexico's Border Industrialization Program was designed by the same Arthur D. Little consulting firm that proposed the plan for Operation Bootstrap in Puerto Rico. Richard Bolin, who managed the A. D. Little contract in Puerto Rico from 1956 to 1961 (and now directs the Flagstaff Institute, whose mission is to "support and encourage world trade," as well as running the World Economic Processing Zones Association), carried out the initial study for the Mexican government on the feasibility of establishing offshore processing there. As in the case of Puerto Rico, one of his tasks was to advertise Mexico's free trade zones to U.S. industrialists. And as in Puerto Rico, much of the funding for the development of the zones came from the U.S. government.[101]

The success of the system—in terms of attracting industry and fulfilling the goal of increased profitability—led to its proliferation in the border region of Mexico, and globally. From Japan, the industry spread to Southeast Asia, Korea, Indonesia, and China; from Mexico to Central America, the Caribbean, and Colombia.

Textiles and Globalization in Colombia

Colombia's textile industry was primarily controlled by Colombian capitalists, yet this industry too operated in a global context. Starting in the nineteenth century, mills established in Medellín imported their looms and spinning machines from England, Europe, and New England; by the twentieth century, the United States was the primary supplier.

Medellín's two largest textile firms were owned by the Echavarría family: Coltejer, founded in 1907, and Fabricato, founded in 1920. Like the capitalists who invested in New England's mills, the Echavarrías had accumulated their capital in the import-export business. They were heirs to the Rudesindo Echavarría e Hijo company, founded in 1872, specializing in wholesale merchandise, in particular imported fabrics. In a sort of inverted precursor to the branded apparel marketers of the 1990s who abandoned production and became marketers of clothing produced by their contractors, the Echavarrías relied on their reputation as importers of quality goods to advertise the new lines they were producing: "The former fabric importers, with their clientele assured and their warehouses well supplied, now began to produce cloth and distribute it themselves."[102]

The Echavarrías' coffee-exporting firm maintained a New York office, where many family members worked; its children were educated at New York private schools and U.S. universities. One of the original partners held a degree from MIT; Carlos Echavarría studied at the Military Academy in Bordentown, New Jersey.[103] Son Jorge Echavarría spent five months training at the Burlington Mills in North Carolina in 1950. "Medellín's industrialists imported the factory model, its machines and floor plans, supervisors and technicians."[104]

The decade of the 1930s brought consolidation, as the Fabricato and Coltejer mills took over smaller factories, as well as the replacement of older machinery by new automatic Draper looms in the newly consolidated plants.[105] A new company, Tejidos El Cóndor, or Tejicóndor, began operations in 1935 with 100 Draper looms; by 1942 it had 687.[106] By 1943 Coltejer was running 1,900 looms.[107] The number of workers skyrocketed, as did worker productivity. In the mid-1940s Coltejer employed six thousand workers, Fabricato four thousand, and Tejicóndor two thousand.[108]

By the 1940s, U.S. investors held an important stake in Colombia's "domestic" textile industry. W. R. Grace had been negotiating for a foothold in Antioquia's textile industry for several years, citing the fantastic profit potential; a Grace representative explained to a U.S. consular official that one Medellín textile mill had made a profit of 400,000 pesos on an investment of 800,000 pesos in 1936, even in the midst of the Depression. He also criticized the Antioquia bourgeoisie for their publicity campaigns against foreign capital.[109] Grace became a partner in Tejicóndor in 1940 (holding 51 percent of the company's stock).

U.S. involvement in Colombia's textile industry increased with the introduction of synthetic fibers. Indurayon built the first synthetic fiber plant in the country in 1939. The North Carolina–based Burlington Mills invested in a joint venture with the Fabricato company in 1944 to establish a synthetic fiber plant, Textiles Panamericanos, or Pantex.[110] Celanese de Colombia (a division of American Celanese) opened a rayon plant in the 1940s, perhaps pressed by growing labor militancy and a long, bitter, and ultimately successful strike in its Rome, Georgia, plant in 1948.[111] Numerous studies have noted the impact of the 1934 general strike, New Deal legislation, and Operation Dixie (in 1946) on the southern textile industry, though they do not in general explore the connection of labor control issues with the industry's first ventures abroad in the 1940s.[112]

In the 1950s "a battery of experts from the prominent U.S. firm Barnes Textile Associates" descended on Colombia's factories to institute neo-Taylorism, or methods time management. According to the historian Ann Farnsworth-Alvear, "Time and motion studies, imported together with new machinery and other labor-saving technologies, were being undertaken in textile mills in Brazil, Egypt, Mexico, and India in the early 1950s, at the same time as in Colombia, and, indeed, the Colombian experience became a model for other textile firms in other Latin American countries."[113]

Ironically, by the 1970s these techniques had been virtually abandoned in the few remaining New England mills. A Colombian immigrant textile worker in Lowell, Massachusetts, described the difference between Medellín's factories and Lowell's:

> Textiles could be much more here [Lowell], but there is no organization of any kind. I was a supervisor at Wannalancit, but I resigned because you can't organize anything or control the workers. You go crazy. It's because of the labor shortage; you practically have to let them do what they want and if you correct them, they leave. . . . I think that there are organized mills here [in the United States], maybe in Carolina. Cadillac is the only organized one here [in New England], the rest are like Wannalancit. It scares me because [some of the practices] were learned from the United States, and they aren't used here. They aren't practiced because of the labor shortages.[114]

The markets for Colombia's textiles were primarily domestic through World War II. Like other import substitution industries in Latin America, Colombia's textile industry flourished during the Depression. During World War II, the U.S. Army contracted Coltejer to supply cloth and granted the company a special license to continue importing U.S.-made machinery.[115] After the war ended Colombia's textile industry became "an avid buyer of used textile equipment." The industry was the largest importer of second-hand equipment in Colombia, encouraged by continued U.S. trade concessions. A 1970s study noted the training of Colombian mechanics to keep the older machinery running smoothly and concluded, "In some of the large textile firms, looms of thirty to forty years are working at about 95 percent of their original capacity."[116]

In the 1970s, Coltejer and other large Colombian companies embarked on a modernization program. "Until a few years ago, we had a very mistaken policy to buy a lot of used equipment from the United States at very low cost, because the machinery was in pretty good condition," a Coltejer official explained at the end of the 1970s. "But the investment savings had very unfavorable repercussions in the costs of operation.... The costs of production were very high, maintenance, lowered productivity, very high labor costs." The new drive for efficiency would "change all the old equipment for new machinery." By this time, however, the United States was no longer the best source of textile machinery, and Colombian factories turned to European manufacturers.[117] Colombia's textile industry was modernizing just as the United States was deindustrializing.

Colombian factories also began to invest overseas. In 1965, Fabricato began an expansion process which included diversification into polyester and other artificial fibers and opened a branch in Nicaragua, called Fabritex.[118] (In the 1980s Fabritex became a center of controversy when the Sandinista government threatened to outlaw a strike at the plant, which was then 48 percent government owned.) When the company merged with Tejicóndor in 2001 it was operating plants in Mexico, Ecuador, and Venezuela as well as several in Colombia.[119]

Building on the relationship established during World War II, Colombian exports to the United States grew exponentially in the postwar period. In 1965, Colombian factories exported 27 million yards of cloth worth $6 million, about two-thirds of it to the United States.[120] In 1967, Decree 444 created structures to support textile exports, including the Fund for the

Promotion of Exports (Proexpo) and subsidies to compensate some of the costs of exporting.[121] By the 1970s, Coltejer was operating ten mills, employed over twelve thousand workers, and exported 60 percent of its finished and 20 percent of its unfinished greige cloth, with a total value of some $36 million. Its Coltefábrica mill produced denim exported to Levi Strauss and Lee factories in the United States. Like U.S. textile companies, Coltejer diversified as well as integrated: it bought foundries, energy plants, an apparel plant, food processing plants, and even a flower exporting business.[122]

In 1958, Colombia opened its first free trade zone in Barranquilla to allow offshore manufacturing—the first in the world outside Puerto Rico.[123] The zone offered "exchange rate incentives, allowed free repatriation of profits for the foreign investors, and granted preferential rates on utility use." In the 1970s five others opened, in Buenaventura, Cartagena, Cúcuta, Palmaseca, and Santa Marta.[124] By 1991 there were seven, in 1999 eleven, and in 2003 fifteen.[125] In 1991 Colombia eliminated import duties on cotton which, in conjunction with the 1990 Step 2 program by which the U.S. government provided huge subsidies to cotton exporters, allowed Colombian textile producers to import U.S. cotton more cheaply.[126]

Levi Strauss, which had been using denim cloth from Colombia since the 1960s, began shifting some of its clothing manufacture from Asia back to Colombia in 1993. The move cut in half the time between placing the order and receiving the shipment in the United States; for Asia, the lead time was eighty to a hundred days, for Colombia, it was forty-five days.[127] Liz Claiborne also began to contract in Colombia in the early 1990s.[128] Ralph Lauren children's wear followed suit in 1998, for the same reason: "We decided to have Colombia as a short lead, short replenishment base," explained Susana Gutiérrez, director of the company's Colombian operations.[129] In 2000, Colombia was producing about $250 million a year in apparel destined for the United States, for Levi Strauss, Ralph Lauren, and Liz Claiborne, but the companies were paying a duty of 17 percent to 20 percent.[130] Until 2002, only items produced with U.S. materials were granted U.S. tariff benefits, and even these only in limited quantities.

As part of the war on drugs, the Andean Trade Preference Act of 1991 (ATPA) claimed to encourage economic alternatives to coca production in Colombia, Bolivia, Ecuador, and Peru by allowing many items produced in those countries to enter the United States duty-free. Textiles, apparel, and petroleum products, however, were excluded. When the Caribbean Basin

Initiative countries were granted tariff-free access to U.S. markets for garments produced with U.S. materials in 2000, retailers prepared to shift their production from Colombia to these countries, and Colombia protested sharply.[131]

In October 2002 President George W. Bush responded with the Andean Trade Promotion and Drug Eradication Act (ATPDEA), which expanded the ATPA to cover petroleum, textile, and apparel products. (Bolivia, Ecuador, and Peru were also included in the Act, but Colombia consistently accounted for the largest portion of imports, some 40 percent, as well as over 50 percent of U.S. exports to the region. In 2004, the Colombian share rose to 47 percent.)[132] Unlimited apparel products assembled in Colombia of U.S. materials could be imported duty-free; those made from Colombian-produced fabrics were duty-free up to from 2 percent to 5 percent of total U.S. apparel imports. (As of 2005, this limit had never been reached.) The ATPDEA also extended the new provisions through 2006.

The U.S. International Trade Commission found that the ATPA and ATPDEA had negligible effects on drug-crop eradication. Why, then, was the program continued, and expanded? Several sectors of the U.S. economy did stand to benefit from the program. Retailers of cut flowers and of apparel, the two products whose imports from Colombia to the United States were significantly increased under the program, were pleased with its results. Petroleum products accounted for almost two-thirds of the duty-free imports from the four countries. Petroleum was by far the largest ATPDEA import from Colombia, followed by coal—and much of the production of petroleum and coal was in fact in the hands of U.S. producers, as discussed in chapter 7. After apparel products were included in 2002, their importation too increased dramatically, to 14 percent of the items imported, and the amount was expected to continue growing rapidly.[133]

The relationship of the ATPDEA to the war on drugs was "indirect" because "much of ATPA/ATPDEA investment has flourished in regions where there is no presence of illegal crops." However, according to the U.S. International Trade Commission, "In many cases, displaced persons fleeing from violence in drug-producing regions are recruited to work on flower plantations." In addition, "the Colombian government estimates that over 140,000 new jobs will be directly created because of efforts to take advantage of new benefits for textiles, apparel, shoes and leather goods. These jobs are focused in areas where people displaced from successful counter-narcotics efforts are settling."[134] A cynic might be forgiven for asking if one of the goals of these "successful counter-narcotics efforts" funded by the United States might be precisely to displace people, to provide a cheap labor force for these new industries, from which U.S. corporations directly benefit.

In the first year of the ATPDEA, Colombian textile and apparel producers spent $100 million importing new capital goods from the United States, and U.S. investors were well on their way to reaching the $500 million in new investment in textile and apparel production expected.[135] From 2002 to 2004 Coltejer invested $22 million in expanding its production of denim and cord and was preparing to open a new $32 million denim plant in 2005. Fabricato-Tejicóndor was planning on spending $47 million by the end of 2004 and another $20 million by the end of 2005 and employing six hundred new workers.[136] Both hoped to expand output rapidly to supply U.S. clothing producers who, under the ATPDEA, could now use cheaper Colombian fabrics and still be able to take advantage of the duty-free import rules. In a curious twist Levi Strauss, which had previously imported Colombian-made denim for its jeans factories in the United States, was now making the jeans in Colombia and transporting the more expensive U.S. fabrics there. In 2004 Levi Strauss used U.S. fabric in 80 percent to 90 percent of its Colombian jeans production because the Colombian factories simply couldn't produce enough denim quickly enough.[137] Levi Strauss also offers a clear example of the effect of outsourcing on U.S. jobs. In 1999 it closed eleven of its twenty-two plants in the United States and Canada, laying off 5,900 of its 19,900 workers.[138] Five years later it closed its last remaining factory in the United States, leaving 800 workers in San Antonio jobless.[139]

Despite Colombian textile manufacturers' expansion, U.S. textile producers also stood to benefit from the ATPDEA. Colombia was already the largest South American market for U.S. fabrics in 1999, with denim the top cloth exported.[140] The Cotton Council International, the export arm of the National Cotton Council of America, ratcheted up its advertising to consumers in Colombia and its presence at trade fairs courting Colombian and other South American manufacturers as markets.[141]

U.S. retailers also favored the continuation of the ATPDEA. The American Apparel and Footwear Association, citing "strong growth" in apparel and footwear imports from Colombia, urged that the Act be extended. Likewise the J. C. Penney Purchasing Corporation reported that "as a major retailer doing business in the Andean region, its experience in the apparel factories of these countries has been very favorable."[142]

While it might appear logical that U.S. clothing manufacturers would oppose a policy that facilitated the import of finished clothing, in fact virtually all of them were multinational enterprises, poised to take advantage of production opportunities anywhere in the world. By 2004, The Gap, VF Corporation (makers of Lee and Wrangler jeans), Tommy Hilfiger, Kenneth Cole, and Benetton had joined the list of those outsourcing to Colombia.[143]

The AFL-CIO was the lone voice of protest when the ATPDEA was evaluated in 2003, noting that "a systematic denial of certain basic labor rights and human rights for workers throughout Colombia has continued."[144] In 2005, not even the AFL-CIO objected to Colombia's inclusion in the program.[145]

Arms for the World

The relationship between U.S. foreign policy and the profits of the textile industry went beyond programs that used taxpayer money to facilitate profit making abroad. Military spending played an enormous role in the development and structuring of U.S. industry in general, and the textile industry in particular. Wars created demand that counteracted the problem of overproduction inherent in a system where constantly increasing automation meant fewer workers produced more goods. Wars also created new spheres for markets and investments. Military aid maintained investment-friendly climates in those spheres even in peacetime. Wars also provided ideological support for the concept of "Americanism" and national unity that nourished the AFL's conciliatory form of unionism. As jobs in the United States became more and more linked to the war industry, unions found it difficult to challenge the ideological complex underlying it.

As far back as the Civil War, the military served as an important market for the textile industry. During the two world wars the industry's reliance on military contracts was made painfully obvious. The cold war, and what Seymour Melman has termed the "permanent war economy," created a rush into military production that affected the entire industrial structure of the United States. Almost every textile company that stayed in business relied on military contracts. They produced uniforms, fabrics for military aircraft and vehicles, parachutes, tents, and a plethora of other items for military use. Some, like Textron, diversified into military industries. Others developed interlocking directorates with major military contractors, like Milliken & Co., whose CEO, Roger Milliken, has also sat on the board of directors of Westinghouse.[146] Some sold out to major military producers, like Draper, and some, like Spartan Mills, the ultimate owner of Naumkeag's southern plant, went bankrupt and had their assets seized by military-producer credi-tors.[147]

During World War I, the U.S. government bought 75 percent of New England's textile factories' output, and many mills expanded production dramatically to fill the orders.[148] The Draper Loom Company seemed posi-tively gleeful in its pronouncements. Its Northrop loom, one long advertise-ment proclaimed, was essential to supplying "our boys at the front."

> The aeroplane service is provided with machines covered with cloth wo-ven on Northrop looms,—and the men have uniforms woven on Nor-throp looms. In the Army the soldiers are clad in goods woven on Nor-throp looms; they sleep in tents made of duck from Northrop looms under Northrop loom blankets; they use Northrop loom bath towels; Northrop loom powder bags hold the powder used in our artillery. In the Navy our sailors have Northrop loom blankets; Northrop loom towels; and Northrop loom garments. Northrop loom cloth finished for raincoats protects all branches of the service from the weather. Northrop loom surgeon's gauze, and bandage cloth, are indispensable when wounded. Northrop loom gas masks protect our boys from poisonous gases.

The coup de grace was a photograph of a Northrop loom, entitled "The Loom which is helping Win the War."[149]

While many people celebrated the end of hostilities, Draper sounded an ominous note. "The cessation of war," an editorial in the company newsletter warned, "which we expect to be followed by Peace brings the textile manu-facturers of this Country new problems."[150] The textile depression of the 1920s and 1930s confirmed Draper's gloomy prognosis.

World War II brought a new round of government contracts. "Those looms in your weave room that were built for peace time products can be changed over to looms for war contracts," Draper exhorted its customers. "The textile industry has done a splendid war time job so far; but as our armed forces increase and their needs multiply, we face a further change to a war basis. It looks, in fact, as if our Government is about to require that the larger part of the looms of our country shall fall in line on its pro-gram for war fabrics." Draper provided instructions for converting sev-eral of its looms to produce shelter tent duck and advice on which looms were appropriate for nylon parachute cloth and other "war time fabrics" for which "big contracts" were being offered. "Remember Pearl Harbor!" the

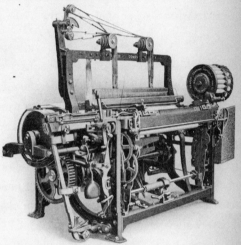

Our Corporation takes pride in the fact that it has been able to provide

AN IMPORTANT ESSENTIAL
TO HELP
WIN THE WAR

The Loom which is helping
Win the War

Figure 10. The Draper Corporation advertises "The Loom which is helping Win the War." Draper Corporation, *Cotton Chats* 191, September 1918. Reprinted by permission of the Bancroft Library, Hopedale, Massachusetts.

company's March 1942 issue concluded patriotically. "Our first job is to lick Hitler and the Japs."[151]

"Almost every day now some branch of the military is contracting to buy, or signifying its desire to buy, large supplies of textile goods," *Business Week* reported in 1940.[152] Robert Ten Broeck Stevens, a son of the J. P. Stevens textile magnate and later CEO of the company until 1969, took a break from the company to serve as deputy director of purchasing for the army during World War II—a move that surely did not hinder his company's access to wartime contracts—and later as secretary of the army from 1953 to 1955.[153]

Textron's predecessor Atlantic Rayon "gained large profits during the war by manufacturing rayon parachutes," as did the Beaumont Manufacturing Company of Spartanburg, another piece of the Montgomery textile empire and later part of the same Spartan Mills that purchased Whitney. The U.S. government gave Beaumont $800,000 to refurbish its facility for production of "tents, rafts, ammunition belts, medical equipment."[154] "The Army and Navy Must Have Millions of Yards of Duck . . . NOW!!" a Beaumont employment advertisement proclaimed. Another showed a smiling GI in front of a huge target centered on Tokyo. "Give us the duck and we'll give you the victory," he promises. An editorial in Spartanburg's *Textile Tribune* echoed what was to become a familiar theme in the postwar period: the Asian threat to U.S. industry and the need for patriotic labor-management collaboration to counteract it. Exhorting workers to work a seven-day week, the *Tribune* explained:

> Now there may be some people working in textile plants who conscientiously object to working on Sunday. Well, just remember this: the next time you are called to work on Sunday and refuse to do it when your work is needed for war goods, that over yonder in Japan the textile workers are working EVERY Sunday and every other day of the week; not just 8 hours a day, but 12 or more, making goods that will go to supply the Jap soldier that the American boy who used to work right there in your mill must face and FIGHT. And remember, too, that Japan has some big cotton mills and has boasted that she will outproduce America.[155]

A year later, Draper was also producing weapons, becoming one of only a few plants in the country that could produce the 75 mm pack howitzer. The army "went 'shopping' for a plant that could turn out the pack howitzer, and its experts wound up in Hopedale. . . . It was no soft job the Army laid out for the Draper Corporation. . . . Ordnance experts call Draper's production of the 75-mm. howitzer one of the best tooling jobs in the country."[156]

The synthetic textile industry also has deep roots in wartime production. The Celanese company, one of the first producers of rayon, had its origins in the British Cellulose and Chemical Manufacturing Company that produced airplane paint for the British government during World War I. In 1918 the company opened a branch in Maryland. When wartime contracts evaporated, the company shifted to the production of acetate fibers. By the 1920s it expanded into plastics and chemicals, becoming one of the largest chemical producers in the United States. In 1944 American Celanese began producing acetate fibers in a new plant in Mexico, and in the 1940s it became one of the first rayon producers in Colombia.[157] (Celanese closed its Georgia plant in 1977 and its Maryland plant in 1983, though it continued to produce in other U.S. locations.)[158]

By the 1940s the entire U.S. economy revolved around what President Eisenhower called "a permanent armaments industry of vast proportions." As one critic explained, "In the mid-'80s, at the height of the Reagan administration's planned $2.3-trillion defense buildup, the Pentagon was spending an average of $28 million an hour. By mid-1985, this huge spending spree had produced a backlog of orders in the defense and aerospace industry of $133 billion. By 1990 . . . the total defense-spending boom for the Cold War years will total $3.7 trillion in constant 1972 dollars—nearly enough to buy everything in the United States except the land: every house, factory, train, plane and refrigerator."[159]

The president of the Wannalancit textile factory in Lowell, Massachusetts, which imported Colombian workers to keep its old Draper looms running in the 1960s and 1970s, described its production line this way:

> We have about a dozen customers . . . mostly industrial cloths, such as going into industrial diaphragms, rubber-coated both sides, military life rafts. . . . A satin we make that goes into the Air Force life jackets, Navy flight jackets. We once in a while get an order from the Post Office Department for mail bags . . . heavy. We sometimes get a few yards, maybe ten, fifteen thousand yards of what they call bullet-proof ballistics cloth, that's a fabric that is woven out of heavy yarns that are laminated together for bullet-proof vesting. You never know. We wove the first . . . uniforms of the astronauts.[160]

Textron: Speculation, Capital Flight, and Helicopters

Always in the forefront, Textron was poised to feed at the public trough and to take advantage of the arms race. In 1960, Textron acquired Bell Aircraft and changed the name of its helicopter division to Bell Textron.[161] Textron Huey helicopters and Lycoming engines found a ready market in the U.S. war in Vietnam.

The end of the Vietnam War meant a search for new markets for military helicopters, and Textron began what would become a long history of arming, and sometimes paying off, the militaries of some of the more unsavory U.S. allies, including El Salvador and Indonesia. In 1979 the company admitted making payments to companies and officials in Iran, Ghana, and the Dominican Republic to support helicopter sales to those countries, and there were reports of similar payoffs in Ceylon (today Sri Lanka) and Mexico.[162] In 1980, the U.S. Securities and Exchange Commission filed suit against the company for millions of dollars of payments made through secret European bank accounts between 1971 and 1978 to government officials of Ghana, Mexico, the United Arab Emirates, Morocco, Ceylon, Iran, Indonesia, the Dominican Republic, Iraq, and Colombia in support of its contracts.[163]

The Colombian government, engaged in its own long U.S.-supported counterinsurgency, was another Textron customer. In a complex deal in 1984, just as the U.S.-government-financed and Exxon-owned Cerrejón Zona Norte coal mine was going into production (see chapter 7), the U.S. Export-Import Bank arranged to guarantee a loan of $12 million by Textron to the Colombian government to finance the purchase of nine Bell helicopters. Textron made the loan in Japanese yen, and it was to be repaid with the sale of Colombian coal to Japan.[164]

By the end of the 1990s Textron was one of the top ten arms exporters in the United States, and the thirteenth largest Defense Department contractor (the third largest in New England), receiving $1.2 billion worth of contracts in 1996 and $1.4 billion in 1999.[165]

The arms export industry is the primary face of globalization for some of the world's poor. "I have often encountered refugees from destroyed villages in southeast Turkey whose only English—delivered in a thick Kurdish accent—were the words 'Sikorsky' and 'Cobra,'" noted a journalist. "Villagers know that the soldiers who burn their houses land in Blackhawk helicopters, the troop transports that are made by the Connecticut-based Sikorsky Co. And they easily recognize the rocket-equipped Cobras, which are manufactured at the Bell Textron plant in Fort Worth, Texas."[166]

The War on Drugs in the 1990s also proved lucrative for Textron. In 1994, Canadians protested a secret deal to sell twelve Bell helicopters to the Colombian army, bypassing the country's defense export licensing regulations by claiming that they were for antidrug purposes.[167] In 1999, the company reported with satisfaction the sale of twenty-four helicopters to Mexico. In some cases, the U.S. government itself purchased Textron products for foreign militaries, as when it provided twenty-five Huey II upgrade kits for the Colombian National Police fleet in 1999.[168]

But the real boon for Textron in Colombia came in 2000, with the Clinton administration's $1.3 billion "Plan Colombia" aid package. Textron lobbyists, and Texas congressional representatives, pressed to have the package approved, and more important, pressed for it to include Bell Huey helicopters.[169] Lobbyists from United Technologies, makers of the Blackhawk helicopters in Connecticut, and from Bell Textron vied for votes in Congress with gifts of hundreds of thousands of dollars.[170] *Newsweek* reported that Textron's efforts included giving congressmen free rides in helicopters that they brought to Washington for the purpose.[171] Both companies were rewarded for their efforts: the bill as passed included forty-two Bell and thirty Sikorsky helicopters.

The U.S. military has been a key, if often ignored, player in the process of globalization. Military buildup helped to restructure the U.S. economy, and it fostered the loyalty of the AFL-CIO to the corporate system in a number of different ways. The military was the leading source of economic expansion and job creation during several periods of U.S. history. Militarization and wars contributed to a culture in which dissent could be dismissed as disloyalty and repressed. It also fostered a double standard by which government spending on social programs could be reduced—creating a more desperate, thus more docile, workforce—while government spending on the military, in which profits went directly into the coffers of major U.S. corporations, increased.

Militarization also contributed to creating and enforcing a global system that favored U.S. corporations. The dollar followed the flag, and the flag followed the dollar, as the military, directly and indirectly, worked to impose conditions congenial to corporate profits around the world. U.S. unions proved to be willing collaborators in the process.

Class Harmony and Free Trade

The regional differential that had undermined textile union organizing for so long turned global when textile factories began to relocate in Puerto Rico and outside U.S. borders. But U.S. unions were deeply committed to nationalism and to a global economic system that maintained an inordinate concentration of resources inside the United States (which, according to George Kennan, comprised 6 percent of the world's population but consumed 50 percent of the world's resources in 1948).[172] This worldview stymied their ability to ally with movements worldwide that sought to reduce global inequality.

Radical unions, from the IWW to the NTWU, proclaimed class struggle, international solidarity, anti-imperialism, and racial justice. The AFL, and later the AFL-CIO, urged labor-management collaboration, national unity, adherence to corporate-defined U.S. foreign policy goals, and racial and ethnic exclusivism. Protectionist and "Buy American" campaigns, based on the idea that labor and management shared an interest in maintaining corporate profitability, fit in with this worldview. It is no coincidence that the Pequot mill and UTW Local 33 experimented with union promotion of the mill's products as part of the labor-management collaboration project in 1933.

The textile unions that urged government protection of the textile industry trod a treacherous path, which frequently led not to labor internationalism and solidarity, but in the opposite direction. The tension between an inward-looking protectionism that sought to privilege U.S. jobs and a stance of genuine solidarity plagued the AFL-CIO's relations with unions in other countries throughout the century. Labor-management collaboration in the interest of corporate profits could also, as Local 33 discovered, jeopardize the relationship between the union and the workers it supposedly represented.

U.S. industry's position on free trade has varied widely. Protectionism served the interests of industry if manufacturers elsewhere were producing items of better quality or at cheaper prices; free trade, on the other hand, helped industry acquire cheap inputs, sell its products, and, later in the twentieth century, produce goods abroad. Led by the textile and garment industries, which had already experimented with outsourcing within national boundaries, the spread of outsourcing beyond U.S. borders meant that many companies were positioned simultaneously on both sides of the fence: they were domestic *and* international producers.

Free trade could also enable manufacturers to impose speed-ups and wage cuts on the argument that if they did not, they would be destroyed by "foreign" competition, even if they themselves were the "foreign" competitors because of their investments abroad. Manufacturers could paint themselves as the victims, rather than the perpetrators, of an unequal system and proclaim their partnership with labor.[173] In all of these respects, the issues mirrored those that arose in the textile industry starting in the late nineteenth century, when New England textile factories confronted (and contributed to) the growth of the southern textile industry.

As far as labor was concerned, protectionism could, in theory, serve to promote better working conditions and wages, but only if manufacturers were willing to share the profits they gained as a result of such policies. Likewise, to the extent that free trade benefited industries, workers could hope that the benefits would be shared. When workers' organizations have joined management in a struggle to save their industries, however, they have often been the losers. The shuttering of New England's textile industry showed how regional differentials undermined the rationale for labor-management collaboration.

Anti-immigrant politics could put U.S. labor in alliance with some of the most right-wing and racist—and anti-union—sectors among U.S. industrialists, like the Draper Corporation and its Pioneer Fund. Likewise, protectionism served to ally the AFL-CIO with actors ranging from William Randolph Hearst to Roger Milliken and the American Textile Manufacturers Institute. Yet if Draper set the standard in Massachusetts for crushing unions, Milliken played the same role in Spartanburg, South Carolina. Racism and nationalism made strange bedfellows, indeed.

Milliken and Company: Mobilizing Nationalism

The "Crafted with Pride" movement that Roger Milliken inaugurated in 1984, with $100 million from the textile industry, hearkened back to the "Buy American" campaigns of the 1930s in emphasizing nationalism and labor-management collaboration. Textile companies launched an advertising campaign, urged their workers to contribute money and write letters, and targeted retailers to promote U.S.-made products and protectionist legislation.[174] The American Textile Manufacturers Institute (ATMI) put in another $45 million in 1987. The Crafted with Pride Council came to include three hundred companies. In addition to textile manufacturers it included cotton growers, garment manufacturers, distributors, and retailers such as, for a time, Wal-Mart.[175]

Also on board were the ILGWU and the Amalgamated Clothing and Textile Workers Union (ACTWU; formed by a merger of the Amalgamated Clothing Workers and the TWUA in 1976).[176] Just as the UTW local at Salem's Naumkeag mill committed its members to promoting sales of the mill's Pequot sheets, the ILGWU urged its members to "promote pride in American-made goods." It was labor-management collaboration all over again: "Labor and management were pulling together as a team to compete in the global marketplace against workers abroad."[177]

Despite the ATMI's initial endorsement of the project, textile manufacturers began to retreat during the early 1990s as they began to see more profits in moving their production abroad than in economic nationalism. First, individual companies began to drop out, then in 1992, the ATMI decided to endorse the North American Free Trade Agreement (NAFTA), with Roger Milliken's as the lone dissenting voice.[178] The reasons are not difficult to discern.

Like New England textile producers confronting the regional differential with the South in the early part of the century, textile manufacturers in the South found many benefits in international competition, even as they decried it. They could use it as an excuse to clamp down on their workers at home; they could deflect worker resentment away from management and on to foreign competitors; and they could take advantage of the multitude of U.S.-government-sponsored opportunities to become the very competition they were complaining of. In 1993, South Carolina exported $373.4 million worth of textile products, much of it to U.S. outsourcers.[179] Burlington "bet on NAFTA to drive business to Mexico, and built factories there."[180] Levi Strauss purchased denim in North Carolina to produce jeans in a new $9 million plant in South Africa, for local sales.[181] Even Milliken himself had global ties, sitting as he did on the board of directors of Arthur D. Little and W. R. Grace.[182] The southern textile industry was going global.[183]

The ATMI did not abandon protectionism altogether; it still took a strong stance against Asian, especially Chinese, imports. Justifying his organization's support for NAFTA, the ATMI's president in 1992 explained, "A Nafta can curb the steady increases in imports from the Far East."[184] In its anti-China posture in the 1990s, the industry once again found a useful, if problematic, way to foster a relationship with the unions it refused to allow in its plants.

Following the Pendulum

If the founders of the AFL adhered to a protectionist position in the early years of the organization, its leaders proved willing to adjust this position over the course of the twentieth century. Between the 1880s and the 1920s, the AFL took no official position on the issue of the tariff. As the country fell into the grips of the Depression in the 1930s, many in the AFL, including its top leadership, followed the lead of William Randolph Hearst and President Herbert Hoover, supported by business interests, in reviving a campaign to raise tariffs and to "buy American" as the solution to the Depression. (Anti-immigrant sentiment, culminating in the deportation of Mexican immigrants, coincided comfortably with this analysis of the causes of the economic crisis.)[185]

By the middle of the decade, however, the tide had shifted as Franklin

Delano Roosevelt, who took office in 1933, advocated an entirely different analysis and approach. Rather than maintaining inequality but sealing borders, the New Deal proposed redistribution of income inside the United States and increasing trade.[186]

The idea of free trade had powerful allies in the corporate world among those who sought markets and investment opportunities abroad. By the end of World War II, the AFL had swung full circle to endorse free trade and the promotion of U.S. products abroad as part of the "guns and butter" pact between labor and capital in the postwar period. Unions joined management's drive for "high productivity and imperial expansion" as a way to sustain profits, for their benefits were dependent on industry's profits. The CIO, representing workers in mass production industries, argued that the future of these industries rested on exports, and endorsed the free trade agenda in 1953, as did the AFL in 1955.[187]

Some unions, however, had their doubts about the salutary effects of the free trade, high-productivity, and imperial expansion model, and the textile workers were prime among them. "Whereas union leaders in core industries could allow industrialists to assume broad managerial prerogatives without endangering the material well-being of rank-and-filers, experience had taught textile unionists that they could not stand by and hope that management would do the right thing."[188] But even the textile unions adhered to a worldview that made it very difficult for them to challenge high productivity or imperial expansion. Instead, they focused on attacking free trade.

By the late 1950s the TWUA and the ILGWU were agitating for some form of protection for their industries and reviving the "Buy American" idea. At the 1961 AFL-CIO convention, George Baldanzi, president of the UTW, warned that the crisis affecting the textile industry would soon affect others:

> When there are corporate interests . . . investing billions of dollars . . . that are establishing plants that are more modern than ours today, unless we get some safeguard against wholesale importation into this country, there is no guarantee that five years from now these same automated factories that are being built by American capital in many parts of the world that are utilizing slave labor, that they will not curtail operations in this country and dump all the cheap goods right back here in the United States. . . . Don't feel that you are immune against this problem, because capital is a heartless beast. . . . It finds the level that is measured only by the dollar bill.[189]

Heartless or not, the union turned to industry as an ally in the anti-import struggle.

By the 1970s, the ILGWU and the ACTWU were spearheading an anti-import approach to the crisis affecting their industry. The AFL-CIO too, in 1970, "turned a sudden about-face on the trade question" and abandoned its free trade stance for one advocating protectionism as part of a drive to protect U.S. jobs. The unsuccessful Burke-Hartke Act of 1972, which labor strongly supported, did far more than close U.S. borders to imports: it also attacked U.S. government incentives for capital flight, calling for the elimination of tax incentives for U.S. corporations operating abroad and presidential powers to restrict capital flight.[190]

The unions' public campaign accompanying Burke-Hartke, however, did not emphasize restricting U.S. capital; instead, it pointed the finger of blame at U.S. consumers for buying foreign goods and at other countries, especially Japan, thus re-creating and playing on the racist/nationalist undercurrent of previous "Buy American" campaigns. The strategic alliance between the labor movement, Roger Milliken, and right-wing anti-immigrant and protectionist activists from Ross Perot to Pat Buchanan underlines the contradictions inherent in the protectionist solution that sees workers in other countries as threats to American privilege rather than potential allies in a struggle for a more just global order.[191]

From NAFTA to CAFTA

The debates over free trade agreements like NAFTA, which went into effect in 1994, and the Central America Free Trade Agreement (CAFTA; the Dominican Republic was added in 2004, and it became known as CAFTA-DR), approved in mid-2005, underscore the cross-cutting interests of U.S. textile and apparel manufacturers who operate abroad and those who operate only at home. They also illustrate the ways that issues of protectionism can sometimes unite unions with investors, and progressive solidarity activists with right-wing racist nationalists, and the fragile commitment of some of these forces to better conditions abroad.

One group of textile manufacturers joined forces to form the American Manufacturing Trade Action Coalition (AMTAC) to oppose CAFTA. The coalition incorporated industry associations including the American Textile Manufacturers Institute, the Cotton Textile Institute, the National Textile Association, the National Cotton Council of America, the American Yarn

Spinners Association, and the American Fiber Manufacturers Association. In September 2003 they were joined by the Union of Needle Trades, Textiles, and Industrial Employees (UNITE).[192]

The coalition proposed a variety of measures to promote manufacturing in the United States, including requiring the military to "buy American" and opposing any easing of restrictions on textile and garment imports. Union and management argued that CAFTA would result in the outsourcing of more textile and garment manufacturing jobs.[193] In particular, they emphasized aspects of the agreement that would allow offshore manufacturers in these countries to import yarns and textiles from China.[194] UNITE also argued for improving conditions of workers in Central America so that they could become a market for U.S. exports.[195]

Bruce Raynor, president of UNITE, sounded some of the old themes of labor-management collaboration and a stance that relied more on blaming foreign countries than solidarity with workers abroad: "We look forward to working hand-in-hand with textile and apparel industry management to change U.S. trade policy for the better," he said in 2003. "It is unacceptable for countries like China, that don't respect basic human rights or environmental standards, to flood our market, destroy entire industries, and put hundreds of thousands of men and women out of work."[196] This position is a far cry from other initiatives taken by U.S. unions in the 1980s and 1990s that have emphasized organizing international solidarity for union struggles across borders.[197]

The anti-CAFTA lobby also included the United States Business and Industry Council, founded in 1933 and made up of mostly small businesses that support protectionism because they are not in a position to expand globally themselves. The Council goes beyond protectionism, however, to oppose all forms of internationalism, including the United Nations, the International Court of Justice, and the Kyoto Agreements, while insisting that the United States "maintain its pre-eminent position in the world" and also its "access to resources and markets."[198]

On the other side were textile and apparel manufacturers like Sara Lee Branded Apparel, based in Winston-Salem, North Carolina, which maintained extensive operations abroad, including in the Palmaseca export processing zone in Cali, Colombia, and VF Corporation, the world's largest apparel manufacturer, based in Greensboro, North Carolina. The VF Corporation operated in twenty-two countries, including fifteen plants in Central

America and the Dominican Republic, making Lee, Wrangler, and North Face brands. For companies that operated assembly plants abroad, CAFTA offered incentives that they were positioned to take advantage of. These two companies led the lobbying effort in favor of CAFTA in the U.S. Congress.[199]

Even as the National Cotton Council of America joined the coalition against CAFTA, it was also working to increase U.S. cotton sales in the CAFTA countries. The Caribbean Basin Initiative (CBI) had spawned the Cotton Council's "Cotton USA CBI Program and NAFTA parity for Central America and Caribbean Region" to promote U.S. cotton to companies outsourcing in Central America and the Caribbean. "Total U.S. exports of cotton textiles, fabrics and apparel in 1999 to target countries reached 1.2 million bale equivalents valued at $2.5 billion, or well above the 1 million bales and $2.1 billion level reached in 1998," the Council enthused.[200] In 2001 the Council sponsored its first "Sourcing CBI" fair in the Dominican Republic, bringing together U.S. cotton textile manufacturers, forty-three Caribbean basin apparel manufacturers, and buyers from retailers like Target and Eddie Bauer.[201] The Council's 2003 "Sourcing USA" fair in Guatemala similarly tried to showcase U.S. cotton mills to manufacturers and retailers.[202] North Carolina shipped $1.7 billion worth of goods to CAFTA-DR countries in 2004: 11 percent of the total U.S. shipments. And 75 percent of what North Carolina shipped was textile products.[203]

The U.S. government has long provided billions of dollars a year to subsidize U.S. cotton growers. In 1990, the Step 2 program began to subsidize those that buy U.S.-grown cotton as well, both textile mills and cotton exporters. Step 2 is another way federal policy supports outsourcing: by making artificially cheap, taxpayer-subsidized U.S. raw cotton and also cotton fabric available to U.S. producers everywhere. Step 2 payments rose dramatically, from $70 million in 1995 to $480 million in 2003, as the rush to outsource accelerated.[204] The three largest recipients, who received well over $100 million each, were the Allendale Cotton Company, Dunavant of California, and Cargill Cotton, the world's three largest cotton traders. (Milliken & Company was number 38 on the list, receiving over $12 million.)[205]

The Sewn Products Equipment Suppliers of the Americas Association, based in Raleigh, North Carolina, and supplying machinery to the global textile industry, announced cheerfully, "China will grow, and so can you. . . . Winning in a quota-free world," as the theme for its 2005 annual meeting. A VF Corporation representative there spoke on "Post-2005 Sourcing Strategies" along with representatives from Nike and Liz Claiborne, all celebrated as "leading contract managers who contract manufacturing in numerous countries."[206] Retailers too opposed protection for the U.S. textile industry. The American Apparel & Footwear Association, the International Mass Retail Association, the National Retail Federation, and the U.S. Association of Importers of Textiles & Apparel jointly urged President George W. Bush to ignore pleas from the governors of North and South Carolina, Georgia, and Alabama to take action to stem the hemorrhage of textile production out of the United States.[207]

Conclusion

Jane Collins argues that overall, the proliferation of opportunities and subsidies for outsourcing strengthened large companies at the expense of small companies that did not have the resources to compete in the sourcing game. The complex quota system favored companies that were large enough to maintain production at multiple sites worldwide and adjust production and imports in accordance with quota opportunities.[208]

Capital mobility also strengthens the hand of capital over labor. As New England textile workers and unions discovered early in the century, regional differentials can increase companies' leverage over workers in various ways: companies can impose more onerous conditions, claiming they need to do so to remain competitive, and they can move to places where they can make greater profits, thus undermining the workplace and societal gains made by unions and working people.

Regional differentials harm workers everywhere. In the low-wage regions, the harm to workers is obvious. In the high-wage regions, the availability of cheaper, more exploitable labor elsewhere constantly undermines workers' ability to maintain or improve their conditions. Government policies that encourage the mobility of capital exacerbate the degree to which regional differentials enhance the power of capital over labor.

Some analyses, particularly in the mass media, approach globalization in terms of *place*, encouraging us to think primarily in geographical terms. The shift of production from one region to another is seen as a loss for one city, region, or country and a gain for another. The analysis proposed in this chapter (and this book) suggests that it is also important to approach globalization in terms of the relationship between labor and capital. Capital mobility is part of a long-term strategy that enables businesses to earn more profits at the expense of their workers and limits the ability of workers to fight back.

The language of place, nation, and nationalism suggests that there exists a commonality of interests between labor and capital based upon place. Protectionist campaigns have promoted this sense of commonality. Workers and businesses, however, have very different relationships to place. Workers live in a place; corporations rely on governments, rooted in territories, to use workers' identification with place to justify and generate popular support for policies that benefit capital. Actions by governments—in particular the U.S. government, the most powerful in the world—have encouraged capital mobility in various ways. Tax incentives and trade policies and military interventions and military aid that crush popular movements, thus maintaining regional differentials, are strategies that rally nationalism and a fiction of common interest based on location to achieve corporate goals. Protectionist policies may favor some businesses that are unable to partake in capital mobility, but they do little to strengthen the interests of workers.

Governments do not play a diminished role, as is commonly asserted, in the current complex of globalization. On the contrary, governments played a key role in constructing the system, and they play a key role in maintaining it. They create tax structures and legislative apparatus, they serve as the major market for many products, and they provide the physical (military) force necessary to enforce the regional inequalities that are at the heart of the system.

ROGER MILLIKEN

Roger Milliken's textile empire, based in Spartanburg, South Carolina, had its origins in New England. Seth Milliken hailed from Maine, a potato farmer who became a "jobber" selling textile products to dealers, first dealing with Maine factories, then investing in textile factories in the South. His company, Deering Milliken (later Milliken & Company), bailed out many southern mills during the Depression and ended up owning them, making it by 2001 the largest textile company in the United States.[209] As a buyer from the mills, Seth Milliken was well positioned to know which ones were in economic trouble and could "snatch them up at bargain prices."[210]

Seth Milliken's grandson Roger was named director of Deering-Milliken in 1941 and became president of the company in 1947. If Textron owner Royal Little's cavalier treatment of workers and unions illustrates the work of a businessman who is more of a speculator than a producer, Roger Milliken could be said to represent the opposite end of the spectrum: he was determined to defend the productivity of South Carolina's textile industry (much of which he ended up owning). For Milliken, maintaining production in Spartanburg County, and in South Carolina and the United States in general, meant an utter adherence to two political tenets: any union organizing must be absolutely obliterated, and the U.S. textile industry must be protected with federal legislation.

During the 1940s and 1950s, Milliken & Company mills established their reputation as among the most recalcitrant union-busters among southern mills. In early 1945, the U.S. Army took over and ran Milliken's Gaffney Manufacturing Company mill in South Carolina when the company refused to accede to War Labor Board orders to negotiate with the TWUA. Three months later, when the war ended, the WLB returned the mill to its owners, who continued obdurate. In mid-September workers at Gaffney went out on strike.

> Strikes were a risky enterprise for southern millhands under the best of circumstances, but under the conditions in Gaffney, once the company's power and influence were fully deployed, strikers found it nearly impossible to defend their cause. The forces of local government, presided over by a mayor whose father was a local mill owner, made no pretense of neutrality. Local police harassed and arrested strikers without provocation, a pliant city council enacted special ordinances designed to impede the strikers' efforts, and servile local judges issued one injunction after another to keep the union off balance.[211]

So far, the situation and the tactics were not terribly different from those reigning in Hopedale, Massachusetts, in 1913.

The company's next tactic was also familiar: it threatened to close the mill. At Gaffney, however, the management went beyond the timid threats employed at Naumkeag: it promptly sold off half of its machinery to back up the threat.[212]

Although Milliken succeeded in breaking the union and continuing operations at Gaffney, the company proved that it was willing to take the next step at its Darlington mill in 1956. In September, the mill's five hundred workers voted in favor of the TWUA in a National Labor Relations Board (NLRB) election. Five weeks after the election, Milliken announced the mill's closing.[213]

The TWUA launched a legal challenge which worked its way all the way up to the U.S. Supreme Court, with the union winning at every level. In 1980 Milliken finally settled with the NLRB and agreed to pay $5 million to the workers or their heirs; by the time of the settlement, over one hundred of the workers had died. The original NLRB ruling, that a company may not close a plant to destroy a union, was upheld. But as one study points out, "In practical effect, the delay of justice proved the opposite" given the twenty-five years that passed and the small amount of the final settlement.[214]

The impact of the Darlington case went well beyond Milliken's workers. Seven years later, when the epic TWUA (later ACTWU) organizing drive against J. P. Stevens began, the company's multifaceted campaign against the union relied heavily on the threat of plant closings, and it frequently held up the Darlington example. Stevens was a company that had begun in New England and closed its unionized northern plants to move into the South, so when it threatened to repeat the pattern, workers and community members took it seriously. The company capitalized on this fear during its long battle against the union, including making explicit threats of a move to South America should workers vote union.[215] When, faced with mounting labor law violations and legal delays, the union took its struggle into the public sphere, launching a boycott and corporate campaign against Stevens, the company was able to use this to bolster its argument that the union was harming the company, thus threatening workers' jobs.[216] (This line of argument could also backfire against the company, however. Public support for the union's cause against Stevens, especially in the North, was bolstered by the company's history of capital flight.)[217]

In addition to crushing unions, Milliken & Company pursued other paths to maintaining its production and profitability. Like other textile producers, Milliken diversified. Milliken mills moved from cottons into synthetics, and by the 1990s had contracts with companies ranging from Avis and Hertz to McDonald's and Burger King.[218] Like Royal Little, he was not averse to closing some plants to increase the profitability of others, even when no union was involved.[219]

Milliken, as well as other textile producers, also pursued a public relations, political, and legislative campaign to protect the southern textile industry. Leading a new wave and complex of political activism, Roger Milliken spearheaded the South's "vocal, indeed downright xenophobic," protectionism of the 1960s and beyond.[220] In this stance, Milliken found a not totally unexpected ally: the very unions he had spared no effort to eliminate from his factories. From the "Crafted with Pride" movement of the 1980s to the opposition to CAFTA in the first decade of the twenty-first century, Milliken and the textile unions found common ground in nationalistic campaigns that emphasized labor-management collaboration.

Milliken ranked number 38 on the 2005 *Fortune 500* list of best employers to work for, based primarily on workers' evaluations of the company. Still adamantly anti-union, and with hourly employees earning about $30,000 a year, the company nonetheless maintained a high degree of worker loyalty. "Thankfully, someone in this country cares about the American worker and what he stands for," one worker told the *Fortune* interviewers.[221]

CHAPTER 4

INVISIBLE WORKERS IN A DYING INDUSTRY

Latino Immigrants in New England Textile Towns

It is too late for the Draper Co. to raise the question of American citizenship, as they have been notorious in displacing American with foreign labor for the simple reason that they could hire these poor foreigners cheaper than the American citizen . . . It is not a question of citizenship or nationality. It is a question of humanity.

—JOSEPH COLDWELL, *MILFORD DAILY NEWS*, APRIL 5, 1913

A continuous stream of migrants from economically backward areas is critical to the process of economic growth as it has occurred in the Western world.

—MICHAEL J. PIORE, "IMMIGRATION, WORK, AND MARKET STRUCTURE"

A Changing Labor Force

The regional inequalities that encouraged capital mobility, and that led some U.S. unions into a stance of protectionist nationalism, also infiltrated the domestic U.S. labor market from the very origins of the factory system. Manufacturers relied on an influx of labor from poorer regions to create and maintain a cheap workforce at home. U.S. unions faced a similar ideological dilemma on the home front as on the international front: Was class or national/ethnic identity their main organizing principle? Were immigrants working-class comrades or were they threats to the precarious benefits American workers could obtain?

Chapters 1 and 2 looked at specific early twentieth-century examples of how unions struggled with these issues. This chapter takes a long-twentieth-century view of how New England employers have used regional and global inequalities to manipulate the domestic labor market through the cycle of industrialization and deindustrialization, and of how unions have often failed to take advantage of potential alliances with new immigrants fighting for labor rights.

Industrialization created new jobs and, perhaps more important, new kinds of jobs, and it sought new workers, and new kinds of workers, to fill them. New England's textile industry initially relied on two systems for staffing its factories. Rhode Island's early mills sought men with large families so that each male employee brought a contingent of lower-paid family members into the mill. The "Lowell system" sought instead to import temporary migrants: young women from surrounding farming communities who were willing to work in dead-end jobs for low wages in order to return home with enough savings to achieve specific economic goals.[1]

Although the composition of the labor force changed significantly over the years, several aspects of this initial system persisted. First, industrial societies have consistently relied on a dual, or segmented, labor market. A large number of jobs belong to what sociologists call the secondary sector: low-paid, dangerous, unregulated, and with little or no opportunity for advancement.[2] To fill these jobs, employers have consistently sought migrant workers from poorer regions, inside and outside of the country, who have been willing to work very hard for very low wages in order to achieve specific economic goals.

This willingness to work under substandard conditions is characteristic of the first generation of migrants, who intend to earn their money and return home to enjoy it. Some migrants do just that. But those who remain seek to better their working conditions, either through labor organizing or by leaving the secondary sector and moving into more stable, better paying jobs. Yet the persistence of a secondary sector labor market of dangerous, underpaid, and unregulated jobs has remained characteristic of industrial societies, as has the persistence of migrant workers to fill those jobs.[3]

Young farm women were followed by southern and eastern European immigrants from the late nineteenth century through World War I. The "great migration" of African Americans into northern industrial cities began when European immigration was cut off, first by the war and then by the immigration restrictions of the 1920s. Mexicans, who were deliberately exempted from the restrictive legislation, and Puerto Ricans, who were U.S. citizens, followed. In the 1960s and 1970s, employers looked further into the Caribbean, Colombia, and Central America.

Several factors structured these waves of migration. Regional differentials meant that migrants could hope to earn more money more quickly and return home with significant savings. Regional differentials, however, have never historically been sufficient to spur migration. In all cases, the migrant stream was initiated through intensive recruitment efforts on the part of employers.[4] Capital flight, involving the movement of industry to a cheaper wage area, has also frequently set the stage for the movement of workers to the source of the industry. This pattern was repeated in the U.S. South, in Puerto Rico, in Mexico, in Colombia, in the Caribbean, and in Central America as the twentieth century progressed.

Deindustrialization in New England after World War II was accompanied by a new wave of immigration from Latin America, and the immigrants followed deindustrialization in a clear geographical pattern. Yesterday's mill and factory cities became magnets for Latin American immigrants.[5] In these cities, where unemployment and poverty rates where high, Latino immigrants found work, and worked very hard. Yet they not only remained poor as the economy expanded; they got poorer.

Latino immigrants played a role in the Massachusetts economic boom of the 1980s, but they did not benefit from it proportionately. The poverty rate for Latinos in Massachusetts doubled in the 1970s, to 37.6 percent. (The rate for whites was 8 percent and for blacks 25 percent in 1979.) And while the rates for non-Latinos declined significantly in the 1980s, the Latino poverty rate remained stubbornly at the same high level. "Massachusetts had the dubious distinction of having the highest rate of Latino poverty of any state during the late 1980s—almost twice the national average . . . The tide of 'the Massachusetts Miracle,' as this period of economic expansion is popularly known, did not lift all boats."[6] As Piore argued in 1979, the dual labor market is deeply embedded in the structure of the U.S. economy, and post-1979 developments confirmed its persistence.

From the Sweatshop to the Middle Class

Two structural aspects of the U.S. economy allowed for the upward mobility and assimilation of the 1880–1920 generation of immigrants. First, they entered an expanding industrial economy, with ample and growing opportunities for work in the manufacturing sector. Second, union organizing, New Deal social legislation, and the creation of a social safety network including social security, protective labor laws, and unemployment insurance together contributed to the transformation of factory labor from the sweatshop to the middle class. Despite these structural transformations, it's important to also recognize what stayed the same. The opportunities of the mid-twentieth century were racially defined. De jure and de facto, those not defined as white were excluded, and while factory work conditions improved, the dual labor market as a whole persisted.

Immigrants to the United States today face a very different picture. They are entering a society in the throes of deindustrialization, where the last manufacturing jobs are quickly evaporating. And they are entering a society whose social safety network is being deliberately dismantled as organized labor struggles to recover from a generation of anticommunist somnolence. The service sector jobs that employ most new immigrants share many characteristics with factory work at the beginning of the century: low pay, little security, dangerous working conditions, and lack of regulation. Yet the two factors that helped to change the nature of factory work—labor organizing and social legislation—show little sign of being able to carry out a similar transformation of service sector work in the foreseeable future. Finally, the new immigrants—primarily from Latin America, the Caribbean, and Asia—belong precisely to those categories that have been racially excluded from the U.S. polity since the country's founding.[7]

Anti-immigrant sentiment in the United States today often crystallizes in the complaints "They come here to take our jobs, they depress the labor market because they are willing to accept hours and conditions that Americans would not" and "They are lazy, they come here to take advantage of our welfare system." Clearly the two claims are contradictory. Yet it is ironic that the same people who criticize immigrants for failing to follow the path of assimilation and upward mobility of past generations seem to resent new immigrants for doing precisely what allowed previous generations to assimilate and join the middle class: work and benefit from the social welfare system.[8]

Popular opinion further stigmatizes certain immigrants for being "illegal," sometimes used as an adjective, as in "illegal immigrant," and sometimes turned into a noun, "an illegal." Immigrants' rights groups have challenged this formulation on several grounds, yet the term remains in common use. "Ningún ser humano es ilegal"—no human being is illegal—a slogan that came into use in the 1980s among Central American immigrant activists and was immortalized in a song by the Salvadoran immigrant Lilo González and in a 1998 etching by Mark Vallen, challenges the concept inherent in the

Figure 11. "Ningón ser humano es ilegal / No Human Being Is Illegal." City Council member Lucy Corchado joins other immigrants at May Day 2006 rally in downtown Salem, Massachusetts. Photo by Aviva Chomsky.

phrase: that not only is an act illegal, but that a human being becomes illegal by engaging in the act of immigration.

In fact, U.S. immigration law is blatantly discriminatory, unlike any other law. Most acts that are defined as crimes are illegal by definition, regardless of who carries them out. Advocates of immigration restriction argue that immigration, while not inherently illegal, must be regulated in the same way as driving a car or opening a business, restricted to those who have obtained permission and fulfilled certain requirements. The difference, of course, is that the law also protects all citizens by giving them equal rights to obtain permission to drive or open a business. In fact, the law prohibits discrimination in this regard. Discrimination, however, is the cornerstone of immigration law. A driver's license cannot be denied based upon where one was born, one's political beliefs, or who one is related to, while place of birth and citizenship status of one's relatives are key factors in determining whether permission to immigrate is granted. The simple act of crossing the border thus becomes illegal for enormous numbers of people. Like the Draper strikers in 1913, immigrants who rallied on May Day, 2006, appealed to natives to accept a more inclusive vision of who in the country deserved rights.

But, readers will protest, as my students often do, if we eliminate immigration restrictions, too many people will come here! Perhaps. Or perhaps we could think about social and economic conditions that cause migration and the policies that create and sustain those conditions. Very few immigrants are motivated simply by adventure, curiosity, or pleasure. For the vast majority, the decision to leave their home, family, and culture is difficult and heart-wrenching, undertaken only because the migrant sees few alternatives. Additionally, we should think about the structure of our economy, which has throughout its history relied on a secondary labor market of low-paying, precarious jobs, in which the hard labor of some creates wealth and comfort for others. Perhaps instead of decrying those who fill those jobs—and who therefore create far more wealth than they consume—we could consider whether the exalted standard of living of some sectors of our society is being subsidized by the underpaid labor of others.

From Radical Immigrants to Anti-immigrant Americans

The way Italian American workers and their unions responded to immigration and capital flight over the course of the twentieth century exemplifies the trajectory of many others, though perhaps in an extreme form. Popular opinion, one study argues, stigmatizes today's Italian Americans "as reflexive conservatives who are hostile to political, racial, ethnic, and sexual minorities."[9] Yet only a few generations previous, the opposite stigma prevailed: Italian Americans were "anarchistic bastards," leftist subversives epitomized by Sacco and Vanzetti.[10]

As the editors of *The Lost World of Italian-American Radicalism* argue, this radical past has not only been repudiated, but it has been deliberately submerged and erased. They recount the story of Cammella Teoli, a young Italian immigrant textile worker in Lawrence, Massachusetts, who testified to Congress during the 1912 Bread and Roses strike there about how she was "scalped" by a machine that caught her hair and ripped the skin off her head, landing her in the hospital for seven months. "Newspapers across the country carried Cammella's story on their front pages. Her testimony prompted a federal investigation of factory conditions and added a human face to the strikers." In the 1970s, after Cammella's death, a *Village Voice* reporter interviewed her daughter. "He was stunned to discover that Cammella's daughter, whom he called Mathilda, knew nothing at all about Cammella Teoli's political past."[11] Assimilation into the mainstream of U.S. society meant obliterating immigrants' radical histories.

The general contours of the process of immigrant "assimilation," and its counterpart, the shift from oppositional political radicalism into the mainstream, are fairly well known. The Red Scares following World War I and World War II, with their repression, deportations, and executions, destroyed two generations of leftist leaders, sent many underground, and convinced others that survival lay in collaboration. Nativist movements also threatened those who challenged dominant ideologies and identities. New Deal politics, the opening of the Democratic Party to immigrants, and the real gains made by working people and their unions in the post–World War II period all contributed to the attraction of a particular form of assimilation.[12]

Elizabeth Votta, the Salem resident quoted in chapter 2 recalling Anne Burlak's speech ("Boy, she was really the 'red flame.' . . . I was excited, to meet this woman who was so active, so . . . fire and brimstone. She really was something else"), also had something to say about the Dominican immigrants who had moved into the Point neighborhood abandoned by the textile mill and its French Canadian workers: "My mother came from Canada, and my father came from Canada. Of course my mother went to work at the Pequot mills. . . . And then they lived down what they call the Point. My mother used to tell me in the Point it was all Canadians then. They were living in this housing that the Pequot mills used to own. They used to wash their porches, their steps, their sidewalks, everything was so nice and clean. Now all it is is all knives and dope." Votta also had an explanation of the mill's closing, which coincides with many others: "By her [Burlak's] inflaming all the people who were striking, that's why they closed the mill."[13] A rejection of one's own radical past and an antipathy toward today's immigrants often go hand in hand.

Massachusetts state representative Marie Parente, who was raised by Italian immigrants in Milford only a couple of decades after the Draper strike, became a leading anti-immigrant voice in Massachusetts politics at the beginning of the twenty-first century. Like so many former factory towns, Milford has received an influx of Latino immigrants in recent years.[14] Nativism among Milford's white residents runs high, and a spate of local anti-immigrant regulations has made Milford "among the most aggressive Massachusetts communities on the issue." "I'm hoping that Milford's story gets out across the country," Parente announced. "And maybe if all the towns hold hands and say, 'We will have no more of this overcrowding and disease and broken laws,' I think then maybe the Congress will understand."[15] Wickliffe Draper would have been proud.

The story of the two "Italian locals" of the ILGWU in New York City, Local 48 (cloak makers) and Local 89 (dressmakers), illustrates how responses to capital flight and to immigration contributed to a union's shift from radicalism to accommodationism.[16] Founded by Italian socialists in the early twentieth century, these locals exemplified aspects of immigrant radicalism in their early years. They "contributed to a host of humanitarian causes and built bridges to immigrant workers in other industries, in the New York area and nationally. They led the anti-Fascist crusade within the Sons of Italy, protested state and federal government policies and actions during the period of the first 'Red Scare,' supported workers' education."[17] According to one study, "By the 1920s, New York City's garment unions became one of the primary centers of Italian American radical activity."[18] In the 1930s, however, the growing threat of capital mobility in the industry and the changing racial composition of the workforce edged the leadership into increasingly accommodationist positions. Wage restraint, top-down control, and collaboration with management became hallmarks of ILGWU policy by the 1950s.

Even in the union's most radical years, ILGWU locals and leadership had a difficult time coming to terms with a new generation of immigrant workers. By the 1930s women were replacing men as the mainstay of the garment industry labor force, and Italians were being replaced by new Puerto Rican and African American migrants to New York. In 1933, women made up 80 percent of Local 89's membership (with forty thousand members, Local 89 was the largest local in the country).[19] The new members, however, confronted an entrenched male leadership that left little opening for their participation in union affairs. Like the Irish male leadership of the UTW in Salem in the 1930s, who mistrusted the newer, mostly female French Canadian and Polish immigrant workers, "into the 1940s and beyond, Jewish and Italian men continued to hold most offices in the ILGWU and maintained control over a predominantly female and increasingly non-European membership."[20]

Both of the Italian locals remained closed to Puerto Rican workers. The union did try to organize Puerto Rican workers, "but only in the locals of those trades where they had begun to pose a threat to white organized labor. In job categories where Puerto Rican women already predominated and where few white workers remained—such as pinking (garment edging), floor work (cleaning and distributing work), and packing—the union made no effort at organization. In 1933 and again in 1934, ILGWU president David Dubinsky denied a petition by Hispanic garment workers for the right to organize their own ethnic local on the model of the Italian locals."[21]

The shift was ideological, political, and racial. As Jennifer Guglielmo writes,

> By the 1930s, Italian American workers in socialist unions no longer sought to dismantle private property, the government, and other systems of oppressive authority, but to utilize the apparatus of the state, community institutions, and labor unions, to assert identities as Americans. New Deal reforms were critical in cementing this transition, since these programs channeled workforce protections and benefits to white industrial workers. . . . In the decades following the Second World War, whiteness guaranteed access to federally subsidized loans, which they used to abandon the inner city for segregated suburbs and maintain positions of authority in the newly empowered trade unions.[22]

The structure of the ILGWU pension funds also contributed to a divide wherein newer Puerto Rican and African American workers, in lower-paid positions and with a high turnover rate, subsidized the pension funds of older members because they did not remain in the industry long enough to cash in on the benefits they paid.[23]

Guglielmo maintains that "by the late 1940s, Italian American women and men garment workers in New York City began to insist on their whiteness, entitling them to privileged political rights, better-paying jobs, and leadership of the union. They often did so by practicing and institutionalizing policies of racialized exclusion in the union and industry, which enabled them to gain control over higher-paying jobs and deny democratic representation to African American, Puerto Rican, and West Indian women and men in the union."[24] Rather than challenging the dual labor market, the union actually supported it. Policies of labor-management collaboration and wage restraint that had become the norm were smoothly transferred to Puerto Rico as the industry accelerated its shift away from New York.

In 1947 the New York Commission against Discrimination ruled that the Italian locals could no longer legally exclude non-Italians. Nevertheless, through the 1980s the ILGWU was accused again and again of discrimination. A 1953 study of Seamstresses' Local 22 "revealed that Jewish and Italian 'old timers' resented the 'newcomers' and 'grumbled' at the prospects of the union being 'flooded' with 'non-union elements.' They thought these 'aliens' were 'selfish', 'lazy', and 'irresponsible.'" The NAACP testified at Congressional hearings in 1962 that the ILGWU kept Puerto Ricans in the lowest-paid and least-skilled positions. "The basic problem with the union is that the union is very tight with the bosses," one Puerto Rican worker concluded in an interview in the late 1970s.[25]

The ILGWU continually accepted low wages and even opposed raising the minimum wage for city workers in New York in the 1960s. Whether because of Dubinsky's anticommunist alliance with capital, or out of fear of jobs relocating, or out of racism against the union's own black and Latino membership, the "overall effect was to create distrust between union leaders and Puerto Rican workers" comparable to that seen between UTW leaders and immigrant workers in the 1933 Salem strike. In two cases, in 1957 and 1958, Puerto Rican workers launched protests against the sweetheart contracts agreed to by the ILGWU and "demanded that the courts replace the ILGWU as their bargaining agent." Even into the 1960s and 1970s, "in spite of the obvious reality that the ILGWU's wage-restraint and nonstrike policies had not contained relocations, the union still maintained these as the cornerstone of its bargaining philosophy."[26]

Industrialization, Deindustrialization, and Immigration

The demand for factory workers created by the expanding industrial economy of the late eighteenth century and early nineteenth was a major factor in stimulating the enormous southern and eastern European immigration of those years. The deindustrializing economy of New England in the late twentieth century also created a demand for low-paid workers. Deindustrialization created a new sweatshop economy, as manufacturers tried to pare their labor costs down to a minimum to survive and compete with offshore assembly plants. The high-tech Massachusetts miracle created another layer of low-paying jobs, servicing the high-wage economy: restaurant work, janitorial work, domestic services, child care, and health care workers.[27]

Like the factory jobs that employed generations of immigrant workers a century earlier, the jobs that the new immigrants came to fill belonged to the secondary labor market: low wage, unregulated, physically demanding, and sometimes dangerous. Some of these were in the textile and garment industries, which were able to evade the postwar labor-management compact precisely because they were prematurely adept at capital mobility. Their evasion of the pact led them to seek new sources of immigrant labor.

As working conditions improved in other sectors, it became difficult to attract a domestic labor force in an industry that was unwilling or unable to improve its wages and conditions. World War II and the New Deal created the conditions for significant improvement in working conditions in other industries. The war also created opportunities for travel, and then education (through veterans' benefits) that expanded textile workers' horizons.[28] The war, and the postwar arms race, created better-paying jobs in shipbuilding, steel, and aircraft manufacture that spurred migration out of textile towns into new industrial centers.[29] New opportunities emerged in declining textile towns like Lowell, Massachusetts, as "glamour industries" in electronics and high technology moved in.[30] By offering substandard conditions in a society that provided alternatives, the textile factories that did remain in New England found themselves facing the labor shortages that Ted Larter bemoaned in the 1970s.

In some cases, late twentieth-century immigrants found work in the sweatshops and "fly-by-night enterprises" that moved into the empty mill buildings.[31] In other cases, they helped declining industries like textiles remain in New England. "Since the early 1970s the simultaneous decline of the [manufacturing] sector and the heavy growth of the Latino population in Lawrence and Holyoke provided firms with the necessary cheap labor to 'ride' the decline (which often ended in plant closings)." In one case, "Latinos grew to 80 percent of the firm's labor force during the time the firm was being readied for shutdown."[32]

In Lowell, Massachusetts, and Central Falls, Rhode Island, textile manufacturers actually went to Medellín to contract Colombian workers who breathed a last gasp of life into a dying textile industry in the 1970s.[33] Joan Fabrics, which opened a factory in Lowell in 1957, began to transfer Puerto Rican workers there from its other plants in the late 1960s.[34] In Lawrence, "the closing of the mills in the '50s and the urban renewal of the '60s caused a void in the city—with empty apartments and no unskilled labor."[35] Merrimack Valley farms sent recruiters to Puerto Rico; Lawrence's shoe factories offered $50 referral fees to those who could bring in new workers.

Lawrence's Latino population rose from 68 to 2,327 between 1960 and 1970, half of these from Puerto Rico. By 1980, the number was up to 10,296.[36] In the small town of Turner, Maine, the Decoster Egg Farm (one of the largest egg producers in the country) recruited two hundred workers from the U.S.-Mexico border in the late 1980s.[37] In Salem, the first Dominicans arrived in the 1960s, moving into the old mill tenements after Salem's giant Naumkeag Steam Cotton Company closed its doors in 1953. By 2000, the census counted over 4,500 Latinos in Salem (two thousand of them Dominican); local residents and analysts were sure this was a serious undercounting.[38]

The labor shortages that plagued New England's textile industry from the 1960s on reached the South in the 1970s, as civil rights legislation and new industries opened opportunities there too. In Spartanburg, Draper increased production, and two Swiss textile machinery manufacturers also established plants. Synthetic textile manufacture, linked to the chemical and petroleum industries, was more capital intensive and offered higher wages than the traditional cotton textiles. The new industries "offered greater opportunities for advancement than the textile economy had traditionally afforded. . . . A strong industrial base, population growth, and rising incomes allowed increasing numbers of Spartans to leave manufacturing altogether and seize other opportunities." Spartanburg's cotton textile industry began to suffer from the same labor shortage as New England's, and manufacturers began to advertise for workers. "By the 1970s, mill personnel offices would begin posting signs in English and Spanish."[39]

The same process was occurring in other textile centers in the South. In the carpet factories of Dalton, Georgia, for example, "manufacturers believed that the labor shortage threatened the continued existence of the heavy concentration of mills." The solution was the same: "During the late 1980s and 1990s manufacturers found a solution to the vexing labor shortage: Hispanic workers, many of them illegal immigrants. . . . As Georgia's carpet industry entered the new millennium, a large portion of the mill workforce consisted of Hispanic immigrants. . . . Mill owners regarded Hispanic workers as the 'saviors' of the industry, allowing the mills to remain in Dalton and keeping labor costs in check."[40]

The J. P. Stevens Company resorted to subterfuge to lure immigrants from Medellín, Colombia, to its South Carolina plants in the midst of the epic union organizing campaign there in the 1970s. As one worker in Medellín recounted:

In 1973 . . . a manager from the Stevens Company in South Carolina . . . came here. He came with an assistant, a Colombian guy who had been a U.S. citizen for ten years. He was helping the company to *enganchar* [contract] weavers, loom fixers, and some spinners. . . . I don't know how, but somehow they got visas. . . . The manager talked with us, took all the information and we quickly got the visas. . . . We went legally with a contract for two years. . . . There were ten of us. We were the first and the last also . . . because we were taken with the objective of doing an apprenticeship to later work in a mill they were going to open here (in Medellín). . . . But that wasn't true. . . . Those of us who went knew absolutely nothing, but that was the means that the company's assistant used.[41]

Mill owners in the 1970s, just like the Drapers earlier in the century, had reason to welcome cheap immigrant workers at the same time that they might use racist appeals to unions to oppose immigrants. While they could benefit from paying lower wages to recent immigrants, they were also sometimes threatened by their militancy. Thus industries have maintained a dual stance of publicly opposing immigration (and fostering anti-immigrant racism) while privately encouraging it, supporting policies that limited legal immigration and fostered undocumented immigration and promoting guest-worker and contract labor programs that created a sub-working class of immigrants without full legal rights.

Yet restrictive immigration legislation had contradictory effects on northern industries. The progressive restriction of immigration from 1917 to 1924 and the loss of a ready source of cheap labor was one reason behind the textile industry's abandonment of the northeastern United States.[42] The few textile plants that remained in the Northeast after the 1950s actively recruited a new generation of immigrant workers, taking advantage of the unique situation of Puerto Rico, various labor contracting exemptions to immigration restrictions, and the relaxing of immigration restrictions after 1965. Harassment by the Immigration and Naturalization Service in the late 1970s was one factor that led Lowell's last mills, which employed significant numbers of Colombian immigrant workers, to make their final decision to close.[43]

The Puerto Rican Link

In the same way that Puerto Rico served as a sort of controlled experiment for what later became a hemorrhage of outsourcing, Puerto Ricans in the 1950s prefigured a huge new wave of Latino immigration into the U.S.

Northeast in the second half of the twentieth century. Puerto Ricans were the first group of Latino immigrants in New England and have remained the largest group, even as their relative proportion has declined in recent decades.[44] The origins of large-scale Puerto Rican migration to New England lie in the intertwined political, agricultural, and industrial histories of Puerto Rico and the United States. New England agriculture lacked easy access to a subordinate labor force enjoyed by the South (blacks) and the West (Mexicans), leading farmers to look to the Caribbean for migrant workers.[45] New Englanders, through trade and direct investment, were also crucial in the transformation of Puerto Rican agriculture, before and especially after 1898, that set the stage for out-migration.

New Englanders developed sugar plantations in Puerto Rico and imported and refined sugar at home. Cambridge was "the candy capital of the U.S.," with "over 100 candy companies, a chocolate mill and a sugar refinery in the area. They took ships' holds full of sugar or molasses from the West Indies and turned it into gooey, sticky or chocolatey treats."[46] U.S., and in particular, Boston capital underlay the expansion and mechanization of the sugar industry.[47] Four U.S. corporations dominated sugar milling in Puerto Rico by 1930: Central Aguirre Sugar Company, originally organized as a Massachusetts trust in 1901; South Porto Rico and Fajardo, both based in New Jersey; and United Porto Rico Sugar (after 1934, Eastern Sugar Associates).[48]

It might appear that agriculture and services have been the exception to the twentieth-century trend of disinvestment and runaway plants. Because they cannot simply move to where cheap labor and lax regulation are available, these industries have had to find ways to preserve or create profitable conditions at home. Traditionally, the agricultural sector has enjoyed its exemption from labor and environmental legislation in the United States, and it has maintained significant government protections and subsidies, including provisions for the importation of workers obliged to work under substandard conditions (the 1942–64 Bracero program, and the H-2 guest worker program after the Bracero program was ended). The service sector has also succeeded in maintaining a low-wage, unregulated, and invisible stratum of mostly immigrant workers.

Despite the greater obstacles that agriculture and services have faced with respect to geographical mobility, however, even these apparently immobile kinds of employment have found ways to move. Telephones, the

Internet, and faxes have allowed services like customer service and technical support to spread around the globe. New England investors planted crops in Latin America, brought seeds and techniques in both directions, brought Latin American workers to their New England farms, and relocated their farms to Latin America. The sugar and tobacco industries—as well as the banana industry, described in depth in the next chapter—provide excellent examples.

The expansion and capitalization of sugar production in Puerto Rico led, inevitably, to unemployment and migration. Subsistence lands were turned over to sugar, expelling peasants; with increasing mechanization, the harvest season shrank while the *tiempo muerto* expanded over the first decades of the twentieth century. Oral histories place the first Puerto Ricans in Rhode Island in the 1920s, when they began to come on annual contracts to work the summer season on local farms.[49]

It was not only in sugar production that U.S. investors, many from New England, decisively shaped Puerto Rico's agricultural landscape. Three Connecticut tobacco growers dominated the state's industry and formed the backbone of the Shade Tobacco Growers Association: The General Cigar Company, Consolidated Cigar Corporation, and Meyer and Mendelsohn. Like the garment manufacturers and retailers that outsourced finishing to Puerto Rico in the 1920s, they sent leaves grown in Connecticut to Puerto Rico for processing, establishing plants in Puerto Rico. "By using island labor to sort Connecticut-grown leaves and roll cigars, companies could pay less than minimum wage and avoid income tax. In fact, General Cigar was a major employer of Puerto Rican workers on the island in the 1950s and 60s." Many of the Puerto Ricans who went to work in tobacco in the Connecticut River Valley in the 1950s and 1960s had already worked for the same companies—minus the minimum wage—in Puerto Rico.[50]

In 1947 Puerto Rico's Department of Labor created a Migration Division to recruit seasonal workers for farms in the northeastern United States. "Recruiters logged many miles on the winding roads of small-town and rural Puerto Rico. Cars with bullhorns cut into the sounds of nature, squawking the promise of good jobs for those who wanted them. Leaflets spread around the island and advertisements in newspapers held the same enticing message." The numbers of immigrants skyrocketed, from 4,906 in 1948 to 22,902 in 1968.[51] Although 1968 was the peak year for workers contracted by the Department of Labor, the pattern grew and continued well beyond the program. A Connecticut tobacco grower commented in 1999 that "labor's the biggest expense" and that her farm housed migrant workers from Puerto Rico and Jamaica in a company dormitory during the July–August harvest season.[52] Another major Connecticut River Valley tobacco grower took the opposite route, relocating operations in Brazil in 1981.[53]

The "great migration" of Puerto Ricans to the continental United States that accompanied Operation Bootstrap brought perhaps a million migrants from the island, primarily to New York, in the 1950s. From there some found their way to Boston, Providence, and other New England cities. In 1959 Boston had fewer than one thousand Spanish speakers; in 1969, estimates ranged from seventeen thousand to forty thousand. A study of Puerto Rican immigrants in Boston in the early 1970s found that Boston employers were actively recruiting on the island. "Generally, this meant that they had hired a Puerto Rican worker on the mainland and paid his fare to his native village to recruit employees for the shop."[54]

Most of the Boston employers who sought Puerto Rican workers in the 1960s did so to replace an earlier generation of African American workers who had come north to fill the low-wage, dead-end jobs abandoned by still earlier generations of European migrants. The sociologist Michael Piore argues that the cycling of immigrants through the lower end of the economy is in part a generational phenomenon: first-generation immigrants (or internal migrants) are willing to work under inferior conditions because their frame of reference is the much poorer home society, while their children, born into the receiving society, are no longer willing to accept conditions that are inferior by its standards.[55]

Dominicans followed the trail blazed by Puerto Ricans from New York to New England. In the 1970s "it was said that jobs were so abundant that factory owners took to the streets to look for workers" in Providence.[56] "When I got here in 1973, men would be outside the factories saying, 'Do you need a job?'" one Colombian reported in 1996.[57] Dominicans in Salem, Massachusetts, give similar testimonies.[58] Some Latinos were brought from New York by interregionalist companies. Joan Fabrics, for example, operated in New Jersey, where it first recruited Puerto Rican workers, and Lowell. When Joan closed its New Jersey plants, it transferred its Puerto Rican workers to Lowell. "By the late 1970s, about half of the workers at Joan [in Lowell] were Puerto Rican."[59]

Out-migration was an inherent component of the low wage, export-oriented model of industrialization imposed through Operation Bootstrap and recapitulated in later decades in Mexico, Central America, and the Caribbean. Puerto Rico enjoyed two major advantages over other countries that followed it in this process: in Puerto Rico, industrialization-by-invitation was financially underwritten by the United States, and Puerto Ricans, as U.S. citizens, could engage in a massive, legal migration to the metropolis. Out-migration served to relieve the unemployment caused by the economic development model and also to mitigate the poverty through a growing reliance on remittances. The financial underwriting began as U.S. tax dollars funded the construction of infrastructure and reached mammoth proportions as the federal government extended welfare and food stamps to Puerto Rico. In 1970, federal transfers to Puerto Rico were about $500 million a year; by 1990 they had reached $6 billion a year (about $1 billion of that in food stamps).[60]

Some have argued that the system of federal transfers has benefited the population of Puerto Rico at the expense of taxpayers in the continental United States. The fact that Puerto Ricans pay no federal income tax contributes to the notion that U.S. taxpayers are subsidizing Puerto Rican citizens. This position, however, neatly bypasses the role of U.S. corporations in the system. U.S. corporations operating in Puerto Rico also pay no federal income tax, thus are the main beneficiaries of the "free ride" available in Puerto Rico (because they make much more money than individual citizens). Just as important, U.S. corporations benefit from the subsidies to Puerto Rican citizens because this frees them from having to pay a living wage to their workers. Like the textile companies that located on the outskirts of cities in the U.S. South, they could benefit from the services provided by the taxes they themselves managed to evade. The companies benefited directly (by using the services) and indirectly (by relying on the services to supplement the wages they paid their workers).

Other countries that followed the Puerto Rican model did so without the advantages of U.S. financial aid and U.S. citizenship. This meant that the poverty that accompanied the model was infinitely more desperate and the immigrants smaller in relative numbers and more vulnerable as noncitizens. Despite these obstacles, out-migration and reliance on remittances have been an inherent component of the export-processing model of economic development everywhere in Latin America. As Saskia Sassen notes, "Measures commonly thought to deter emigration—foreign investment, or the

promotion of export-oriented agriculture and manufacturing in poor countries—have had precisely the opposite effect. Such investment contributes
to massive displacement of small-scale agricultural and manufacturing enterprises, while simultaneously deepening the economic, cultural and ideological ties between the recipient countries and the United States."[61]

One study of Mexico's maquiladoras found that foreign companies deliberately seek to locate in zones of high out-migration. "The factories employed family members of migrants—those who remained at home. In other
words, labor migration and maquiladora work became, for many families,
part of an intertwined strategy of social reproduction, made necessary by the
insufficiency of the wage paid by the factories."[62] For the factories, this
meant that they could pay less than a living wage and their workers could
still survive.

If other Latin American countries have lacked federal transfers in the
form of welfare for their citizens, this does not mean that the U.S. government has not contributed funds to ensure that the model functions. Outside
of Puerto Rico, however, economic and military "aid" has worked somewhat
differently. Instead of putting money into the hands of the poor, it has put it
into the hands of the wealthy—and the military—to help enforce an unjust
social order. Corporations in Colombia, for example, can pay low wages not
because families supplement wages with welfare and food stamps, but because paramilitaries will obligingly kill workers who try to organize a union.
Foreign military aid is itself an important form of corporate welfare, since it
sustains military production inside the United States.

Central Falls and Lowell: The Long Road to Colombian Workers

Two of the oldest textile centers in New England, Central Falls, Rhode
Island, and Lowell, Massachusetts, became magnets for Colombian textile
workers in the 1960s. The causes were at once structural and fortuitous. In
both cases, a chance encounter at a single mill opened the door to a con-
certed effort to recruit Colombian workers, which evolved into a chain
migration that ended up creating significant Colombian immigrant communities in both cities. The Colombian presence is more dramatic in tiny
Central Falls (population eighteen thousand in 2000), where Latinos constituted almost half of the city's population (and Colombians about half
of the Latinos in 1990; a smaller proportion in 2000 because of dramatic
growth in the Puerto Rican and Guatemalan populations during the decade)

than in much larger Lowell, with a population of over one hundred thousand, where only 14 percent of the population is Latino. (Almost ten thousand of Lowell's close to fifteen thousand Latinos were Puerto Rican; only 1,167 were Colombian.)[63]

Central Falls adjoins Pawtucket, where Samuel Slater built the first U.S. cotton mill in the eighteenth century, often termed "the birthplace of the cotton-textile industry in the United States." With the depression in the cotton industry in the 1920s, its factories began to close or diversify to silk and rayon production.[64] As the national secretary for the communist National Textile Workers Union in the late 1920s, Anne Burlak was based in Olneyville, next door to Central Falls and Pawtucket. She led a 1931 strike at the Royal Weaving and General Fabric mills in Central Falls and ran for mayor on the Communist Party ticket in Pawtucket in the early 1930s (see chapter 2).

Textile jobs contracted precipitously in the Central Falls/Pawtucket area, as in the rest of Rhode Island, after the 1920s. In 1950 there were over sixty thousand textile workers in the state; in 1960 twenty-eight thousand. By 1980 the number had shrunk to twelve thousand; by 2001 it was down to 6,400.[65] The mills that survived into the second half of the century tended to be small and specialized in niche markets. Elizabeth Webbing Mills, founded in 1929 and run by the Lifland family from 1959 until it closed in 2001, made suitcase straps, pet collars, seat belts, and truck tie-downs.[66] The Pontiac Weaving Company in Cumberland, one of the three to participate in the initial recruitment drive in Medellín in the mid-1960s, produced satins and taffetas since 1951. At its height Pontiac employed 140 workers. By the time it closed in 1994, its workforce was down to thirty-five.[67] Cadillac Textiles, also an early recruiter of Colombians, dated to 1921 and closed in 1986.[68] One of the few survivors into the twenty-first century was Hope Webbing, founded in 1883, which produced industrial textiles. Hope was both global and small: with plants in Mexico and France, as well as Rhode Island, it employed six hundred people worldwide (380 of them in Rhode Island).[69]

Lowell, known as "the Spindle City," shares with Pawtucket/Central Falls an important spot in the history of the U.S. textile industry. A classic study of Lowell in the 1940s characterizes it as "the first instance in America of the development of a city of the primarily industrial type, a city which owes its existence to its mills."[70] Like Central Falls and other textile mill cities, Lowell

Figure 12. Colombian textile workers at the Wannalancit mill in Lowell, Massachusetts, 1989. Copyright © James Higgins. Reprinted by permission.

experienced early deindustrialization as cotton mills moved south, while some mills moved into woolens and worsted, and later silk and synthetic production. By the late twentieth century the city was in severe industrial decline, but a few mills held on.

Lowell's Ames Manufacturing Company was founded by members of the J. P. Stevens family and marketed its products through Stevens until the 1940s. Unlike Stevens, Ames remained in New England, continuing to operate two mills in Lowell through the 1970s, when it became one of several Lowell companies to import Colombian labor.

Although it maintained a presence in New England, Ames operated at a national and global level. Lawrence Manufacturing Company, which Ames purchased early in the century, imported polyester yarn from Brazil to produce knit fabric for the General Tire Company. When southern U.S. manufacturers succeeded in obtaining tariff protection on polyester yarn, Ames shifted back into clothing production.

In the early 1950s the company built a mill in Georgia (the Cleveland Mills), which began making army uniforms. In the 1960s, Ames began to expand production of knits developed at the Lawrence mill into Europe, operating nine mills there by the 1970s. In 1975, the company bought the Synthetic Yarns Company in Taunton, Massachusetts, and moved it back to Lowell. Synthetic Yarns produces fabric for labels using yarns produced by Dupont, Monsanto, and Celanese.[71]

Joan Fabrics had its roots at the beginning of the century in a furniture upholstery weaving plant in Central Falls. Like so many other textile manufacturers, it expanded into South Carolina, buying a mill in Hickory in 1952, but it also expanded in New England, buying a factory in Rhode Island in 1955 and one in Lowell in 1957, then four more in Lowell and two in New Jersey in the 1960s.[72] By 2000, Joan also operated plants in Fall River, Massachusetts, in North Carolina, and in Mexico.[73] In September 2001 Joan was purchased by Collins and Aikman; the Lowell plant was later closed.[74]

Wannalancit too had its roots early in the twentieth century, but unlike the others, was always based in Lowell and did not expand elsewhere. Like so many others in the textile industry, however, it relied heavily on government contracts, producing synthetic fabrics for parachutes and space suits. It was also a factory filled with old Crompton and Draper shuttle looms, which Colombian workers were experts at fixing.[75]

The Creation of a Migrant Stream

The ties between the U.S. textile industry and the Colombian, and the unequal relationship between the two countries, created a generation of Colombian textile workers primed to be recruited for migration just as the U.S. textile industry was facing a labor shortage. Medellín's textile workers were trained on Draper looms and in industrial relations techniques imposed by Boston's Barnes Textile Associates; they spent their lives weaving denim for Levis jeans and canvas for the U.S. Army. Colombians tend to be acutely aware of their country's long unequal relationship with the United States, beginning with the taking of Panama. This relationship intensified after World War II, as U.S. advisors began to help the Colombian government develop counterinsurgency techniques, while the Alliance for Progress made U.S. material aid a palpable presence in many individuals' lives.[76] In addition, the U.S. Department of Labor included loom fixers and weavers as job categories for which employers could import workers in the 1960s and 1970s, which facilitated the contracting of Colombians.

Paradoxically, Colombian workers left some of the world's largest and most modern, integrated, and diversified textile plants in Medellín to come to "the personalized, eclectic management of a small-scale, single product company" in Lowell.[77] Colombian entrepreneurs had brought in U.S.-made machinery and U.S.-developed labor-management techniques to modernize their industry in the mid-twentieth century, just as the largest and most "modern" plants were closing in the United States. Those that remained— or relocated—in New England were the smaller companies with older machinery.

The modern textile industry's search for cheap, unregulated labor took two forms: those that could afford to, moved or outsourced abroad; those that could not afford to move or outsource brought in new workers from abroad. Rather than being the one-way street toward industrial organization and upward mobility painted by many accounts, modernization in fact has been a continuing process of creation, and exploitation, of regional differentials. The development of the department store and the regulation and abolition of homework in New York led garment manufacturers to create a home needlework industry in Puerto Rico in the 1920s; Colombian workers trained on imported U.S. machinery and methods in Medellín came to some of the earliest centers of the U.S. textile industry, Lowell and Pawtucket/Central Falls, to find that machinery and those methods in decay.[78] One Colombian supervisor quit his job at Wannalancit in Lowell because he could not adjust to the disorganization of the plant in comparison with Medellín: "Textiles could be much more here [Lowell], but there is no organization of any kind. . . . It scares me because [some of the practices] were learned from the United States, and they aren't used here."[79] (See chapter 3 for a longer version of this quote.)

CENTRAL FALLS

In fortuitous terms, the recruitment began with a visit by an MIT student, Jay Giutarri—son of Central Falls Lyons Fabric Company's owner—to his Colombian college roommate's home in Medellín in the early 1960s. (Of course, Medellín's textile oligarchy had been educating its sons at New England schools for several generations already.) "It was then that he saw first-hand the highly-skilled work of the textile workers in Medellín. He called his father back in Rhode Island to share his excitement, and soon recruited four men to work in his father's mill in Central Falls."[80]

A slightly different version of the story explains that Giutarri was a partner in a business in Barranquilla and spent the years 1961–63 there. When he returned to Central Falls in 1964 and was confronted with the labor shortage, he was prompted to return to Barranquilla to try to recruit a few workers from a textile factory down the street from his business. As a result of this trip, he requested visas for a supervisor, two weavers, and a mechanic.[81]

"Personally, I think I have brought about one hundred," Giutarri explained years later. "But what happened was that some of the workers we brought were very good, very acceptable, and well trained, so we wanted to bring more, as did some of the other, larger mills here in Central Falls. So they sent people to Colombia to interview prospective workers as well. So everybody began bringing their own personnel . . . the other factories went to Medellín to find workers, and I went there too, to find workers experienced in the operation of a certain machine, of which there are none in Barranquilla." Giutarri described "a line blocks long" when he placed an advertisement in a local newspaper inviting potential recruits for interviews.[82]

Two other Central Falls mills, Pontiac and Cadillac, facing the same labor shortage, soon followed Lyons's example. Some of the early immigrants became "worker-recruiters" whom the companies paid to go back and bring in more immigrants.[83] By the mid-1970s, the mills no longer had to recruit: the migrant stream had been established. "The promise of jobs were always available to the Colombians who came to Central Falls, and many of the mills employed generations of families."[84] For two decades, from the early 1960s to the early 1980s, these Central Falls mills, like a few of their counterparts elsewhere in New England, survived by importing Colombian workers. "Mill owners expressed their appreciation by stating that without the immigrants, their businesses would not have survived."[85] By the early 1980s, however, most of these remaining mills also closed. Some of Rhode Island's Colombian workers followed the textile industry to South Carolina, but others stayed and have turned Central Falls into a thriving enclave or niche economy.[86]

LOWELL

The Lowell migrant stream originated with twenty loom fixers recruited in Medellín in 1969 by Fabio Agudelo, a Colombian hired by the Connecticut-based Ponemah Company for that purpose. A small Colombian immigrant community was already taking root in New York in the 1960s, and Ponemah's owners were also aware of the Rhode Island experiment.[87] The company owned five mills, and it sent Agudelo home to Medellín, accompanied by Ponemah vice president Samuel Cruppnick, with twenty H-2 visas in hand to bring back experienced loom fixers for its Taftville, Connecticut, plant. As a former supervisor in a Medellín mill Agudelo knew many workers, and he handed out fifty invitations to a select group, asking them to come for a test and an interview at a local hotel later that week. Twenty were then selected and offered jobs at Ponemah, complete with work permits.[88] Seven came from Coltejer, seven from Fabricato, four from Tejicóndor, and one from Pantex.[89]

Ponemah wanted workers willing to put in long hours, and it found them in the Colombians who had left their homes and families precisely to make as much money as they could in as short a time as possible. "In an incredible display of endurance, the Colombian loom fixers spent most of their time working. Cash accumulation was their principal motive for coming to the United States in the first place . . . All of them worked at least ten to twelve hours a day, most worked six or seven days a week, and many worked double shifts at least several days a week."[90]

Within months Ponemah decided to close the Taftville plant and transferred the twenty Colombians to its Florence Mills in Greenville, New Hampshire, a small town in the Manchester-Nashua metropolitan area. When Florence also closed only months later, the workers moved on to other mills in New Hampshire and Rhode Island. One, Mario Quiceno, followed a lead given by one of his supervisors who had once worked at Wannalancit and introduced himself to the owner, Ted Larter. Larter not only enthusiastically hired Quiceno on the spot, but also urged him to bring some more Colombians with him. Soon seven of the group had been taken on by Wannalancit and settled in Lowell.[91]

Fifteen years after the *primer enganche*, the political scientist Eleanor Glaessel-Brown found that most of the original group of men had experienced numerous textile mill closings, but most of them had remained textile workers, moving from one mill to the next, mostly in New England. Meanwhile, the New England communities where they originally settled, in particular Lowell and Pawtucket/Central Falls, had become magnets for increasing numbers of Colombian immigrants. In Lowell, Wannalancit relied on its first Colombian hire, Mario, to set up a recruitment network that brought in dozens of Colombian workers. From Wannalancit they moved to Joan Fabrics, which also used the older Draper shuttle looms that the Colombian-trained workers were so adept with, and to Ames Manufacturing's Lawrence and Synthetic Yarns mills. By the end of the 1970s, Colombians made up 10 percent of the workforce at Joan Mills, 15 percent at Lawrence, over 25 percent at Synthetic Yarns, and over 50 percent at Wannalancit. Even the continuing influx of Colombian workers, however, could not save Wannalancit. In December 1980 the mill closed permanently.[92]

Wage Differentials and Remittances

The wage differential alone does not explain why Colombian workers would leave thriving Medellín for declining Lowell, but it provides part of the explanation. A textile worker in Lowell earned about $5 per hour in 1980; in Medellín, he or she earned just over $1. Overtime hours were unrestricted and often available in Lowell and paid at an even higher (time-and-a-half) rate.[93] Taken alone, these figures are not necessarily very meaningful, for the cost of living is also considerably higher in the United States. However, the wage differential becomes more meaningful if we place it in context.

First, Latin American immigrant workers frequently maintain a transnational identity and household income strategy. Most workers migrate not with the idea of permanent relocation, but rather to create a temporary influx of cash. A significant portion of the migrant's income is sent home in remittances, or saved for the eventual trip home. In Colombia, remittances are the second largest source of national income, after petroleum exports. In 2004, petroleum brought in $4.2 billion and remittances $3.9 billion. Coal exports followed at $1.8 billion, and coffee at $1.1 billion.[94]

Low wages in Colombia have historically been compensated in part by an extensive social security system.[95] This system has been very important in the "reproduction" of the workforce and in family survival strategies in the long term. In the short term, however, a young, healthy worker might be willing to temporarily sacrifice the social safety network in favor of a higher cash flow. If other family members remained employed in Colombia, the risk was further reduced. One of the Colombians from the 1969 primer enganche explained his decision: "My wife and I talked about it. Then we got excited because I had begun to build a big house and had no hope of fixing it up soon. Maybe if I went up there I could earn enough to finish the house and then return here for good."[96]

Various studies of Latino immigration into the United States have noted the fact that immigration allows the costs of reproduction of the labor force to be absorbed by the sending society, while corporations in the receiving society receive no-strings-attached adults who are in their prime working years.[97] The costs of bearing, raising, educating, and training the textile worker, and of raising and educating the textile worker's children to produce a new generation of workers, are borne by families and society in the sending country. Businesses in New England can pay minimal benefits and advocate for minimal taxes and minimal social services at home because they can depend on a supply of educated workers produced by other societies, either through moving their production abroad or through bringing the workers to New England. As one Colombian immigrant suggested, "The role of Colombia, really, is to train manpower for industry in other countries."[98]

The average age of the Ponemah Colombians was 39.5. Eighteen of the nineteen were married, and they had an average of 4.8 children. All of them had completed "numerous" textile training courses, and almost all of them had over twenty years experience working in textiles.[99] Thus although textile workers do not fit the typical picture of "brain drain" in which the highly educated flee the third world for better opportunities in the first, they did bring with them substantial investment that the U.S. companies could benefit from.

Immigrant workers often find ways to survive with much lower levels of consumption than native workers generally do, because they consider their condition temporary. Piore described the typical arrangement as "twenty men leasing three rooms, eight beds, which they slept on in shifts, eating canned food uncooked out of tins, working two jobs and occasionally three, and sending home every month two or three times what it costs them to live."[100]

Indeed, the Colombians in Lowell eschewed consumption and sent home significant amounts of money, from $40 to $50 a week at the beginning, and up to $100 a week after their initial expenses had been covered. "It was really through leaving the family at home, living ascetically and working consistent overtime, or by adding wage earning members to the family income force that the textile worker immigrants could achieve their cash accumulation goals."[101]

One of the workers explained his living arrangements:

In Lowell the mill had a large air-conditioned hall with beds and so we slept there on the second floor, above the offices. . . . There was an electric hot-plate and we cooked there. . . . In the beginning I could send

$120/week because we didn't have to pay. . . . Of course our food was bad, and we slept poorly because we all slept in the same room. . . . We earned more because we worked so many extra hours, generally twelve, but there were people who worked fourteen, sixteen and eighteen. . . . Since it was in the same mill you only had to change clothes. . . . We suffered, but one is very stuck on dollars.[102]

When they were dispatched to Medellín a year later to receive their permanent residency papers from the U.S. consulate there, most of the migrants were sorely tempted to stay. A combination of pressure from Ponemah president Sam Cruppnick and the U.S. consulate, and the refusal of the Medellín factories to rehire workers who had been "corrupted by the dollars," however, led them back to the United States. "Very few of the men had intended to stay permanently in the United States when they signed Ponemah's contract. . . . Most . . . had specific cash requirements intended to change their destinies in Medellín: cash to build a house, start a business, or provide their children with an education. . . . But life in the U.S. was addictive."[103]

The AFL-CIO and Immigration

Textile workers and unions have struggled with the question of solidarity versus exclusivism with respect to immigrant workers since the early twentieth century. English textile workers in Fall River felt threatened by unskilled French Canadian immigrants willing to work for lower wages; French Canadians in turn felt threatened by a new wave of Polish immigrants. The advantages that older workers had struggled to achieve through their unions seemed threatened by the arrival of new, unorganized workers, who could constitute a cheaper, more exploitable workforce. At the same time, established unions felt threatened by the radicalism of newer workers. Was it the union's job to exclude low-wage, immigrant workers, to socialize them into the union's accommodationist stance, or to be reenergized by their radicalism?

Since its founding in the 1880s, the AFL advocated restrictions on immigration, including the Chinese Exclusion Act (passed in 1882), a literacy requirement for immigrants (enacted in 1917), and the restrictive Immigration Acts of 1921 and 1924. These positions were quite in keeping with its orientation as an exclusivist, craft-oriented organization committed to a dual labor market.[104]

Anti-immigrant legislation supported by the AFL-CIO, culminating in its support even for the Employer Sanctions portion of the 1986 Immigration Reform and Control Act, had a contradictory effect. In the words of the labor journalist David Bacon:

> The position, which reflected the federation's cold war, business union policies, created a color line. It sought to protect wages for native-born workers by excluding immigrants, rather than by organizing everyone.... Employer sanctions have played a central role in holding down the price of labor. . . . In an economy in which whole industries depend on an abundant supply of immigrant labor, maintaining a subclass of undocumented workers with fewer rights and less access to benefits is an important source of profit. As sanctions have made that subclass much more vulnerable, the labor of the undocumented has become much cheaper for employers.[105]

Thus in domestic policies toward immigrants, as in foreign policies, the AFL-CIO supported a domestic and a global structure whose inequality benefits employers at the expense of workers.

An ACTWU union leader interviewed on the subject of immigrant textile workers in the 1970s had this to say: "They have real problems in terms of our society: lack of language skills, lack of education. This is still an entry industry in the sense that people come, and can become very productive and high earners, despite their lack of language ability, education, and experience and so on." While expressing sympathy and solidarity with immigrant workers, this official also demonstrated a profound misunderstanding of the skills and education of Colombian immigrant workers, given that the very reason they were recruited into the textile industry was because they brought education and skills that native workers lacked. Furthermore, although the textile industry in Colombia is almost completely unionized, while unions are very weak in the industry in the United States, the same official went on to suggest that immigrant workers, especially undocumented immigrants, were extremely difficult to organize: "They don't trust people, we can't go after work and talk to them, to explain to them what a union is about and how it functions. Many of the countries they come from . . . the trade-union movement there is either non-existent or corrupt, so they have a very bad taste when one mentions unions."[106]

Immigrant workers' alienation from unions, however, is frequently due to the way U.S. unions have treated them. The New York garment industry became notorious for organizing over the heads of Puerto Rican women workers. In Boston in the 1960s, close to half of Puerto Rican workers were in unions but received little benefit. In their workplaces, "either the plant had a bimodal job structure itself or was part of an industry that did. The heart of the union organization and the focus of its influence on job characteristics was the skilled job. Unskilled jobs were organized as a byproduct. For example, unskilled workers lacked real access to the formal grievance procedure, forcing them to resolve their problems personally with their foreman."[107]

It was not until 1993 that the AFL-CIO began to move beyond a position that identified immigrants as a threat to U.S. workers and unions. The organization started to develop a more critical analysis that blamed the anti-immigrant policies, discrimination, and racism that kept immigrants marginalized as the real problem.[108] In 1999, the federation passed a resolution pressed for by unions and central labor councils, especially those on the West Coast that were organizing among immigrants, reversing its prior support for employer sanctions.[109] Since then it has consistently emphasized the rights of and the need to organize immigrant workers.

The AFL-CIO's foreign policy (discussed in chapter 6), its stance on protectionism and free trade (discussed in chapter 3), and its stance on immigration, have been linked in various ways. To the extent that the organization defines its agenda as promoting the immediate interests of its members—and defines the interests of its members as congruent with maintaining the profitability of the plants where they work—a punitive and exclusive stance on immigration may coincide with a foreign policy designed to promote the interests of U.S. businesses operating abroad and a position on trade that sees workers abroad as a direct threat to workers at home and seeks to resolve the competition through trade policies that will privilege U.S. workers over their counterparts abroad. In contrast, if the organization sees the interests of its members as linked to a broader program of social justice and equality, then support for immigrants' rights, and a position on foreign policy and trade that seeks to protect and enhance the rights of workers abroad, would make more sense. The AFL-CIO's anti-immigrant stance was interwoven with its generally pro-imperial attitude toward U.S. foreign policy, which also came under question in the 1990s, in part because unions began to recognize how U.S. foreign and trade policies aimed at maintaining low wages abroad were contributing to capital flight.[110]

A COLOMBIAN IN PAWTUCKET, RHODE ISLAND

Carlos (a pseudonym) was one of the second wave of Colombians to come to Central Falls, those recruited by friends who were part of the primer enganche. He told his story in a 1977 interview in Central Falls, as part of a National Institute for Mental Health Study conducted by Louise Lamphere.[111]

Born in 1944 in Barranquilla, Colombia, Carlos went to work at age 14 at a local hammock factory, tending a machine for making loose-weave hammocks. A year later a friend alerted him to a better-paying opportunity at a textile factory, Tejidos Ahuichagre, and a few years after that he moved again, to Tejidos Celda. In 1967, shortly after he had married, he received a letter from a former coworker who had been recruited to work at Pontiac Weaving in Central Falls, offering him a contract and a visa to work as a weaver tender. He decided to take the opportunity, and four months later the company sent his working papers and he set off for Central Falls, where his friend helped him find a place to live. Eight months later his wife joined him. Their first child was born in 1969, and his wife's sister and her family moved to Central Falls around the same time, with the help of a contract that Carlos obtained for his brother-in-law at Lyon Fabrics.

The job at Pontiac lasted only a year, but after being laid off there he quickly obtained a similar position at Lyon Fabrics. Two years later he was laid off from Lyon as well and moved on to Pansey (Pansy) Weaving Company, where his wife was already working and where he still worked when he was interviewed in 1977.

"Here in textiles, almost all of the laborers are Colombians," he explained. "All, all of them . . . around here, there are almost no Americans left; the work is very heavy, and Americans don't like to work like that. . . . There is a lot of work, but one is paid very little. . . ."

"Because of the exchange rate, [American salaries] seem inordinately high . . . but that's with respect to what things cost there [in Colombia]. But here it's like almost, I see it as pretty much the same: one works to eat, to pay for an apartment, and that's it; the same as in Colombia—one works to eat, and . . . it's the same thing. . . . But in terms of services, in Colombia—services for workers, there are more benefits there—significantly more. The union helps you a lot. Here all you get is your vacation time, and that's it. Work is work, wherever you go."

Summarizing Carlos's testimony, his interviewer described a life of isolation.

[Carlos] has lived in [Central Falls] for the past ten years, and he likes nothing about it. When he left his native land, he was full of life, full of desire to enjoy things, to go to parties, to dance. But when he got here, he found the place dead, and it has rubbed off on him; now, even though there are parties held quite often, he doesn't even go. But the most uncomfortable aspect of living in Rhode Island is the cold. It's just not like being in his native land. He doesn't have much contact with his neighbors, other than the Colombians who live in the same building. They greet each other when the meet on the street, but they don't hold conversations. . . .

It is this solitude that constitutes the biggest difference between life in Colombia and that of the U.S. . . . One of the biggest limiting factors . . . of life in the U.S. is the limitation which is presented by the absence of his family. He would really like to have more chances to see them; in this respect, life is poorer in the U.S.

Like most Colombian workers in the United States both Carlos and his wife regularly sent money home to family in Colombia—Carlos $120 a month, and his wife $60 a month. Carlos also purchased a house in Colombia in 1973, which he rented out.

Shortly before the interview, Carlos had tried to secure a contract to bring his younger brother to Rhode Island, but "things are starting to get tougher," he explained; this time he couldn't find a company willing to offer working papers.

"I'd like to have them *all* here so they can see how the cash is earned . . . they just send their requests . . . and since I send it to them, they think that I have plenty. . . . The bank cashier considers me a friend by now . . . It's hard to earn money here, hard to work. . . . They send their requests, I always send them, send them, send them, send them, send them. . . . I tell them the situation is difficult here, but they say 'you have dollars!' I have dollars, but here that means nothing!"

CARMEN RUIZ RÍOS, JUNE 2006

Puerto Rican native Carmen Ruiz Ríos is a bilingual teacher in the Salem, Massachusetts, school system and has observed the growth of Salem's

Figure 13. Carmen Ruiz drives local students through a magical version of Salem's Dominican neighborhood in a mural she worked on with them. The Colombian author Gabriel García Márquez sits in the back seat, while the popular Dominican singer-songwriter Juan Luis Guerra appears in the bottom-right corner. Photo by Heather Cahill. Reprinted by permission.

Dominican community from that vantage point. Ruiz Ríos recounted her experiences in an interview with the author in June 2006 in Salem, Massachusetts.

I came to Salem in 1978 to work as an outreach worker for the old Salem Youth Commission. They placed me at the High School, in a drop-in center, so I used to see the students all the time. The students would come to me and talk to me, and sometimes I would make home visits, and that's how I started relating to the Spanish-speaking population in Salem.

The following year I started teaching social studies and history in Spanish, in the bilingual department. When I started working in the bilingual department at the high school, I had about 100 students. And then it went up to probably 200.

I had to teach all the grades, 9th, 10th, 11th and 12th grades. I taught all the classes, the history and social studies classes in Spanish. The students would take all of their classes in Spanish, with the exception of English, gym, music, and art.

The majority of the students were from the Dominican Republic. They came from families that had just arrived into this country, looking for jobs. I think a lot of the families were related, they were cousins, or very good friends, back home. They came to Salem because their friends said "Come down, the kids can go to school, they can do it in their own language while they learn English, and we can get you a job." That's how the network started.

A lot of the parents would come, and they came with their families, like the mother, the father, maybe a grandmother, a grandfather, maybe an aunt, a cousin, and they would all live in the same apartment, because they couldn't afford to go live separately. I had cousins and siblings in my classroom. I taught a family of seven children in different years, and cousins as well.

They mainly worked in factories. In the Shetland, and Harbor Sweets. I had mothers and fathers that still work there. Harbor Sweets was a very big attraction for the Spanish-speaking community as well as stores, but I think at the time, more than anything, it was factories. In Salem, in Peabody, and in Lynn. Jobs in the service industry came later.

The students that I had at the end of the '70s and the beginning of the '80s were first generation. They were all born back in the Dominican Republic. They all came not really knowing the English language. I re- member they had to go with their parents to see the doctor, to the pharmacy, to agencies because they had to translate. I don't hear that now, from my students, as much as I did at the beginning. Some of them would say "Well, maestra, I didn't come to school yesterday because I had to go with my mother to the doctor," or to Welfare, or any kind of service that the family needed.

Before, it was more needy, financially. I saw a lot of kids who I knew didn't eat a good nutritious meal at home. The parents didn't have jobs, or well paying jobs. Then as the younger kids became more adults and teenagers, they started getting jobs and then things got better, they were able to contribute to rent. I remember they would work when they were at the high school, and they would contribute to pay the rent, to maybe get a better apartment, right in the Point, get their own cars.

Sometimes I ask one of my students, "where do you live?" and they say "Missy, I live down the Point." It doesn't surprise me, but it's hard for them to leave their community, even if they have a sound financial posi- tion. It's hard for them to leave the Point because that's where they're comfortable. That's where their families are. They like to live next door to their cousins, to their aunts, their grandmothers, their grandfathers.

The neighborhood is mainly a Dominican neighborhood. In the summertime you drive by the Point, and you see the culture in its biggest splendor, because that's when they go out on the streets, they're dancing, they're talking to each other, some men are playing dominoes, you go to the parks and you see the kids, it's like a little part of the Dominican Republic or Puerto Rico, right in Salem. That's where they really feel comfortable exposing their own culture. I don't see that happening anywhere else in the city. Only in the Point.

I bet if we went down to the park right now, most of my students are going to be playing in the park, playing baseball, which is very big in the Dominican Republic. Today we went to the library, most of the boys took out books about baseball! You're going to see the neighbors talking in the streets, you're going to probably see the clothes hanging from the clothes-lines, you're going to hear a lot of music, either in the cars, or from the apartments. And you're probably going to see the police patrolling a lot. That's the community. That's probably typical of what would go on. A lot of music, a lot of talking, a lot of movement. Loud. We don't mean anything bad when we do that, but it's going to be loud. Our pitch is louder when we speak Spanish.

The community is so tight, they probably know each other well. Everyone knows each other.

I think there was a lot of resistance from Salem residents from the very beginning. "Oh, you're going to the Point? Why are you going to the Point? I wouldn't go to the Point ever!" and "I'm afraid to drive by the Point at night, and during the daytime, how can you do that?" There were a lot of people surprised that I worked with the community. Sometimes in school I heard "those kids . . . those kids."

In the schools I see it . . . some of the teacher sometimes think that maybe we're louder, maybe they have more trouble, learning, and the other [Anglo] kids are quieter. Yes, I see that, comments . . . teachers' attitudes . . . you see that. Even among the teacher population, you can see it. I believe is a reflection of how some people feel in the population at large.

People come here, basically, because of the financial situation in the Dominican Republic. Some of them come from the capital, Santo Domingo, others come from Santiago, Baní, or El Cibao. A lot of the early generation came from the countryside. I remember a lot of mothers and fathers did not know how to read and write. Why do they come? Looking for a better financial situation, a better education for their children. They want a better life for the kids! They are willing to sacrifice their way of life to give better chances to their children. A lot of them say to me, "when I'm done with the kids, I'm going back to the Dominican Republic."

Now, the composition of the community has changed in many ways. The city of Salem is much more diverse, in the sense that, even though a lot of them live in the Point, they integrate into the Salem society and participate as full citizens. Before, I saw them doing everything in the Point. Now I see that they go to the parks outside. They go to the stores, they go to Walgreens, consuming American products. The parents, and the grandparents, when they cook, it has to be the Dominican food, it has to be the Puerto Rican food. However, the new generations love pizza, hamburgers, cupcakes and the like. So they go out and buy pizza.

The students that I have now were born in this country. They do know Spanish, but their dominant language is English, and they're totally different, their needs are different. Their parents have jobs in services, a lot of the parents work at stores. A lot of them at the fast-food restaurants. I happened to be in the hospital yesterday. I was surprised to see that most people that clean, and that work in the cafeteria, spoke Spanish, all of them. Salem residents servicing their community.

A lot of them are professionals or even own their own business, which I didn't see that at the beginning. Some of my former students have their children at my school. I can see that they have better financial situations than their parents had or have now. Financially, they are much better than they were before. However, not everyone has attained financial security.

Also for the kids, the main language now is English. It saddens me a little bit to see this. Yesterday, one of the students said to me, "maestra, I'm speaking more in Spanish now because of you. *Por culpa tuya*, I'm talking more in Spanish." Because his parents were born in DR, but he told me that he talks to them in English. The other generation, the ones from the early '80s, spoke Spanish at home. Now parents are making the effort to talk to them in English because sometimes the kids do not understand Spanish when they talk to them in Spanish.

I think that Salem has changed a lot, the Hispanic population has changed. The classroom that I hear now is completely different from the classroom that I heard when I started working in Salem. When I started working in Salem you sat in my classroom, in breaks, and everything was spoken in Spanish. Students were very close to me. But now you can see mostly everything is in English, and the students are more detached from the teacher. I remember, when I was at the high school, we used to go on field trips, we used to go bowling, we used to go to the movies, because we were very close to each other. We had collective thinking, I am not sure if this is the case now.

If something happened to my students in school some staff members would come to me, like I was their mother or responsible for them. "Look what happened to him!" "Look what he's doing! Talk to her!" "Do this, do that." I use to go to their houses to share time with the families, "come over, my mother made this," or "here, my mother brought you this from our country, she made this for you," and you don't see that now, the community has changed.

The day of May 1 [2006] immigrants rights demonstrations, a lot of us wore white shirts in our school. I told my students that they must wear white shirts to show solidarity, and even our principal wore it too, but nothing was talked about or mentioned over the school intercom. People are still very afraid of speaking up and talk[ing] about it, why this is going on. It's still very much a white Anglo-American society. Very much.

People from Puerto Rico . . . we're citizens for some things, but for other things we're not. What I'm saying, like I always say, that I am an American citizen by birth, but I feel very much an immigrant, and very much a Hispanic. You know what I'm saying? I don't see myself as an American because I'm not. And although we are legal in this country, and we carry the American passport, and we are American citizens by birth, people don't see that. They say, "Oh, the Puerto Ricans, why are they here, let them go back," and "Puerto Rico belongs to the United States," and you know, the whole, the whole thing. So, they look at us the same way they look at the rest of the Latin American population.

I think the majority of Puerto Ricans feel like they are immigrants. I think I might be speaking for a lot of them, they feel [like] immigrants in this country. In many ways, I feel like a foreigner, completely a foreigner. I mean, I've been living in this country for many years, and I'm very used to the system, and I like the system and everything else, but still, in many ways I don't feel that I belong, and I don't think I ever will.

That is the thing. I think that the message is that "if you're going to come here, you have to learn about us, and you almost have to forget who you are to become us." And I think one of the things that I always try to teach my students is number one, you have to be very proud of your language and your culture, don't ever forget it, don't ever forget who you are, where you come from, where your parents came from, and your culture. And always be proud of that. And sometimes you're going to encounter a lot of resistance, a lot of it.

PART II *Colombia*

CHAPTER 5

THE CUTTING EDGE OF GLOBALIZATION
Neoliberalism and Violence in Colombia's Banana Zone

An unnamed skipper of an unnamed merchantman first brought Caribbean-grown bananas to our shores in 1690. This shipment probably came from Panama [i.e., Colombia], and it is said to have been delivered at Salem, where the Puritans boiled the bananas with pork to complement a boiled New England dinner. The citizens reported with great indignation that the bananas tasted like soap.

—CHARLES MORROW WILSON, *EMPIRE IN GREEN AND GOLD: THE STORY OF THE AMERICAN BANANA TRADE*

People have been eating since God made the world. . . . An automobile can get you places same as a horse, only faster. A readymade suit can cover a man same as a tailor-made suit, only cheaper. But nothing man is apt to think of can substitute for fruit and vegetables. . . . When you buy a stem of bananas from Bart Judson, you know you're buying the best the market offers.

—EARLY TWENTIETH-CENTURY BOSTON BANANA SELLER, IN DOROTHY WEST, *THE LIVING IS EASY*

The Fruit Company, Inc.
reserved for itself the most succulent,
the central coast of my own land,
the delicate waist of America.
It rechristened its territories
as the "Banana Republics"

—PABLO NERUDA, "THE UNITED FRUIT COMPANY"

This chapter shifts the focus from New England to Colombia, in particular the Urabá banana export region and the social and labor struggles there. Urabá in the 1960s offered investors an extreme version of the neoliberal dream: an ample supply of very poor migrant workers, virtually no government regulation or taxes, and ready access to military force to crush any kind of protest. It was the opposite of the social welfare state that expanded workers' economic and political rights.

Investors in Urabá found, however, that maintaining social control solely through violence had its drawbacks. Some textile magnates chose to make peace with conciliatory unions in order to undermine the more militant ones and maintain labor peace, and many acknowledged that some level of social welfare was necessary to maintain their productive system. In Urabá, a several-decades-long assault on the left gave way to an increasing state presence and accommodation with a union controlled by right-wing forces by the end of the 1990s.

The events described in this chapter could be seen as the flip side of globalization: if the New England cases illustrate the departure of capital from an industrialized region, the Colombian cases illustrate the attempt to create a neoliberal paradise to attract capital. Or they could be seen as a continuation and recapitulation of patterns that emerged in the struggles of New England textile workers. They are both, and they are also linked in a multitude of chronological, conceptual, and direct ways.

To live in Colombia's northern Urabá region in the 1980s and 1990s meant to live in a land where private paramilitary forces worked openly with the army, and both in the service of the landlords: it was "the most violent place in the hemisphere," according to human rights organizations.[1] It meant to live in a land with no law except violence, with no government except the different armed actors, with no alternative except to work on the banana plantations. It meant that every attempt to bring social change was criminalized, and that the death sentence came without warning and without trial. And it meant that the perpetrators of violence operated with absolute impunity. One woman tried to explain her decision to make peace with right-wing paramilitaries after they killed her father by slitting his throat from ear to ear, slicing open his chest with a machete, pulling out his intestines, and cutting off his testicles: "The only way you can protect yourself is to live with them and accept them. If you don't, your home is gone forever."[2]

Although the violence in Urabá may appear senseless, it in fact follows a very clear political-economic logic. Violence cleared the area to allow ranchers and banana growers to move in; violence in neighboring regions pushed peasants into Urabá, where, with no access to land, they went to work under horrific conditions for the banana plantations. Violence greeted their first attempts to organize unions. Two armed left-wing guerrilla movements found allies among the workers, and the violence escalated as the army and paramilitaries collaborated to crush every form of social protest. Many hundreds were killed in the process of imposing a neoliberal order in Urabá. The violence in Urabá is one face of globalization.

All over Latin America (as elsewhere in the third world), contemporary globalization has been associated with neoliberal economic policies and structural adjustment programs, imposed by international financial institutions, and a shift away from the protectionist, populist, and redistributive policies of the mid-twentieth century.[3] As in the United States, the mid-century reforms primarily affected the urban working classes. While Medellín's textile workers enjoyed unions and benefits, rural workers in Colombia were overwhelmingly excluded from the process. Neoliberalism and globalization forced both urban and rural workers into a system that increased integration in the world economy through welcoming foreign investment, emphasizing exports, and scaling back the social welfare aspects of the state.

For workers in the United States, globalization has meant the extension of a process that began in the early twentieth century with New England's textile industry. It has meant shuttered factories and lost jobs, as companies have closed shop and moved abroad in search of cheaper workers, lower taxes, and fewer rules and obligations. The neoliberal project has created and enforced these conditions in Latin America, amply supported, when necessary, by U.S. military aid to counteract popular opposition. In the third world as in the first, today workers are frequently confronted with management threats to close plants and seek cheaper, more pliable labor elsewhere if they refuse to comply with management demands. Governments face the same conundrum: if they attempt to raise taxes or increase regulation of foreign investors, or approve laws protecting workers or the environment, the investors threaten to leave.

Poor people in Latin America have been the first victims of neoliberal policies, as land reforms have been stalled, prices have risen, wages have fallen, subsidies have been cut, and access to basic food, health care, and education has withered. Resistance has also grown among other social groups, including students, intellectuals, journalists, and artists, who object to what they have seen as the selling of their country to foreign enterprises.

The belief that foreign domination has led to poverty and inequality at home is deeply rooted in Latin American nationalism.

The neoliberal model has engendered protest everywhere it has been implemented. Where the rights of the poor to survive have been subordinated to the rights of foreign capital to make a profit, the poor have fought back. They have organized peasant leagues to press for land reform, and they have organized unions to struggle for their rights as workers. When legal means have failed, they have often turned to more militant, sometimes extralegal (but peaceful) means like land invasions and strikes. And when peaceful protest has been met with violent repression, some have turned to armed resistance. Urabá has seen all of these developments since the 1960s.

Colombia leads the hemisphere and in some cases the world in human rights violations, death squads, massacres, forced displacement, and killings of journalists, unionists, and human rights activists. Not coincidentally, Colombia also leads the hemisphere in U.S. military aid. As other Latin American countries, including Bolivia, Brazil, Chile, Argentina, Venezuela, and Uruguay, have moved to the left in elections since the 1990s and softened or even reversed their own neoliberal experiments of the 1970s and 1980s. Colombia remains the cutting edge of the U.S.-supported project of contemporary neoliberalism. The trajectory of events in Urabá exemplifies the process.

Industrial New England and Bananas

If the initial capital for New England's textile industry was amassed partly from the West Indies trade in slaves and sugar, the links between New England capital, New England workers and consumers, and Latin America only increased thereafter. With the shift from agriculture to industry in New England, food production was increasingly outsourced, much of it to Latin America. The same coal that powered the Naumkeag Steam Cotton Company allowed bananas to become a reliable source of food in New England through the use of steamships to transport the perishable fruit.

In the nineteenth century the United States replaced Europe as Latin America's main trading partner as the European industrialized countries began their push into Africa. U.S. multinationals moved into Latin America to produce (or extract) copper, tin, and later petroleum and coal, and agricultural products like rubber, coffee, and bananas, and later a huge array of fruits, vegetables, and cut flowers. "The banana, as an article of import and consumption in the United States, is purely a product of what I designate as the Machine," explained an official UFCO biographer in 1914. "Jefferson and Franklin never had a chance to eat a banana. There did not then exist the machinery of production and distribution by which it was possible to raise bananas in commercial quantities in the tropics and transport them to Philadelphia, New York, and Boston. . . . [Moreover,] there were no industrial enterprises with a capital and a scope fitted to undertake the huge task of producing and importing bananas."[4]

If any single company represents the U.S. industrial empire in Latin America, it is the Boston-based United Fruit Company (now Chiquita Brands), known as *el pulpo* or "the octopus" for its relentless tentacles. Like the textile industry, the banana industry had its roots in New England, and by the late nineteenth century was moving capital, people, and products around the globe in the search for optimum conditions of production and markets. The industrial order required a secondary labor market at home, and an even cheaper secondary labor market abroad, to feed the workers and the factories.

Like the textile companies, United Fruit in the early twentieth century imported workers from poorer regions, maintained production in numerous sites, and used the threat of relocation to induce government and worker cooperation. It also prefigured the later maquiladoras by exporting labor conditions that were not acceptable in the United States and producing items abroad for export to U.S. markets. Like Wal-Mart, United Fruit was committed to increasing markets by keeping prices low—which meant keeping the costs of production low.

Two New Englanders, the Wellfleet-born ship captain Lorenzo Dow Baker and the Boston fruit marketer Andrew W. Preston, combined their enterprises in 1899 to form United Fruit. Born in Beverly Farms, Massachusetts, Preston became president of the new company; Victor M. Cutter, who succeeded him in 1924, hailed from Lowell. According to a UFCO biography, "Andrew Preston was to the Hub's fruit trade what the Lowells and the Cabots were to Beacon Hill."[5]

These men, however, belonged to a second generation of industrialists. Rather than genteel urbanites, they saw themselves as twentieth-century conquerors, taming savage lands with their industry, "applying the methods of a high civilization and scientific industry to great tropical sections which have remained undeveloped," and, incidentally, expanding U.S. power

Figure 14. Family in the Santa Marta banana region, 1925. United Fruit Company Photograph Collection, Baker Library, Harvard Business School. Reprinted by permission.

abroad. "Any enterprise or any statesmanship which increases the productivity of these tropical sections adds directly to the assets and welfare of the people of the United States," explained the official company biographer in 1914.[6]

Immigrant factory workers were Preston's target market. "Boston and its factory suburbs were growing. Factory workers were eager buyers of bananas, so long as the fruit was cheap. Andrew Preston proposed to keep it cheap." Textile factory owners welcomed immigrants as cheap labor; Preston saw them "as a potential source of good banana customers."[7] Supplying the market led to vertical integration. "The successful [retailing] company of the future is the one that controls the growing of its own fruit," Preston wrote in 1892, expressing the same sentiment that led sellers like Seth Milliken, J. P. Stevens, and Liz Claiborne to integrate their retail enterprises in the North with production in the South—first in the southern U.S., then in Latin America and Asia.[8]

In the countries where the United Fruit Company operated—Central

America, the Caribbean, and Colombia—workers' democratic rights have been much more severely circumscribed than in the United States, and the role of violence in labor control greatly magnified. From its very entrance into Latin America, the United Fruit Company has manipulated states and employed violence to keep its production profitable, often enlisting the support of the U.S. government.[9] Yet despite, or because of, the lack of workers' rights in Latin America, U.S. companies there have often faced much greater radicalism abroad than at home.

As the twentieth century drew to a close, Colombia took the dreary first place as the worst humanitarian disaster in the Western Hemisphere, with horrifying rates of human rights violations, including massacres, forced displacement, and assassinations of journalists, human rights advocates, and union organizers. One of the most violent regions in this country assailed by violence was the Urabá banana zone, perhaps the most extreme example of contemporary neoliberalism. If the neoliberal state is a state that has relinquished all redistributive attributes, established optimum financial security for corporations, and privatized virtually all of its functions, then that is precisely the state that has existed in Urabá, where even the military and police have been essentially privatized. A close examination of labor and violence in the Urabá banana zone reveals the nightmare of neoliberalism gone mad.

There are parallels between the textile industry cases described in the first chapters of this book and the Urabá banana zone, and there are also links. There are direct links, in the ways that capital, products, and people move between the two regions and the ways that industrialization at home relied on and supported the multinationals that provided food for workers and raw materials for factories. There are also fruitful comparisons and connections that emerge from examining the ways that capital-labor relations have evolved over time. The expansion of workers' rights in the United States in the middle of the twentieth century was intertwined with the cultivation of export-processing zones abroad, where sweatshops could thrive. But as the expansion of workers' rights contributed to the taming of labor radicalism at home, U.S. companies continued to face radical unions, communists, and even revolutions and expropriations abroad.

In Colombia, the movement for workers' rights in the second half of the twentieth century was met by U.S.-supported militarization and counterinsurgency. By the end of the century, Colombia was the showcase for neoliberal reform—the modern version of what southern towns were offering New England textile companies in the 1900s—with Urabá as its cutting edge. Yet it was also the site of dramatic resistance to the neoliberal model. As in the early twentieth-century United States, it has often been the most marginalized workers who were the most radical.

The events this chapter describes are horrifying and tragic, but they are worth considering in some detail. They depict one possible future for all of us. They portray labor-capital conflict at its most raw and violent. They suggest that violence and repression are an integral part of the economic model of globalization, built into its very structures. If Colombia plays a crucial role in U.S. foreign policy in the twenty-first century, examining the course of labor relations in the banana zone can help us understand why— and what the logical result of such policies may be.

Using Violence to Establish a Banana Zone: Urabá 1945–60

Urabá was home to a small population, mostly Afro-Colombian migrants from the Caribbean coast, when the civil war known as *la violencia* struck in the 1940s.[10] In a pattern that recent studies have identified elsewhere in Colombia as well, landowners and paramilitaries drove armed peasants and squatters from the lands they had cleared. Urabá's population shrank as inhabitants fled. By 1953 the region was essentially in the hands of the paramilitaries.[11] In conjunction with the violence came the construction of a highway through the region (finished at the end of World War II but not opened to automobile traffic until 1954), which "emerged as a central locus of violence" in the late 1940s and early 1950s.[12]

Today's right-wing paramilitary groups and Colombia's oldest and largest guerrilla organization, the FARC (Fuerzas Armadas Revolucionarias de Colombia, or Revolutionary Armed Forces of Colombia), which played central roles in Urabá's violence in the 1980s and 1990s, both had their origins in la violencia. The landlord and rancher militias went through several incarnations, emerging as the AUC (Autodefensas Unidas de Colombia, or United Self-Defense Forces of Colombia) in 1997. The FARC was founded in 1964 with close links to the Colombian Communist Party, in part to defend peasant-occupied territories. A second guerrilla organization, the EPL (Ejército Popular de Liberación, or Popular Liberation Army), founded in 1967 by a Maoist splinter group, also emerged as an important player in Urabá in the 1980s.

The city of Medellín—the capital of Antioquia province, where the Urabá region is located, and the center of Colombia's textile industry described in chapter 3—remained largely immune to the violence. Paternalism, labor peace, and compliant unions characterized the textile sector, even as the industrialists "seem to have tacitly condoned violence in the far-flung municipalities where they owned ranches."[13] Certainly, Medellín's textile magnates were in a position to profit from the results of the violence in Urabá, where they became important players in the development of the banana industry.

Although a study of la violencia in Urabá concludes that "it is impossible to draw an absolute correlation," it is clear that property values and land concentration both increased dramatically in the areas where paramilitary violence achieved "worker elimination and land usurpation" at the behest of "sectors of the economically powerful." Banana investors were a prime beneficiary of the newly cleared land. The first planters arrived in the early 1950s, and United Fruit began to shift its Colombian operations from Santa Marta to Urabá in the early 1960s, turning the region into what one observer called "an immense sea of bananas."[14]

Two basic patterns characterized United Fruit operations throughout Latin America. In Santa Marta, where the company established operations in the early twentieth century, it directly owned land, employed workers, and ran plantations. In its new operations in Urabá, it chose to contract out part of the of land, while still controlling the transport, purchasing, and marketing of the fruit. The second method offered the company greater flexibility, requiring less initial investment, less risk, and the ability to shift rapidly among sources of supply.[15] Like the textile and garment manufacturers who relied on contracting out, it also removed the company from direct responsibility for labor or human rights violations connected to their insistence on high quality and low prices.

To establish the Urabá plantations, the company extended credit and loans to Colombian investors on the condition that they acquire and title land and fulfill the company's requirements as far as improvements, drainage, roads, and so on.[16] Most of the investors came from the Antioquia elite, including the powerful Echavarría family, coffee exporters who had profited in the first half of the century by building Colombia's textile industry.[17] A politically and socially cohesive group, they formed the Association of Banana Growers of Urabá (Augura) and dominated the region's politics until the late 1980s.[18]

Peasants who had cleared the land without title generally lost it during the 1960s, and small banana farms were gradually swallowed up by larger ones throughout the 1970s and 1980s.[19] A Colombian study explained that "the UFCO loan policy created pressure by those who fulfilled the company's requirements to take over the lands of those who did not, sometimes through offers to purchase, but also through violent pressure and death threats. In addition to increasing conflicts and violence, the massive expulsion of peasant farmers in the banana region increased the demand for land in the urban areas."[20]

Employment in the banana industry and the completion of the highway attracted a new wave of migrants, mostly from the neighboring, predominantly Afro-Colombian province of Chocó.[21] Poverty, violence, and the spread of ranching continued to push migrants from neighboring provinces into Urabá into the 1990s.[22] Regional inequalities operated at two levels: poverty and displacement in the Chocó made Urabá's wages look high to many migrants, while the same wages were still low enough by U.S. standards to keep bananas cheap for U.S. consumers.

By 1984 Urabá was producing 92 percent of Colombia's banana exports, and Colombia had become the fourth largest exporter in the world.[23] By 1995, the region had a population of 350,000, with twenty-nine thousand hectares [about 71,661 acres] planted in bananas, in 409 farms belonging to 310 owners. Sixteen thousand people worked on these farms, some four thousand of them directly for Chiquita Brands subsidiary Banadex, which also owned and operated the port in Turbo.[24]

Two-thirds of the workers in the 1960s and 1970s were Afro-Colombians who had previously been peasants, small miners, or fishermen. The workday lasted eighteen to twenty hours; most workers lived in camps on company property, with no water or electricity, sometimes sleeping in cardboard boxes.[25] Even in 1979, very few of these barracks had running water, electricity, or latrines.[26] Urban centers were practically nonexistent, and housing and public services were scarce.[27] Housing conditions in the region's main town, Apartadó, were even worse than on the plantations in 1979, and even in 1993 only 31 percent of houses there had access to running water.[28] Nevertheless, in part because of growing violence on the plantations, by 1987 75 percent of Urabá's banana workers had moved off the plantation into the inadequate urban centers.[29]

URABÁ'S FIRST UNIONS

Immigrant workers in New England's factories faced employer and institutional resistance to their struggles for more sustainable living and working conditions, but workers at U.S. export enterprises abroad have faced far greater obstacles. Yet, as Charles Bergquist has shown, workers in foreign-owned export industries have often been the backbone of radical labor movements in Latin America and have been able to mobilize nationalist sentiment in their support. The origins of Latin America's leftist and communist labor movements have often been among workers in the foreign sector.[30] (See chapter 6 for further discussion of Colombia's divided labor history.) Like New England's early factory workers, Urabá's banana workers found allies on the left willing to support them in the face of employer intransigence.

Communist Party sympathizers founded Sintrabanano among a small number of UFCO construction workers in Urabá in 1964, and the union affiliated with Fedeta (Federación de Trabajadores de Antioquia) and the leftist CSTC (Confederación Sindical de Trabajadores de Colombia, or Trade Union Confederation of Colombian Workers).[31] The company quickly fired organized workers and succeeded in having them, as well as communist leaders in the region, jailed. "The general pattern was first to fire workers, and if this was not enough, to appeal to the military authorities or the police."[32] Local arrest records from the 1960s show waves of arrests for such crimes as "posting communist flyers" and "having foreign and subversive literature."[33]

During the 1970s, militarization, firings, assassinations, and the enforcement of "collective pacts" between owners and workers that excluded unions undermined every effort at union organization on the banana plantations.[34] "The army presence was ubiquitous in worker assemblies, searches, and in the occupation of banana fincas."[35]

A second Urabá union, Sintagro, was founded in 1972 among workers for contractors growing African palm for the Dutch-Colombian company Coldesa. Sintagro affiliated with the conservative Catholic UTC (Unión de Trabajadores de Colombia, or Union of Colombian Workers), but "in spite of its moderation, the response was the militarization of the plantation" and the exile of its officers when it presented its first bargaining proposal in 1976. The union was crushed, but this time a new factor entered the equation: the small EPL guerrilla movement responded by assassinating the Coldesa's director of industrial relations.[36] In the context of the violence that had greeted peaceful and legal attempts at organizing, some members of Sintagro were also ready to begin to work with the guerrillas.[37] The union became linked to the EPL after 1980 when the latter began to actively seek alliances with the banana workers.[38]

What was missing in Urabá, according to one study, was a state presence. Urban areas like Apartadó were established through a series of squatter invasions and settlements; public services were virtually nonexistent.[39] The absence, or selective presence, of the state had advantages for the UFCO and the banana growers' association, Augura: low or uncollected taxes, nonexistent environmental controls, and subsidized credit.[40] In 1991 Urabá was declared a free trade zone, eliminating all state controls on rents, food prices, energy, and telephone rates. Rents quadrupled, and energy and phone costs became the highest in the country.[41]

When Mr. Seamans visited Alabama in 1926 to explore the possibility of moving the Naumkeag mill there, he advocated locating just outside city limits so that the mill could evade taxes and regulations but still take advantage of city services. Tacitly, he was acknowledging the need for a public sector to sustain the reproduction of the workforce. By the mid-1990s, even the banana growers were decrying the lack of state presence in the Urabá region. In part, this was because they themselves were being called upon to provide the social services that the state had failed to create. "They denounced the lack of state presence in the zone, the weakness and incapacity of the local governments, the lack of public services and the rise in invasions. They warned that 'a deterioration in the Urabá region . . . complicates the peace processes that are being attempted with the different armed groups.' "[42]

However, the state was not absent altogether: its military was omnipresent. In 1976 the national government imposed military mayors in the four major *municipios* of the region. Several battalions stationed there maintained the heavy military presence even after civilian government was restored in 1986.[43] "The handy notion of the absence of the State is inexact and hides something even more serious than its absence, which is a partial presence that ignores the universal principle of public assistance," explains the Colombian scholar William Ramírez Tobón. "The State in this region, at least in the first decades of its development, has been on the side of those who invested to modify the zone with commercial crops. The infrastructure network, the credit and monetary support for invested capital, the friendly tax structure, and the pro-export tilt of macro-economic policies have been the main forms of state presence in Urabá."[44] In other words, Urabá has enjoyed an extreme version of the neoliberal conception of the state.

According to a Colombian human rights investigation in 1993, "Official policies in the region, including those of regional development, have been more geared towards programs of military pacification to provide security to the businessmen and latifundistas [large landowners], than towards plans for social rehabilitation. . . . The military presence in the zone, consisting of six battalions, in addition to the police and military intelligence units, has not served to put a brake on the crimes. There are approximately seven thousand members of the armed forces serving in Urabá."[45]

The selective presence of the state has also fostered corporate lawlessness. United Fruit's subsidiary Banadex has been accused of multiple private business deals in violation of U.S. and Colombian law, ranging from bribing Colombian customs officials for use of government storage facilities, to transporting large quantities of cocaine to Europe on Chiquita ships, to smuggling in arms for paramilitaries through their ports.[46]

MILITARIZATION

Prior to 1980, left-wing guerrillas had established a very small presence in Urabá—perhaps some thirty to forty men under arms divided among three fronts of the FARC.[47] In the 1980s, labor struggles became a venue for growing guerrilla activism, and the EPL also established a presence. According to the political scientist Mauricio Romero, this relationship brought mixed results to the workers: "The use of force by the guerrillas offered a predictable invitation to official repression, but it also brought concrete gains to the inhabitants of the region. In effect, the guerrillas forced the banana companies to accept unions and collective bargaining."[48]

In the absence of any rule of law, both workers and management turned to force. By 1980 Sintagro had become a constant target of official and paramilitary violence. The political scientist Jenny Pearce offers a typical example: "In 1979, on receiving a list of demands from the workers on the Revancha Gaolfre plantation, the owner offered the estate's union leader, Armando Tobón, 50,000 pesos to withdraw the list. Tobón refused and, five days later, was murdered. The workers then went out on strike, whereupon the army moved in and forced them back to work."[49]

The lawyer Luis Asdrúbal Jiménez Vaca, who assisted Sintagro and other progressive organizations in the region, wrote that in 1980 he "began to be summoned, harassed and temporarily detained by the Voltígeros military battalion. The arbitrary detention of workers became common practice, as did the presence of soldiers at union meetings." Soldiers captured those attending a Sintagro meeting in December 1981, taking several workers to the Voltígeros battalion quarters and torturing them. Despite escalating threats, harassment, and assassinations in the mid-1980s, Sintagro continued to negotiate and sign agreements with the banana companies.[50]

A human rights investigation in the 1990s found divergent opinions regarding the impact of the guerrilla presence on social movements in Urabá. Some argued that guerrilla presence weakened the social movements; people were afraid of becoming involved because they would be accused of supporting the guerrillas. Others argued that only the small-scale armed actions of the guerrillas in the 1960s and 1970s forced the companies to open their "feudal hacienda regime" and negotiate with their workers.[51]

The Peace Process of 1984

Negotiations between the FARC and President Belisario Betancur (1982–86) led to an agreement in May 1984 that opened the country's political structures to the left, inviting the armed left to demobilize. The accord allowed for direct election of Colombia's mayors and provided amnesty for FARC members who agreed to lay down their arms. This process led to the November 1985 founding of the UP (Unión Patriótica, or Patriotic Union), a new unarmed leftist party which, despite unremitting military pressure, participated in elections from the mid-1980s to the mid-1990s. In August 1984 the government signed a similar agreement with the EPL.[52]

A human rights study concluded that the cease-fire created a space for the union movement and alternative political parties to flourish. With the threat of armed pressure reduced, banana growers were more willing to negotiate and workers better able to channel their actions toward political and union organizations.[53]

Both Sintagro and Sintrabanano grew astronomically. The end of 1984 saw the first industrywide strike in the banana zone—1,500 workers at eighteen plantations—and the first joint accord between Augura and the unions. In 1985, 127 contracts were signed, covering 60 percent of the workers in the industry, a total of 4,000 workers.[54]

The cease-fire also had other, unanticipated consequences. When the guerrillas laid down their arms, the region was opened to right-wing paramilitary forces, which were not slow to fill the vacuum. A 1985 bomb attack against Sintagro's offices and the assassination of the EPL spokesperson Oscar William Calvo ended EPL participation in the cease-fire.[55]

The peace process may have also inadvertently contributed to reorienting the guerrilla presence in Urabá. As Colombian analyst Fernando Botero explains, it created an opportunity "for the guerrillas to 'breathe' and to gain political influence in the main unions of the region. When the peace accords were broken . . . the guerrillas did not simply return to their traditional areas of colonization. Now they also controlled the workers movement in the region and they were prepared to engage in mass political work."[56]

The guerrilla movements were changed in other ways by the peace process. Many of the more optimistic, and idealistic, members of the FARC were the first to lay down their arms and join the political process. Huge numbers of them became victims of right-wing violence. This left the FARC in the hands of those less committed to social change and more committed to a military solution.

The *Guerra Sindical* and the Arrival of the Paramilitaries: 1985

The first public denunciation of paramilitary activity in Urabá came on the heels of the peace process, when Sintrabanano's president Alberto Angulo condemned paramilitary actions in 1985. Two years later Angulo himself was assassinated by the paramilitaries.[57] Fidel Castaño's Muerte a Revolucionarios del Nordeste (Death to Revolutionaries of the Northeast, a predecessor to the AUC) appeared in northeast Antioquia and Urabá in 1986, and its threats and assassinations of UP leaders began in earnest.[58]

Tension between the two leftist guerrilla groups also emerged. The EPL maintained a strong influence in Sintagro, which had organized the majority of banana workers. The FARC, through the UP, dominated the political sphere, winning important local representation in the 1986 and 1988 elections.[59] The EPL accused the FARC of a series of assassinations and of using violence to try to establish its political influence in the union movement. The FARC accused the EPL, which had withdrawn from the peace process, of ideological rigidity in its refusal to engage in the political opening or dialogue; the EPL countered that the FARC was inciting official violence against it by its accusations.[60]

The two groups also competed for workers' loyalties and territorial control, forming "EPL farms" and "FARC farms." Plantation owners were able to take advantage of these divisions, "signing agreements with one union to weaken the other, taking advantage of the conflict and inflaming it further."[61]

Both Sintagro and Sintrabanano affiliated with the CUT (Central Unitaria de Trabajadores de Colombia), Colombia's new national labor confederation, in 1986.[62] But 1986 also saw the replacement of the Conservative president Betancur by the Liberal Virgilio Barco, who ended the peace process with the guerrillas and the shaky cease-fire with the FARC. If the peace process had led to increased violence on the part of the recalcitrant right and its paramilitaries that opposed Betancur's initiatives, its end increased the levels still further. The army established a military governance in Urabá in 1987, taking over civil and political powers.[63] That same year, twenty-four union leaders were assassinated during contract negotiations and Sintagro's headquarters was destroyed a second time by a bomb. By September, another sixteen unionists were killed.[64] Violence against unionists typically increased during contract negotiations: two Urabá mayors reported that "assassinations of trade unionists and workers decrease after an agreement has been reached with the plantation workers."[65]

In 1987 there were two hundred political killings in Urabá, the majority of victims banana workers and unionists. Most of the founders of Sintagro and Sintrabanano were dead by the end of 1987.[66] Observers testified that there were clear links between Fidel Castaño and other drug traffickers, the paramilitaries, and the police in the banana zone. Some mentioned a paramilitary training school in Carepa, where the Israeli mercenary Yair Klein provided military instruction.[67]

Augura appears to be deeply implicated in the entrance of the paramilitaries in Urabá. Its new president in 1987, José Manuel Arias Carrizosa, was an outspoken supporter of the creation of civilian paramilitary "self-defense" committees. Urabá landowners publicly "proclaimed the need and the right to eradicate violence by their own means if the State was incapable of doing so through institutional means."[68]

Nevertheless, the April 1987 agreements were a milestone in labor relations in Urabá. The Ministry of Labor agreed to mediate and achieved the first industrywide accords, signed by Sintagro and Sintrabanano and Augura.[69] They covered far more workers: 6,730 represented by Sintagro and 1,685 by Sintrabanano, or 85 percent of all banana workers.[70]

The agreements also brought significant advances in workers' rights, including the eight-hour day, wage increases and the dismantling of the company barracks system of housing and the financing of urban housing for workers. With few public resources, however, the urban infrastructure was woefully inadequate. Urabá's cities, one study notes, "grew as part of the 'boom.' These towns reflect their frontier origins. In spite of having a distorted modern and urban character, they are not really towns . . . In Apartadó, there is no plaza where any minimal sociability could take place, and the church is situated practically in the middle of a highway with heavy traffic."[71]

Although the coincidence of the series of union victories with increasing violence against the unions at the end of the 1980s may appear paradoxical, it in fact makes perfect sense in the Colombian context. The peace accords and the growing strength of the unarmed left in the political sphere provoked a ferocious response from the armed right throughout the country. Nowhere was this response as violent as in Urabá, where the paramilitaries already had strong roots, and both foreign and domestic capital were accustomed to wielding uncontested authority over labor. It was the success of nonviolent labor organizing that fueled the grower-paramilitary violence at the end of the 1980s.

New Strategies: The Left Unites, the Right Undermines

In 1987 the EPL's political wing and the UP reached an accord in Urabá which allowed Sintagro and Sintrabanano to unite in Sintrainagro in 1988.[72] The new Sintrainagro, representing some fourteen thousand banana workers, like its predecessors affiliated with the CUT.[73] From 1982 to 1988, 699 people, mostly banana workers and especially union leaders and activists, had been killed in Urabá.[74]

Despite continued attacks by the right, the left focused on building collaboration inside Sintrainagro in preparation for what promised to be a difficult negotiating process in the fall.[75] In early 1989 the FARC and the EPL jointly called for "political guarantees for a regional dialogue with full participation of the popular organizations. Given the economic importance of the region . . . and the worsening of the social conflict . . . the central government must promote and participate in this regional dialogue."[76] The different factions in Sintrainagro collaborated on a bargaining proposal, and the different factions of the left seemed to be united as never before.[77]

After a series of assassinations accompanied the beginning of contract negotiations in September, fourteen thousand workers began a strike, joined by a two-day civic strike called by a "broad-based political, peasant and union coalition" in Urabá to demand investigation of the extraordinarily high number of political murders in the area.[78] Three workers and a farm administrator were killed on the first day of the strike. While the initial purpose of the strike was to protest the murders, it extended through the month of November, as Augura, the banana growers' association, refused to bend on the union's demand for a 30 percent increase in their $165 monthly wage.

At the end of the month, a reporter found the region under heavy military control and many strikers living in a makeshift camp in the center of Apartadó, where they had fled from official harassment on the plantations.[79] The strike ended in early December with an agreement granting a 29 percent wage increase in the first year and 27 percent the following year, recognition of agreements previously signed with Sintagro and Sintrabanano, and attention to the housing problem.[80]

The tentative attempts at unity on the left led to renewed violence from the right. Nine unionists were killed during the strike. As the 1990 election season began shortly after, Apartadó's UP mayor Diana Cardona was killed, and massacres occurred in Chigorodó and Pueblo Bello.[81] The right wing also began to pursue another strategy: landowners, the army, and the paramilitaries joined together to cultivate dissident sectors of the left and guerrillas to try to foster divisions and bloodshed. They were particularly successful with the almost decimated EPL.

Despite—or because of?—paramilitaries' documented authorship of the 1990 massacres, some EPL leaders were receptive to the appeal from the right and began negotiating an accord with the paramilitaries.[82] The murders of so many leaders and activists of the unarmed left, combined with this dramatic shift on the part of the EPL leadership, resulted in a major realignment of forces in the region, in which both the armed and the unarmed left virtually ceased to exist. By the first decade of the twenty-first century the unarmed left had been obliterated, and the armed factions that remained of the FARC and the EPL essentially ceased to represent any leftist position.

The EPL leader Mario Agudelo explained his organization's about-face:

> We decided that faced with the problem of paramilitarism and the offensive of the right, the best response was not to make war.... We concluded that we had made many enemies who potentially were not enemies.... We understood that we could not maintain a war against [paramilitary leader] Fidel [Castaño] because there was a social movement at stake that was showing signs of exhaustion, of not wanting more violence. That was when we suggested the slogan of regional salvation and defense of banana production. We thought that those ideas could create an opening with the

growers, bring them into dialogue. Bring in all of the factors in the conflict, even the right, with Fidel Castaño. We proposed the need for a unilateral truce and a dialogue with the government, as a condition for the democratic recovery of Urabá. . . . For the first time we proposed the possibility of allying with the banana growers.[83]

Although the level of violence in Urabá was unique, Agudelo's logic was familiar, and it was the same logic employed by advocates of labor-management collaboration in Salem in the 1930s, Puerto Rico in the 1950s, and South Carolina in the 1980s. Workers' real interests lay with their employers, not with their class. Class interest must be transcended by geographical interest, and labor and management should unite around the goal of local productivity and profitability.

The Demobilization of the EPL and the "Social Pact": Labor-Management Collaboration under Paramilitary Control, 1991

The second EPL demobilization, in 1991, looked very different from the FARC demobilization in 1984. Perhaps taking a lesson from the right-wing assault on the UP, and perhaps because of the increasing paramilitary strength in the region, the EPL leadership committed itself to political accommodation with the right and drew the union Sintrainagro along with it.

Outside observers note that by 1990, the EPL had been close to decimated throughout the country due to attacks by the army and paramilitaries and internal divisions. In 1991 2,100 members (592 in Urabá) accepted a government amnesty, supported by Fidel Castaño and the paramilitaries, who agreed to likewise turn in their arms and to donate land, money, and cattle to hundreds of demobilized guerrillas.[84] (The paramilitary demobilization was short-lived: Fidel Castaño and his brother Carlos soon revived their army as the AUC.)

The right also took a lesson from the past and took advantage of the EPL demobilization to establish complete armed control over the region. "Castaño's move into the banana area was aimed at a drastic private project of restoration of public order," explains Ramírez Tobón. "The radicalness of his actions came from the lessons learned in Córdoba when the space left by the demobilization of the EPL and the disarming of a large portion of the Auto-defensas was filled by the FARC, which moved several companies to the area. 'Here there is no alternative,' the Castaños said. We will 'retake the arms in order to return them to the government only when the guerrillas are gone.' "[85]

Demobilized EPL guerrillas formed a new party with the same initials, Esperanza, Paz y Libertad (Hope, Peace, and Freedom), and in May 1991 signed an agreement with Sintrainagro and Augura "to work jointly towards the celebration of a 'social pact,' which they describe as the starting-point for the 'integral development'" of the region.[86] The pact was signed by "the economic and union sectors in Urabá who, committed to a joint project, will link capital and labor to promote the project of peace and development."[87] The banana industry also agreed to establish a social security fund and to provide 23 million pesos for the reinsertion process for demobilized EPL members.[88]

In 1993 the state social security system began to offer medical services to workers, shifting this out of the hands of the banana companies. The companies also agreed on a levy on each exported box of bananas to support a housing fund, contributing to the elimination of the plantation barracks system.[89]

Agudelo described the social pact in the following terms: "It was a first step to link the entire society to the process and to reduce tensions and channel the conflicts. It was necessary to create an atmosphere of opening beyond just demobilizing; also in the political customs, labor relations, state presence, and the unprecedented possibility to create a space for discussion. . . . We were talking about transcending individual interests in order to strengthen a process of democratic coexistence in the zone . . . We received a positive response from the banana growers association. It created a new atmosphere in labor relations, and we can say that these problems were dealt with in new ways."[90]

Although Esperanza's relations with Augura and the paramilitaries were eased, relations with the FARC and the Communist Party worsened. "The Communist Party began to attack us, accusing us of being conciliators, of renouncing the class struggle and of selling out the interests of the workers. . . . They criticize us not only because of the peace process, but also because of the social pact. They said, 'how can you make a pact with the enemies of the people? Arias Carrizosa is a fascist. You can't create a dialogue with the enemies of the people, because that sells out their interests.'"[91] In the early 1990s "the divide between the Left that defends its traditional positions and those who have adopted a shift to a policy of collaboration and national agreement, became quite clear," wrote two Esperanza analysts.[92]

Esperanza's swing to the right was facilitated by the assassination of most of its more left-wing leaders. A human rights commission found that "the majority of the Esperanza, Paz y Libertad activists who were assassinated were outspoken members of union negotiating committees. . . . The para-militaries took advantage of the situation to assassinate the most radical unionists who were causing them the most trouble."[93]

A study of the EPL reinsertion process also notes that many demobilized EPL combatants remained quite isolated and skeptical of the shift in their organization's orientation: "They don't recognize the current leadership of some of their former superiors. The credibility of the new political move-ment Esperanza, Paz y Libertad, which grew out of the accords between the EPL and the government, is very low. . . . The total discrediting by the ex-combatants of their own political movement, Esperanza, Paz y Libertad, is very surprising."[94]

Esperanza soon dominated Sintrainagro. "We decided to take a different approach to the conflict," explained a Sintrainagro leader. "We knew that Augura had a clear plan to resist the union, crush it and destroy its gains. . . . We learned from experience to change our vision, to calm things, to open spaces for agreement and for dialogue."[95] Further, Esperanza and some union leaders argued that they needed to form a united front with Augura to prevent the flight of the banana industry to the greener pastures of Central America.[96] "We proposed the possibility of allying ourselves with banana growers, around issues of economic development, social problems, and human rights," Agudelo explained.[97]

OPPOSITION TO THE "SOCIAL PACT"

The EPL demobilization and social pact did not end the armed conflict in the region: "The EPL reinsertion destabilized the delicate balance among the territories belonging to the different guerrilla groups. . . . The military fronts abandoned by the EPL were inevitably reoccupied by either government forces, the paramilitaries, or one of the remaining guerrilla groups."[98] Thus, as the EPL demobilized, both the FARC and the paramilitaries increased their activities.

Competition between the UP and Esperanza at the electoral level was also bitter and punctuated with violence. Two UP mayors were assassinated in the late 1980s and early 1990s. In the 1992 elections, the first in which Esperanza participated, the party won several city council positions.[99] The party gained further support in the 1994 elections.[100]

One factor in the bloodshed was the fact that not all EPL members had accepted the amnesty, so some one thousand remained in arms. Unlike the FARC, which in the 1980s had supported the demobilization and the formation of the UP, the armed EPL immediately declared the new Esperanza party to be a military target.[101] By the middle of 1991, some Esperanza members rejoined the EPL and began a "wave of homicides" against their former comrades.[102] The Defensor del Pueblo wrote in 1992, "The dissident [armed] EPL group . . . is attempting to finish off those who were their former comrades in the armed struggle, but who have now reentered the political life of the country."[103] After eight months of respecting the EPL reinsertion in early 1991, members of the FARC joined with dissidents to target Esperanzados.[104]

The government's weak commitment to the reinsertion process contributed to its fragility. Many ex-combatants were unable to find work that had been promised in the banana sector; government investment in social development and economic infrastructure, as well as in economic projects proposed for reinserted combatants, was also inadequate.[105] And, "in what is considered the most fragile aspect of the reinsertion process, personal security for the leaders has been practically nonexistent."[106]

Agudelo believed that EPL dissidents were responsible for the vast majority of the attacks on Esperanzados.[107] According to an Esperanza human rights report in mid-1992, "Though there are many cases where the authors are still unknown, we have testimony that places clear responsibility for violations of human rights [of reinserted EPL members, including assassinations, threats, and displacement] on private justice groups, paramilitaries, members of the State security forces and, in greater number, the residual EPL groups that have decomposed into banditry. Some of these are also being mobilized by the small, but extremely radical, dissident faction, which is trying to reconstruct an armed force with the same name, EPL. Also, in several cases we have found unfortunate levels of involvement by FARC."[108] These attacks strengthened Esperanza's allegiance to the government and its various armed forces, including the paramilitaries.[109]

ESPERANZA REARMS: 1992

Despite its peaceful rhetoric, Esperanza formed yet another paramilitary force in mid-1992, directed against the EPL and the FARC.[110] Agudelo explained:

We discovered that some people were organizing clandestinely, without actually creating an organization, just groups in which workers and ex-combatants began to defend themselves from the attacks by the EPL dissidents. In some areas, there was an attempt by the party's bases to create what they called "worker autodefensas." Later they saw that these autodefensas could be confused with the paramilitaries. So they began to call themselves "Comandos Populares." . . . They don't represent a political alternative, but are just a self-defense group. When the tension with the dissidents disappears in an area, the presence of these muchachos also disappears. They have turned to this type of response because they have suffered attacks by the dissidents, not for any other reason.[111]

By 1995 the Comandos were operating throughout the banana zone. Two human rights investigations came to similar conclusions. One wrote, "They are made up of reinserted and non-reinserted members of the political movement Esperanza, Paz y Libertad. . . . They were at first formed to protect [Esperanzados] from attacks from EPL dissidents, but they . . . have degenerated into an offensive group that selectively kills opposition politicians and union leaders, like those from the Communist Party and the Unión Patriótica."[112] The other concluded that the Comandos were "acting as paramilitaries, armed and supported by the Army and the national government," and that they targeted especially plantations where the communists or the UP were strong.[113] Clear links emerged between the Comandos and plantation owners, as well as the DAS (Departamento Administrativo de Seguridad, or Administrative Security Department). Some plantations seemed to maintain members of the Comandos—who were not workers—on their payrolls.[114]

Local inhabitants accused the Esperanza party of "coordinating and financing the actions of the Comandos Populares" and believed that "the economic aid that the government has given to the ex-guerrillas as part of the peace plan has been diverted" to the Comandos. "The State's armed forces protect the Comandos, and have authorized their members to act as bodyguards for Esperanza leaders, with salaries and safe-conduct guarantees allowing them to carry arms supplied by state entities. . . . Regional officials complain that Esperanza members' reliance on private security guards has become an inappropriate challenge to the State's monopoly on arms. The Comandos patrol the streets of Apartadó, discrediting the reinsertion process and becoming a provocation."[115]

In January 1993, EPL dissidents kidnapped and murdered Sintrainagro vice president Alirio Guevara, a reinserted Esperanzado, accusing him of links with the Comandos Populares.[116] Perhaps in retaliation, the Comandos Populares killed three family members of a local EPL commander. In February, Sintrainagro's secretary general was also assassinated, apparently by the Comandos. In April, the EPL killed an overseer and three workers on a banana plantation, claiming that the three had been working openly with the Comandos Populares. After 40 workers were killed in a single week in April, 3,500 workers spent six days occupying the Apartadó sports coliseum in protest.[117] To outsiders, the violence appeared inexplicable: leftist organizations and guerrilla groups turning on each other and on unionized workers. This interpretation, though, discounts several crucial elements: the violent imposition of paramilitary control, the purging of the left from Esperanza and Sintrainagro, and the warming of relations between the latter two and Augura.

The struggle for control of the union and of local governments became even more bloody over the course of 1993. The two political factions, UP/PC (Partido Comunista, or Communist Party) and Esperanza, each accused the other of promoting the violence. "Nevertheless, both sides agree that not all of the victims are due to the struggle between the two sides. There appears to be a mysterious third force, which some believe consists of the paramilitary groups and the death squads. The President of the Republic acknowledged their presence in the region at the end of November, even though the military command in the region denies it."[118]

The divisions inside the union, as well as the violence from outside, severely hampered its viability. "The union in the past has been an ally to the community in defense of human rights and in civic protests for public services," a human rights commission wrote in 1994. But now "these organized responses . . . have lost their effectiveness. A civic strike called because of the killing of a union leader couldn't be carried out because members of a political organization, also leaders of Sintrainagro, refused to participate. The division of the union movement among internal political forces is reflected in the weakness in the responses that workers can give to human rights violations."[119]

The Autodefensas moved decisively into the banana zone in the beginning of 1995. Although there had been paramilitary activity in Urabá from the mid-1980s, they became a permanent, controlling presence in the northern municipios of Urabá in 1993 and in the banana municipios in 1995.[120] The level of violence increased sharply in late 1994 through early 1995, provoking a veritable flood of displacement—over twenty thousand people became refugees between November 1994 and May 1995.

Hundreds of deaths followed in the wake of paramilitary takeovers of Turbo, Carepa, and other cities in the banana region.[121] (The last was Apartadó, in June 1996.)[122] Esperanzados or people living in areas controlled by them or known as sympathizers were the main victims of violence in 1994; now the paramilitaries turned with a vengeance against the Unión Patriótica and its areas of influence.

Human rights organizations have repeatedly shown ample evidence that the army (in rural areas) and the police (in urban areas) work openly with the paramilitaries in their counterinsurgency actions. "In Carepa, for example, members of the so-called autodefensas maintain a public establishment only a few meters from the police station, and uniformed police are frequently seen leaving with them. . . . Likewise in Turbo, the so-called autodefensas maintain public establishments that are well known by local inhabitants, but ignored by the civil authorities and the police."[123]

The paramilitary advance coincided with the installation of General Rito Alejo del Río as commander of the army's 17th Brigade in Urabá in December 1995. According to Amnesty International, the 17th Brigade openly carried out joint operations with the paramilitaries, which resulted in "numerous human rights violations and the forced displacement of thousands of civilians."[124]

Esperanza viewed del Río's activities positively. Agudelo complained that the army previously had taken little action to protect the demobilized EPL members or communities under Esperanza influence. Under del Río, however, "the relationship between the communities and the army strengthened."[125]

Human rights organizations were less enthusiastic. "The public forces do not understand the situation of the campesino in the midst of an armed conflict," concluded one investigation. "Sometimes civilians collaborate [with armed actors] out of fear of losing their lives, their possessions, their family's safety, or their land. The police and army look for evidence and information by attacking the communities, pressuring them, just like the other armed actors, the guerrillas and the paramilitaries. The civilian population suffers the demands and attacks of all the actors, and nobody recognizes its rights." Both the police and the army worked openly with the paramilitaries, and the DAS, made up partly of reinserted EPL members, worked closely with the Esperanza-affiliated Comandos Populares.[126]

In 1995 approximately three hundred banana workers were killed—the FARC and EPL murdering supposed Esperanzados, and the Comandos Populares, paramilitaries, and the army killing supposed guerrilla supporters.[127] The Comisión Verificadora found 856 homicides between June 1994 and April 1995, or 244.5 per 100,000 inhabitants—the highest rate in the country.[128] Sintrainagro claimed that 600 banana workers had been killed as of September 1995. In the third massacre of 1995, 17 workers were forced off their bus on the way to work and executed at the end of August, leading to a six-day strike. Colombian President Samper added four hundred soldiers to the one hundred already patrolling the plantations, but the union spokesman Ramón Osorio said, "It's impossible to talk about improved security when the paramilitary groups continue killing people."[129]

In late September yet another massacre, of twenty-four peasant farmers, took place. This time, union president Guillermo Rivera blamed the FARC. He noted that the union had begun to accuse the FARC of "intimidating people by force" and "losing their social support among workers and the broader population," and that this massacre, like the one on August 29, was carried out just prior to a union assembly to discuss the region's economic crisis and the role of the union. (The Communist Party, however, blamed the paramilitaries for the massacre, pointing out that it would be impossible for a large group of armed men to evade the heavy presence of the Colombian army in the region unless they were working *with* the army.)[130]

Both the FARC and the paramilitary-Esperanza alliance contributed to the carnage, but their participation was lopsided. During the 1990s, over 1,000 members of the Communist Party and the Unión Patriótica were killed in Urabá.[131] Esperanza reported 274 of its members killed from 1991 to 1994, primarily by the FARC.[132] The paramilitary self-defense groups "were responsible for thirty-two of the fifty-five massacres that took place [in Urabá] between October 1995 and September 1996; thirteen, in contrast, were attributed to the guerrillas."[133]

The result was also lopsided: by the end of the 1990s, the paramilitaries, in alliance with Esperanza and the army, were in almost complete control of Urabá.[134] Leftists were systematically purged, assassinated, and displaced from Sintrainagro and from the region. "The majority of those assassinated in the last two months have been from the union movement or from the Unión Patriótica," explained one of the two surviving members of the union's executive board. "We think this is a plan of extermination supported by the empresarios, other political forces, and with the complicity of the national government since it is not taking any measures to stop it."[135] A 1995 investigation concurred, writing that the paramilitaries "contribute to a counterinsurgency action with broad collaboration and participation by the national Army and Police in the region. They defend private property and are supported economically by ranchers, businesspeople and the owners of some banana plantations, who they claim to represent."[136]

The UP areas of Apartadó were also purged. The Bernardo Jaramillo neighborhood, for example, was turned into a ghost town. "Anybody walking through it towards the end of 1997 could see the empty houses, stores and cooperatives, that were once vibrant projects, closed. On the corners, listening to loud music and drinking, were men who were not from the neighborhood. People call them 'paracos' or paramilitaries, and nobody wants to go near them. They are the owners of the area . . . An analysis by the mayor's office revealed that by August of 1997 there were over 1000 uninhabited houses and lots in this sector, and almost 300 businesses closed in the town."[137]

The Remaking of a Union

Romero notes the unusual correlation of forces in Urabá: "The alliances that the paramilitaries consolidated [elsewhere in the country] . . . have usually been with economic and political elites threatened by the insurgency, and with sectors of the state security forces. . . . In Urabá, however, the coalitions included Sintrainagro, the most important and consolidated workers' organization in the region, and the Esperanza, Paz y Libertad party."[138]

Sintrainagro had already begun a process of rapprochement with the banana growers, the army, and the paramilitaries as its left-wing leaders and members began to be systematically assassinated in the late 1980s and early 1990s, leading to the social pact of 1992. With the paramilitary takeover and the shift in political forces in Apartadó, the union's new leadership aligned itself decisively with the right wing, and with Augura. The presidential advisor for peace in Urabá announced in early 1994 that "worker-management relations are no longer the main source of violence as they were between 1987 and 1989. This type of violence has been transcended."[139]

As the military and paramilitary takeover of the region took root, Esperanza and Sintrainagro solidified their identification with these forces. On June 20, 1997, Sintrainagro joined a "peace march" called by the army. The growers gave workers the day off and provided transportation to the Apartadó stadium for the event. The Comandos Populares also "invited" workers to attend. There Sintrainagro's leaders—now with an Esperanza majority—joined with Augura, Esperanza, and the traditional parties in calling on the population to support the military.[140]

When General del Río was removed from Urabá in 1998—and then forced into retirement in 1999—because of his links with the paramilitaries, Sintrainagro president Guillermo Rivera was a featured speaker at an event organized in his honor by Augura at the upscale Hotel Tequendama in Bogotá. In the October 2000 local elections, with the UP destroyed and displaced, the EPL made significant advances, winning two out of four mayoral races in the banana zone, including Mario Agudelo as mayor of Apartadó. When Colombian president Alvaro Uribe Vélez visited Urabá in 2002, Agudelo lauded his "contribution to the pacification of Antioquia" when he was governor.[141]

A journalist contrasted the panorama in 1993 and 2003: "In September–October 1993 I visited Urabá and the town of Nueva Antioquia. It was a Sunday, and some one hundred of its 954 inhabitants were meeting in the school. I will never forget the pride with which the humble peasants and banana workers explained that in Nueva Antioquia, which belongs to the municipio of Turbo, the Communist Party had 15 base organizations with 154 members, that is, one in every six inhabitants was a communist. In every street in the town there were party cells with active members."[142]

In 2003, the scene was very different. "Between 500 and 800 members" of the paramilitaries planned a gathering in Nueva Antioquia. "This demonstration will reinforce the attempts to demobilize this group under the leadership of landlord Carlos Castaño Gil. . . . The paramilitaries patrol openly in the very center of Nueva Antioquia. Thus their 'reinsertion' process should be very easy under the vice presidency where Carlos Franco, one of the 'reinserted' Esperanzados [members of the EPL] from the early 1990s now works."[143]

By allying itself with the far right, Sintrainagro became isolated from the majority of Colombia's trade union movement. In 2003 the division came to the fore on two occasions. First, in July, when the Coca-Cola workers union Sinaltrainal called for an international boycott of Coca-Cola products to protest the violent repression of their union in the bottler's Urabá plant, Sintrainagro and the International Union of Food and Beverage Workers (IUF) publicly opposed the boycott. Second, in late 2003, when President Uribe presented a referendum supporting his neoliberal economic package to Colombian voters, the CUT and the left campaigned actively against the referendum, while Sintrainagro came out in support of Uribe. Oswaldo Cuadrado Simanca, Sintrainagro's president, appeared on the presidential news agency on September 25 to publicize his union's stand.[144] (The referendum did not pass.)

Sintrainagro reaffirmed its identification with the Uribe government and the army after a February 2005 massacre in the Peace Community of San José de Apartadó. The community is one of several in Colombia's war zones, established with the help of the Catholic Church, to create a space that rejects the presence of all armed actors. Echoing President Uribe's comments in the wake of the massacre, a Sintrainagro press release derided the concept of peace communities, insinuating that they collaborated with the FARC, that they were subversive by virtue of rejecting the presence of the army, and that the international nongovernmental organizations that supported them, including Amnesty International and Peace Brigades International, were also suspect.[145]

Romero argues that the banana companies, the Liberal Party, and the army successfully made concessions to the union and Esperanza in order to break the alliance between the FARC and the banana workers. The companies agreed to grant significant workplace and wage improvements, while the Liberal Party agreed to share its political control with Esperanza (but not the UP). Yet, he argues, "it is most likely that [the banana workers] were not really as revolutionary, before, as the authorities accused them of being, and that today they are not really as reactionary as their opponents claim. Rather, they have had to adjust according to changes in the relational contexts in which they have had to act." However, Romero may exaggerate when he suggests that "the last decade's revolutionaries have today opted for citizenship."[146] This chapter shows that many of the "last decade's revolutionaries" may have been killed and displaced, or they may have been terrorized into silence or acquiescence.

UNITING AROUND PROTECTIONISM

Protectionism became an arena in which Sintrainagro could elaborate an agenda and pursue its goals in the international sphere without challenging the local status quo of paramilitary control and fierce repression of the left in Urabá. As did U.S. textile factories during the Depression and through the 1990s, Augura urged its union to make common cause around protecting the industry's markets in the face of competition. The militarization of Urabá coincided with global shifts in the banana trade that threatened Colombia's markets. Banana multinationals had anticipated a growth in European markets with the fall of the Soviet Union in 1989 and increased production accordingly. When the eastern European markets failed to materialize, prices crashed. This context, along with the European Community's decision to favor its members' former colonies, contributed to a 1992–93 "banana crisis" of overproduction in Colombia.[147] The decline in exports affected every aspect of Urabá society: 30 percent of local businesses were closed, unemployment skyrocketed, and the mayor of Turbo noted that the number of street peddlers in the city seemingly doubled overnight.[148]

Augura, meanwhile, announced $80 million in losses in 1992, and pleaded inability to honor the salary gains previously agreed upon in the upcoming union contract. At the same time, the association emphasized labor's and management's common interest in protecting Colombia's place in the global banana trade. Augura's president offered to send Sintrainagro representatives on a European tour to press for more favorable treatment for Colombian imports.[149]

Surviving members of the left "wanted to confront the growers' association and demand a real improvement in working conditions. Unionists close to the Esperanza, Paz y Libertad movement believe, on the contrary, that workers should take into account the situation that the business association is facing and be cautious in their demands."[150] In this stance, they echoed the arguments of the UTW in Salem in 1933.

The continued struggle through the first decade of the twenty-first century over the European Community's policies on banana imports has contributed to an environment in which employers can insist that the interests they share with their workers in maintaining their share of the markets must transcend workers' class goals. Upon the signing of a two-year contract in May 2002—after a one-day strike by Sintrainagro—the minister of labor noted that "the agreement did not only deal with labor issues, it considers the future of the zone. . . . The agreement supported the idea that the businesses and the workers of Urabá must be united for the good of regional economic development." For his part, Sintrainagro president Oswaldo Cuadrado Simanca "emphasized the harmony and good will in which the negotiations took place, and declared that the agreement benefited both parties."[151] As Sintrainagro General Secretary Hernán Correa explained in 2004, "we came to see that the boss was not an enemy, he was a partner."[152]

Labor Internationalism in the Banana Zone

Global competition may have contributed to Sintrainagro's rapprochement with management, the political far right, and the paramilitaries on the domestic front, but the banana industry's multinational nature also offered the union an avenue for a different kind of innovative organizing internationally. In 1993, Latin American banana workers, responding to the relentless downward pressure that the companies were exerting on their wages and working conditions, united in a region-wide confederation aimed at challenging corporate strategies of pitting workers against each other in the proverbial "race to the bottom." Just as Sintrainagro was cementing its ties with the far right and the banana growers at home, its leaders joined banana unions from Honduras, Guatemala, Nicaragua, and Panama in Costa Rica to form the Latin American Coordinating Committee of Banana Workers Unions (Colsiba). "Colsiba is itself an unprecedented achievement," writes the historian Dana Frank, "the product of new global strategic thinking on the part of trade unions. . . . In all of Latin America, Colsiba is the only organization that joins unions in the same sector across national lines in an autonomous regional coalition."[153]

In 2001 Colsiba signed a historic agreement with Chiquita—by far the largest banana producer in Latin America, although not in Colombia—guaranteeing labor standards and worker rights.[154] In some ways it resembled the kind of result that U.S. textile unions had struggled for in the twentieth century, arresting the race to the bottom by standardizing wages and working conditions throughout the industry. Labor organizations and their supporters worldwide hailed the agreement as a pathbreaking achievement with a historically notorious union-busting company, and a landmark for cross-border solidarity among workers in multinational corporations.[155] Solidarity organizations from the U.S. Labor Education in the Americas Project (US/LEAP) to the European Banana Action Network and BananaLink (United Kingdom) have acclaimed Colsiba, and Sintrainagro's role—but remained rather silent on the context that created today's Sintrainagro.[156]

As unions worldwide are confronting global corporations like Chiquita, and groping for new ways to confront the rapidly evolving global economy, Sintrainagro and Colsiba's transnational work truly seems to develop a potential model for global labor solidarity. Yet, paradoxically, Sintrainagro's transnational initiatives have not challenged the local social order, and Augura has looked benignly on Sintrainagro's international activism. Colsiba and its international supporters have focused much of their attention on Ecuador and Guatemala, which they consider to be the leaders in the "race to the bottom" because of their low wages and non-union plantations. Like the northern textile "persisters" in the first half of the twentieth century and the southern textile protectionists in the second, Colombian producers actually stood to benefit from challenges to poor conditions and cheap costs elsewhere.

Voluntary standards agreements like those signed by Chiquita offer one way that workers can move beyond traditional forms of organizing when confronting multinational corporations. However, practical experience with the Chiquita agreement reveals the continued importance of unions. Because no real enforcement mechanisms exist, the agreement has been truly meaningful only on those plantations where a strong union could insist on observance. Otherwise, it is up to the company itself to evaluate its compliance. Even as Colsiba and Chiquita signed their agreement, and labor solidarity organizations applauded Chiquita for taking the "high road," the company was maintaining its version of labor peace in Urabá by funneling money to the paramilitaries.[157]

A Colsiba study five years after the 2001 Chiquita agreement concluded rather gloomily that the company had sold off its Colombia operations (in 2004), was threatening to abandon its Panama and Honduras holdings as well if workers there refused to renounce their collective bargaining agreements, was shifting its Guatemala production to non-unionized Pacific coast plantations, and was exploring expansion in non-unionized Angola. "A company can be certified in one country and benefit from the publicity of this certification in consuming countries for all its range of produce, while they misbehave in a neighboring plantation or shift plantations to non-unionized areas." Such an agreement, Colsiba concluded, "only works effectively in countries where unions are (still) strong enough to come to the negotiating table."[158]

Sintrainagro's experience suggests that internationalism may be a strategy for a union that has little leverage on the home front, even one that has been forced into a cozy relationship with management. As chapter 3 showed with respect to textile unions' strategies, internationalism can tend uncomfortably towards protectionism, especially when management joins or leads the struggle against labor violations elsewhere. As globalization undermines the capacity of individual unions to confront challenges locally, it consequently weakens the links in any international alliance.

ASSESSING THE NEW SINTRAINAGRO

Several European unions, and the International Trade Secretariat IUF (International Union of Food and Beverage Workers), which the union joined in 1998, have been particularly active in developing links with Sintrainagro. The Federation of Danish Workers and the Danish government began a three-year joint training program with Sintrainagro in 1997, and extended it for six more years in 2000. The Finnish Center for Union Solidarity runs a similar program, while a Spanish union built a 450-student elementary school for the union in La Chinita, an Esperanza-dominated barrio of Apartadó.[159]

Alistair Smith of BananaLink had only praise for the "experiment in peace" in Urabá. "Genocidal massacres have given way to an inspiring process of peaceful reconstruction," he wrote in 2001. Sintrainagro has moved

> out of the ideological trenches and into new struggles. . . . Plantation supervisors and their families drink and dance in the same bars as unionized workers.
>
> At the heart of the rebirth of Urabá is the banana union. To the distaste of some in the labour movement, it promotes itself as an *empresa social de los trabajadores*—a workers' social enterprise. The fact is that Urabá banana workers enjoy an annually renegotiated collective employment contract, good worker management relations, increasing productivity, improving health-and-safety provision, and, from last year, an employer-led environmental and social programme called "Banatura." Of the 300-

or-so plantations, 5 are successfully run by workers' co-operatives supported by Sintrainagro. The union's educational and training programmes are the envy of other unions.[160]

The situation looked very different to a Canadian trade union delegation that visited Urabá in 1997. Members were "deeply disturbed" by the situation of the union there. Their report merits extensive quoting:

> Throughout our meetings with Colombian trade unionists in all regions visited, we witnessed an incredible determination to carry forward the struggle against virtually impossible odds. . . . In only one instance were we troubled by anyone involved in the labour movement and that instance deserves mention. While visiting the northern region of Urabá, members of our delegation met with the leadership of the National Agricultural Union, Sintrainagro. . . . Sintrainagro members, both leadership and rank-and-file, have been deeply affected by the intense level of political violence in Urabá. The killings have only escalated in recent years. . . . While in the past, Sintrainagro's leadership reflected the various political tendencies in the region, today, we were told, the leadership is comprised uniquely of militants from the EPL [i.e., Esperanza] party.
>
> During our interview with the Sintrainagro leadership, our delegation was deeply disturbed both by the tone and content of the discussion. We were struck by the fact that the briefing provided by the union leaders represented an interpretation which was diametrically opposed to that provided to us by all the other NGOs with whom we met in the region. Specifically, the leaders expressed little concern over the incursion of paramilitary groups into the region (which has resulted in countless massacres and tens of thousands of refugees). Furthermore, they never acknowledged the abuses committed by the military in the region nor the links between the military and paramilitary forces which has been well documented by Colombian and international human rights organizations. The Sintrainagro leaders whom we met also launched a vociferous and slanderous personal attack against the courageous mayor of Apartadó, Gloria Cuartas, a woman who is well known as a strong advocate for peace and a defender of the rights of the civilian population. . . . Before we left the meeting, we were essentially warned that we would not be wise to travel in the region (under the auspices of church-based human rights organizations) without the prior approval and direction of the Sintrainagro leadership.

Our concerns regarding the Sintrainagro leadership were only heightened the following day when we met with the army commander of Urabá, General Rito Alejo del Río. Here, we were struck by the fact that General del Río's briefing of the situation in Urabá coincided exactly with that provided by Sintrainagro leaders. Moreover, in referring to that union under its present leadership, General del Río had only words of praise, describing the union as "the model of models."

The group concluded by noting, "There are hundreds of former members of this union who are now displaced in other regions of the country who would undoubtedly have a very different story to tell regarding the particular leadership that currently heads Sintrainagro. In our view, their testimonies should form part of the final assessment of the role this union is now playing in the Urabá region."[161]

Chiquita and Colombia Today

In 2003, Chiquita subsidiary Banadex employed 4,400 workers in paramilitary-controlled Urabá and exported 11 million boxes of bananas a year, accounting for almost 10 percent of Chiquita's global production.[162] But Urabá's armed peace brought its own form of difficulties to the multinational. In May 2004, Chiquita publicly admitted that it had made payments to an illegal armed group in Colombia that the U.S. State Department had designated a "terrorist organization." The company subsequently clarified that the payments had totaled almost $2 million between 1997 and 2004 and had gone to the right-wing AUC paramilitaries. Although the company claimed that these were extortion payments, necessary to protect their workers, nobody could deny that in fact banana workers were the paramilitaries' primary victims. "This was a criminal relationship," Colombia's attorney general explained. "Money and arms and, in exchange, the bloody pacification of Urabá."[163]

Only weeks after it first acknowledged the payments, Chiquita announced that it was selling its Colombian operations to Colombian producer Banacol. "In terms of the sale, there are many business reasons for considering the sale of the operation, and the [U.S. Department of Justice] investigation [of the illegal payments] is a factor," explained the company spokesman Mike Mitchell in June. Chiquita would continue to purchase and market Colombian bananas from its former plantations, but its shift to contracting was complete.[164] In August, company CEO Fernando Aguirre announced, "We are making good progress in transforming Chiquita into a more consumer and marketing centric organization."[165] A conflictive, century-long history of corporate involvement in Colombia was entering a new phase. The very conditions that the UFCO had fostered in its zones led to its demise. The company that had moved into production to guarantee a supply for its markets at the end of the nineteenth century was giving up production altogether in the twenty-first.

Urabá and the Future of Unions

For some corporate and state powerbrokers, Urabá suggests the wave of the future. As the *Houston Chronicle* reported, "the paramilitary rampage in Urabá had implications far beyond the banana fields. According to a recent Colombian government report, the paramilitaries' strategy and tactics in Urabá served as their 'modus operandi' when the militias took their anti-guerrilla campaign to new areas of Colombia. 'It became a national model and many people applauded,' said León Valencia, a political analyst in Bogotá."[166] The United States considers Colombian president Álvaro Uribe its closest regional ally, continues to pour money into Colombia's military, and declared the Colombian case a "good model" for U.S. efforts elsewhere in the world.[167]

A delegation of U.S. trade unionists visiting Colombia under the auspices of the AFL-CIO Solidarity Center in February 2005 had the following to say about the situation of unions there:

> We were devastated by the DEATH & DESTRUCTION that has been leveled on Colombian workers, especially women and children. Hundreds of union leaders and activists have been, and are being, arbitrarily executed, detained and displaced. Meanwhile, the Colombian government is systematically outlawing the rights of workers to form unions and bargain collectively.
>
> We believe that we must begin to educate our members about the billions of dollars appropriated by the U.S. Congress to support "Plan Colombia" and the havoc it is wreaking on workers and the Colombian people. Finally, alliance between President Bush & Colombian President Uribe leads to our conclusion that in areas of union busting, anti-union legislation, and court decisions, we are potentially seeing our future.[168]

Although the case of Urabá is unique in some ways, it is all too representative in others. Unique in the degree of violence, it nonetheless represents the ways that, far from the view of the U.S. public, violence has ensured the availability of the cheap products U.S. consumers enjoy. Unique in the virtual absence of any state protections, it nonetheless represents the natural culmination of the neoliberal policies that are attempting to reduce state social protections of citizens everywhere in the world. Unique in the levels of paramilitary violence employed to tame a union, it nonetheless recalls the types of violence and threats that have been used by employers, governments, and private security forces to control workers in many other contexts, especially, today, in the poorer parts of the world. Unique in competing to undersell other poor countries producing the same fruit, it nonetheless represents the trend that has spread from agriculture and manufacturing even into the service industry in the era of globalization, in which workers, and countries, compete to offer the most concessions in order to placate investors.

The case of Urabá is also sadly representative of the ways in which U.S. workers and citizens are complicit in creating the very conditions that have led U.S. jobs to move abroad. U.S. military aid, sometimes culminating in direct intervention, sometimes remaining at the level of financial support, advisors, and training, has been a crucial element in the complex that created and sustains the global system under which we all live.

BRIGADIER GENERAL RITO ALEJO DEL RÍO ROJAS

General del Río gave his perspective on the situation in Urabá to a delegation organized by the Colombia Support Network in August 1997 at the headquarters of the Colombian Army's Seventeenth Brigade in Carepa, Antioquia.

I am Brigadier General Rito Alejo del Río Rojas, Commander of the 17th Army Brigade.[169] First of all I'd like to tell you what my jurisdiction is.

I command the troops that are quartered and that carry out operations all throughout the Antioquian and Chocoan regions of Urabá. This jurisdiction encompasses 24,000 square km [about 9,266 square miles] of land, and more or less from 4,000 to 5,000 kilometers [about 1,166 to 1,458 nautical square miles] of sea. The region is characterized by a lack of adequate means of transportation. Eighty percent of it is jungle, with, as I said before, few roads. Much of the transportation is carried out through the rivers that naturally come from the jungle.

The region is completely lacking in resources. There are no means of education, very rudimentary health services, and a very serious problem with disease and lack of education for the population. In the same way, the houses, in general, outside of the municipal centers, that is, in the rural areas, the houses are very primitive, they don't provide for basic human needs. It is a population that lacks the means for recreation, for entertainment. Here one can easily see that in the municipal centers, where there are population centers, the principal means of entertainment in general is the consumption of alcohol. I would say that people don't have any other form of recreation.

There are some very isolated communities where really the hand of civilization has not arrived. They are totally isolated in the jungle. The only agency of the state that has arrived there is the armed forces. So you see this is quite a complex problem.

On the other hand, because of the different problems that exist in the region, it's a zone that has been characterized for a long time by the control of groups outside of the law. They have been very radical, and they have tried to impose their hegemony through force. It's a zone that was dominated at first by the EPL. They demobilized 5 months ago. But before they demobilized, groups from the FARC also invaded the region. And at the same time, ELN [Ejército de Liberación Nacional, or National Liberation Army] groups came in.

Because of the demobilization of the EPL, which created a political party, Esperanza, these other groups began a process of extermination against those who had chosen the path of reinsertion. That is, the reinsertados renounced all of the activities carried out by the guerrillas, and they turned themselves into the Colombian justice system. So they were considered to be traitors. A persecution began against them, and a struggle to exterminate them. The FARC and the ELN began the struggle to exterminate them.

This is what caused the beginning of the massacres in Urabá. There had been some massacres before, but they began to get worse after 1990, more or less. I must clarify that really, part of the problem is the lack of a functioning judicial system, which could have reined in this situation in time, using the legal system against these groups. Most of the time, when they committed crimes, they had complete impunity. This created a more complex situation, in which all of the people at all levels started to organize groups outside of the law. So the phenomenon of organized delinquency appeared. That is, those who are mistakenly called "paramilitaries."

I want to clarify this, because that name is a name created by the narco-terrorists, who are trying to convince the community that these groups work with the army. But the position of the government and the armed forces is very clear. We consider all of these groups to be the same as the narco-terrorists: we consider them as disturbing factors and elements outside of the law. The narco-terrorists are the FARC, the ELN, all of those that are dedicated to the drug traffic, to terrorism, which I will explain to you in a moment.

There are narco-terrorists from the drug cartels, and there are narco-terrorists from these criminal organizations, that are committing the same horrific acts as the drug traffickers like Pablo Escobar . . . that are so noxious for the nation. Some of the narco-terrorists are only involved with drug traffic, and some are involved with subversion. There is a group that carries out terrorism along with the group that carries out armed resistance. And they dedicate themselves to cultivating and the control of the drug cultivations. That is why they receive payments from the drug traffickers, so that they can buy arms and equipment.

This region especially is seen as very lucrative, because it has the advantage of being surrounded by two seas. The Caribbean Sea, along the Gulf of Urabá, and also the Pacific, along the Chocó coast. The Caribbean touches Antioquian and Chocoan coasts. For narco-subversive elements, this area is so important, because of these two coasts, and taking advantage of the border of Panama, they bring all kinds of arms and munitions. And at the same time, they export great quantities of coca and other elements of the drug trade. They exchange some of these cargos for arms that sometimes are left over from guerrilla demobilizations in other countries.

This region also became a very special place to negotiate kidnappings. Because it was easy to take the kidnapped people into the jungle, and since the roads were so difficult, they had the security that it was almost impossible that the public forces could come into this area to rescue them.

This situation, and the wealth of the land, have attracted the armed actors. I can guarantee that any person who establishes himself here who wants to start a business, either industrial or agricultural, has a high probability of succeeding, because the climate, the weather, and the land are favorable for these kinds of commercial activities.

The zone has approximately 32,000 hectares [about 79,074 acres] planted in bananas. But around these plantations is rich pasture land for cattle. At the same time, it is good for cultivating any kind of produce. It has different altitudes. The plains are used for cattle and bananas, and along the mountainsides, plantains, which are different from bananas, fruit trees of all kinds, corn, and other products are cultivated.

When banana production was established here, the union began, and that's how the current problem with the agricultural workers here in the region began. Some people were trying to carry out a program for the cultivation of African Palm. But the guerrillas practically burned down all of these plantations, and they were destroyed.

So what predominates now is banana plantations. And we believe that there are about 11,900 workers dependent on this product. This means there are 11,900 heads of households. We calculate that on the average, each one has 5 to 6 dependents. These are people who really have a very high salary, much higher than what a normal worker makes. But because of the lack of education, of preparation, they do not manage their money well. They spend most of it on alcohol.

In general, all of the people have a very low standard of living. These citizens have established homes through "invasions" in different towns. I think you have already seen part of Apartadó, and have seen these invasions, and how primitive most of the houses are. I think that this is the most serious social problem that we are faced with in this region.

I think that the serious problem is that which you have seen. In Apartadó, there are invasions within invasions. That is, people invaded a section to build houses. Then more people come, and they invade the invasion. They settle inside the invasion.

The problem began when different currents confront each other.

That is, at first, the EPL demobilized, and the FARC begin to attack them. And then this began to cause the confrontation between organizations and between parties. In general, the FARC has stood out as the bloodiest group here in the region. I can prove this with statistics, I have three copies of this book that explains everything. The book describes how human rights have been violated, and what are the real facts as far as human rights violations by these different groups. . . .

I also want to point out, that normally, the information that comes out of the country, and that comes to some organizations, is not really true. Some of this information is partial or one-sided, and members of these groups blame other factors or other elements for the crimes that the organization itself has committed. . . .

We want the world community to know who is really committing assaults against human rights, and who is really committing attacks against the community. . . .

I must clarify this here, it is very important. When we began to detain these people, there began to be pressure from all of the organizations, especially the FARC, to defame the actions that the public forces were carrying out, because of the capture of these subjects who had carried out all of these horrifying massacres during a long time here.

And they even told some organizations that we were committing atrocities against the population of Urabá. But we have the great satisfaction to be able to show you clearly the kind of people who were captured. With the literature that they had in the moment of capture, completely disproving any lies they were trying to promote. . . .

Here I would like to emphasize a very special situation. In some opportunities they begin to send out communiqués; irresponsible ones, I would say, to different parts of the world. By some people linked to those organizations. Of course they make it look like there are atrocities. But when we investigate, they are just lies, they don't have any foundation. When we ask the person to bring charges to the competent authorities, they usually refuse, because all they want is to defame the Armed Forces, to defame the nation. And there are people who are interested in maintaining this situation, because they gain resources from it. They even commit violations of international humanitarian law when they ask, in these communiqués, for reprisals against relatives of people linked to the army and police, including minors, sanctions against minors who have nothing to do with the problem.

I think that this is a true violation against human rights, because when an individual commits a crime, it is the individual, not the family, and even less so if it is a child.

CHAPTER 6

TAKING CARE OF BUSINESS IN COLOMBIA

U.S. Multinationals, the U.S. Government, and the AFL-CIO

The international situation is about more than multinational corporations. Corporate globalization and military intervention are intertwined. In the labor movement there's an absence of understanding about the relationship between the two.... Unions in the rest of the world are not simply asking us whether we will stand with them against General Electric, General Motors, or Mitsubishi. They want to know: What is your stand about the U.S. empire, about aggressive wars or coups d'état? If we have nothing to say about these things, how can we expect to have any credibility?

—BILL FLETCHER, "LABOR NEEDS A HARD LEFT TURN: BILL FLETCHER SAYS THE CUR-
RENT DEBATE OVER LABOR'S FUTURE IS DOMINATED BY AN OUTDATED CONSERVA-
TISM." INTERVIEW BY DAVID BACON. *TRUTHOUT/INTERVIEW,* 2005

The nature and policies of the AFL, and later the AFL-CIO, at home have always been intertwined with the nature and policies of the organization abroad. The clash of the AFL's mainstream leadership with radical immigrant workers in the Northeast in the early twentieth century was part of a worldview and orientation that also excluded African Americans, Puerto Ricans, and Mexican Americans (immigrants of a different sort) and tacitly or explicitly acquiesced to U.S. imperialism. As the labor historian Paul Buhle put it in a recent study, the mainstream U.S. labor movement adhered to a notion of " 'American exceptionalism,' meaning the avoidance of class struggle, which was conceptually attached to a notion of the right and proper U.S. domination of the hemisphere and ultimately the planet."[1]

The AFL's philosophy was based on protecting the jobs of skilled workers. This meant what Buhle called "a national rather than class definition of 'the American standard of living' or 'American wage,'" which privileged a notion of a white male working class and nurtured racism, sexism, and support for U.S. expansionism, as well as labor-management collaboration, in the emergence of a unique culture of business unionism in the United States.[2] European immigrant workers "became white" as they assimilated into this culture and philosophy.

The alienation of Salem's and Hopedale's radical immigrant workers from the AFL of the early twentieth century is part of the same story as that of the organization's suspicion of immigrants, its commitment to labor-management collaboration, and its embrace of the expansion of U.S. power abroad. If U.S. multinationals in Latin America could support the "American standard of living" by bringing in cheap bananas, cheap rubber, cheap petroleum, or cheap coffee, great. More radical unions that called for labor internationalism were routinely denounced as "red." Vulnerable immigrant workers were called upon to declare their loyalty to the racial order of the United States, to the government, and to its foreign policies.

Moreover, when U.S. unions confronted issues of regional and/or global inequalities, it was frequently from the standpoint of protectionism. From the "Buy American" campaigns of the 1930s to the United Steelworkers' "Stand Up for Steel" campaigns at the end of the century, unions joined with employers on parochial grounds. Too often, narrow protectionist campaigns were also imbued with racism against workers in other countries.

Samuel Gompers expressed the AFL's stance on imperialism at the end of the nineteenth century. "The nation which dominates the markets of the world will surely control its destinies," he stated in 1898, as the United States embarked on its first overseas expansion, taking Cuba, Puerto Rico, and the Philippines. "We do not oppose the development of our industry, the expansion of our commerce, nor the development of our power and influence which the United States may exert upon the destinies of the nations of the earth." He demurred, however, on the need to annex the Philippines, "with their semi-savage population." Economic domination was a laudable goal, but it could be achieved without annexation. "Neither its gates nor those of any other country of the globe can long be closed against our constantly growing industrial supremacy. The higher intelligence and standard of life of the [U.S.] workers will largely contribute to the highest pinnacle of industrial and commercial greatness."[3]

This early statement incorporates the complex of racism, nationalism, and identification of the interests of unionized U.S. workers with U.S. business that was to characterize the AFL's, and later the AFL-CIO's, foreign policies for the next century. In contrast, unions on the left, like the IWW and communist unions, embraced an agenda of social justice, proclaiming antiracism and inclusion at home and internationalism abroad.[4]

Anne Burlak's critique of the UTW southern campaign in the 1930s denounced William Green's courting of "bankers, politicians and mill owners," his meetings with the chambers of commerce, and his emphasis on "the 'patriotism' of the AFL, of its dedication to the free enterprise system, its no strike policy, and [its advocacy of] union-management cooperation in the mills." He also, Burlak wrote, "painted the horrors of 'communist' organization as an alternative, if the AFL was not accepted." (See profile in chapter 2 for the full quote.) Sounding something like the Esperanza leadership of Sintrainagro, Green "told southern business leaders that 'we come preaching the doctrine of cooperation and good will. . . . We know that success to us must come out of success in industry; the greater the earnings to industry, the greater the benefits we enjoy. . . . We offer to management and to the owners of industry a cooperative organization willing to give the best we have in training and service and skill in order that the industry might be made profitable.'" He "flay[ed] the communists with a venomous scourge as 'a force that would destroy our country, that would strike at the very soul of our institutions.'"[5] The stance that the UTW took in its southern campaign prefigured precisely the stance that the AFL, and later the AFL-CIO, would take in Latin America a decade later.

The difference was that the UTW (AFL) and later the TWUA (CIO) confronted a white southern workforce that was nonunionized and whose commitment to the racial order of the post-Reconstruction South was strong enough to make them little interested in any fundamental social change. Nationalist ideology in the United States encouraged them to support the projection of U.S. power abroad. In Latin America, in contrast, unions and workers frequently challenged not only their employer, but also foreign imperialism and capitalism. Some were nationalists, some were communists, and many had a coherent and well-grounded analysis of global inequality and foreign exploitation. In short, they were very, very interested in fundamental social change, not only in the national, but also in the global order.

After World War II, the AFL joined wholeheartedly into collaboration with the U.S. government in cold war policies that sought to undermine labor radicalism abroad. The union's enthusiastic embrace of military Keynesianism, or government military spending to create jobs, and the dependence of so many of its members' jobs on military production contributed to a dependence on a virulent anticommunist ideology to justify military spending that would protect jobs at home.[6] Anticommunism also served to demonize Latin American activists who challenged U.S. economic domination in their countries—the very economic domination that upheld the "American standard of living" that the AFL was committed to. The making of the white working class in the United States was inextricably intertwined with racial and national distinctions that privileged the primary labor force—regulated, unionized, and white—whose prosperity depended upon a secondary labor force: unregulated, nonunionized, and consisting primarily of people of color, whether African American sharecroppers and domestic workers, Mexican migrant farmworkers, or workers in Latin America who produced goods for U.S. companies and U.S. consumers.

The AFL's exclusionary orientation has overall weakened the position of organized workers in the United States. By defining social benefits in terms of union membership—creating a "private welfare state"—it has supported the existence of an unequal society that dependably provided a more exploitable group of workers: racial and ethnic minorities, recent immigrants, women, and workers abroad.[7] These inequalities allowed employers to find or import cheaper workers or abandon their organized workers for cheaper labor elsewhere. Union organizing drives in the U.S. South in the 1930s, 1940s, and 1950s were predicated on the understanding that low wages and the absence of unions there undermined their strength in the North as well. Yet until the 1990s, the AFL-CIO leadership followed a course of support for U.S. foreign policies that imposed low wages and weak unions abroad, despite growing evidence that this corporate-sponsored project undermined workers' jobs in the United States as well.

It is not coincidental that the New Voices slate that took the helm of the AFL-CIO in 1995 viewed an overhaul of the federation's foreign policy as integral to the recovery of an organization decimated by job losses in manufacturing. Other aspects of the New Voices platform included a shift toward organizing new workers, particularly immigrants, women, and minorities, and revising the federation's stance on immigration. Voices for a more inclusive unionism and a more radical vision of unions' role in society had never been absent in the U.S. labor movement. But they have been marginalized, again and again, in the country's major labor federation.

The tension between nationalist/protectionist and internationalist perspectives on globalization was visible at the 1999 anti–World Trade Organization demonstrations in Seattle, among other occasions. Many analysts hailed labor participation in the activities as a significant shift away from labor's cold war alliance with U.S. foreign policy. Some noted, however, that protectionism still challenged solidarity, as in the "Seattle steel party," in which steelworkers symbolically dumped Chinese-made products into the harbor.[8]

This chapter looks at the AFL's and AFL-CIO's complex relationship with labor internationalism over the course of the twentieth century, focusing particularly on the case study of Colombia. The Colombian example presents a clear picture of how the AFL-CIO's adherence to an anticommunist, business-supported international agenda led it to play an important role in undermining Colombia's union movement. U.S. companies with investments in Colombia like United Fruit, American Celanese Corporation, Standard Oil, Shell Petroleum, Coca-Cola, and W. R. Grace generously funded AFL-CIO programs there. Sometimes they were also the direct beneficiaries of these programs, as when the AIFLD helped to destroy a leftist union at Celanese's Medellín factory in the 1960s.

"An American Union": The AFL Defines Its Foreign Policy

The case of Panama presents a telling prelude to later AFL-CIO policy in Colombia. At the AFL's 1902 convention, as the United States was negotiating the site for an interoceanic canal, a member proposed a resolution stating that the AFL was "unalterably opposed to any encroaching upon the independence of any Latin American states . . . feeling that it must lead to war, bloodshed and hatred, in and through which the workers must be the chief sufferers." The resolution was tabled by the organization's Committee on Resolutions and its Executive Council.[9]

By the time of the next convention, in November 1903, events had overtaken the AFL leadership. The Colombian Senate rejected the U.S.-proposed canal treaty in August, and in November U.S. President Theodore Roosevelt orchestrated a revolution in the province and quickly recognized a new government there, which just as quickly accepted the proposed canal treaty.

Colombian representatives pressed the AFL to denounce the events, and there was an attempt to reintroduce the 1902 resolution at the 1903 convention. Gompers, however, argued that the seizure of the Canal Zone represented "the organized expression of the American people." The Committee on Resolutions introduced a substitute measure, supporting the canal and asking that union labor be used in the construction process. The committee's substitute resolution passed ninety-nine to forty-seven (although fewer than half of the delegates present voted at all).[10] These events illustrate another phenomenon that has lasted until the present: in the top-down organizational structure of the AFL/AFL-CIO, the rank and file has had little input into, and often little knowledge of, the federation's international activities.

Foreign Corporations and Colombian Labor Radicalism

U.S. corporations, particularly in the oil and banana industries, had had an important presence in Colombia since the beginning of the century and helped to shape the labor movement there. Foreign companies brought with them a common complex of characteristics that frequently led to strong anti-imperialist sentiment among Latin American labor movements: poor working conditions, unequal pay scales, racism, repatriation of profits, meddling in national politics, and reliance on U.S. political and military support. U.S. businesses and the U.S. government pressured Latin American governments to enforce a low-wage, high-profit economic model, with little regulation of foreign capital. Latin American social justice movements saw foreign domination as a major cause of domestic poverty and inequality. Anti-imperialism frequently put Latin American labor movements on a collision course with the AFL. Because the American standard of living increasingly promoted by the AFL depended on cheap imports—produced by cheap labor—from abroad, the federation perceived its interests as congruent with those of U.S. businesses operating abroad.

For Colombians, a massacre during a strike in the UFCO banana zone in 1928 came to symbolize the malevolent impact of foreign investors and U.S. imperialism. Apparently at the behest of the UFCO, the Colombian army attacked without warning, killing hundreds, possibly thousands of striking workers and their supporters. The populist politician Jorge Eliécer Gaitán rose to national prominence after dramatically denouncing the massacre before the Colombian Congress and calling for controls on foreign capital. Many Colombians attribute his 1948 assassination, which set off the decade-long violencia, to the CIA. The Nobel Prize–winning author Gabriel García Márquez further immortalized the strike in *One Hundred Years of Solitude*.

Colombia's mining and petroleum industries were overwhelmingly in foreign hands by the 1920s, and the United States was the main beneficiary. The Tropical Oil Company, a subsidiary of Standard Oil of New Jersey, and Shell Oil Company controlled the extraction of Colombian petroleum. Various smaller U.S. and British companies operated gold, platinum, and emerald mines.[11] Both the products and the profits were exported.

Tropical began explorations in Barrancabermeja in 1919. Production began in 1922, and the Unión Obrera (later Unión Sindical Obrera [USO]) was founded in early 1923.[12] The communist labor leader Ignacio Torres Giraldo described Barrancabermeja's social milieu: "The situation was polarized between two opposing forces: the imperialists of the Tropical Oil Company and the mass of its workers united with the rest of the population. Even the local government—council, mayor, and judge—were part of the population or supported it, except in the periods of conflict with the company when the governments in Bucaramanga or Bogotá replaced the legal local government with the military regime that the Yankee oilmen demanded."[13] Whereas U.S. employers like Naumkeag or Draper could call upon nationalism to try to rally worker and community loyalty, nationalism cut the opposite way in Colombia, where it was the employer who was foreign.

Another observer describes the social geography of the oil camps: "The foreign personnel, Canadian and U.S., the so-called gringos, in their houses, sports and recreation fields, social clubs and other exclusive services, protected by barbed wire fences. In communal barracks with no services, imprisoned by more barbed wire, the Colombian workers. In better endowed camps, the higher level Colombian employees, submissive adulators of the foreign bosses." Still more barbed wire separated the entire installation from any outside vendors or businesses.[14]

The 1920s saw what one Colombia labor historian described as the "period of the great strikes" against Tropical in 1924 and 1927 and against United Fruit in 1928.[15] Organized against U.S.-owned companies, they had a strong nationalist and anti-imperialist thrust and went far beyond the workplace, bringing together local peasant and business communities against the multinationals. As in Salem and Hopedale, communist and socialist activists played an important role. In both Barrancabermeja and Santa Marta, company payment in scrip and exclusion of local businesses through the use of company stores drew local entrepreneurs to join workers. The extraordinary and violent use of state power against strikers, as in Santa Marta in 1928, further contributed to the radicalization of workers' movements.

During a December 1935 strike oil workers took over the city of Barran-cabermeja. "Businesspeople and the majority of the population supported the oil workers; a shop-owner, in fact, managed the money and funds that the workers had accumulated to finance the strike; the strike committee gave orders controlling the prices of basic items to prevent speculation; it created vigilance brigades made up of strikers themselves to conserve, defend and protect the petroleum installations, it prohibited alcohol, and it organized the supply of food to the population and communal kitchens." Local peasants donated food.[16]

If the first strikes combined bread-and-butter with political issues, the January 1948 oil strike was overwhelmingly dominated by politics. Tropical workers led a national protest against the company as it sought to extend its contract with the Colombian state, due to expire in 1951. While the immediate issue in the strike was the laying off of a large number of workers, the strike also called upon the Colombian government to take back the country's oil resources.

The City Council of Medellín passed a resolution in favor of the strikers, explaining, "The striking oil workers are not only defending their own interests as workers. . . . Their movement has also served to denounce the fact that the Tropical Oil Company . . . is applying a calculated policy of slowly dismantling its technical installations for exploration and exploitation, which in the end will affect our country's important economic interests." A government arbitration tribunal ruled two months later in favor of reinstating the workers and requiring the company to restore all of its operations. Shortly after, the Congress created Ecopetrol (the Empresa Colombiana de Petróleos, or Colombian Petroleum Company) to prepare to take national control of the oil fields.[17]

The oil workers union became a rallying point for leftist and anti-imperialist organizing in Colombia. The debate over Ecopetrol symbolized a debate over national sovereignty and the question of who was to profit from the extraction of Colombia's resources: foreign companies or the Colombian people?[18]

U.S. oil companies did not hesitate to appeal to their government on the issue of Colombian labor discipline. In September 1948, a Texas Petroleum executive protested Colombian workers' "determination to share in the management [of the company]. He said the company would 'not stand for this' and would 'pull out of Colombia rather than submit to it.' He urged a cutoff in all U.S. loans to Colombia if its government did not act decisively to curb labor's excesses."[19] Three days later, the U.S. ambassador informed the Colombian government that its failure to support the interests of U.S. companies in conflict with their Colombian workers "raised the question of whether Colombia was entitled to receive loans from the United States."[20]

The U.S. government continually sought to limit Ecopetrol's control over Colombia's oil sector. In late 1962 the U.S. ambassador met with Colombian President Valencia to make the same veiled threat to him that New England textile factories were making to their workers fifty years earlier: give us what we want, or we'll pull out. He warned against Ecopetrol's plan to increase its refining capacity in Barrancabermeja, urging the president to instead consider favorably proposals by Mobil and the Texas Petroleum Company to build new refineries. He pointed out that Ecopetrol would have to rely on foreign loans to finance its project. "Particularly at a time when the Colombian balance of payments was so unfavorable, I had wished to call to the President's personal attention this possibility of realizing a further substantial investment in Colombia by foreign private capital which would obviate the necessity of a further drain on Colombia's limited foreign exchange. I also mentioned the possibility that, if Ecopetrol were to expand its refinery capacity . . . it might well discourage the foreign companies from making any further investments in Colombia."[21]

From the 1950s until the 1990s, foreign companies had to enter into joint ventures with Ecopetrol to invest in Colombian oil. High on the agenda of the 1990s neoliberal reforms was dismantling Ecopetrol to allow investors more autonomy and full repatriation of profits. "The conditions of contract concessions have been made more attractive for foreign investors," eliminating production sharing and reducing royalties, boasted a Colombian government publication in 2004.[22] Once again, USO stood at the forefront of national protest.

"Ecopetrol was born from the premise that the oil is Colombian, and that the wealth it generates should contribute to the wellbeing and development of the Colombian people, thus the sovereignty and development of our country," wrote two Colombian journalists that same year. "We can call Ecopetrol our own thanks to the enormous struggle of the USO workers. . . . USO plays a central role in society and in social initiatives. In Barrancabermeja to be a worker is not only a labor issue, it also has a political dimension, because they are responsible for the defense of the nation and its resources."[23]

The U.S. union activist Fred Hirsch, who has spent a quarter of a century challenging AFL-CIO Latin America policies, met with USO leaders during a delegation his union participated in to Colombia in 2002. "A young USO leader said, 'Globalization attacks everything we've built. They want to privatize Ecopetrol and do away with our labor laws. They want us out of the way to do it. That's what it's all about.' "[24]

U.S. Multinationals and Counterinsurgency in Colombia: The 1960s

Threats of disinvestment may have convinced Colombia's government of the wisdom of submitting to U.S. multinationals, but they did not succeed in undermining the popular nationalism of radical workers, the Communist Party, the left wing of the Liberal Party, and an increasingly prominent armed guerrilla movement. Colombia became a centerpiece of U.S. policy in the hemisphere well before it began to enter the news and the public consciousness in the 1990s. The globalization complex—foreign loans, privatization, opening to foreign capital, and military aid and counterinsurgency to enforce these conditions on an unwilling populace—advanced in Colombia during the entire second half of the twentieth century.

In 1949 Colombia became the first Latin American country to receive a World Bank mission to prescribe its economic future.[25] In 1958, as described in chapter 3, it was the first to open a free trade zone for offshore manufacturing. With Chile, Colombia led the continental experiment with neoliberal economic restructuring in the 1970s.[26] A 1988 U.S. government study applauded the degree to which "Colombia gradually opened its economy to the outside world" starting in the 1960s.[27]

The strength of the armed and unarmed left in Colombia posed an ongoing challenge to this corporate agenda. By 1952, with Colombia sending a battalion to support the U.S. war effort in Korea, the United States began to heavily outfit Colombia's military (including supplying bombers and napalm), on the grounds that Colombia's internal security was key to hemispheric stability. The United States founded Latin America's first antiguerrilla training school in Colombia in 1955 and increased its counterinsurgency activities there throughout the decade.

Brigadier General William P. Yarborough headed a U.S. Army Special Warfare Center team to Colombia in February 1962, which set the groundwork for a counterinsurgency program that continues to this day. Among other things, Yarborough recommended the creation of clandestine civilian and military units to carry out "paramilitary, sabotage, and/or terrorist activities against known communist proponents."[28] Another goal was "integrating viable Colombian doctrine and techniques into counterinsurgency instruction presented at the U.S. Army Special Warfare School" so that U.S. counterinsurgency experts could apply lessons from the Colombian situation elsewhere in Latin America.[29]

Based on the Yarborough team's recommendations, U.S. advisors designed the antiguerrilla "Plan Lazo" in June 1962, calling for "aggressive, offensive patrol activity" as well as "psychological operations" against the so-called bandits. The plan also created the Intelligence and Counterintelligence Battalion, one of whose goals was to "find, destroy or eliminate communist and extremist activities through a network of clandestine agents."[30] The battalion became notorious for its human rights violations and its role in supporting the right-wing paramilitaries in subsequent years.[31] Much of Colombia's official and para-official violence is deeply tied to U.S. counterinsurgency efforts there.

Peaceful, legal organizing, including union organizing, was a key target of counterinsurgency. U.S. officials considered the oil workers federation, Fedepetrol, in which the USO was a leading voice, to be a symbol of communist subversion: "No doubt at all Marulanda [a guerrilla leader who later founded the FARC] and his followers genuine communists. Are currently receiving propaganda support Bogotá and other parts country from Communist Party, Fedepetrol union, Communist youth, and other extremists," the embassy telegrammed in 1964, urging the U.S. State Department to augment its support for the Colombian army incursion against the areas under guerrilla control.[32] At the same time, the U.S. ambassador reminded the State Department, "Communism even now is not principal enemy to U.S. interests in Latin America but rather enemy is extreme and unreasoning nationalism."[33] U.S. policymakers found democracy itself troubling in Latin America, as a secret report on the situation in Colombia in 1962 suggests: "The emphasis which democratic government places on the rights of its citizens makes it peculiarly susceptible to attack by organized subversive efforts."[34]

Colombian government and paramilitary violence have continued to dovetail with the interests of U.S. companies in Colombia and have been financed by U.S. aid. In the first decade of the twenty-first century the United States provided aid and training explicitly for military protection of

Occidental Petroleum's Caño Limon-Coveñas oil pipeline, which had been repeatedly bombed by the FARC.[35] Paramilitaries patrol the outskirts of the Drummond coal mines in Cesar province and have been accused of selectively murdering union activists at Drummond as well as in several Coca-Cola bottling plants in Colombia.

In 2003, the Canadian company Greystar Resources utilized a private Colombian security firm with the open cooperation of the Colombian army to sweep through an area claimed by the company, displacing peasants, small miners, and guerrillas, so that it could take advantage of the rising price of gold and resume mining operations. "In the Angostura area, the new security initiatives resulted in many hundreds of government troops returning this year and locally manned militias being set up in seventeen nearby communities. In September, a large contingent of police also returned. And finally, in a strong statement, the government has built a battalion-size military base in the mountains, just 8 km from Angostura, and is building two more bases 20 km away." With this backup, the Greystar manager of investor relations Eduardo Baer announced cheerfully, "Things are now turning around in Colombia, and there's a lot of American investment and interest, certainly in oil and gas, and in coal." "We have a comprehensive security program which has taken us more than three and a half years to put in place," said Greystar's vice president Frederick Felder. "It's quite exceptional and we've been fortunate to have support from all levels of government—all the ministries have helped us, and that goes all the way up to the president."[36]

U.S. Labor in the Cold War

After World War II the AFL, and later AFL-CIO, threw itself wholeheartedly into promoting a U.S. government and corporate agenda abroad, leading it to frequently support the most right-wing and anti-union forces in Latin America. As one of several critiques published in the 1980s argued, the AFL-CIO "adheres to an anticommunist, pro-U.S., and pro-capitalist agenda that shapes their choice of beneficiaries. Unfortunately, this agenda often pits the labor institutes against nationalist and popular movements that are struggling to redistribute economic and political resources in a more equitable fashion."[37]

By working to undermine labor radicalism and foster compliant unions that complemented the interests of U.S. capital abroad, the AFL-CIO also reinforced the labor-management pact at home, at least temporarily. But by strengthening U.S. companies' positions abroad, the federation also unwittingly helped to set the stage for the wholesale flight of U.S. manufacturing abroad in the later years of the century. The AFL-CIO's stance was never without its challengers, inside and outside of the labor movement. Some of the challenges came from the left, from the older communist and IWW brand of internationalism. Others took the form of labor-management nationalist protectionism, of the Roger Milliken and Pat Buchanan variety: Protect American Jobs!

In general, though, union workers in the United States knew very little about their federation's foreign policy. Foreign policy decisions were made at the top, by a leadership entrenched in a cold war ideology, and AFL-CIO foreign policy activities were funded directly by the U.S. government. Abroad, labor representatives worked closely with the labor attachés at the U.S. embassies. The budget for these activities was huge: during the 1980s, it was greater than the federation's entire domestic budget.[38] Still today, AFL-CIO foreign policies are funded by the government and developed, and carried out, without oversight or input from the membership.

The AFL worked through several different international bodies to pursue its agenda in Latin America. It was instrumental in founding the International Confederation of Free Trade Unions (ICFTU), an anticommunist global confederation organized to challenge the World Federation of Trade Unions (WFTU), in 1949.[39] Its first Latin America representative was the ILGWU organizer Serafino Romualdi, who had previously worked for the Office of Strategic Services to encourage and develop links between conservative (anticommunist and antinationalist) unions in Latin America and U.S. labor. This effort led to the formation of ORIT (Organización Regional Interamericana de Trabajadores, or the Interamerican Regional Organization of Workers) in 1951. In 1962, the American Institute for Free Labor Development was created to coordinate labor support for the U.S. government's antirevolutionary policies in Latin America.

The role of AIFLD in Colombia corresponded to the organization's pattern elsewhere in the hemisphere, where it worked to undermine radical labor organizations, create and promote conciliatory alternatives, and liberally hand out favors to individuals and unions that were willing to support a counterrevolutionary and pro-business agenda. From the 1950s through the 1990s, where there were radical unions or a government that challenged

U.S. hegemony, AIFLD was on the scene to try to restore what U.S. policy-makers saw as the proper social order. On numerous occasions, AIFLD contributed actively to the overthrow of governments that promoted a nationalist and redistributive agenda that challenged the desires of U.S. corporations.[40] At times, AIFLD explicitly helped to undermine unions at the Latin American facilities of some of its U.S. corporate sponsors.

The organization itself exemplified labor-management collaboration. As AFL-CIO President George Meany explained in 1969, "The AFL-CIO Executive Council decided unanimously that we should bring enlightened American business into this institution. . . . So we went to American business, and we told them why we thought they should cooperate. We got a most encouraging response. The result is that we have some outstanding American businessmen contributing to the work of the AIFLD." Indeed, on AIFLD's board of trustees and among its financial backers, major U.S. multinationals with operations in Latin America were prominently featured.[41]

The alliance also placed AIFLD in the forefront of promoting U.S. cold war policies that consistently worked against popular movements for social justice in Latin America. When questioned about the value of AIFLD "training" programs that brought (carefully selected) Latin American unionists to the United States, AIFLD Social Projects Director William Doherty explained how AIFLD graduates had played an important role in the 1964 overthrow of left-wing populist president João Goulart in Brazil. "When they returned to their respective countries," he explained, they promoted AIFLD's agenda of business unionism, "helping unions introduce systems of collective bargaining, and modern concepts of labor-management relations. As a matter of fact, some of them were so active that they became intimately involved in some of the clandestine operations of the revolution [i.e., the military coup] before it took place on April 1. What happened in Brazil on April 1 did not just happen—it was planned—and planned months in advance. Many of the trade union leaders—some of whom were actually trained in our institute—were involved in the revolution, and in the overthrow of the Goulart regime."[42]

In Central America too, where the AFL-CIO leadership remained committed to supporting the Reagan administration's interventions in the 1980s, critics inside and outside the labor movement have argued that the AFL-CIO supported a U.S. corporate and imperial agenda, working to undermine labor radicalism in the name of anticommunism.[43] Recent declassified documents have shown the role of AIFLD in countering leftist unions and undermining the Allende government in Chile in 1973.[44] Other studies have criticized the AFL-CIO relationship with anti-Chavez unions involved in the 2002 coup attempt in Venezuela.[45]

Given this history, it is not surprising that many Colombian unionists view AFL-CIO programs in Colombia with suspicion, or that labor activists in the United States and Latin America are also skeptical of the AFL-CIO's claims that its funding of the conservative Venezuelan CTV (Confederación de Trabajadores de Venezuela, or Confederation of Venezuelan Workers) in the months before that federation supported the April 2002 coup attempt against populist president Hugo Chávez was completely innocent.

International Trade Secretariats, the AFL-CIO, and Latin American Unions

International trade secretariats (ITSs) are international federations bringing together unions from the same industry. Linked to the ICFTU and heavily reliant on the AFL-CIO and its affiliates for funding, they began to enter Latin America in the 1950s. "Their utility as a political instrument was underscored by a U.S. Labor Department official in the late 1950s and early 1960s, who noted that: 'ITS flexibility, inner cohesion and conviction makes the Secretariats especially effective anti-Communist organizations . . . and thus extremely important to U.S. policy objectives.' "[46]

Although virtually invisible in the United States, the checkered history of the international trade secretariats in Latin America is well known to union activists there. In Brazil, the International Federation of Petroleum and Chemical Workers (IFPCW) came into the country after the 1964 coup to "'clean up' Communist-infiltrated unions"; in the Dominican Republic, "the ITS came to play a larger role as AIFLD's activities met increasing criticism from nationalist and anti-imperialist labor elements. Several ITSS expanded their activities through funds from U.S. affiliates, which, in turn, received monies from AIFLD. The International Transport Workers' Federation and the Postal, Telegraph, and Telephone International (PTTI) both worked to strengthen reformist unions against existing progressive unions in their respective sectors." In Guyana under the leftist government of Cheddi Jagan in 1963, "CIA agents worked as labor people, AIFLD maintained anti-Jagan trade-union leaders on its full-time payroll, and the American Federation of State, County, and Municipal Employees supplied almost $1 million in strike benefits to anti-Jagan forces through the Public Services International."[47] Several ITSs, including the IFPCW and the Retail Clerks, received covert CIA funding until the system was publicly revealed in the mid-1960s; when this funding was cut off, USAID, through AIFLD, stepped in to fill the gap.[48]

Many Colombian unionists remain suspicious of the activities of ITS in their country. The IUF's recent support for the purged Sintrainagro and its ally, the newly formed SICO, which replaced a leftist union in the Carepa Coca-Cola factory (discussed at the end of this chapter), are not seen in Colombia as isolated events, but rather as part of a long history of U.S.- and Western European–dominated organizations' meddling to undermine movements for social change.

A History of Colombian Unions

Labor historians have frequently noted the weak and fragmented nature of organized labor in Colombia. With only a small portion of the labor force working in the formal sector, labor legislation that made both organizing and dues collecting difficult, and low wages, unions have frequently turned to alliance with one of Colombia's two political parties (Liberal and Conservative) or foreign bodies (Comintern, the WFTU, the ICFTU, ORIT, AIFLD) for ideas and resources. Repression, and the subservience of Colombia's major labor federations, the Confederación de Trabajadores de Colombia (CTC) and the UTC, to the Liberal and Conservative parties, respectively, greatly weakened Colombia's labor movement in the twentieth century, despite the strength of a small number of independent unions like USO. By isolating more radical unions and activists and promoting leaders whose sole attraction was their anticommunism, ORIT and AIFLD further divided the movement.

Yet twice during the course of the twentieth century, in the 1930s and in the 1980s, Colombia's unions have managed to transcend political differences and create a national body. Colombia's first national confederation, the CTC, dates back to the reformist climate following Liberal Party victories in the 1935 elections. The group split almost immediately between the communist and noncommunist members. However, in 1935 the Comintern called for its member parties to join in Popular Front movements with bourgeois political parties against fascism, opening the door for collaboration among communist and noncommunist unions as well. The Nazi-Soviet

Pact of 1939 temporarily split the organization again, and the liberal and communist wings held rival congresses in 1940. By 1941, however, the Soviet Union was at war with Nazi Germany, and the Colombian Communist Party had recommitted itself to the Popular Front.[49]

Further complicating the terrain, partisan competition led Colombia's Conservative Party to sponsor a rival confederation, the Church-affiliated UTC, in 1946. U.S. officials were in close contact with the Catholic advisors to the UTC at the time of its founding and soon began to fund the federation.[50]

When the conservative Mariano Ospina Pérez won the 1946 election, the level of violence against the labor movement, especially the liberal-backed CTC, rose immediately: "Regional authorities had made a habit of deploying police agents to break up strikes and protect private property against the interests of labor since around 1910," explains the historian Mary Roldán. "But when animosity between workers and police took on partisan overtones, the tensions between these two groups rose to new heights."[51]

Simultaneously, the AFL made its first direct foray into Colombia. The federation sent Serafino Romualdi to Latin America in 1946 to "look for friends and allies" and attempt to "launch a new inter-American labor group" with an anticommunist agenda.[52] In Colombia, Romualdi's project was to purge the left from the CTC.

At the August 1946 CTC congress in Medellín, Romualdi encouraged what he called "democratic labor leaders" to take over the organization, "pledg[ing] AFL assistance" to these leaders—also supported by the Liberal Party—as they claimed ownership of the CTC name and funds. In October, the Ministry of Labor recognized the anticommunist faction, under Juan C. Lara, as the legal CTC. However, in December, when Lara was visiting the United States as the guest of the AFL Free Trade Union Committee, left-wing liberal and communist CTC members reclaimed the organization and were duly recognized in February 1947. "What was left of the anti-Communist CTC refused to accept the Liberal-Communist pact and announced a fight to the finish to be carried to the next CTC convention. Of course, Lara and his followers counted on, and promptly received, support from the AFL Free Trade Union Committee." This attempt to dominate the CTC was short-lived. Although Romualdi claimed that Lara's faction "clearly represented a majority of the bona fide membership" in 1946, by 1951 he was calling it a "splinter CTC group" that "had been quietly dropped and was no longer functioning."[53] The AFL, however, was just beginning its campaign to eradicate Colombia's leftist unions.

It is worth pausing to contrast the roles of the United States and the USSR in Colombia. The U.S. government, and its AFL/AFL-CIO ally, maintained organizations, offices, and personnel in Colombia and poured money into their programs and the allies they wished to cultivate. The USSR did none of these things. The only communists in Colombia were Colombian communists. Many of them were pro-Soviet (and later, some were Maoists). But like the IWW in Hopedale and the National Textile Workers Union in Salem, their actions were shaped largely by local realities. The strength of communism in Latin America in general, and in Colombia in particular, grew from the nature of capitalism there. In its New Deal, social welfare incarnation, U.S. capitalism succeeded in fulfilling the needs and aspirations of the majority of the population at home. In its savage, foreign-dominated Latin American version, capitalism spelled misery and hunger for far too many.

The 1948 violencia that cleared Urabá for the banana planters also opened the doors to an all-out attack against the labor movement nationwide. In November 1949, President Ospina declared a state of siege that lasted for ten years, "during which the government could legislate by decree, restrict the right of assembly, censor the press, and make arbitrary arrests."[54] During those ten years, the labor movement was decimated.

The 1949 electoral season brought a wave of official violence against organized labor. Railroad union officials wrote, "Those attacks are not all the product of private citizens in an exalted state of partisan fervor, the majority are led . . . by the very public employees and agents charged with protecting the tranquility, honor, life and goods of the union's membership."[55] After the 1949 election, in which the conservative Laureano Gómez was elected unopposed, "public sector workers—the primary targets of official harassment between 1946 and 1949—increasingly took up arms against the state or colluded with and protected armed Liberal groups operating in their geographic vicinity."[56]

The May 1950 CTC Congress—the only one held during the decade-long state of siege—further engaged Colombian workers in the cold war. Under pressure from the U.S. government, working through Romualdi, Liberal Party leaders demanded that the CTC expel communist affiliates, withdraw from the Confederación de Trabajadores de América Latina, and join the ICFTU.[57] Perhaps unsurprisingly, the confederation complied.[58]

In the period of the violencia and conservative hegemony after 1948, the CTC lost ground decisively to the UTC. The IFCTU and ORIT helped by funding the conservative confederation, providing 15 percent of its budget from 1956 to 1958 and 8 percent of a much larger budget from 1961 to 1963.[59]

When Vice President Richard Nixon visited Colombia in 1955, the UTC and the CTC held a joint reception to honor him as he "presented a 500-volume library on U.S. labor history and related subjects to Colombia's free labor movement." Romualdi also spoke at the UTC convention in Cali in 1956.[60] The battle to control Colombia's labor movement, however, was far from over.

AIFLD in Colombia

Since Colombia was a laboratory for U.S. countersubversion techniques in the 1950s and 1960s, it is not surprising that the AFL, and later AIFLD, played an active role there. Colombians formed the largest contingent of unionists trained through AIFLD programs—over seventy thousand.[61] Certainly one impact of AFL/AIFLD intervention has been, until 1986, to keep Colombia's labor movement weak and divided.

One of AIFLD's prime goals in Colombia was to promote anticommunist unions, leaders, and policies within the CTC. First ORIT, and after 1962 AIFLD, developed a warm alliance with the CTC leader José Mercado, whom even Andrew McLellan, the AFL-CIO international representative in Washington, characterized as "vicious."[62] Despite his numerous failings as a person and as a union leader, he fulfilled what the United States saw as the most important characteristic. "I have a great deal of respect for José's intelligence and guts when it comes to standing up and being counted on the issue of Communist intervention," enthused the U.S. labor attaché in Bogotá in a missive to McLellan in 1966.[63]

Indeed, Mercado could always be counted on to express an almost sycophantic support for U.S. policies. An embassy official reported in late 1962, "Mercado stated that labor is fully committed to the democratic system—and is 'on the firing line in the fight against subversion. There is no better investment in democracy and the goals of the Alliance for Progress than in strengthening the free trade union movement.'"[64]

Colombian analysts have taken a much dimmer view of the CTC under the sway of AIFLD and José Mercado. What U.S. observers saw as anticommunism, many Colombians saw as selling out to foreign capital. Iván Osorio O. critiqued the confederation's 1960 conference in Cartagena: "By this time imperialism had deeply penetrated some CTC leaders, [bringing about] the political and economic submission of our country and the domination of our unions, under the pretext of anti-communism. This was the U.S. policy after World War II."[65] A 1963 UTC analysis acknowledged the unpopularity of the official CTC leaders: "The most recent Congress in Cartagena in 1960 was a demonstration of the strength of the Government to protect a tiny number of union leaders who were incapable on their own of overcoming the Communists."[66] It was all too easy for the United States, and the AFL-CIO, to label as communist any voice challenging U.S. corporations in the country. This meant that the AFL-CIO threw its support behind a few corrupt union officials and worked to undermine Colombia's strongest and most militant unions.

At Cartagena the CTC expelled the leftist Antioquian federation Fedeta (with which Sintrabanano affiliated in 1964), as well as the federations of Valle, Caldas, Tolima, Santander, and Norte de Santander, and Fedepetrol and the National Federation of Construction, Cement, and Building Materials Workers.[67] This meant that some of the largest and strongest unions in the country—representing some 100,000 workers, while 60,000 remained in CTC unions—were now outside of any federation. (The UTC claimed to represent 350,000 workers in 1963.)[68] Some of the unions expelled from the CTC, along with other independents, formed the Confederación Sindical de Trabajadores de Colombia in May 1964. Paradoxically, the drive to expel leftist unions from the CTC may have in fact encouraged these more radical unions to ally with the communists.

Its single-minded pursuit of an anticommunist agenda frequently put ORIT at odds even with its supposed allies. In 1962, for example, the UTC protested vociferously and even moved toward withdrawing from ORIT when the organization pushed Mercado's candidacy in the organization. "They feel sure that [Arturo] Jauregi [secretary general of ORIT] pressured other nations to go along with Mercado because of Mercado's position in relation to the Commie threat in his unions. . . . Jauregi should know that Mercado's anticommunism does not necessarily make him a good labor leader and it certainly does not make the CTC the proper organization to represent Colombia," Colombia's AIFLD director Emilio Garza protested gently, noting that the CTC only comprised 120 affiliates, while the UTC had 600.[69]

At the UTC's eleventh plenary later that year, a resolution declared that ORIT "has discriminated many times against the UTC," noting also that the CTC had greatly disproportionate representation in ORIT's educational program. "We believe that this discrimination is primarily due to a few representatives of the AFL-CIO, who favor those individuals who place themselves unconditionally at the service of their pretensions."[70] To McLellan, however, focusing AIFLD's programs on the CTC was entirely justified: "There is a degree of urgency for such a program with the CTC because of successful Communist penetration and control of a number of CTC affiliates."[71]

In 1963 Garza noted that "things do not look good for the CTC Congress.... Unions were so disgusted with the last Congress and how well the machine was oiled that they are using this as an excuse for not going this year." Garza went so far as to suggest that the AFL-CIO "send a man down here to do the coordinating" of the Congress and the elections, which had clearly been orchestrated beforehand to assure Mercado's continued presidency. "I would love to do the job myself, Andy," Garza commented, "but one goof and AIFLD is shot in Colombia."[72]

The AFL-CIO's ideological straitjacket led it to suspect communist influence even within Christian unions. By the 1960s, in line with the progressive tendencies in the Catholic Church embodied in Vatican II, some Catholic unions in Colombia joined the new Latin American Confederation of Christian Unions (CLASC), using anticapitalist and anti-imperialist language. "The communists . . . have even managed to capture those who call themselves Christians," a UTC analyst wrote in 1963.[73] The AFL-CIO's George Meany heartily seconded this opinion, declaring that the "CLASC maintains that the fundamental economic structure of Latin American society is all wrong and that there must be a social and economic upheaval in order to effect change. . . . This philosophy of CLASC has frequently made their policies all but indistinguishable from extremist revolutionary elements including the communists."[74] The archbishop of Medellín joined the fray, criticizing unions that chose to affiliate with the CLASC and announcing, "We consider any attempt to disaffiliate a union from the UTC . . . as a serious attack against unionism that follows the social doctrine of the Church and the orientations of the church hierarchy, and a benefit to Communism."[75]

Later in the 1960s U.S. officials even began to worry about the orientation of the UTC. "The UTC position is more and more that of the 'Third World,'" the U.S. labor attaché in Bogotá reported in 1966. "This is the kind of stuff which José Mercado throws up to us once in a while, as a reason we shouldn't support the UTC."[76]

In 1965, the AIFLD report noted proudly that an AIFLD student, Hugo Solón Acero, eliminated "the last vestiges of Communist influence in the regional [CTC] federation of Cundinamarca."[77] Despite, or because of, its repeated purges of the left, however, the CTC continued to lose ground. Its sole strength seemed to reside in Mercado's personal control of the organization. "If he [Mercado] leaves the CTC, I am convinced as you must be that the whole structure will fall apart," McLellan informed the embassy in early 1966.[78] And a year later, the labor attaché expressed the same sentiment:

> Our friend José is in the peculiar position of being at one and the same time the man who can keep the CTC from falling apart, and the man who is responsible for its weaknesses. Both José and the Liberal Party appear to be more interested in maintaining the CTC as a political force than in building an economically strong labor movement. Eventually, the UTC and the Communists will benefit from this situation. . . . As long as José rules the roost, the CTC will probably not make the structural changes which are required if it is to meet the needs of the times. I refer, of course, to the need for building strong national unions and federations.[79]

McLellan could not differ:

> With reference to Mercado and the CTC, I quite agree with you. Mercado is directly responsible for the inherent vacancies in the CTC but by the same token appears to be the only leader within the organization capable of holding it together even as a loosely-knit organization. . . . When I discussed the situation of the CTC with [UTC President] Tulio Cuevas . . . he quite frankly told me that if he were a delegate to the CTC Congress he would certainly vote for Mercado's reelection on the grounds that the disintegration of the CTC under Mercado's leadership is inevitable and to some degree the UTC is benefiting from this fragmentation of the CTC. By the same token, while the CTV of Venezuela publicly praises him for his militant stand on the Cuban boycott in glowing terms, privately they find him objectionable and unacceptable as a spokesman for any sector of the American labor movement.[80]

If corrupt leadership, ideological vacuity, and political subservience limited the CTC's appeal to its affiliates, ORIT and AIFLD sought to keep their loyalty through material rewards. Yet it seemed to be a losing battle. "It must be obvious to you watching the situation day by day," McLellan wrote to O'Grady in 1967, "that more and more dissident groups are withdrawing from the CTC and those not aligning themselves with the UTC are aligning themselves with organizations of rather dubious orientation."[81]

Several examples from the late 1960s illustrate the ways that Colombian unions negotiated the ideological and material pulls that frequently tugged in opposite directions, and also the ways that the international trade secretariats collaborated with AIFLD's anticommunist agenda. In one case, a union left the UTC with a significant debt; in the other, the PTTI succeeded in expelling communists from a union, and AIFLD rewarded the purged union with a loan.

At the U.S.-owned R. J. Reynolds Company in Barranquilla, a union affiliated with the UTC secured a 100,000 peso loan from the Banco Popular for a strike fund during a three-month strike in early 1966. However, "no sooner had the strike been settled with an average wage improvement of 40% when the union leadership went over to the Commies," the U.S. labor attaché complained to the AFL-CIO International Office. "The union has now been expelled from the UTC, which is stuck with a note for the 100,000 pesos. I haven't investigated the situation thoroughly, but wonder if it is a matter of money or Communism, or perhaps a little of both," he mused.[82]

In another case, Sittelecom, the leftist union of workers in the state telecommunications agency Telecom, withdrew from the Communication Workers Federation, which was "all but destroyed" by its departure. U.S. officials, working through PTTI, launched a campaign to bring Sittelecom back under control. The labor attaché was able to report with satisfaction in 1966 that "in a recent Congress democratic leaders knocked out the Communists. This was in great part the result of work done by PTTI representatives in Colombia." He added that AIFLD should thus quickly reward Sittelecom with a loan for a housing cooperative project.[83]

The IFPCW, with U.S. funding, tried to carry out a similar takeover in the oil workers federation Fedepetrol, long a center of resistance to U.S. corporate goals in Colombia. The IFCPW budget proposal to USAID explained that it planned to create a rival federation and at the same time "assist the free, democratic trade unions currently in Fedepetrol to recapture their organization from its present Communist leadership control. We must continue to work with key persons employed by Ecopetrol, Colpet and Intercol (the three oil companies where the rival union has its membership strength)." In addition, the IFCPW intended to work to strengthen the rival federation "and assist it in developing a closer relationship with the government of Colombia. Eventually, merge Fedepetrol into our affiliate."[84] Fedepetrol, however, remained fiercely independent, and the attempt to establish a rival federation foundered.

An example from the Medellín textile industry shows even more explicitly how AIFLD helped a U.S. corporation and deliberately undermined unionized workers in Colombia. A U.S. Senate investigation uncovered the following case: "The local union in Celanese Colombiana S.A. (a subsidiary joint venture of the Celanese Corporation of America which is a contributor to the AIFLD) had been debilitated by its Castroite orientation. Within a few months several illegal work stoppages had taken place, plus a sympathy strike in favor of Castro. The company retaliated with mass firings." Rather than support the union in the face of illegal firings, AIFLD saw this as an opportunity to purge the left from the union: "AIFLD graduates, together with other democratic leaders, were able to gain control of the union. Since that time the union has affiliated with the UTC."[85]

Celanese had opened its Colombia plant in the 1940s in the context of a lengthy, ultimately successful strike at its Rome, Georgia, facility aimed at bringing the plant's wages in line with its northern counterparts. The all-white TWUA local in Georgia took a militant stand on wages, but at the same time adhered solidly to the racial, religious, and political order of the South—no threat of Castroism there.[86] The factory could pay lower wages in Colombia, but it could not count on worker docility, at least not without the help of AIFLD.

The institute was also on hand to undermine radical peasant organizing. Colombia's independent peasant movement grew out of the National Peasant Association, or Asociación Nacional de Usuarios Campesinos (ANUC), created in 1966 as an official vehicle to incorporate peasants into government-sponsored land reform programs and undermine radical peasant and guerrilla organizing in the countryside. By 1970s, however, ANUC had escaped the confines set up by the government and become a radical organization itself. Its 1971 call for a comprehensive agrarian reform, including collectivization, and for direct action to achieve it, signaled the organization's definitive break from its official sponsors.[87] As the ANUC turned more and more to revolutionary language and action, including land invasions, official and unofficial repression against the organization increased. By the middle of the 1970s, rural death squads organized by landowners or local politicians began to emerge to target the organization.[88]

Both the CTC and the UTC openly opposed ANUC and its activities. The UTC organized a rival federation, the Federación Agraria Nacional, receiving money from both USAID and AIFLD for its efforts.[89] The latter was also quick to establish its own counterpresence in the rural areas, creating campesino centers to offer "educational programs, vocational training, and legal assistance"—and to lure peasants away from the ANUC.[90] By the late 1970s, a combination of isolation, co-optation, and repression had greatly weakened the ANUC. At the end of the 1970s "literally thousands of ANUC . . . and other militants and their urban supporters were rounded up by the military and accused of active ties with guerrilla organizations. Dozens have claimed they were tortured. Scores remained in jail without trial or the possibility of bail for a year or more."[91] And AIFLD offered not a whisper of protest.

One Colombian study of labor internationalism voiced the ongoing suspicion that Colombia's unionists feel toward international bodies, in the context of the founding of the Central Unitaria de Trabajadores de Colombia in 1986. The ICFTU, the authors explain, "placed its organization at the service of one country's political interests, in this case, those of the United States. This has meant that the ICFTU has lost credibility in union struggles. . . . The ICFTU continues to exist today, though it is plagued with serious problems originating precisely in its political orientation."[92]

Toward Trade Union Confederation: The 1970s

While Colombia's economic and political policies have catered to foreign investors and the export economy throughout the twentieth century, the modern neoliberal project began in the 1970s. The government began to dismantle the welfare benefits described in chapter 4. Assaults on peasant and worker movements coincided with new incentives to the export sector. "For the first time the priorities of the new neo-Liberal orientation of Colombian capitalism were spelled out as the priorities of official economic policy." Reducing the cost of labor was an integral element of the program.[93] These policies further de-legitimized—or else radicalized—the officialist unions.

The 1970s saw the slow growth of independent unions, especially in the public sector, as well as growing grassroots independence in the UTC and

CTC. The independent Colombian Federation of Teachers, FECODE, was at the forefront of labor militancy. Independent unions grew from representing 25 percent of the organized labor force in 1967 to 35 percent in 1974 and over 50 percent in 1984, and they tended to be stronger and more active than those in the confederations.[94]

The push for independence and unification grew in the 1980s. The peace process that opened the political system to a left party, the UP, helped to create a political space for independent unions as well. Although the CTC continued to command significant resources because of its support from the Liberal Party and AIFLD, its disaffected member unions began to explore alternatives. As Pearce explains, "three unity processes got underway— within the independent sector itself, between the independents and the Communist Party, and between these and the dissidents of the traditional union confederations." In 1986 seventeen federations from the UTC and three from the CTC broke with their organizations and joined the Communist CSTC and the independents, including FECODE and Fedepetrol, to found the Central Unitaria de Trabajadores de Colombia (CUT).[95]

The CUT vigorously rejected affiliation with any political party or international labor body, but also made its political orientation clear: "The CUT is a UNIFIED, CLASS-CONSCIOUS, DEMOCRATIC, and PROGRESSIVE union . . . Its primary task will be to unconditionally defend the conquests and existing rights of workers and the people [*pueblo*] in general, and seek to better their conditions of work and life. It will struggle for full national independence, democratic freedoms, social justice, respect for human rights, and the social transformations that will allow the development and progress of our people."[96] Clearly, this was not to be solely a bread-and-butter union, and while rejecting political affiliation, it saw its political role as extending well beyond what AIFLD had been promoting as the appropriate role for unions.

The formation of the CUT coincided with an increasing neoliberal assault in the 1980s and 1990s. IMF (International Monetary Fund) demands and U.S. military aid combined to enforce a further restructuring of the state sector toward the demands of foreign capital. As the U.S. Department of Energy enthused in 2004, "Since 1999, Colombia's government has taken measures to make the investment climate more attractive to foreign oil companies."[97] Similar legislative changes, mandated by the IMF, reduced state control over the mining industry as well.[98] Unions, and the newly organized CUT, were at the forefront of national protest against the neoliberal model.

Not coincidentally, this was also a period of extraordinary violence against organized labor; by 2002 over three thousand CUT members had been killed.

New Voices in the AFL-CIO: 1995 to the Present

Several structural changes began to chip away at the AFL-CIO's cold war orientation in the 1980s. By the 1970s, AFL-CIO member unions were beginning to voice their dissent over the federation's Latin America policy. "The rank and file are not consulted on AFL-CIO activities abroad or informed about their intent," Hobart Spalding explained in a 1977 study. After the 1973 coup in Chile, the rank and file began to pay more attention. Individual unions, led by the Communications Workers of America (CWA), began to raise questions at their conventions regarding the federation's foreign policy. Some members joined together to form the Union Committee for an All-Labor AIFLD, seeking to sever the organization's ties with business and government.[99] Fred Hirsch from the Plumbers and Fitters Local 393 in San Jose, California, began what was to become a decades-long struggle to force the federation to open the records on its activities in Chile.[100]

Dissent against the official AFL-CIO foreign policy grew in the 1980s. Within the federation, leaders of some important unions came together in the National Labor Committee to challenge the federation's cold war position on Central America and press for, and develop, an alternative agenda. The National Labor Committee built ties with unions, including leftist unions, in Central America and collaborated with church-based and other progressive organizations within the United States to oppose U.S. military support for El Salvador's right-wing government and the Nicaraguan Contras.[101]

"The 1985 debate was the first open floor discussion of a foreign policy issue at an AFL-CIO convention, and in 1987 over fifty percent of the membership opposed the federation's Central American policy platform."[102] At the same time, the federation was beginning to respond to structural changes in the U.S. economy and the flight of U.S. corporations to the low-wage havens that U.S. foreign policy had contributed to creating. One recent study sees the debate on foreign policy issues as one of the keys to the emergence of the New Voices movement in the AFL-CIO and its victory in 1995.[103]

At the forefront of the dissent was John Sweeney's SEIU (Service Employees International Union). Still, after taking the helm of the AFL-CIO in 1995, Sweeney took two years to restructure the organization's international apparatus. In 1997, the federation's international institutes, including AIFLD, were disbanded, replaced by the American Center for International Labor Solidarity, or Solidarity Center, which was to be led by reformers and fundamentally reorient the AFL-CIO's international agenda.[104]

Colombia quickly became an important focus for the Solidarity Center. The imposition of the neoliberal economic agenda there, the huge upsurge in U.S. military aid to the country, and the fierce repression of organized labor that led to thousands of assassinations during the decade all contributed to focusing U.S. labor, as well as human rights and solidarity organizations, on Colombia. Yet not all Colombian unionists were willing to take at face value AFL-CIO solidarity, and its new program for providing temporary refuge for Colombian unionists through invitations to the United States to participate in training sessions at the Meany Center in Washington, followed by internships with U.S. unions.

THE SOLIDARITY CENTER'S COLOMBIA PROGRAM

Few analysts in the United States have raised any questions about the Solidarity Center's Colombia program, despite the fact that it has been funded, and touted, by the U.S. Department of Labor. U.S. Labor Secretary Elaine Chao's statement announcing the program in 2001 reiterated the sentiment of labor's cold war alliance with government: "This program supports our foreign policy goals and national security interests in Colombia and in the hemisphere overall."[105] Now, though, the AFL-CIO clearly articulated its opposition to U.S. policy in Colombia, not only to U.S. military aid, but also the neoliberal economic agenda there.

The federation's opposition crystallized in a 2000 Executive Council statement that "the [Colombian] government's program of privatization and economic deregulation to create 'flexible' labor markets, as required by the IMF, has also undermined freedom of association and taken a severe toll on working families" and that "the United States should not deepen its entanglement with a military which has been responsible for the violence perpetuated against trade unionists."[106] Furthermore, the unionists who have come to the United States through the Solidarity Center have clearly not been of the ilk fostered by the cold war AFL-CIO, nor have they spent their time in the United States being indoctrinated with anticommunist ideology and tactics. Because the more militant unions in Colombia are those that have suffered the severest repression, many of those invited by the Solidarity

Center come from those sectors. And because of the confluence of progressive community-labor organizations like Jobs with Justice, unions focusing their organizing efforts on low-wage, often Latino, immigrant workers, and a solidarity and human rights movement in the United States actively opposing U.S. policies and military involvement in Colombia, visiting Colombian unionists have tended to find their niches within these progressive coalitions, rather than in programs aimed at grooming them for collaboration with the status quo in their country.

The Colombia program may be the best known element of the Solidarity Center's work because of the activism that participants have engaged in while in the United States. Some have been placed in very visible positions with progressive labor organizations, and several of them have taken advantage of the opportunity to maintain a high profile of speaking and involvement with Colombia solidarity events.

Héctor Giraldo, for example, a leader of Sintraofan, a public employees union in Antioquia, spent his internship in Boston in 2002 working with the SEIU on an organizing drive among mostly Latino janitors and collaborating with the progressive labor organization Jobs with Justice. He returned to Colombia accompanied by a labor delegation from the unions he had worked with and with a commitment from CWA District 1 for a long-term relationship, including an innovative program by which District 1 locals vote yearly to continue supporting Giraldo's union with 10 cents per year deducted from each member's dues.[107] The delegation met with U.S. Embassy personnel in Colombia to demand protection for Héctor, and noted clearly, "When we asked union leaders and members what we could do back home, they all told us to stop our government from sending military aid."[108]

Miguel Fernández, from the Colombian teachers union FECODE, long one of Colombia's most militant unions, continued Héctor's work the following year in Boston. He noted wryly that the SEIU, which was hosting his stay, had committed enormous resources to the presidential campaign of John Kerry, a strong supporter of U.S. military aid to Colombia. Nevertheless, Fernández also worked closely with a local Colombia solidarity organization, Colombia Vive, which had a completely contradictory agenda. Through campus and public talks, he made it clear that he was quite opposed to U.S. policy in Colombia.[109]

Two others in the program came from Colombian unions currently working with the United Steelworkers of America (USWA) and the International

Labor Rights Fund (ILRF) on lawsuits against their U.S.-based multinational employers for human rights violations against their unions: Francisco Ruiz from Sintramienergética at the Drummond Coal mine (see chapter 7) and Luis Adolfo Cardona from the Coca-Cola bottling plant in Carepa in the Urabá banana zone. While placed with unions in Chicago and Los Angeles, respectively, both became active spokesmen for their unions and the lawsuits. Cardona worked closely with local solidarity organizations, including the Chicago Jobs with Justice Global Justice Committee, in support of the Coca-Cola boycott called by his union, Sinaltrainal, in 2003. Ruiz, in Los Angeles, collaborated with U.S. unions and a new project launched in support of Drummond workers and their lawsuit, drummondwatch.org.

Some leftist Colombian unionists are still dubious, however. They claim that the AFL-CIO has continued to favor "yellow" or company unions. Regarding the banana zone, they say, the AFL-CIO remained silent about the slaughter of hundreds of leftists and the transformation of Sintrainagro into an ally of the paramilitaries and the banana companies.

Some U.S. observers also remain skeptical as to what extent the AFL-CIO has repudiated its past. Critics have focused on a continued reliance on U.S. government funds, which they believe contradicts the organization's claim to political independence, and a lack of transparency, both in an unwillingness to open the archives on AIFLD's past activities and in the present. Revelations about the Solidarity Center's ongoing links with the anti-Chávez Venezuelan CTV and use of National Endowment for Democracy funding for rather unclear purposes in aiding that organization created a wave of criticism after the 2002 coup attempt in which the CTV appeared complicit.[110] Several West Coast labor federations, impelled by the indefatigable Fred Hirsch, have passed increasingly urgent resolutions asking the national leadership of the AFL-CIO to "clear the air" and openly repudiate AIFLD's past policies, and open the documentary record.[111] At its 2005 convention, the leadership once again quashed the resolution before it could reach the floor.[112]

The 2005 convention was also the occasion of a major split in the federation, as several important unions, including SEIU, UNITE-HERE, the UFCW, and the Teamsters left the AFL-CIO to form the Change to Win Coalition. As of mid-2006, Change to Win had little to say about international policy. Rather, new forms of solidarity and of reconceptualizing global labor relationships have emerged from individual unions, inside and outside the federation, and in independent labor organizations like the National Labor Committee, Jobs with Justice, the U.S. Labor Education in the Americas Project, and the International Labor Rights Fund.

Events surrounding the August 2006 CUT congress illustrate both the heavy weight of the past and, perhaps, tentative steps toward a different future for AFL-CIO relations with the Colombian union movement. Solidarity Center representatives in Colombia openly supported a move to restructure the confederation—a move that the left believed was a ploy to increase the weight of the right in the organization. "They're just up to their old tricks," one Colombian union leader told me disgustedly before the meetings, suggesting that the left might simply split from the confederation once again in order to maintain its independence.[113]

The message that the AFL-CIO brought to the congress, though, was very different from the one it had promoted in the 1960s. In 2006, the U.S. federation asked the Massachusetts Labor Council president, Jeff Crosby, who had just returned from leading a Witness for Peace labor delegation to Colombia, to represent it at the congress.

"In our view the issue is not simply one of offering support," Crosby told the assembled delegates, offering a radical, alternative vision of solidarity. "If you have come to help me," he quoted an indigenous leader's response to outside aid, "you are wasting your time. If you have come because your liberation is bound up with mine, let us work together." He noted the common struggles against privatization, deregulation, and free trade that unions in both countries were waging, lauded the activism of some of Colombia's more militant unions like the USO and the Coca-Cola workers, and insisted that the AFL-CIO would respect any internal decisions made by the CUT and continue to support the confederation regardless. "We also continue to offer our support for the struggle of the Colombian people to determine their own model of economic development and their use of their own resources. We hope to work with you, as equals, to develop a model of economic development and relations between our two countries that will benefit the workers and people in both our countries," he concluded.[114] This was clearly a different face of the new AFL-CIO.

The ITS in Colombia Today: The Case of the IUF and Coca-Cola

Some Colombian unionists remain suspicious of affiliation with the ITS, as well as with the Solidarity Center. The role of the IUF in the food sector can illustrate the complexities of the situation. Certain Colombian unions, in particular the purged Sintrainagro in the banana zone, have affiliated with the IUF, while more left-leaning unions in the sector have not. This situation has placed the IUF squarely in the center of some of the major fault lines in the Colombian labor movement.

In July 2003, the Colombian Food and Beverage Workers Union Sinaltrainal called for an international boycott of Coca-Cola products. The decision came two years after Sinaltrainal joined the USWA and the ILRF in a lawsuit against the company for the murders of union activists in its Colombian plants. "Cases that are thirteen years old have still not been cleared up," explained union president Javier Correa. "No one has been detained and the cases have not been resolved."[115] The impossibility of achieving justice through the legal system in Colombia pushed the union to move to the international level, joining a number of human rights cases filed in the United States using the Alien Tort Claims Act, which allows legal action in the United States for crimes committed outside of the country if redress is impossible where the incidents took place. The boycott took the campaign to yet another level, asking the public to become involved in insisting that Coke take moral responsibility for crimes committed in its Colombian facilities.

The charges stem from a wave of paramilitary killings in Coca-Cola bottling plants following the paramilitary takeover of Urabá. The union charges that the manager of Coke's plant in Carepa, Colombia, openly met with paramilitaries inside and outside the plant, announcing that "he had given an order to the paramilitaries to carry out the task of destroying the union." Shortly after this, threats against union leaders began; two months later, paramilitaries killed Sinaltrainal executive board member Isidro Segundo Gil at the plant's gate. That night, they burned the union's headquarters. Two days later, paramilitaries took over the plant and informed workers that they had to sign letters of resignation from their union or be killed. They took workers into the manager's office, where they signed the prepared letters.[116]

The IUF had played a key role in supporting the boycott called by Guatemalan Coca-Cola workers in the 1980s. In Colombia, however, the organization demurred. While it was willing to raise its voice to protest threats and murders at Colombia's Coca-Cola plants, the IUF quickly voted to "strongly condemn" the boycott.[117] Sinaltrainal's accusations against Coke

Figure 15. Salem State College students and community members display Stop Killer Coke posters as they demonstrate to get Coke products off campus, May 2004. The author is second from the right. Photo by Hope Benne. Reprinted by permission.

were "unsubstantiated and unverified," the IUF statement said. Without directly criticizing Sinaltrainal for its independence—the union has not affiliated to the IUF—the IUF noted that "Coca-Cola workers internationally and their unions, through the IUF," should be the ones to make a decision about the boycott. Further, unions "must take account of the global environment in which the company operates, a factor overlooked by supporters of the boycott." And finally, the statement notes that after Sinaltrainal was crushed, the bottler brought in a new union which did affiliate to the IUF. The new union, SICO, explained the IUF, was closely linked with the banana workers union Sintrainagro, also an IUF affiliate.[118]

While the boycott movement has caught on on college campuses and a number of important unions have signed on, other unions have been quite reluctant. The Canadian Labor Congress (CLC) issued a lengthy question-and-answer document explaining that although it strongly supported Sinaltrainal and the lawsuit, it would adhere to the IUF's position on the boycott itself because this was the stance of its shared affiliates, the Canadian Auto Workers, and the UFCW. One of the questions asked, "Why has the IUF statement regarding Sinaltrainal been posted on the CLC website? This article does not present a balanced view of the current situation in Colombia. It is our belief that it should be removed immediately, as it has the potential to undermine solidarity with Colombian workers." The slightly evasive reply was that "IUF affiliates represent thousands of Coke workers around the world, including two more Coke unions in Colombia whose members are also Colombian workers. In a situation where several unions in a particular country have conflicting positions on issues such as the calling of a boycott, it is not the practice of the CLC to intervene on behalf of one side." Interestingly, despite this disclaimer, the contested IUF statement did not appear on the CLC website when I consulted it.[119]

While some U.S. unions and locals have joined the boycott or expressed public support for Sinaltrainal, the AFL-CIO Solidarity Center has not.[120] When the Solidarity Center's assistant director, Stan Gacek, left the center for a position at Coke in 2006, some Colombian unionists professed little surprise.[121]

Conclusion

U.S. multinationals operating in a global context, U.S. policies forged in the cold war, and U.S. labor policies interacting with U.S. government policy, global labor issues, and internal U.S. union politics have played a major role in the Colombian labor movement and in the violence it has been subject to. At the same time, Colombian workers have, through their organizing and their actions, shaped the options and responses of U.S. multinationals, government, and unions. Developing effective strategies and visions for global solidarity is crucial to the survival of organized labor in both countries.

Colombian unions today are the most embattled on the planet. Union activists there feel, with some justification, that they are on the front lines of a global struggle against corporate power and a global economic order that relentlessly sacrifices human needs in search of profit. U.S. union activists are rightly worried about the loss of manufacturing jobs and the chipping away of hard-won union benefits in their own country. Yet to Colombian unionists it is abundantly clear, as Bill Fletcher suggested in the epigraph to this chapter, that "the international situation is about more than multinational corporations. Corporate globalization and military intervention are intertwined." For too long, the AFL-CIO has adhered to a narrow vision and joined U.S. corporations and the U.S. government in opposition to Colombian and other third world workers as they have led the fight for a more just global order.

Figure 16. Jeff Crosby, president of IUE-CWA Local 201 in Lynn, Massachusetts, represents the AFL-CIO at the summer 2006 CUT Congress in Bogotá. Photo by Cathy Crumbly. Reprinted by permission.

At a 2006 conference on Global Companies–Global Unions–Global Research–Global Campaigns, sponsored by the Cornell Institute for Labor Relations, the division between union leaders from the global North and those from the South was still painfully clear. From the North there was talk of coordinated bargaining, and even "the strong helping the weak."[122] From the South there was talk of creating a new form of global economic integration. José LaLuz from AFSCME concluded, "So far, I haven't heard anyone from the North acknowledge that what we need is a different kind of global economic system. The problem is, that the South in the North (i.e., immigrants) are not yet visible as leadership in the unions of the North. When the South in the North take the lead, then we will hear different voices coming from the North."

The connections between North and South are far deeper, and a more fundamental part of the U.S. economy, than most of the northern conference attendees acknowledged. Understanding the ways that regions like New England and Colombia are linked through labor histories and the role

that the United States and the AFL-CIO played in contributing to the violence facing Colombia's labor movement can help to explain, and perhaps
help transcend, the disjuncture in how many U.S. and Colombian unionists
imagine solidarity today.

JEFF CROSBY, JUNE 2006

*Jeff Crosby is president of IUE-CWA Local 201 in Lynn, Massachusetts,
which represents some 2,400 mostly manufacturing workers at General
Electric (GE), Ametek Aerospace, and the Lynn Waste Water Treatment
Plant. He has also been a leading activist in proposing new forms of labor
internationalism. He discussed the links between local and global union
work in an interview with the author in Lynn, Massachusetts, in June
2006.*

The [GE] plant includes primarily machinists and aircraft engine as-
semblers. They're all highly skilled. Along with that there are a bunch
of other things, we have a few nurses, we have firefighters—the plant is
like a small city. And so we have some secretaries, we also have craft
people, electricians, who maintain the building, plumbers, pipe fitters,
iron workers, all that stuff, so it's a very varied workforce. It's typically
male, probably 90 percent, and it's typically white, and typically in their
fifties. They haven't hired any significant number of people in the last
20 years, which means that the newer immigrant groups, Latinos and
Asians, have only a small representation in our workforce. But there is an
African American population. The union always fought against discrimination in hiring back through the UE days, the thirties, so I have, for
example, a third generation African American GE worker. It's been a kind
of a family place, so it's not unusual that you have second and third
generation workers.

When I first punched in, in 1979, we had 8700 members at GE. Now
even including Ametek and the Water Treatment Plant we have about
2400. Some of it's just increased productivity, and doing more with fewer
people. Some of it is they moved out most of the power generation work
to other places, in the mid 80s. But a lot of it is outsourcing, and people
are desperately aware of that. I mean they physically see work going out
of their buildings. You're working on a job and the next day it's in South
Korea, or Russia, or China, or well, Sweden, or Italy.

It's the work going overseas that probably is the hardest for people to swallow, 'cause they look at it, understandably, as "we pay taxes to the government, the government takes that money, gives it to GE, and we are paying GE to transfer our jobs. So we are actually paying for our own destruction."

For our manufacturing workers now, the world is a much smaller place than it used to be. Practically speaking, it makes a lot more sense now to talk about an internationalist labor movement. There really isn't any argument anymore that you can deal effectively with a multinational corporation only from one country. So that issues about trade, or international solidarity, are much more widely acceptable as legitimate discussion for even your average member who may not be active in the union.

Parts from Ametek got moved to Mexico, where GE was building a big aircraft engine center. General Electric actually came to Ametek Aerospace management and said, "you will move these parts to Mexico. Or you will do no more business with GE." And their leverage was they require their vendors to reduce costs, sort of like Wal-Mart, you know, in their industry. If you don't reduce costs, you're out of business. And you can't reduce costs in the way that they want you to if you're paying somebody 26 dollars an hour when you can pay, to do the same work in Mexico, four dollars a day. They said, "we'll support you, we'll explain to you how you do it, but people in Mexico make less money, even their engineers, and the unions there are friendly"—as opposed to us—"and the health and safety regulations are more reasonable."

So then we would talk about internationalism, or the world economy, or "hey maybe we have to link up with Mexican workers," or "it's really not a great system if they can do what we do for 4 dollars a day, then obviously we have a problem with maintaining our livelihood." The kind of things that we would talk about in the '80s, and it would fall on deaf ears, are now reaching much more fertile ground.

It seems to me that the corporations got to a certain point and they said, (a) we need to have a more ruthless kind of extension of the market into all corners of the economy to make the kind of profits that we want to make, and (b) there's no Soviet Union anymore, so whatever you thought of that, good, bad, ugly, or indifferent, at least it's not there anymore, therefore we can extend a fairly brutal form of the market into every corner of the earth. So they had a need and they had an opportunity, and they had a weakened opposition domestically AND internationally, and they took advantage of it.

Depending on what element of the trade union movement you're speaking to, you start with the aspect of neoliberalism that they know about: privatization, deregulation, and free trade. The school employees in Lynn are concerned about privatization. You know, airline workers are getting killed by deregulation. My people understand free trade pretty well. The only people that understand that it's a systémic thing, a coherent set of policies, are people like [the economist and former World Bank official Joseph] Stiglitz and people that work for the World Bank. And the Colombians! Actually the trade union movement in the whole rest of the world gets it, you know, we're a little bit behind.

Neoliberalism also has an ideological component, which is really critical. In this country, the dominant view is that the market can solve everything. So if you deregulate the airlines, and let the market play itself out, you'll get a more efficient airlines, prices will go down, and oh by the way, workers aren't going to make any money, but hey. And same thing with free trade, same thing with privatization. So the theory is that economically, that the market can make everything rational, that an unregulated market is the greatest form of efficiency, somehow everybody will benefit somewhere sometime by having cheap stuff. I think neoliberalism has an effect on everybody's life right now, not just their jobs but the schools, everything.

So the question facing the trade union movement is, what kind of internationalism are we going to build? The current hegemony of neoliberalism has made the old kind of national chauvinism, chauvinist policy, of supporting U.S. foreign policy in order to maintain our privileged position, obsolete. My view is that that's not going to work any more. It may have worked in the short term for some people, in the United States, but it never worked for everybody, particularly African-Americans. There were always people that were excluded. And that's not AFL-CIO policy any more.

The fact that U.S. unions are reaching out to trade union movements around the world to put joint pressure on multinational corporations is a big advance. It's a lot different than using whatever energies and funds we have to divide the trade union movements in other countries in order that our favored players rise to the top whether or not they're doing anything for workers in their own countries. So that in and of itself is a huge advance. It's a good thing, and that's pretty much the dominant thinking right now. By U.S. standards that's a breakthrough of immense proportions.

How to make that effective, beyond sort of "hey we should really work together," that's really difficult. But there's work going on to find those ways. What we have not addressed as a group, as a whole, at least, in the trade union movement, is building an internationalism that is what I would call social justice internationalism. And you hear this from trade unions from the global south quite a bit. I heard this back into the '90s, from a Brazilian friend of mine who was at the Harvard trade union program. One of the things he said is that trade unions like the CUT in Brazil, and COSATU in South Africa, are saying, "yeah, that's really good, let's bargain together. But by the way, your soldiers are all over the world, they're causing war, you're supporting apartheid, we need more than simply a pragmatic, narrow internationalism."

But I'll just give you an example. I escorted a Colombian trade unionist who's from a teachers union to visit teachers union leaders here in the United States. So, I would take her to meet the NEA and the AFT. And the NEA and the AFT people would say things like, "well how do you negotiate for in-service trainings?" And the woman from Colombia would respectfully respond, and then she would say, "um, by the way, a lot of us are getting killed. What does your union think about Plan Colombia?" And, you know, it was like ships in the night.

So to go to a trade union movement like the CUT in Colombia, or the teachers unions, who suffer at least half the fatalities and the murders by the death squads in Colombia, and say, "hey we're internationalists too, let's talk about in-service training," somewhat misses the point.

And I heard this also at the Global Unions conference, in February of this year, where Secretary Treasurer Trumka gave a fairly explicit, and what was by U.S. standards a pretty radical speech about we have to not only get outside the neoliberal box, the set of policies that I mentioned before. So he said not only do we have to get outside the neoliberal policy box, we have to destroy it. And he gave a pretty clear picture of what those policies are and how they hurt us.

Then we got to Berta Luján, who had been a staff person of the FAT, one of the independent trade union federations in Mexico, who was now working for the PRD candidate, the mayor of Mexico City, who's running for president, and she said "that's not enough. We need to join with the unions of the global south that are trying to seek an alternative model of integration." Which is actually a better way of saying things than "fighting globalization" because that doesn't sound like you're a Neanderthal. We need to help find alternative models of integration. She said, "there's all those alternatives out there, we've got to be a part of that, we all of us have to join that conversation and help create alternative methods of integration. And we'll fall short if we don't do that."

And the South African spokesperson was even more extreme, more forthright. He comes out of the South African experience where the COSATU was allied with the communist party, and he said, "we need to talk about socialism." So anyway, that's the kind of conversation we need to have. And that's the thing we need to change in the U.S. trade union movement, so when they talk about international solidarity, it will not be seen as just self-serving. And it will deal with the actual political complexities, the actual realities, the actual oppression, that we're facing. From those three legs of the neoliberal policy that we're trying to deal with.

And if we do that, that doesn't just change the trade union movement. That changes the country. And you have a very different debate, and you shine a little light onto what has been an extremely narrow set of policy discussions in the United States.

Part of the importance of Colombia, or the opportunity to do work around Colombia, is created by the Solidarity Center which I think has an exceptionally good program around building solidarity with Colombia. They brought Colombian trade unionists who needed respite from death threats to the United States for a year. It's very different from what the AFL-CIO did in the past, because these people were not vetted for their politics. This wasn't "bring people here, train them so they can go back and destroy the left in their own country." That wouldn't have been particularly new. These were people from all different political persuasions, from all different sectors of the trade movement in Colombia (a) who needed protection, and (b) who needed protection from U.S. policy.

The AFL-CIO was very, very clear that part of this is an effort to undermine, to defeat U.S. aid to Plan Colombia. And the AFL took a position against U.S. military aid to Colombia. It was a solidarity based on human rights, at least.

Part of the goal of the delegations I've participated in is to bring people back to educate other folks and to become organizers, and to build solidarity with the Colombian trade union movement. And then in my view, it's partly to help build the anti-neoliberal current in the trade union movement here. Colombian economist Hector Mondragón said to us that just as fascism came to South America on the jack boots of the Chilean coup in 1973, so did neoliberalism, the final integration of South America into the U.S. corporate economy, come to South America carried by Blackhawk helicopters as part of Plan Colombia.

So Plan Colombia is armed globalization, it's just the continuation of politics by other means. If people can understand that, then that will contribute to the current of thinking in the trade union movement that our enemy isn't just a specific violation of human rights policy over there, but our enemy is neoliberalism. And neoliberalism is the specific form of capitalism that we're dealing with right now, and that's what we have to change. So it has several different aspects for me: to educate people, to encourage them to become activists around Colombia solidarity when they come back, and to contribute to a broader kind of understanding of neoliberalism and what we're up against to survive as a trade union movement in the United States.

Today, you look around in the global south, where to me most of the creative thinking is going on, and you see a whole variety of experiments, sort of anti-neoliberal electoral victories, ranging from [Brazilian president Luiz Inácio] Lula [da Silva] to [Venezuelan president Hugo] Chávez and a whole bunch of things in between. You could use old terms, which is all we've got, unfortunately, because of our poverty of theory . . . but you could say there are moderate alternatives, there are social democratic alternatives, there are more socialist, more left socialist alternatives like Chávez, Evo Morales in Bolivia, and I think what we need to do is say, in response to neoliberalism, we need to join that search for alternatives. You need to join the search of other workers and trade unions in the world for an alternative. And so where that will go, I don't know, but I know it's not what we've got now, and I know it's radically different. And we'll have to see and we'll have to put our heads to work [to] help create it.

In the short run you're just fighting to survive, fighting one attack after another. But you can't sustain that without an alternative strategy or you're just a bunch of dinosaurs trying to rebuild the rust belt that nobody thinks will ever happen again. And I think that's the position we're really in in the labor movement. We're seen as relics from a bygone era, even by our friends! Even by Democratic Party politicians, for example, who might support us. But they do it out of the kindness of their hearts, "yeah, it's really too bad, it's not their fault they're dinosaurs, and so we should give them some benefits while they look for another job."

There is a crying need for a political education program and a change in the framework for U.S. trade union movements for very practical, immediate reasons. Not just because it's a nice thing to do or it's a good idea, both of which are true and would be sufficient in themselves. But in the trade union movement if you're lucky, things that are pragmatically in your interest are also morally right. And that's why I like the trade union movement.

MINING THE CONNECTIONS
Where Does Your Coal Come From?

I n August 2001 armed security guards and police dragged residents of the village of Tabaco from their homes as bulldozers followed and razed them. The Cerrejón Zona Norte mine in Colombia's northern Guajira province had been pressuring residents for months to leave Tabaco to make room for expansion of the mine. Some residents gave in and sold their homes to the mine, but others organized themselves into the Committee for the Relocation of Tabaco and demanded that the community as a whole be granted land to reconstruct their collective livelihoods. The company refused. The following spring, two representatives of Tabaco and other displaced communities came to the United States to speak at the shareholders meeting of Exxon, half-owner of the mine, and in Salem, Massachusetts, where the local power station burns thousands of tons of coal from that mine every year.

In March of the same year, paramilitary forces boarded a company bus taking workers home from their shift at the La Loma mine in the neighboring Colombian province of Cesar and pulled off the union's president and vice president. Valmore Locarno Rodríguez, the president, was killed in front of his coworkers; the vice president, Víctor Hugo Orcasita, was taken away, his tortured body found several days later. Union officials had been requesting permission to stay overnight inside the mine facility for weeks, but the company refused. Soon after, paramilitary forces visited the home of the union's secretary treasurer, Francisco Ruiz. When they realized he was not there, they killed his younger brother. Francisco managed to gain a spot in the AFL-CIO Solidarity Center's protection program and fled to the United States, where he was later granted political asylum.

Colombian Coal in a Global Context

Both of these events are related to globalization in myriad interlocking ways. Frequently, discussions of globalization focus on the very visible topic of manufacturing, where labels clearly tell you whether a product was "made in the USA" or not. But energy, while less visible, is another crucial area in which globalization shapes lives, in the United States and abroad. The story of the runaway coal mines fits right into a pattern of globalization in which governments in the first world and the third have facilitated the mobility of capital, lending agencies have imposed neoliberal policies that are enforced at gunpoint, and workers in both worlds have struggled to achieve decent lives.

Although Colombia is better known for its coffee exports, its major export is actually oil, followed by coal, with coffee now trailing in third place. The Cerrejón Zona Norte mine, the largest open-pit coal mine in the world, began as a joint venture between Exxon, a U.S. corporation, and the Colombian government in 1982. The privately owned La Loma mine was a project of the U.S.-based Drummond company, begun in 1985. In the 1990s, both mines entered full production, with rapidly rising exports to the United States.

There were several reasons that U.S. mining companies wanted to shift their production to Colombia and that U.S. power plants, the main consumers of coal in the United States, wanted to import Colombian coal. It was cheaper to produce coal in Colombia, where wages were low and regulation lax. In the United States, although mining continues to be dangerous work, the epic struggles of the United Mineworkers in the first half of the twentieth century brought living wages and decent conditions to mining. Like manufacturers, mining companies have looked abroad—with ample support from the U.S. government—for ways to increase their profits. Like the southern cities that wooed northern textile companies, Colombia offered, in addition to low wages, low taxes, subsidized infrastructure, and minimal regulation.

Coal purchasers had additional reasons for turning to imported coal in the 1990s. The Clean Air Act mandated lower emissions from U.S. power plants, and Colombian coal was high quality: low sulfur and low ash—clean-burning coal. According to the U.S. Department of Energy, coal imports "increased dramatically" at the end of the 1990s because of "the heightened

demand for low-sulfur coal to meet the stricter sulfur emission requirements of Phase II of the Clean Air Act Amendments of 1990." Colombia was
the major source of imported coal (61 percent of the 12.5 million short tons
imported in 2000), and much of it went to Alabama utilities, to replace the
coal formerly produced by Drummond's Alabama mines.[1] Coal-fired power
plants in New England, in particular the Salem Harbor and Brayton Point
plants in Massachusetts, also became major importers of Colombian coal.
As in so many other cases in U.S. history, movements for social change may
have had clearly defined goals, but they occurred in a global context that
meant that they sometimes brought unintended results.

Another piece of the globalization puzzle lies in the actions of international financial institutions and the U.S. government. Over the course of
the 1990s, the International Monetary Fund entered into a series of agreements with Colombia, reinforced by structural adjustment loans, to improve the country's investment climate. What is best for foreign investors—
low taxes, privatization, deregulation, and low wages—is not, of course,
always what is best for the population. Contrary to the declarations of pun-
dits who associate free markets with free societies, neoliberal economic
policies in Latin America have often been enforced by the most dictatorial
and violent of governments, beginning with Pinochet's Chile in the 1970s.

Colombia has been no exception to this rule. Neoliberal economic policies, backed up by structural adjustment loans, were also supported by huge
influxes of U.S. military aid in the 1990s, turning Colombia into the largest
recipient of such aid in the Americas, and the third largest in the world. Human rights organizations like Amnesty International and Americas Watch
have consistently noted the links between the U.S.-funded Colombian army
and the paramilitaries, Americas Watch going so far as to call the paramilitaries the "Sixth Division" of the Colombian army. These armed actors have
played a key role in repressing popular movements that have protested the
economic model being imposed on the country.

As was the case in manufacturing, the U.S. government also contributed
directly to the ability of mining companies to move abroad. The construction of the Cerrejón mine, for example, relied heavily on U.S. government
funding. In February 1982, the Export-Import Bank approved a $12.3 mil-
lion loan to a Spanish company to purchase U.S. earth-moving equipment
for Colombian mining; Canada's Export Development Bank followed with
a $160 million line of credit to the Colombian government to purchase

Figure 17. A bird's-eye view of the Cerrejón mine. Photo by Aviva Chomsky.

Canadian equipment, and the Export-Import Bank countered with another $375 million in August.[2] In the end the Export-Import Bank lent $1.5 billion to the Colombian government, paying for its entire share in the project.[3]

U.S. military aid to Colombia has also contributed directly to the welfare of U.S. companies there, as described in chapter 6. The U.S.-supplied Colombian army guards the Cerrejón Zona Norte mine from a base built nearby for that precise purpose.[4] The consortium that took over the state's portion of the mine under an IMF loan agreement in 2001 (privatization of the mine was one of the conditions for a $2.7 billion loan) and purchased Exxon's portion in 2002 openly acknowledged maintaining a contract for "logistical support" with the Colombian army.[5]

U.S. coal imports increased dramatically and steadily between 1998 and 2004, from 3.5 million short tons to 16.6 million short tons. More than half of that coal came from Colombia every year.[6] Colombian coal produced by foreign companies went all over the world. In the first half of 2004, El Cerrejón exported almost 10 million tons. The largest single recipient was the Netherlands, which received 2.5 million tons; the United States followed with close to 1 million. Drummond, in the same period, exported 8.5 million tons, with over 3 million going to the continental United States and another 500,000 to Puerto Rico.[7]

Chapter 6 described the trends of the 1980s and 1990s that led U.S. labor unions to develop a more internationalist perspective and become increasingly critical of U.S. support for repressive governments in the third world. In the 1980s, when U.S. workers, their unions, and their supporters in Congress addressed the development of coal mining in Colombia, they voiced their concerns primarily in terms of protecting their own jobs.[8] By the 1990s, a more global perspective of the race to the bottom and the need for international solidarity became more characteristic of the U.S. labor movement. The United Mineworkers of America (UMWA) and the International Federation of Chemical, Energy, Mine and General Workers' Unions (ICEM) began to develop active programs in support of Colombian coal miners. Sometimes these consisted of union-to-union coordination and help with collective bargaining; occasionally they went beyond these to confront the larger questions of the global economic order.

The People behind the Coal: Cerrejón

Coal mining in the Guajira peninsula severely disrupted the livelihoods of the Wayuu people, an indigenous group of approximately 120,000 that have lived since before the Spanish conquest in the northern tip of South America, including the Guajira peninsula. Over the course of the centuries, the Wayuu territory has shrunk as they have been pushed out of the more fertile southern Guajira lands into the dry deserts of the northern Guajira. Despite centuries-long contact that included involvement in the smuggling trade and continued encroachment on their ancestral lands, the Wayuu remained an ethnically, culturally, and linguistically distinct people—the largest indigenous group in Colombia.

The Wayuu adopted horses and cattle from the Spanish and developed a seminomadic lifestyle that, in conjunction with the Spanish weapons they acquired and the desertlike character of the northern part of the peninsula, allowed them to remain substantially unconquered into the late twentieth century. They were not isolated: involvement in trade and smuggling, also a tradition since colonial times, meant that in the 1980s traditional weavings and handmade *rancherías*—temporary dwellings of wattle and daub—coexisted with pickup trucks and wage labor on Venezuelan farms. Some Wayuu lived in fishing villages along the coast and farming villages in the southern part of the peninsula. The Wayuu also have a tradition of working as middlemen in lucrative smuggling operations, ranging from black market consumer goods to marijuana in the late twentieth century.[9]

The southern portion of the Guajira peninsula is more fertile and has been home to both small farming communities, many of them Afro-Colombian, and large ranchers. Oral histories of the village of Tabaco, for example, place its founding in the 1790s, when enslaved Africans overwhelmed their captors at sea and escaped to the Guajira, following the river inland until they found land they could farm. Residents of Tabaco, and numerous other small settlements, farmed small plots of coffee, maintained kitchen gardens with fruit trees, and relied on hunting and work on neighboring ranches prior to the arrival of the mine.

The contract of association establishing a partnership between the Colombian government's Carbocol (Carbones de Colombia) and Intercor (International Colombia Resource Corporation), a fully owned subsidiary of Exxon, was signed in 1977 and consisted of three phases: exploration (1977–80), construction (1980–86), and production (1986–2009).[10] The project included the mine, a 150 km (ninety-five-mile) railroad from the mining area in the lower Guajira peninsula to the coast, and a port. Each of these operations is huge in scale. The mine itself was to occupy 38,000 hectares (94,000 acres); the 150 km railroad was designed for three locomotives, each pulling one hundred cars carrying one hundred tons of coal each, along with a twelve-meter-wide support road running parallel to the railroad at an elevation of four meters, and Puerto Bolívar, on the western shore of the entrance to Bahía Portete, equipped to receive ships of 300 meters by 45 meters—the largest port in the country.[11]

An anthropologist described the state of the mine in 1983:

The road has been completed since 1981, and the construction of the port, warehouses, workers' camps, hospital, water treatment facilities, etc., is considerably advanced. Less construction is visible at the mine area, where the task of clearing the land of vegetation for the mine and mine infrastructure is immense—much greater than that required for the port. Temporary workers' camps have been erected and more are being built to accommodate the projected peak workforce during the construction phase of about 7,000 (although more recent estimates placed the eventual construction work force at 10,000). Once production begins in 1985–1986, the permanent workforce of about 3,000 workers will be housed in several towns located along the southern part of the mine-port road. The infrastructures of these towns will be expanded to accommodate the influx of workers.[12]

The mine itself is in the southern part of the peninsula and thus did not directly affect most of the Wayuu. The road and railroad, however, cut through the heartland of Wayuu territory. The pastoral nomadic Wayuu lacked legal title to their ancestral lands; thus, when the potential for profit arose in those lands, the government declared them to be *baldíos*, or untitled land, and in 1981 granted Carbocol twenty-nine thousand hectares in four *reservas* (areas claimed by the government for economic development purposes) that it had requested for the railroad, road, port, and construction materials. Some two hundred Wayuu families were in fact offered compensation for their *ranchos* that were confiscated. The compensation was minimal (much smaller than that offered to ranchers in the southern part of the peninsula); it was also culturally inappropriate because the lands taken were in fact part of a much larger system of migration and kinship, not just the location of specific residences.[13]

Along the northern coast, fishing in the Bahía de Portete was halted as the harbor was dredged and turned over to the shipping of coal. Media Luna, a Wayuu community of approximately 750 on the southern end of the bay, was the first permanent community to be displaced by the mine. After negotiations with Intercor in 1982 (punctuated by "angry discussions and physical threats"), residents agreed to move their homes, their farms, and their cemetery to a nearby location to allow for the construction of the port. Despite a constant struggle with the pollution caused by the construction, when the company demanded that they move again a few years later, seven families (forty-two people) refused. The company walled off and locked the area and surrounded it with armed guards. Despite constant harassment, including lack of water, refusal of building permits, and blacklisting of community members from employment, residents have remained there, living in conditions described in 2001 as "like a Nazi concentration camp."[14]

In 1982 the Wayuu formed Yanama—a Wayuu word meaning "collective work"—an organization to defend their rights in the face of the incursions on their lands. Yanama was successful in preventing Carbocol from leveling the Cerro de la Teta, though the sacred mountain remains inside the company's reserva. Some Wayuu also tried, mostly unsuccessfully, to appeal to government agencies charged with the defense of indigenous rights. The major strategy was *invasión*, or the construction of residences directly along the railroad strip designed to establish a presence and prevent construction. In the summer of 1983, over one thousand ranchos had been built, effectively halting railroad construction. Yanama also worked to have Wayuu territory declared a *resguardo*, or indigenous reservation.[15]

In 1996, a Wayuu representative described the impact of the mine on his people at a meeting in Wisconsin: "The construction of the mine had a devastating effect on the lives of approximately 90 Wayuu apushis (matrilineal kinship groupings) who saw their houses, corrals, cleared ground and cemeteries flattened for the construction of a road from El Cerrejón to the new port of Puerto Bolívar, with no respect for indigenous rights. The excavation of the open pit has also caused the adjoining rivers and streams to dry up, along with people's drinking wells."[16]

A 2001 report documented the depressingly predictable long-term effect of the mine on the indigenous Wayuu communities: the proliferation of alcoholism and prostitution, the loss of sacred spaces, a rise in death rates due to poisoning and contamination from the mine and its wastes, loss of cultural integrity and identity, and increasing poverty.[17]

Early in the twenty-first century a new factor entered the picture in the Guajira: paramilitary forces, which until then had been absent from the remote peninsula. The equation was more than coincidental. Throughout Colombia, where there was profit to be made, the paramilitaries established a presence. In the Guajira, they came first in the fall of 2003 to Bahía Portete, a Wayuu community near the company's port. "They began to arrive in civilian dress, in groups of three or four," recounted a villager. "We never imagined that they were paramilitaries. But a few months later, they began to identify themselves. Especially at night, they would put on their uniforms and say that they were paramilitaries." (For the source of this and the quotations in the following paragraph, see Débora Barros Fince's testimony at the end of this chapter.)

By the spring of 2004, rumors were circulating that the paramilitaries wanted to eliminate the community and take over the port. "People were getting nervous because they were saying that they were going to kill people, that they were going to finish up this job, because it wasn't much, they could do it, there were only two families, they could kill them, and the land would be freed up." On April 18, 2004, 150 men in army uniforms arrived at the village and began a killing spree, quickly turning the task over to the thirty newcomers whom villagers now clearly identified as paramilitaries. When the carnage was over, twelve people were dead and thirty missing. "We found hair, we found arms," explained a survivor, who fled the village but returned days after to search for survivors. The village was abandoned, with most of its three hundred inhabitants fleeing to Maracaibo, Venezuela.

Local Peasants and the Cerrejón Mine

Indigenous people were not the only ones displaced by the mine and its infrastructure. By the 1990s, Yanama had formed links with local farming communities that were primarily Afro-Colombian and mestizo in population. They are not pastoralists, but rely on subsistence farming and wage labor on the surrounding farms and ranches, many of which have slowly been taken over by the mine in the past decade.[18]

As mining expanded throughout the 1990s, pollution from the mine, and then the mine itself, began to encroach on surrounding villages. In 1992 the lawyer Armando Pérez Araújo, representing the towns of Caracolí and El Espinal, brought suit against the Colombian Ministry of Health because the contamination of coal and other dust and the constant noise of the machinery were prejudicial to the health of the residents. He argued that in February 1991 the Ministry had declared a 1,000-meter strip of land to be "uninhabitable," and a 4,500-meter area "dangerous" because of the contamination, but had not taken any action to protect the residents, who included both Wayuu Indians and peasant farmers.[19] Yanama argued that between 1984 and 1991 the health of the community had deteriorated significantly and that twenty-four deaths (out of a combined population of about 350) had been caused by exposure to toxins from the mine. After several appeals, the court ruled in favor of Yanama and ordered the company to guarantee the protection of the inhabitants of these towns. However, with the collaboration of the head of the Office of Indigenous Affairs of Uribia, the company's "solution" was to remove people from their homes to a nearby indigenous reservation.[20]

Two British solidarity activists who visited the region in October 2000 to investigate conditions in the villages near the mine discovered that the towns that had protested the mine's effects in 1992 no longer existed. Manantial and Caracolí had been dispersed by violence; at Viejo Oreganal residents were pressured to sell their land as the companies that were operating the mine purchased surrounding pasture and destroyed the church, school, and community center. At Espinal, police had ordered residents to relocate without warning to a new site; those who refused were forcibly removed. The pattern seemed consistent: first, blasting, dust, and contamination made life unpleasant, then pasture land disappeared, harassment of residents followed, and finally, if residents refused to leave, forcible eviction destroyed the community.[21] Beginning in 1997 and culminating in 2001, the community of Tabaco suffered the same fate.

In May 2001 Armando Pérez Araújo, representing Tabaco, attended a meeting in London as one of several representatives of Yanama. The declaration that emerged from the meeting, signed by delegates from twenty-three countries, read in part:

> We have seen our peoples suffering for many years from mining in all stages and forms, and from exploration to development through to abandonment. Industrial mining has caused grievous pain and irreparable destruction to our culture, our identities and our very lives. Our traditional lands have been taken, and the wealth seized, without our consent or benefit.
>
> Invariably mining imposed upon our communities has poisoned our waters, destroyed our livelihoods and our food sources, disrupted our social relationships, created sickness and injury in our families. Often our communities have been divided by "imported" civil conflicts.[22]

Residents testified that "their houses are cracking up because of blasting from the mine and that their main water source is polluted with coal dust. Pasture land is being lost as mining operations come closer. Many villagers have already left."[23] Tabaco residents were particularly distressed at the apparent collusion between the company, the government, and the Catholic Church. The priest, Marcelo Graziosi, agreed to sell the church—which had been built by the community—for 38 million pesos ($16,550). Tabaco residents appealed to the priest in Hatonuevo and the bishop, but in vain. The government closed the school (though a volunteer teacher continued to give classes there) and the health center.

In June 2001 five people—two indigenous journalists; the president of Tabaco's Community Council, José Julio Pérez; a community resident; and a volunteer teacher, Mario Alberto Pérez—were accosted by company police while attempting to document company measures directed toward the destruction of the community. The security agents confiscated the film, stating that it must be for the guerrillas, and beat and arrested the five.[24]

On August 9, 2001, private and public police arrived with bulldozers to carry out the destruction of the community. Several video photographers

Figure 18. José Julio Pérez, a leader from the displaced community of Tabaco, at the Salem power plant. Salem received two 40,000-ton shipments of coal from the Cerrejón mine in August 2001, the month that the mine razed his village. *Salem Gazette*—John Harvey. Reprinted by permission.

documented the destruction and its aftermath. Now Tabaco's smaller neighbor, Tamaquitos, fears that the same fate awaits it.

The experiences of the Wayuu of the northern Guajira peninsula and the Afro-Colombian communities of the southern part of the peninsula share both old and new historical elements. For five hundred years economic development in Latin America in the form of mining has displaced and uprooted indigenous communities. Until the middle of the twentieth century mining has also relied on systems of forced labor that have also uprooted and destroyed traditional societies outside of the mining areas in Africa and Latin America. Mining enterprises resorted to forced labor in the colonial period because as long as a subsistence alternative flourished, there was little incentive for peasants to enter the mines. Subsistence economies inside the mining areas were destroyed to make room for the mines, and subsistence economies outside the mining areas were destroyed to bring workers to the mines.

At the end of the twentieth century, however, forced labor in the mines had all but vanished. The destruction of traditional societies has progressed to a point where Colombia, like the rest of Latin America, now has a surplus of landless, available workers and suffers from a high rate of unemployment

—a phenomenon unknown in the colonial period. Still, the Cerrejón mine has spurred migration, as villages have been destroyed, possibilities of work in agriculture, hunting, and fishing have been diminished, and new jobs in the mine have been created that seek educated and skilled workers. With little infrastructure, few schools, and an illiteracy rate of 65 percent, the Guajira peninsula produced few workers prepared to work in the offices or with the heavy machinery of a late twentieth-century capital-intensive strip mine.

International Labor Solidarity at El Cerrejón

By the beginning of the twenty-first century the Cerrejón Zona Norte mining complex employed between 4,500 and 6,500 workers.[25] Reports suggest that during the construction phase, most of the workforce at Cerrejón Zona Norte was drawn from the Wayuu communities, but that once production began they were replaced by nonindigenous Colombians. Armando Valbuena Gouriyu, a Wayuu who worked for the mine, stated that five thousand Wayuu were employed in the construction phase, only to be fired when the mine went into operation. Valbuena himself was trained as a technician and worked in the mine from 1983 until 1988, when he and seven other workers representing a workers organization were fired in the midst of union contract negotiations with the management.[26]

Workers at El Cerrejón were represented starting in 1983 by Sintercor, originally a company union created by Exxon but successfully severed from company control in 1985.[27] (In 1997, Sintercor changed its name to Sintracarbón and its purview from representing only workers at Intercor to seeking to affiliate others in the coal industry.)[28] During the first two rounds of contract negotiations, in 1986 and 1988, the Colombian army entered the mine to enforce union acceptance of contracts that provided minimal protections: in 1988 the wage was $0.95 an hour, and workers did not have the right to stop work when unsafe conditions arose in the mine. Between 1983 and 1994, fourteen workers were killed in mining accidents there.[29]

It was in late 1988 that the United Mine Workers of America began its relationship with Sintercor. A delegation from Illinois District 12 visited El Cerrejón and promised to support the union there during the 1990 negotiations round. According to the UMWA Special Projects Coordinator Ken Zinn, "The union leadership understood that the fate of the Colombian mine workers and UMWA were intertwined. UMWA President Richard Trumka explained, 'Our goal is to strengthen unions in low-wage countries so they are strong enough to fight for decent wages and working conditions to raise their standard of living up to our level. If we don't, the multinational corporations will attempt to lower our standards to the lowest international common denominator.' "[30]

In the spring of 1990, negotiations between Carbocol/Intercor and Sintercor broke down.[31] The key issues in dispute in the negotiations this time were wages and hours—Intercor wanted to reduce work shifts from twelve to eight hours—and a company plan to dismantle company-owned housing and food facilities. Workers engaged in a slowdown as negotiations dragged on, though the company had already been stockpiling coal since November 1989 in anticipation.[32]

On April 25, after a workers' assembly authorized the strike (in compliance with Colombian labor legislation), the workers walked out. (They agreed to allow nonunion workers to continue to load coal for shipment at Puerto Bolívar, for safety reasons.) The company promptly cut off the negotiations, claiming that the strike was "unreasonable."[33]

The day before the strike began, however, the UMWA brought Sintercor's vice president Walter Castillo to the United States to meet with the union's two Illinois locals, Exxon shareholders in Houston, and even CEO Lawrence Rawl, as well as the UMWA's international executive board in Washington, DC. The UMWA agreed to contribute substantially to Sintercor's strike fund, to meet with some of Exxon's principal shareholders to discuss the company's labor rights violations in Colombia, and to work with Denmark's labor federation to threaten a Danish boycott of Colombian coal.[34]

After the workers had been on strike for eighteen days, Colombian President Virgilio Barco invoked an obscure provision of Colombia's Constitution and asked the Supreme Court to empower him to declare the strike illegal because it was "potentially damaging" to the country's economy. (This was only the third time that this provision had been invoked in Colombia's history.)[35] He then authorized the Colombian army to occupy the mine. In May 1990 eight hundred armed soldiers in armored tanks forced the workers to return to work.[36] Subsequently, a military presence during the biannual contract negotiations became the norm.[37] The ICEM launched an international campaign to protest the use of the military in breaking the strike and to ensure a presence in supervising subsequent contract negotiations.[38]

The 1990 experience also led the UMWA to further commit to this internationalist collaboration: "The Colombian military response to the miners' strike brought the UMWA to the realization that simply waiting until a strike occurred was not effective solidarity work." Between 1990 and 1994 the UMWA pursued a multilayered international strategy that included working with European, Australian, and Latin American mining unions and the Miners International Federation to pressure the Colombian government as well as the company, collaborating with human rights and Colombia solidarity organizations, bringing U.S. congressional pressure on Colombia, and bringing a UMWA presence to the 1992 Cerrejón negotiations. According to the UMWA, its campaign was a significant factor in Sintercor's achieving contract victories at El Cerrejón in 1992 and 1994.[39] When union leaders were confronted with death threats by paramilitaries during a new round of contract negotiations in late 2004, ICEM officials wrote in strong terms to the CEOs of the three companies, "We feel that Carbones del Cerrejón as a company has a strong moral responsibility as a matter of urgency . . . to publicly condemn such intimidation tactics." When similar threats against union leaders accompanied the 2006 negotiating round, the Cerrejón company did just that. In a December 2006 press release the company stated unequivocally that it "emphatically condemns and rejects this type of threat against its workers, unionised at Sintracarbón, and reiterates its commitment and defence of the right of free association, to the full exercise of democratic freedoms and to the respect of Human Rights."[40]

The Story of La Loma Mine

Paramilitary activity in Cesar province commenced "aggressive operations" in the mid-1990s, as Drummond's mining activities there began in earnest. As in Urabá, the paramilitaries' stated target was the FARC, which had been active in the area. But, as always, their victims were mainly suspected FARC sympathizers—meaning, frequently, large portions of the peasant population and unionized workers. In October 1996 paramilitaries attacked the village of Media Luna, outside of Valledupar, killing six and abducting seven. (Residents later found the body of one of the seven, castrated, eyes gouged, and fingernails pulled out.) While no specific motive was named, this was part of what Amnesty International called a "wave of internal displacement" following the "paramilitary offensive" in the province.[41] By 2000, the paramilitaries dominated the region and acted with relative impunity against workers and peasants—and, according to many, with tacit support of the Drummond company.[42]

Drummond's 215-mile rail line from the mine to its private Puerto Drummond has been repeatedly bombed by the FARC since it began operations in the mid-1990s, including five times in 2000–2001. The FARC also reportedly levied a tax on Drummond's coal production, although Drummond adamantly denied this, insisting that the company would close down operations before agreeing to pay.[43] After an April 2000 attack, the company began to circulate flyers reading "The multinational Drummond is a source of income and growth for our city, and for that reason it has become part of our heritage," and "*No al Sindicalismo guerrillero* [No to the guerrilla union]."[44]

The political and military polarization creates a complex environment for workers unions in Cesar, as in the Urabá banana region. Faced with Drummond's threats of shutting down operations in late 2000, Colombia's vice president protested that "an outrage is being committed against the work to which all coastal residents have a right, especially those in this section of the country. The company is known for bringing great benefits to the region and it would be a shame and rather painful if it had to leave the country because of threats of this nature." Unions in the region signed on to a government petition to the guerrillas to "stop in their tracks."[45] Survival, both economic and literal, demanded that worker organizations support the company in this context, yet protestations that their unions were not linked to the guerrillas have done little to protect workers from the paramilitaries. Caught between the company's use of the guerrilla threat as an ideological weapon against workers and the paramilitary threat as a concrete and immediate danger, workers have nonetheless persisted in organizing and maintaining a union in the mine.

Drummond company advertising depicts "a chubby, smiling coal miner named Drumino, wearing a bright-yellow shirt, blue pants and a bright-blue mining helmet. It's the company's answer, announced Garry Drummond, to the prototypical Colombian coffee-bean picker Juan Valdez. 'This is Drumino, coal miner, saying hi,' the character says in one company publication. 'I am uncomplicated and hard-working, cheerful and optimistic.' "[46] Reality at Drummond has not been so pleasant. The active presence of paramilitaries there has made the situation even more dangerous than at the Cerrejón mine.

Drummond workers joined the Sintramienergética union early on. In addition to more traditional union issues—wages, hours, working conditions, and health insurance—Drummond workers protested the paramilitary sympathizer the company contracted to prepare their food, saying he prepared "inedible slop," and the fact that they had to take lie detector tests, including questions like "Are you supporting the guerrillas?" In flyers like the one mentioned above ("No al Sindicalismo guerrillero") the company also made it clear that, as far as it was concerned, union activity was subversive activity. Following a FARC attack on the railroad in September 2000, in which three employees were taken hostage, a new company flyer stated, "We know that the heads of the union have a clear nexus with the subversion. . . . Down with the guerrilla union. Down with the subversion that is against investment in the country."[47]

The year 2001 was an especially horrific one for Drummond workers. Union activists received frequent death threats and protested to the company and to the national government. In February a group of armed men claiming to belong to the same paramilitary AUC that controlled the Urabá banana zone broke into the home of the Drummond union activist Cándido Méndez in Chiriguaná, Cesar province, and killed him in front of his family. In March the paramilitaries carried out the bloody murders described at the opening of this chapter.

In early October 2001 the local's new president, Gustavo Soler, was also murdered, the fifth union activist to be murdered at Drummond that year.[48] Soler was a machine operator who had worked at the company for seven years and had taken over the presidency upon the murder of Locarno and Orcasita. He was pulled off a public bus by armed men while traveling from Valledupar to Chiriguaná and taken into a white pickup (*camioneta*); his body was discovered the following day with two bullet holes in the head.[49] Only a month earlier, Aram Roston of *The Nation* had interviewed Soler. He wondered why Soler seemed unduly concerned that his cell phone seemed to be malfunctioning. Soler explained wryly, "This is my security," the only step that the government had taken to protect him. Within weeks of the interview, he was dead.[50]

International Labor Solidarity at Drummond

When Drummond began its Colombian operations in 1985, it began laying off workers at its Alabama mines. By 2001, two thousand Alabama mine workers had been laid off, and the company was importing four million tons of coal a year from Colombia back to its Alabama power plants. United Mine Workers activists in Alabama described the effect of the mine closures on their communities:

"By laying off so many Alabama miners, the company sucked the life-blood out of our region," said District 20 president John Stewart . . ."Many miners lost their homes and cars," said [Local Union 1948 president John] Nolen. "The trickle-down effect forced some local businesses to close. While some miners got jobs through the state employment services, little assistance came from Drummond. The company is not noted for helping anyone."

"We're hurting in Walker County," said L.U. 1948 mine committee chairman Wendell Rigsby of Jasper. "Three shirt factories shut down here because our economy went south." "Drummond's departure devastated many families," stressed L.U. 7813 president Ed Stover of Oakman, Ala., who worked at Drummond 32 years before retiring last year. "Many laid-off miners don't have enough money to pay their mortgages. Some small towns in Walker County no longer have the tax bases to serve their residents."

Drummond's president, Mike Zervos, cited three reasons for shifting the company's production to Colombia: high mining costs, global competition, and environmental laws.[51] (Union miners in Alabama earn approximately $3,000 a month; in Colombia, Drummond pays its workers between $500 and $1,000 a month.)[52] The very accomplishments of unions and other organizations in the United States—higher wages, improved working conditions, safety and environmental regulation—have led U.S. companies to seek conditions more to *their* liking abroad, where government repression has frequently prevented workers and citizens from achieving the standards of the United States.

Exxon too has cut back mining operations in the United States since it began to develop the Cerrejón Zona Norte mine in Colombia. In 1983, just as Cerrejón went into production, the company closed a state-of-the-art mine it had opened in 1979 in West Virginia with the promise of forty years of production there. "Exxon opened a mine in South America," one UMWA worker in Wayne County explained. "That's where my job went. Now, I've been out of work for two years and I can't even get welfare or food stamps." Over the next decade Exxon continued to close or sell mines in the United States, cutting its U.S. workforce drastically. By 1995, Exxon operated only two mines inside the United States, Monterey Coal #1 and #2 in Illinois, employing eight hundred union workers.[53] By 2001, the company employed only 321 workers at its last remaining mine.[54]

U.S. collaboration with a government that human rights organizations have repeatedly and vociferously condemned for its tolerance and/or perpetration of the most egregious human rights violations is part of an unfortunate, but not surprising, pattern.[55] Trade unionists in Colombia have been among the principal victims of right-wing paramilitaries, working in tacit or even overt collaboration with the Colombian government.[56]

The killing of union leaders in the Colombian coal mines was greeted with a wave of union activism in the United States. The USWA, the ICEM, and the UMWA immediately condemned the March 2001 murders at the Drummond mine.[57] A USWA delegation to Colombia to "investigate military involvement in the killing of trade unionists" was informed of the killings at the Drummond mine on its second day there.[58] The AFL-CIO had already taken a stand in 2000 opposing U.S. military aid to Colombia because of violations of human rights and labor rights.[59] The USWA's president Leo Gerard stated, "Our union's commitment to the fundamental rights of workers in every nation is unyielding. That's why we sent a contingent to Colombia to show our solidarity and bring attention to the workers' plight. . . . We are also sending a message to the U.S. government that we are strongly opposed to the amount of military aid being sent to the Colombian army when trade unionists and innocent people are being killed by the very military forces we are financing."[60] Tellingly, the Drummond spokesman Mike Tracy clearly articulated the opposite view: "We've always supported [U.S. military aid through] Plan Colombia. . . . We just think that it's in the best interest of the government and the business community in Colombia, and the general population."[61]

In March 2002 the International Labor Rights Fund, the United Steelworkers, and several Colombian unions brought a federal lawsuit against Drummond under the Alien Tort Claims Act for complicity in the murders.[62] Their purpose went well beyond compensation or retribution. "We aren't doing this to make those victims into millionaires," Terry Collingsworth, director of the Rights Fund, said. "We want to see those companies change."[63] The Drummond lawsuit was joined by similar actions against Occidental Petroleum and Coca-Cola for human rights abuses in Colombia. Like other corporate campaigns, these lawsuits were not aimed only at the companies they targeted. Rather, they sought to make the Alien Tort Claims Act into a viable tool to enforce human rights standards on all companies operating abroad.[64] Collaboration in these lawsuits has taken labor solidarity to new levels.

Coal Consumers Get Involved

The coal that came to the United States had very limited, and specific, destinations. El Cerrejón's coal came to five ports, each one serving a major power station: Mobile, Alabama; Jacksonville, Florida; Baltimore, Maryland; and Salem and Brayton Point, Massachusetts. Drummond's coal also came in large quantities to Salem, Brayton Point, and Mobile, in addition to Garrows Bend (a coal import-export terminal outside of Mobile); Newburgh, New York; Savannah, Georgia; and Tampa, Florida. Even more coal goes to Nova Scotia and New Brunswick, former coal-mining regions themselves, to fire power plants there.[65]

One Colombian union leader got a very different reception when he visited two different regions in New England and Canada that are major consumers of Colombian coal. In Salem, Massachusetts, the union at the Salem Harbor Power Station was initially reluctant to meet. The city of Salem had been battered in recent decades by plant closures: after the Naumkeag mill closed in the 1950s, the two other manufacturers in the city, GTE Sylvania and Parker Brothers, had also closed their doors in the 1990s. Meanwhile, a local environmental organization was pressing to get the plant, one of the dirtiest in the state, to clean up its emissions.

The union insisted that it supported cleaning up the plant: "I don't only represent 119 union members, but 119 environmentalists. There isn't a guy in there that doesn't want clean energy," said James "Red" Simpson, president of International Brotherhood of Electrical Workers Local 326 at the plant.[66] At the same time, the union was deeply suspicious of the environmentalists, who it feared wanted to eliminate the coal-fired plant—and their jobs—entirely.

An unusually close relationship developed between the union and the management at the plant, with many workers convinced that their shared interest with management in deflecting environmentalists' attacks outweighed any labor-management differences. The top-heavy structure of the plant, with 56 managers and 119 workers, and the nature of the jobs—highly skilled and well paid—contributed to the complex, as did the fact that the plant was the largest taxpayer in the city, and city authorities were also committed to keeping the plant running.[67]

In 2003, the Republican state governor stepped in to mandate a resolution to a controversy that had been percolating for several years over a schedule for bringing the plant into compliance with state environmental legislation. Environmentalists wanted the state Environmental Protection Agency to maintain the original 2004 date that had been imposed; the company, Salem's mayor, and the union wanted an extension until 2006. HealthLink, a local environmental organization, circulated figures from a study by the Harvard School of Public Health showing that emissions from the plant contributed to dozens of local deaths every year. Facing heckling by "an angry crowd of plant workers and city officials" in Salem, Massachusetts Governor Romney shouted, "I will not hold jobs or create jobs that kill people."[68] In 2003, state and local officials, the plant, and community organizations arrived at a compromise: emissions would be reduced immediately through increasing the use of imported coal—most of it Colombian—while the plant would receive an extension on installing new equipment.[69]

The president of Local 326 eventually agreed to meet with his Colombian counterpart in 2002—with managers of the plant present—and emphasized that with the jobs of his members at stake, he did not want to do or say anything that could jeopardize the future of the plant. "They were a little bit worried," the Colombian union president explained afterward. "But we said, 'I didn't come here to tell them to close the plant.' "[70]

In Nova Scotia, the United Mineworkers was also decimated by shutdowns, as the Nova Scotia Power Company had shifted its coal purchases to Colombia. Bob Burchell, the Canadian representative of the UMWA in Sydney, had a very strong message. "Nova Scotia, unfortunately, is contributing to that," he stated in a public forum, referring to the violence against union members in Colombia. "Every time we flip that light, we are contributing to what is going on in Colombia. Not because we want to but because we have no choice because we're controlled by a monopoly of power right now in Nova Scotia. We should not be relying on blood-soaked coal from Colombia to turn our lights on when we have ample supplies of coal here."[71] Solidarity, tinged with protectionism?

Colombian Mining Unions Debate Solidarity

The left and right within Colombia's union movement can in some ways be defined by the same question that U.S. unions are grappling with, of whether the union concentrates on bread-and-butter gains for its members or conceives of its mission in broader terms of social and economic justice. An example from Colombia's mining sector unions, and their relations with international entities, can illustrate the difference.

Sintraminercol, the union at the state mining entity Minercol, has taken the most radical stance on multinationals and globalization. Sintraminercol's president is also secretary general of Funtraenergética, the Federation of Mining and Energy Sector Workers. Funtraenergética, formed when the leftist federation Fedepetrol merged with Funtrametal in 2001, continues to work for the vision of national control of Colombia's resources in the tradition begun by the USO in the 1920s. "Our Federation's platform prioritizes the defense of mining and energy resources, the human rights not only of workers but also of the general population. . . . We represent mining and energy sector workers, but also mestizo, indigenous, and Afro-Colombian communities affected by the mining industry."[72] Sintraminercol has an adamant stance of maintaining its independence from any ITS, finding its home instead with the Colombian social movements of the left working for human rights, denouncing the military/paramilitary collaboration, and constructing an analysis that connects the violence in Colombia to the political and economic project of neoliberalism, privatization, and the needs of multinational investors.[73]

Sintracarbón, the union at the Cerrejón Zona Norte mine, and an affiliate of the ICEM, initially adopted a more limited focus on the wages and working conditions of its members. As described above, the ICEM and some of its North American affiliates, in particular the United Mineworkers, have taken a strong and active stance of solidarity with Sintracarbón during contract negotiations at the mine. This role has been clearly circumscribed, however, to workplace issues.

When Francisco Ramírez, president of Sintraminercol, gave a series of talks in Canada in which he accused the consortium that owns the Cerrejón mine of corruption, interference in the Colombian legal system, collaboration with paramilitaries, and displacement of villages in the mine area, the president of Sintracarbón responded with a letter disassociating his union from any criticism of the company. This response, which was immediately posted on the company's website, read in part, "Although in the Colombian Mining Sector there have been inconveniences regarding human rights, this is NOT the case of Cerrejón, a company where there is a current Collective Bargaining Agreement, which, to this date has been upheld, in the same manner the company respects SINTRACARBON as the legitimate representatives of the workers." In addition, the union explained that only the ICEM was authorized to represent it in the international sphere.[74] While the ICEM has consistently supported Sintracarbón in the bargaining process and, like the Steelworkers, has been outspoken in its response to murders and death threats against Colombian union leaders, it has not been eager to pursue the question Sintraminercol consistently raises: the nature of the global economic order.

Both Sintracarbón and its international supporters took a major stride in 2006, when an international human rights delegation accompanied the union in a week of visits to the Afro-Colombian and indigenous communities affected by the mine. "I had no idea anything like this existed in my country," the union leader Freddy Lozano exclaimed in disbelief upon seeing the conditions in the communities. The union's report on the visits stated, "The United Nations has established categories of 'poverty' and 'extreme poverty,' but these communities have been reduced to the conditions that we could call the 'living dead.' They do not have even the most minimal conditions necessary for survival. They are suffering from constant attacks and violations of their human rights by the Cerrejón company."[75]

"Just as the company has a social responsibility for the way it runs its business," wrote the union leader Jairo Quiroz, "our union has a moral and political responsibility before the destruction that the Guajira communities are suffering at the hands of Cerrejón. The company generates huge profits through the misery, poverty, and uprooting of these populations. The communities have to pay a very high price for the company's profits." The union's new relationship with the communities, he continued, "brings us the strength and conviction that we need to continue our struggle against the social inequalities in our country."[76]

"The reality is far worse than we had imagined," the union's report concluded. "The multinational companies that exploit and loot our natural resources in the Cerrejón mine are violating the human rights of these communities. Sintracarbón has committed itself to the struggle of the communities affected by the mine's expansion. We invite all other unions and social organizations in Colombia and especially in the Guajira to join in the struggle of these communities for better conditions and quality of life and to take on the communities' problems as our own problems."[77]

Unions in the North also hinted that they were inspired by Sintracarbón's venture into a more radical path of reaching out to Colombia's social movements. "We support the Sintracarbón union's courageous and unprecedented step in including in its bargaining proposal a demand that the collective rights of the Afro-Colombian and indigenous communities are recognized and addressed," wrote United Steelworkers president Leo Gerard in a statement echoed by Richard Trumka, the AFL-CIO secretary-treasurer, and John Gordon, president of the Public Service Alliance of Canada, which had recently organized workers at another mine owned by BHP Billiton in northern Canada.[78] It remains to be seen whether and how these ties of global and local solidarity can develop in ways that challenge the larger, global neoliberal model.

Conclusion

Unions in the United States and Canada have clearly made giant strides in cross-border solidarity since the 1960s. Solidarity seems to be strongest where union members at home are seeing their plants close and their jobs move abroad, and in cases of egregious human rights violations abroad aimed at crushing unions. Since the 1980s, the link between U.S. policy and the repression of labor abroad, and the implications of the repression of labor abroad for workers in the United States, have become part of the consciousness of the mainstream labor movement. The dismantling of AIFLD in the 1990s and its replacement with the Solidarity Center is symbolic of this recognition. Yet the U.S. labor movement is still grappling with the contradictions inherent in its position of global and even domestic privilege, its definition of its constituency, and its moral compass. Textile unions were the first to confront the stark reality of runaway plants, first inside and then outside the United States. But their experiences, successes, and failures have not been systematically interrogated for their relevance to unions in today's globalized world.

Unions in Colombia are struggling with many of the same issues, but in a context where the consequences are more immediate, and more dire, being on the opposite end of the process. With an unemployment rate of 14 percent, a poverty rate of 55 percent, and an ever-present specter of violence against union and other social activists, the incentive for workers with jobs to accept the status quo rather than risk their meager privilege is that much greater. Given the situation, it is remarkable that so many Colombian unionists have taken on the struggle, not only for bread-and-butter issues, but to challenge the economic and political model their country is pursuing and imagine a different world. Few unions in the United States have been prepared to take this next step.

TESTIMONIES

Débora Barros Fince, August 2004

Débora Barros Fince is a Wayuu indigenous inhabitant of the community of Bahía Portete, where the Cerrejón company constructed its port for the export of coal. Right-wing paramilitaries entered the region in 2003. Barros Fince describes life in a region under paramilitary control and the April 2004 massacre in which the paramilitaries drove out her people from their ancestral lands.[79]

We live in the Guajira peninsula, the northernmost tip of Colombia. Our community is called Bahía Portete. Two families live there: the Fince Epinayuu family and the Fince Uriana family.[80] For a long time our families have lived from fishing and artisanry. Mostly from fishing. We live along the sea coast. People come from Riohacha, and other places, to buy our fish. Or sometimes we trade in the stores. For example, we take our fish to Uribia, and we exchange it for food, to buy rice, oil, sugar, corn. Our two families have been there for over five hundred years. We are the only owners of the land, these two families.

[When the paramilitaries came to the area] they began to arrive in civilian dress, in groups of three or four. We used to see them with a group called the POLFA [Policía Fiscal y Aduanera, or Fiscal and Customs Police], which works with the DIAN [Dirección de Impuestos y Aduanas Nacionales, or National Taxes and Customs Directorate]. But we never imagined that they were paramilitaries.

But a few months later, they began to identify themselves as paramilitaries. Especially at night, they would put on their uniforms and say that they were paramilitaries. That was when they began to disrespect the community, to take things . . . For example they would come to the stores and ask for things and refuse to pay. People would say, "but why aren't you paying?" "Because we're paramilitaries, so shut up, because if you don't we'll kill you." They did the same thing, for example, if someone had a gas station. A lot of cars go through Bahía Portete, going north, to Nazareth. And they began to take that too. The same thing with animals.

Figure 19. Débora Barros Fince returns to the desert near her displaced village of Bahía Portete for a memorial in April 2006. Reprinted by permission of Débora Barros Fince.

They would come to the corrals and get on an animal and just ride away, and because it was them, nobody could say anything. And if you did say something, they would abuse you.

It's a very serious thing to say this, but we are sure that they worked with the police. Because look, the police were there, and they were there too. And the police knew that they were paramilitaries, because they would walk around saying that they were paramilitaries. And the police, none of them said a thing.

What I'm going to tell you next seems impossible to believe. Two Wayuu compañeros got tired of having their animals taken away. They couldn't stand it any more. So they naively went to Uribia, which is the municipal headquarters for our area. They went to the police station and lodged a complaint, saying that there were some people in Bahía Portete who claimed to be paramilitaries, who were abusing people and taking their animals.

So what happened: a half hour later, they were driving their car back to the community, and there was a white Toyota waiting for them. They took the two of them. They knew exactly who they were. "Hey you, informer! Why did you go to lodge a complaint against us?" They tied them up, and they killed them right there in the community.

A few days before the massacre, around the 15th of April, because the massacre was on the 18th, people were getting nervous because they were saying that they were going to kill people, that they were going to finish up this job, because it wasn't much, they could do it, there were only two families, they could kill them, and the land would be freed up. But I, in particular, didn't pay much attention. I said to myself, "it's just talk."

One of my uncles, though, was getting desperate. My mother and my sister refused to leave the house, and he said "there is no reason you can't go out, this is ours, you don't have to give them anything. We haven't done anything to them."

He came, and he called up the Cartagena Battalion in Riohacha on his cell phone. It's almost impossible to believe. He told them that they needed to send some men over. "There are some men here," he said, "who are paramilitaries, and they are threatening to kill everyone, to destroy the community. We need you to send some troops here."

And they said "yes, we know. We are preparing to send some troops over."

So what happened? A half hour later he got a call on his cell phone. They told him they were going to kill him, that they were going to cut him to pieces, they said a whole lot of things to him. We were just paralyzed when we found out they had called him like that.

The massacre happened on a Sunday. I personally had received threats a week before, saying they were going to kill my family. It happened that they were in the house of an aunt of mine, and my aunt couldn't stand it any more, and she said "But why do you have to come here to abuse me?" What happened was that she was serving lunch, and he came and kicked the food. He said, "look what you've done" and I don't know what else. As if people had to cook for them, and they could just come and eat everything. And she spoke rudely to him, she said "I'm going to leave here, I'm going to go somewhere and lodge a protest against you." Because of what she said, the guy mistreated her.

So, they called me, and they said "Tell her to keep her mouth shut, because if she doesn't, we're going to finish her off. And we're going to kill you too." And I don't know what else, a whole bunch of things. And I guess they carried out their threat because they cut all of the women's heads off, they put a grenade in one woman's head. All of that . . . It was a Sunday.

I'll tell you what happened, quickly. At 6:30 in the morning 150 men came. They came down from the Macuira mountain, that's where they came from. And we know that there's a military base there. And they came down from there. A lot of people saw them. For example, one was my grandmother. And she said that she saw men in uniform . . . And that she didn't pay much attention. And I said, "why not?" And my aunt, who was one of those killed, in front of my little cousin, said "why should we be afraid, it's the police, it isn't those sons of bitches who come around here sometimes, it's the police. We should stay where we are, because it's the army." And it was true, it was the army. So they let themselves be grabbed, the men took them by the arms . . . They pushed my grandmother, she had fractures in her legs when we found her.

So what happened. The uniformed men, well, people began to run. The children ran, and that's why there are a lot of children missing. Because people said "look, go tell so-and-so . . ." Because the houses aren't close together, the houses are far apart. So people said "go, tell so-and-so to watch out, that these are bad people, that they are killing people." Because people began to realize what was happening when they began to drag Rubén away.

Rubén Epinayuu. He was 18 years old. And they tied him with a chain to a Toyota, and they began to drag him. And that's when everybody started running. And the majority, practically everybody who escaped, it was because they fled to the mangrove swamps. And they realized that people were running for the sea. People preferred to drown, or whatever, but they ran into the sea. And they hid in the mangrove swamps.

So what happened. The uniformed men didn't kill the women right away. Instead they turned them over to 30 men in civilian clothes, who were the same ones that the community already knew [the paramilitaries]. They are the ones that carry out these massacres.

They do all kinds of things. After they kill them, after they cut them up, like they did, after they burned two children in a car. . . . We were sure that the people who had disappeared. . . . We found too much hair, we found arms. . . .

What happened next seems impossible to believe. It's sad to have to tell this, what happened to us. We called the army, we called everybody. And the army said, everybody said, "No, this is just a conflict between two families, they'll have to work it out." That's what they said, and so. . . . We went to get the corpses on April 21, three days after the massacre. We decided, we were over near the salt mine, and we decided, if we're going to die, we're going to die, but we were going to go in, just us women, to pick up the bodies. Because at first we thought that they had killed the whole community. Because nobody was coming out, and . . .

It turned out that all of the children, and some of the women, were in the mangrove swamps. They were there for almost three days, drinking salt water, with nothing to eat, with nothing. That's why many of the people, when we arrived, were dehydrated.

All of us who survived the massacred decided to go to Maracaibo [Venezuela]. Why Maracaibo? Because we don't trust the government, we don't trust the army. Because it was the army that captured the women so they could be killed. That's why we made the decision to go to Maracaibo, and ask the Venezuelan government to help us. That's where we reported the massacre. Because we were afraid that if they realized we were still in the area, they were going to come and finish us off.

But we want to return to our territories, and we are going to return. But we will return when the government gets the paramilitaries out. But the government is using the strategy of not getting rid of the paramilitaries because they don't want us to return. We know that they have an interest in taking over the land. That's what's going on.

Francisco Ruiz, December 2003

Francisco Ruiz was the secretary-treasurer of the Sintramienergética union at the Drummond mine and the only elected union leader to survive the paramilitary killings in March of 2001. He was offered refuge in the United States by the AFL-CIO Solidarity Center protection program and remained active in Los Angeles organizing labor, community, and legal solidarity with his union. The following testimony comes from a talk he gave at the Gloucester, Massachusetts, YMCA Teen Center in December 2003.[81]

Thank you for giving me this opportunity to speak with you. We want to take advantage of every space there is to speak here in the United States, because it is here that the people who carry out the massacres in Colombia are trained; it is here where the measures that are taken in Colombia are decided upon.

I work for a company called Drummond, which operates the coal mines in the Cesar province of Colombia. This company has its head-

Figure 20. Francisco Ruiz, a former union official from the Drummond mine in Colombia, wears a Salem State College cap on a speaking tour in New England in December 2003. Copyright Mark Wilson—*Boston Globe*. Reprinted by permission.

quarters in Birmingham Alabama. And today we have evidence that this company is responsible for the assassination of three union leaders in one year. Many of us have been affected by the situation. In my case, I had to leave my family, my work, leave my home, and had to come to a totally different world.

This happened just because I wanted to raise my voice to defend my rights, rights which logically affected interests of the company. How would you feel if for the mere fact of exercising your rights, for doing what you are supposedly allowed to do, using legal means, tomorrow you might be captured, you find yourself killed, cut into pieces, or you are exiled from your country? Is that just? Can we live in a society like this? Can we call this a just and democratic society?

I was one of the board of directors of the union in the Drummond coal mine for over seven years. In addition to the economic needs that we had for better salaries and better working conditions, we workers also believed that we deserved respect, because every human being deserves respect. When there is no respect, there can't be a good relationship. That's why we workers at Drummond have struggled, that's why we have organized. And this struggle caused the death of my comrades in 2001. On March 12, 2001, two leaders of the union, the president and vice president, were taken off the bus they were riding. All of the workers were made to get off the bus, and to stand around the bus, and they killed Valmore in front of his co-workers. Víctor was taken away, he was tortured, and then he was killed.

On September 5 two paramilitaries came to my house looking for me to kill me. Fortunately I wasn't there at the time, and so now I am here to tell you the story. If I had been at home that day, I would not be here now. About a month later, on the 6th of October, my compañero Gustavo Soler, who succeeded to the presidency after Valmore and Víctor were killed, was also taken off a bus, and was killed, and also tortured.

All of this, the government paid absolutely no attention to. The company that we work for paid absolutely no attention to this, because the company has been making use of the services of these paramilitary groups to be able to keep control, and to implement the measures that they need to, to make the highest level of profits at the lowest cost. Today I'm in the United States, but not because I want to be here. I have had to leave my family in Colombia.

Four days after they came looking for me to assassinate me they killed my younger brother, just because they couldn't find me. So I'm here because of the force of circumstances, because of the conditions that we are struggling to change. I don't know what's happening to my family. I'd like to be able to be with them for the holidays, but unfortunately my circumstances don't allow it. I don't wish this situation on anybody, because it is very difficult. But it is our reality.

CONCLUSION

The story that this book tells is, from one perspective, simple, linear, and repetitive. Capital seeks inequality, because inequality allows capital to profit from low wages. Over the twentieth century, two principal methods for accomplishing this have been to bring cheap workers to points of production (immigration) and to move production to where workers can be paid less (capital flight). When workers, unions, or governments have succeeded in obtaining better wages and working conditions, industries have repeatedly resorted to these tactics. When workers, unions, and governments have tried to woo industries, or halt capital flight, by granting more advantages to industries, they have found themselves caught in an endless race to the bottom.

Patterns and Paradoxes

There are several aspects of this story, however, that are less well known. First, most accounts place this phenomenon in the second half of the twentieth century. I argue that the events of the late twentieth century continue a pattern begun by the earliest industry in the country, the textile industry, a century earlier. Second, most accounts treat immigration and capital flight separately. My approach insists that they are most fruitfully studied together, as aspects of the same phenomenon of economic restructuring. Finally, despite over a century of evidence revealing how attempts to attract or conciliate industries have contributed to the race to the bottom, policymakers continue to advocate these attempts.

From another perspective, each chapter in this book tries to present a case study that shows the unexpected, the apparently paradoxical, and the complex aspects of the overall picture. Draper, the company that promoted the mechanization and speed-up of the textile industry worldwide, and whose founders created and funded racist and anti-immigrant organizations, fostered the growth of an Italian anarchist community and a chapter of the Industrial Workers of the World out of which Nicola Sacco developed his political passion. The export of Draper looms to Colombia created generations of trained loom fixers who were later recruited by textile factories in Lowell and Central Falls and formed part of a stream of Latino immigrants into New England. Massachusetts State Representative Marie Parente, the daughter of Italian immigrants in Milford, led the late twentieth-century anti-immigrant campaign in the state legislature.

At the Naumkeag Steam Cotton Company, once the paragon of labor-management collaboration, a vigorous strike led in part by the Communist Party led to the overturn not only of the collaboration program, but the AFL union in the 1930s. The Communist Party also contributed to radical labor organizing on the Colombian banana plantations begun by the Boston-based United Fruit Company along with the same Antioquia textile elite that was importing Draper looms. In Urabá, however, the trajectory was the opposite: with ample support from U.S. military aid, much of it in the form of helicopters and matériel produced by former New England textile companies, union organizing was crushed over a bloody two decades and replaced with another version of labor-management collaboration. In addition to violence, the banana industry relied on the time-tested threat of capital flight if conciliatory gestures were not forthcoming.

Coal from the southeastern United States provided the power for the Naumkeag mill, the first in New England to rely on this alternative to water power, as well as the steamships that allowed for the creation of a banana-importing industry in New England. At the end of the twentieth century, Exxon and Drummond, two of the major U.S. coal producers, shifted their coal production to Colombia, closing unionized mines in the United States and shipping Colombian coal back to Salem. The union at Salem's power plant, one of the major U.S. consumers of Colombian coal, hesitated to meet with a Colombian mining union leader when he came to Salem because its leaders feared that any statement on their part could lead to the plant's closing.

What's a Union to Do?

As textile workers discovered very early on, the ability of unions to achieve workers' goals can be undermined in many ways, direct and indirect. And because the global economy has existed for as long as unions have existed, they have always, knowingly or unknowingly, been engaged with it as well as with local and national actors beyond the workplace. At Naumkeag in 1933, while local officials and union officials counseled abdication, outside supporters from the Socialist and Communist parties insisted on the justice of the workers' cause and helped to provide the material support they needed to sustain the strike. The company was reluctant to abandon its modern facility in Salem and also chose not to hire replacement workers (due in part to the low demand for its product during the Depression) or resort to military force to crush the strike. The federal government stepped in with the Cotton Textile Code, which regulated the ability of management to unilaterally impose working conditions.

At Draper in 1913, workers also enjoyed a context of lively, multifaceted radical support from beyond their ranks, including the IWW, anarchists, and socialists. Draper took a much harder line against the strike, however, quickly bringing in replacement workers and relying heavily on antipicketing injunctions, arrests, and police violence.

Workers in the United States today face a formidable array of obstacles: a weakened and discredited labor movement with a history of collaborationism, the legacy of anticommunist crusades that have virtually obliterated the kind of organized radical left that nurtured the strikes early in the twentieth century, a fraying social service system and growing inequality at home, and a global system of debts, economic restructuring, and trade agreements (created and enforced by governments) that give corporations enormous leverage over their workers.

Its focus on narrow, bread-and-butter goals has been both a strength and a weakness of the U.S. labor movement. For a brief historical conjuncture in the 1940s and 1950s, it appeared to be a successful strategy. But its very success was also its weakness: in resting on an exclusivist nationalism and avoiding confronting issues of social inequality at home and abroad, the labor movement weakened its own socioeconomic foundations.

There are many links between the use of immigrant workers and the use of outsourcing. In both systems, businesses rely on the existence of regional and global inequalities to exert a downward pressure on wages and working conditions. In the United States, businesses have invited unions to collaborate with them in maintaining and benefiting from these inequalities.

It has become almost a truism to note that if corporations have become global, unions must also implement global strategies.[1] One thing that the growing global solidarity movements have in common is that, while centered on labor organizations, they also transcend them. As the U.S. labor movement isolated itself from the left in the United States over the course of the twentieth century, it lost the ability to pursue a broader agenda of social justice. Some of the most striking activism in the so-called era of globalization has been that in which the labor movement has extended itself, tentatively, in this direction, as in the World Trade Organization protests in Seattle in 1999.[2]

Grassroots union efforts have been at the forefront of challenging the complacency of the AFL-CIO leadership, sometimes successfully, other times not. The victory of the New Voices slate in 1995 represented for many the success of a radical challenge from within. By 2005 new challenges from the grassroots were arguing that the potential for change had been diffused and another overhaul was necessary. The 2005 AFL-CIO convention was overshadowed by the threat of some of the largest unions to split from the federation if their proposal for restructuring was not accepted. Buried beneath this debate was the "Clear the Air" resolution proposed by the California Central Labor Councils, demanding that the AFL-CIO openly disassociate itself from the anticommunist interventions of the past and open its foreign policy records to public scrutiny.

On the domestic level, militancy emerged in local struggles like that of UFCW Local P-9 in Austin, Minnesota, against Hormel and UPIU Local 14 in Jay, Maine, against International Paper that pitted local unions against more conciliatory internationals. In both cases, radicalized locals turned to the public for support and worked with the organizer Ray Rogers on corporate campaigns based on the one he had developed during the battle to unionize J. P. Stevens.[3] Like the Stevens strike, the International Paper and Hormel strikes turned into social movements, mobilizing the kind of emotion, commitment, and community that the Draper and Naumkeag strikes did in 1913 and 1933, and also attracting the attention of progressive organizations outside the labor movement that lent their solidarity and support. One study of the Jay strike noted the interaction of labor mobilization with outside, progressive support. Jesse Jackson's visit to Jay, for example, "helped to transform the strikers' perception of their struggle. . . . The theme struck by Jackson was that the strike was part of a broader struggle for fairness and dignity that united Local 14 with all who struggle against oppression." Over the course of the strike, the local was transformed "from a traditional business union to a cause. . . . The strikers began to see themselves as point soldiers of the labor movement, and Jay as a place where the decline of unions would be reversed."[4]

Likewise, in Minnesota, "Local P-9 had gone from an apathetic union, like so many others—lucky to get a quorum at a monthly meeting—to a union—unlike almost all others—lucky to find a meeting room big enough to hold those who wanted to attend. The excitement this generated led 3,000 local unions to send aid to P-9. It also sparked the support of farm activists, peace and justice activists, Native American activists, and thousands of others, who saw their hopes reflected in this struggle."[5]

In both Jay and Austin, the strikes were defeated. The array of forces allied against the strikers was formidable, and in both cases, as in Salem in 1933, this array included the national-level leadership of their own unions. It also included a labor law that favored defeat by delay, as in the Darlington textile strike; the use of police and National Guard forces against strikers, as at Draper; and the interregional strategies of both International Paper and Hormel that allowed them to increase production at other plants when one went on strike.

That Ray Rogers went on to run the "Killer Coke" campaign against Coca-Cola as the company was being sued by the International Labor Rights Fund and the United Steelworkers for the murder of union organizers in its plants in Colombia in the 1990s is surely more than pure coincidence. Students United Against Sweatshops, an organization that formed in the late 1990s to challenge the outsourcing of college logo merchandise to third world factories, also took on the Coca-Cola issue in the beginning of the twenty-first century.[6] For many on the left of the U.S. labor movement, Colombia is one of the key battlegrounds where the future of workers everywhere is being fought at the dawn of the twenty-first century.

The Search for Cheap Labor: Migrants and Outsourcing

Looking at globalization as a long historical process, with labor history at it center, asks us to rethink both the nature of change over time and the nature of relationships among places. Never content to pay a "living wage," industry has consistently sought ways to find, or create, a labor force that can meet its reproductive needs beyond the realm of the factory. The strategies have included hiring young women and justifying low wages on the grounds that the wages were supplemental and temporary (in the early textile industry in the United States and in today's export processing zones), bringing in immigrants, and sending work abroad. In all cases, industry has sought to displace the cost of bearing, raising, and educating its workforce onto other sectors rather than contributing its share to the society that bears, raises, and educates them.

Inside the United States, taxes, unions, and the regulation of labor and the environment have forced industry to contribute to the larger project of social reproduction. Puerto Rico presents a unique case in which the U.S. government sustains the social reproduction of the labor force, but industries there are not required to contribute. In other countries, the contribution of the U.S. government has been more to maintain the repression needed to preserve a lower standard of living, as well as to create and enforce trade regulations that facilitate corporate mobility and profits.

The U.S. government has also facilitated the social reproduction of the workforce in places like Puerto Rico, Mexico, and Colombia by simultaneously encouraging and illegalizing immigration. Immigrant workers are "cheap" for several reasons: because their social reproduction takes place in their home country, thus relieving U.S. business from contributing to their reproduction; because U.S. policies maintain poverty in their home countries, allowing the meager wages they earn here to have more value there; and because their remittances relieve U.S. factories operating abroad from the need to provide a living wage there. In addition, anti-immigrant policies facilitate low wages and poor conditions for immigrant workers because the workers lack legal rights and because public antipathy creates a climate in which they find it difficult to claim even the legal rights they do have.

Runaway Plants: Who Gains, Who Loses?

U.S. companies have promoted the view that as consumers, people located in the United States benefit from cheap labor because it provides them with cheap products. Certainly, U.S. society is overwhelmed with subtle and unsubtle promotion of consumerism, and people in the United States are encouraged to think of themselves as, above all, consumers.

Yet even at the level of consumption it is clear that some people in the United States benefit far more than others from the current system. As income inequalities grow and public social services shrink, the consumption gap in the United States becomes more and more glaring.

And people, of course, are more than consumers. They live in communities, they raise families, they seek meaningful relationships, they work, they breathe. Cheap products in the long run may be small recompense for a society in shambles.

The argument is also frequently made that workers in other countries benefit from the outsourcing of jobs. The *Salem Evening News* reminded striking mill workers in 1933, "In these days of such widespread unemployment, persons with a job are mighty lucky and should appreciate that fact."[7] In the 1950s, Governor Luis Muñoz Marín of Puerto Rico insisted that "the worst wage of all is no wage."[8] In the 1990s, a Mexican union in an export processing region reiterated the sentiment: "There is no worse company than one that closes."[9] And in the Colombian banana zone, after ten years of paramilitary terror, a former leftist guerrilla leader concluded that it was time for "regional salvation and defense of banana production" and proposed "the possibility of allying with the banana empresarios."[10]

This position, however, begs an important question: What are the alternatives? And why? Rather than accept the premise that we must choose between poor wages and working conditions or no jobs at all, we must reframe the question to interrogate how we can achieve a better set of alternatives. To do this, we must uncover the historical process that has led us, over and over again in the twentieth century, to this particular conjuncture, in which workers are told, and come to believe, that their only options are concessions or job loss.

To begin to uncover the process, we must first recognize that poverty and inequality are human creations, the results of human actions and historical processes rather than inevitable conditions. Rather than accept poverty and inequality as given, if we can come to understand how these conditions have come into being, we can think intelligently about how to change them.

Thus, rather than beginning with the question: Is it better for Colombian workers to have low pay and dangerous working conditions, or no jobs at all?, we could reframe the issue and ask: Why have U.S. businesses, the U.S. labor movement, and the U.S. government collaborated to crush movements for social change in Colombia? Can this process be changed? How can foreign investment be controlled—from the U.S. end and from the Colombian end—so that it will benefit rather than harm the people who live in the area where investment occurs?

Likewise, if we ask: Is it better for Draper workers to work for inadequate wages or face police violence and lose their jobs?, inadequate wages might appear to be the better alternative. However, the experience of Salem's Naumkeag Steam Cotton Company workers shows that under different circumstances, a strike can also bring victory. In Salem, the question might be reversed: Is it better to strike for improved conditions (and win) or accept the stretch-out and accompanying layoffs?

Instead of either of these questions, however, I would suggest that we ask: What are the circumstances that have allowed workers to improve their conditions, and how can we as a society work to increase the spaces, and the chances, for workers to have a meaningful voice in their workplaces and communities?

Two important factors have been the nature of workers' organizations and the role of government. Clearly, these two factors are interrelated, because government policies, and the way they are pursued, can heavily tilt the balance in favor of or against democratic labor organizations. (By "democratic" I mean organizations in which workers have a strong and meaningful voice. While the AFL-CIO has often joined the U.S. government in defining "democratic" as anticommunist, the cases in this book also show examples in which the AFL-CIO has functioned undemocratically and communist organizations have functioned democratically.) These policies range from outright repression, to taxation and government spending that favor profit and concentration of resources versus those that favor redistribution, to regulations that govern what unions, and what companies, are allowed to do to increase their leverage over each other.

Inequality, Regions, and History

Labor, capital, and products have been mobile since the beginning of recorded history. Similarly, inequality has a long historical pedigree. This does not imply that inequality is inherent in human societies, or in "human nature." Inequality is inherent in the emergence of "civilization"—complex (i.e., unequal) societies where a division of labor allows the emergence of social classes. In early civilizations, the vast majority worked in agriculture, and civilization itself depended on the ability of a group of leaders, often conquerors, to concentrate resources by taxing farmers, turning themselves into a governing class of priests and royalty. At the same time that this tributary system extracted resources from people who worked independently, systems of direct labor control also emerged. Again, conquest frequently played a role: prisoners of war or conquered peoples were turned into slaves. As Sidney Mintz pointed out so eloquently, the plantation slave system was in many ways the prototype for the factory system, because it fundamentally shifted the relationship of people to work.[11] Farmers, even when heavily taxed, controlled their own working lives. Slavery meant that somebody else structured one's work and owned the product of one's labor. But once farmers lost access to their land, enslavement was no longer necessary. Workers had to find jobs working for others in order to survive. Inequality thus opened the door to the race to the bottom.

Region has a relationship to inequality, but it is not an obvious or direct one. As a result of the modern colonial system, which can be conveniently dated, perhaps, to 1492, the world appears to be divided into wealthy areas, the former colonizers who amassed wealth by extracting it from their colonies, and poor areas, the former colonies who became impoverished through the extraction of their resources by the metropolises. The poverty of Latin America, Asia, and Africa today is in large part a result of a massive, five-hundred-year resource shift out of these areas into Europe and the United States.

But to define regions as rich or poor elides the issue of inequality within regions. The regions of the world that are poor are also characterized by vast internal inequalities, and these inequalities are inseparable from their poverty. The regional wage differentials that have encouraged companies to import workers from or move to poorer regions are created and enforced locally as well as globally. Governments in the U.S. North and South, in Puerto Rico, in Mexico, and in Colombia have chosen labor-repressive and poverty-enforcing policies that enhance the opportunities for profit. Local actors as well as outside investors have been able to benefit from these policies. When unions have chosen a stance of wage restraint and conciliation, they have placed narrow, short-term goals over broad, long-term vision. When they have chosen a stance of competing with the unorganized over one of commitment to social justice, they have acquiesced to the race to the bottom in which workers everywhere are losers.

Differentials among and within regions are related and are the result of historical processes in which the search for cheap labor and profit has played an important role. Investors, governments, and even unions have contributed to creating and maintaining these differentials. But unions have also stepped up to the challenge of organizing the unorganized, drawing the line on concessions, and challenging government policies that foster inequality at home and abroad. Whether in radical alternatives to the AFL-CIO, militant locals inside the federation, or labor-community organizations like Jobs with Justice, voices for a unionism that strives to challenge inequality at the local, national, and global levels have repeatedly emerged even in the United States.

Labor movements and movements for social change have been at their most successful when they have understood the idea that "an injury to one is an injury to all." When Salem strikers insisted, "If we lose this strike, all textile workers will be affected," they showed a clear understanding of the way the race to the bottom functioned.[12] It had to do with region, but region was only one factor in the multitude of ways that capital tried to profit at the expense of labor.

Governments, Nationalism, and Globalization

Labor and capital have both been mobile, in different ways; governments, however, have been firmly attached to regions and have played a crucial role in maintaining regional inequalities. Yet the multitude of forms of government intervention—in the case of the United States, often in concert with the labor movement—show that governments also cross regional boundaries.

Labor movements have faced the triple temptation of parochialism, collaboration, and exclusivism. All three are based on the idea that certain workers can benefit through an identification, often based on region or race, with their employer. But labor parochialism, which is predicated on the continuing existence of inequality, inevitably and inherently serves to perpetuate inequality—an inequality that serves the interests of capital but not of workers. When the U.S. labor movement has retreated to protectionism and anti-immigrant policies in order to protect some workers at the expense of others, and when it has collaborated with the U.S. government in programs that maintain inequality abroad, it has weakened its ability to challenge the very conditions that threaten it.

To truly address the global conditions that undermine workers and their ability to achieve a better life, labor movements must challenge the fundamental issue of inequality and the policies that create and promote it. The U.S. labor movement has taken steps in that direction in recent years. In opposing CAFTA or the ATPDEA, it has argued that U.S. trade policies should be predicated on guaranteeing rights for labor abroad. This small step, however, begs a deeper discussion of advocacy regarding the nature and causes of global inequality.

One view of globalization has suggested that the economic integration that accompanies it signifies a loss of power and meaning for the nation-state. If globalization hurts workers, the corollary to this position would hold, then protectionism and strengthening the nation-state against the globalizing forces that undermine it would be the response.

The view suggested by this study is somewhat different. Economic integration is not simply a geographical process that connects different regions, it is a method that capital has used to create and control cheap sources of labor. In the twentieth century, economic integration that linked regions by moving workers and moving capital to bring down the cost of labor took the form of international migrations, internal migrations, and capital flight.

The nation-state, as well as local governments, have played a major role in structuring the form that globalization has taken. The state as an institution has fostered inequality at home and abroad, and at the same time fostered national sentiment that justifies and naturalizes inequality. At home, it creates an imagined community that transcends inequality (and implicitly justifies it); on a global level, the imagined community justifies the notion of labor-management collaboration in the national (or regional) interest.

The most common image of globalization is a lateral or horizontal structure, in which regions become more and more tightly intertwined as people, products, ideas, and technology move ever more quickly among them. But if we look at globalization from the perspective of labor history, inequality replaces horizontalism as its organizing principle. What we have come to call "globalization" has meant increasing inequality and an increasing ability of the powerful to profit from this inequality. Corporate, or neoliberal, globalization creates, thrives on, and re-creates inequality. Understanding how inequality has been created and who it has benefited can help us find ways to challenge it.

Introduction

1. IMF Staff, "Globalization: Threat or Opportunity?," April 12, 2000, http://www.imf .org. This optimistic perspective on globalization is also promoted in popular works like Friedman, *The World Is Flat*, and Barber, *Jihad vs. McWorld*.
2. See, for example, Tonelson, *The Race to the Bottom*. Barber's *Jihad vs. McWorld* portrays the contemporary world in similar terms.
3. The critical perspective on globalization underlies a worldwide popular movement challenging the global economic institutions that promote it. For an example of this critical view, see Brecher and Costello, *Global Village or Global Pillage?* The debate on globalization draws on many of the themes of previous opposing approaches to economic development, perhaps most recently reflected in Landes, *The Unbound Prometheus*, which frames development as beneficial for all, and A. G. Frank, *Re-Orient*, by one of the founders of dependency theory, which emphasizes the inequalities and exploitation at the heart of economic development.
4. Economic Development Data and Information, "Doing Business in Connecticut," http://www.youbelonginct.com.
5. Héctor Mondragón, presentation at "Voces por la Vida" conference, Bogotá, August 26–28, 2004.
6. Piore, *Birds of Passage*, 4.

1. The Draper Company

1. Hartford, *Where Is Our Responsibility?*, makes this argument most explicitly with respect to the New England textile industry and its unions. Others, including Bluestone and Harrison, *The Deindustrialization of America*, argue that deindustrialization began in the post–World War II period, precisely the period that many analysts identify as the golden age of collaboration between labor and management. Both Cowie, *Capital Moves*, and Hartford emphasize that interregional

capital mobility precedes and prefigures today's international capital mobility. As Cowie explains, the "new international division of labor" frequently seen as a phenomenon of the 1980s was preceded by "an earlier but parallel regional division of labor" (34).

2. One of Draper's hallmarks as a company was an aggressive invention and patenting process, placing it high on the list of new patents registered early in the century. Mass, "Developing and Utilizing Technological Leadership," 132.

3. Draper Corporation, *Cotton Chats* 196, February 1919.

4. *Cotton Chats* 208, February 1920.

5. Dalzell, *Enterprising Elite*, 11.

6. Ibid., 33, 13.

7. Tucker, *The Funding of Scientific Racism*, chap. 1

8. In some ways the closest cousin to Hopedale was the Oneida community founded in 1848 in upstate New York, which sought to combine manufacturing and eugenics. For more on Oneida, see Carden, *Oneida*.

9. Tucker, *The Funding of Scientific Racism*, chap. 1.

10. When William returned from Italy he founded the Hopedale Manufacturing Company with James H. Northrop, inventor of Draper's Northrop automatic loom. After George Alber's death in 1923, Eben's sons B. H. Bristow and Eben S. Jr. ran the Draper company, while Clare and George O., sons of William, remained involved with Hopedale Manufacturing. In 1927 the two companies merged. See *Worcester* (Mass.) *Telegram*, February 28, 1927.

11. Tucker, *The Funding of Scientific Racism*, chap. 1; Malloy, Malloy, and Ryan, *Hopedale*, 21.

12. Malloy, Malloy and Ryan, *Hopedale*, 41.

13. Tucker, *The Funding of Scientific Racism*, chap. 1.

14. See Gould, *The Mismeasure of Man*, for a discussion of the widespread nature and acceptance of this school of thought.

15. Tucker, *The Funding of Scientific Racism*, chap. 2.

16. Ibid., chaps. 3, 4; quote on 130. The federation was founded in 1978 by John Tanton, formerly president of Zero Population Growth, who went on in 1983 to create U.S. English with California Republican S. I. Hayakawa. Tucker puts the date at 1988, but every other source, including the organization's website, gives the 1983 date. Tanton actually left U.S. English in 1988 to found another organization, ProEnglish. See http://rightweb.irc-online.org.

17. See Minchin, *Don't Sleep with Stevens!*, for a discussion of how the civil rights legislation that opened the doors of textile employment to African Americans also opened the doors to union organizing; African Americans were the textile unions' staunchest supporters in the South in the 1970s.

18. *Milford* (Mass.) *Daily News*, April 3, 1933.

19. Danker, "The Hopedale Strike," 78. Strikers later requested that the Massachusetts legislature investigate whether Draper had violated U.S. laws forbidding contract

labor, but the legislature declined. *Milford* (Mass.) *Daily News*, April 23, April 26, 1913. Eben S. Draper, then president of the company, denied any irregularity in the hiring or contracting of Italian workers, insisting that the company hired only Italians already living in the Milford area. When William Draper was ambassador, from 1897 to 1900, Eben Draper stated, the company had only a thousand employees, none of them Italian. *Milford* (Mass.) *Daily News*, May 8, 1913. If Draper did not do any recruitment in Italy, that would make the company exceptional. In Lawrence, for example, "almost all of Lawrence's largest mills used recruiting agents" in Italy, placing posters in villages and advertisements in newspapers. See Cameron, *Radicals of the Worst Sort*, 77.

20. Avrich, *Sacco and Vanzetti*, 21. Foggia was also home to an ethnic minority of Albanians, many of whom also migrated to Milford. Jennie Paglia in Avrich, *Anarchist Voices*, 97.

21. Ralph Piesco in Avrich, *Anarchist Voices*, 98.

22. "About Our Church," http://www.sacredheartmilford.org.

23. Gemmo Diotalevi, Milford, Massachusetts, September 19, 1987, in Avrich, *Anarchist Voices*, 95.

24. Avrich, *Sacco and Vanzetti*, 21.

25. According to his trial testimony, posted by Professor Doug Linder of the University of Missouri, Kansas City Law School, http://www.law.umkc.edu. For a detailed description of Sacco's voyage to Milford and its context, see also Avrich, *Sacco and Vanzetti*, chap. 1.

26. Avrich, *Sacco and Vanzetti*, 27; *Milford* (Mass.) *Daily News*, April 28, 1913. For Coldwell's later life and influence on the Woonsocket, Rhode Island, labor movement, see Gerstle, *Working-Class Americanism*, 161.

27. Jennie Paglia in Avrich, *Anarchist Voices*, 97.

28. Concetta Silvestri, ibid., 107.

29. *Milford* (Mass.) *Daily News*, April 28, March 20, 1913.

30. Cameron, *Radicals of the Worst Sort*, 128.

31. *Milford* (Mass.) *Daily News*, March 22, 1913. Coldwell also spoke to the Fortnightly Club at the local Universalist Church early in 1913. *Milford* (Mass.) *Daily News*, April 9, 1913.

32. *Milford* (Mass.) *Daily News*, March 7, 1913.

33. Ibid., March 20, March 21, March 29, 1913.

34. Ibid., April 1, 1913.

35. Danker, "The Hopedale Strike," 83, 82.

36. *Milford* (Mass.) *Daily News*, March 29, April 1, 1913.

37. Ibid., April 2, April 3, April 8, April 10, 1913. The April 8 article identifies Morris as being a baker from Franklin, Massachusetts.

38. Ibid., April 3, 1913.

39. Ibid., May 5, 1913, describes Haywood's appearance in Milford.

40. Cameron, *Radicals of the Worst Sort*, 126.

41. Ibid., 134–35.

42. *Milford* (Mass.) *Daily News*, April 1, April 3, 1913.

43. *Cotton Chats* 126, April, 1913. For further discussion of the racial history of American identity, see chap. 4 on immigration.

44. *Milford* (Mass.) *Daily News*, April 5, 1913.

45. Ibid., April 3, 1913.

46. Letter from the Committee of Striking Laborers to Mr. Nutting, June 30, 1913, reproduced in *Cotton Chats* 128, June 1913.

47. *Milford* (Mass.) *Daily News*, April 7, 1913. For a discussion of the slippery definitions of "whiteness" in the early twentieth century, see Haney López, *White by Law*.

48. *Milford* (Mass.) *Daily News*, April 8, April 21, 1913.

49. Ibid., April 17, 1913.

50. Eben S. Draper, "We Ask a Careful Consideration," in *Cotton Chats* 127, May 1913.

51. *Milford* (Mass.) *Daily News*, May 9, 1913.

52. Ibid., April 9, April 28, May 5, 1913.

53. Ibid., April 10, April 11, April 15, April 18, April 21, 1913. Similar competing uses of the American and other national flags emerged in the nationwide immigrant rights demonstrations on May 1, 2006.

54. Ibid., April 28, 1913.

55. Ibid., April 29, 1913.

56. Hartford discusses the complexity of the Catholic church's view, which combined antiradicalism with a social vision defending "the rights of labor, and . . . the responsibilities of capital (*Where Is Our Responsibility?*, 49). There were, Hartford argues, "striking parallels between the structure of Catholic social thought and that of mainline trade unionists. Each was cast in a framework of reciprocal rights and obligations; and each accepted the hierarchical nature of the emerging industrial order" (50). In some cases, however, the church took an overt and unambiguously antagonistic stand. In Lawrence in 1882, St. Anne's Church was "a model of patriarchy and a teacher of deference and obedience to authority. From the pulpit French Canadian priests rallied against the strikers and demanded loyalty to the mill" (Cameron, *Radicals of the Worst Sort*, 53). During the 1912 Lawrence strike, Father O'Reilly, "a powerful figure in the city," was "a staunch opponent of the strike" (141). In a 1927 strike in Woonsocket, Rhode Island, a priest at the Notre Dame church "whose parish was one of the hardest hit by the strike, advised his parishioners to 'accept whatever sacrifice was necessary and to have recourse to prayer'" (Gerstle, *Working-Class Americanism*, 57). Gerstle describes the conflict between Woonsocket's radical unionists and the church in the 1920s and 1930s and the eventual reconciliation when the radicals were ousted from the union's leadership in the 1940s (122–23).

57. *Milford* (Mass.) *Daily News*, April 12, 1913.

58. Ibid., April 14, April 29, 1913.

59. Danker, "The Hopedale Strike," 85.

60. *Milford* (Mass.) *Daily News*, April 26, 1913.

61. Ibid.

62. Danker, "The Hopedale Strike," 79; *Milford* (Mass.) *Daily News*, March 22, April 21, 1913.

63. *Milford* (Mass.) *Daily News*, April 3, April 4, 1913. A document dated April 29, ordering the recipient to vacate Draper company housing, is located in the Joseph M. Coldwell Papers, Mss 358, folder 1, Rhode Island Historical Society, Providence.

64. *Milford* (Mass.) *Daily News*, April 5, April 7, April 8, April 15, 1913.

65. Ibid., April 14, April 30, 1913.

66. Ibid., April 14, April 15, April 23, May 2, May 5, 1913.

67. Ibid., April 16, 1913.

68. Ibid., April 10, April 11, 1913. The Granite Cutters also vowed to take up a weekly collection for the Draper strikers for the duration of the strike. Ibid., April 21, 1913.

69. Ibid., April 18, April 21, 1913.

70. Ibid., April 30, 1913.

71. Ibid., May 1, May 2, 1913.

72. Jennie Paglia in Avrich, *Anarchist Voices*, 97.

73. *Milford* (Mass.) *Daily News*, May 3, 1913.

74. C. E. Nutting to Messrs. Santo Bagnoli, John Paccioretti, Nunzioto di Vitto, and S. Ferino, July 1, 1913, reproduced in *Cotton Chats* 128, June 1913.

75. The history of the Queen City Cotton Company can be found in Sharp, "The Transformation of a Working-Class Neighborhood."

76. Racine, "Boom Time in Textile Town," 40, for the founding of Gaffney; *Cotton Chats* 332, October 1939, for a photo of the restored Model A loom sold to Gaffney in 1895.

77. Thomas W. Hanchett, "Chadwick-Hoskins," Charlotte-Mecklenburg Historic Landmarks Commission. http://cmhpf.org.

78. Bridges, "The Draper Story," 257. *Cotton Chats* 294, April 1929, says that the Atlanta facility was only a warehouse, occupying fifty thousand square feet "exclusively used for the storage of repair parts and replacements for Northrop looms."

79. *Cotton Chats* 294, April 1929.

80. In 1912, 78 percent replaced common looms in New England, and only 45 percent were replacements in the Southeast (*Cotton Chats* 124, February 1913).

81. *Cotton Chats* 112, February 1912. There were also a few hundred each in Maryland, Mississippi, and Louisiana.

82. *Cotton Chats* 148, February 1915; *Cotton Chats* 255, September 1924.

83. William P. McMullan, Agent, Naumkeag Steam Cotton Company, to W. I. Stimpson, Agent, Draper Company, February 11, 1916, reprinted in *Cotton Chats* 161, March 1916.

84. Hartford, *Where Is Our Responsibility?*, 53.

85. *Cotton Chats* 252, June 1924.

86. Ibid.

87. Ibid. 253, July 1924.

88. Robert A. Bakeman, letter to the editor, *Peabody* (Mass.) *Times*, June 9, 1933.

89. *Cotton Chats* 253, July 1924.

90. Ibid. 256, November 1924.

91. Ibid. 268, June 1926.

92. Ibid. 296, July 1929.

93. Savage and Lombard, *Sons of the Machine*, 10; Glaessel-Brown, "A Time of Transition," 347.

94. In the process of transporting it to Bello the machinery suffered so much damage that Pedro Nel's son, the historian Luis Ospina Vásquez, wrote that it was "made by Talleres de Robledo," the company that repaired them. Botero, "Tejiendo país."

95. Draper Corporation, "Telares Draper en América Latina," in Draper Corporation, *Telares Draper*, section 4, p. 3.

96. Ibid., section 4, pp. 3–4, 11–13.

97. Glaessel-Brown, "Immigration Policy and Colombian Textile Workers."

98. I have not been able to locate a complete run of *Cotton Chats*. The Hopedale Public Library has an incomplete collection, including one issue in its Spanish version, issue 331, May 1939.

99. Draper Corporation, "Telares Draper en América Latina," in Draper Corporation, *Telares Draper*, section 4, pp. 3–4, 11–13.

100. Ibid., p. 6.

101. Carlton, "Textile Town Settles In," 229.

102. Mass, "The Decline of a Technological Leader," 242.

103. See, for example, Rockwell's description of a successful automation at a Japanese company, http://domino.automation.rockwell.com.

104. Malloy et al., *Hopedale*; Bridges, "The Draper Story," 259. In the early twenty-first century, the heavily debt-ridden Texmaco came under fire for having used its close relationship with the Suharto dictatorship to secure billions of dollars of illegal loans from the Indonesian Bank Restructuring Agency. See Sadanand Dhume, "Texmaco's Survival Guide," *Far Eastern Economic Review* 164 no. 31 (August 9, 2001), 36–40. Draper-Texmaco continued to operate its Spartanburg, South Carolina, plant through the first decade of the twenty-first century. See "Draper-Texmaco Features Loom," *Textile News*, June 18, 2001, http://www.textilenews.com.

105. Avrich, *Sacco and Vanzetti*, 21–23, 25.

106. Ibid., 26–27.

107. Ibid., 27.

108. Coldwell to Eugene Lyons, in Lyons, *The Life and Death of Sacco and Vanzetti*, 33, cited in Avrich, *Sacco and Vanzetti*, 29.

109. Robert D'Attillio, "La Salute é in Voi: The Anarchist Dimension (Historical Context of the Sacco-Vanzetti Case)," The Sacco-Vanzetti Project, http://www.sacco vanzettiproject.org.

110. Avrich, *Sacco and Vanzetti*, 55.

111. Ralph Piesco, in Avrich, *Anarchist Voices*, 98.

112. Avrich, *Sacco and Vanzetti*, 29–30.

113. Ibid., 58–60.

114. Ibid., 66–67.

115. George T. Kelley, in Avrich, *Anarchist Voices*, 100.

2. The Naumkeag Steam Cotton Company

1. Ware, *The Industrial Worker*, mentions in passing strikes at Naumkeag in 1853 and 1857 (119, 161). For the probable shift in the workforce, see A. Chomsky, "Salem as a Global City," 221.

2. Naumkeag Steam Cotton Company (NSCC), "Directors' Records," AB-3, June 21, 1918.

3. Ibid.

4. While wage data by ethnicity for Salem is not available, the U.S. Immigration Commission found around 1910 that overall, French Canadians earned significantly more than Polish immigrants. Hartford, *Where Is Our Responsibility?*, 43.

5. "Some further account of the strike on June 17th and its final adjustment," NSCC "Directors' Records," AB-3, September 18, 1918.

6. NSCC, "Directors' Records," AB-3, November 19, 1919.

7. "Help us win our strike!," undated flyer, circa May 1933. Anne Burlak Timpson Papers.

8. NSCC, "Directors' Records," September 10, 1926.

9. Mr. Seamans to the Directors of the Naumkeag Steam Cotton Company, NSCC Collection, case 3, December 21, 1926, 2.

10. Ibid., 2–3, 5.

11. Ibid., 4, 7.

12. Ibid., 1.

13. Nyman and Smith, *Union-Management Cooperation*, 7, 8; NSCC, "Directors' Records," AB-3, March 11, 1927.

14. Nyman and Smith, *Union-Management Cooperation*, 4. The *Salem* (Mass.) *Evening News*, May 12, 1933, later pointedly noted that the union president Joseph Fecteau enjoyed "the confidence of Franco-Americans" inside the plant and out—with no mention of how he was viewed by the Polish workers.

15. The agreement is reproduced in Nyman and Smith, *Union-Management Cooperation*, 185–86.

16. Ibid., 10–15.

17. Ibid., 17.

18. Ibid., 27.

19. Ibid., 41, 45.

20. Ibid., 59, 68 n. 1, 70 n. 1.

21. The *Boston Globe*, May 11, 1933, stated that 900 of the 1,800 workers at the mill were married women. The *Salem* (Mass.) *Evening News*, May 11, 1933, said over 800. Nyman and Smith discuss the issue of seniority rules in *Union-Management Cooperation*, 68 n. 2.

22. Nyman and Smith, *Union-Management Cooperation*, 68–70. Quote from 70.

23. Ibid., 71, 75, 90.

24. NSCC, "Board of Directors," AB-3, September 23, October 23, November 14, December 23, 1930.

25. Nyman and Smith, *Union-Management Cooperation*, 73–74, 75. Nyman's and Smith's is the most in-depth study. See especially 78–79 for a discussion of national attention to Naumkeag. Their bibliography (210) lists contemporary publications on the Naumkeag experiment. A recent study of textile unionism refers to Naumkeag as "the most significant experiment in labor-management cooperation undertaken by the UTW" (Daniel, *Culture of Misfortune*, 284 n. 27).

26. The mill ordered a 10 percent cut in November 1931. NSCC, "Board of Directors," AB-3, November 13, 1931. The work week was cut again in the spring of 1932, to 3.5 days per week. Nyman and Smith, *Union-Management Cooperation*, 93, 103, 109.

27. Nyman and Smith, *Union-Management Cooperation*, 90, 111.

28. "Total votes cast 1190," Morris L. Cooke Papers.

29. Nyman and Smith, *Union-Management Cooperation*, 126, 127.

30. Ibid., 132.

31. *Salem* (Mass.) *Evening News*, May 9, 1933.

32. Ibid., June 2, 1933.

33. Ibid.

34. Ibid., July 10, 1933.

35. Newspaper clipping identified only as *Sunday Journal* (circa July 12, 1933). Anne Burlak Timpson Papers.

36. "Help us win our strike!," undated flyer, circa May 1933. Anne Burlak Timpson Papers.

37. NSCC, "To Our Employees," reprinted in *Salem* (Mass.) *Evening News*, July 7, 1933.

38. *Salem* (Mass.) *Evening News*, May 9, May 16, 1933.

39. "Agent Smith States Mill Gates Will Not Open Monday Morning," ibid., May 12, 1933.

40. Ibid., May 8, 1933.

41. "A Bird in the Hand," ibid., May 9, 1933.

42. Ibid., June 12, 1933.

43. Ibid., April 19, 1933.

44. Ibid., May 9, 1933.

45. "Strikers Are Firm in Their Determination Not to Return," ibid., May 13, 1933. On

the issue of French Canadian workers' reputation for conservatism and a discussion of how and when their same ethnic values could be mobilized into radicalism, see Gerstle, *Working-Class Americanism*, chap. 1.

46. *Boston Globe*, May 11, 1933.

47. *Salem* (Mass.) *Evening News*, May 11, 1933.

48. Ibid., May 13, 1933.

49. Ibid.

50. Ibid.

51. Ibid.

52. Ibid., May 16, May 27, 1933.

53. "Strikers of the Naumkeag Steam Cotton Company," undated flyer, Anne Burlak Timpson Papers. Although Burlak is silent on this issue, Ned Sparks credited her with having exposed the issue of the numbered ballots. *Salem* (Mass.) *Evening News*, June 2, 1933.

54. Newspaper clipping identified only as *Sunday Journal* (circa July 12, 1933). Anne Burlak Timpson Papers.

55. On the first day of the strike, the pattern was set when the hastily organized strike committee tried to call a meeting: "Police looked into the matter and at the request of City Marshal Harkins, no permit was issued, after it had been found that the meeting had not been called by the union officials, but that it was sponsored by 'Reds.'" *Salem* (Mass.) *Evening News*, May 8, 1933. See also, for example, *Salem* (Mass.) *Evening News*, July 10, 1933. For a discussion of this phenomenon nationwide, see American Civil Liberties Union, "Blue Coats and Reds."

56. *Daily Worker*, June 14, 1933. On the UTW loss of the Lawrence strike and its impact on workers elsewhere, see Gerstle, *Working-Class Americanism*, 103.

57. *Salem* (Mass.) *Evening News*, June 12, 1933.

58. *Daily Worker*, June 14, 1933.

59. On May 27, the *Salem* (Mass.) *Evening News* reported that she had been "in this city and Peabody during the past several days."

60. Ibid.

61. Ibid., May 20, May 27, 1933.

62. Ibid., June 5, 1933; *Daily Worker*, June 7, 1933.

63. *Salem* (Mass.) *Evening News*, June 7, 1933.

64. Ibid., May 19, 1933. Apparently Bates ceded on this point, because the following day's paper reported that Bakeman had in fact attended the meeting. Ibid., May 20, 1933.

65. *Salem* (Mass.) *Tribune*, May 28, 1933.

66. *Salem* (Mass.) *Evening News*, June 17, 1933.

67. Ibid., June 16, 1933.

68. Ibid., July 10, 1933.

69. *Daily Worker*, June 23, 1933. The leaflet is also quoted in the *Salem* (Mass.) *Evening News*, June 21, 1933.

70. *Boston Globe*, June 16, 1933; *Salem* (Mass.) *Evening News*, June 20 [?], 1933.

71. *Salem* (Mass.) *Evening News*, June 16, June 20 [?], June 22, 1933.

72. *Daily Worker*, June 29, 1933.

73. *Salem* (Mass.) *Evening News*, July 1, 1933.

74. *Daily Worker*, July 3, 1933.

75. Newspaper clipping identified only as *Sunday Journal* (July 9, 1933). Anne Burlak Timpson Papers; *Salem* (Mass.) *Evening News*, July 10, 1933; *Daily Worker*, July 12, 1933.

76. *Daily Worker*, July 12, 1933.

77. See, for example, ibid., June 23 and July 8, 1933, articles urging readers to contribute to the strike relief fund set up by the strike committee.

78. *Salem* (Mass.) *Evening News*, May 20, May 22, June 22, 1933.

79. "Help us win our strike!," undated flyer, Anne Burlak Timpson Papers.

80. Comments made at public presentations at the Salem Council on Aging (June 2004) and the Salem State College Enterprise Center (July 2004).

81. *Salem* (Mass.) *Evening News*, May 20, May 22, May 31, June 1, June 7, June 8, July 15, 1933.

82. *Daily Worker*, June 9, 1933.

83. *Salem* (Mass.) *Evening News*, July 19, 1933.

84. Ibid., July 15, July 17, 1933.

85. Ibid., July 17, 1933.

86. Interview with Elizabeth Votta, June 2004.

87. *Salem* (Mass.) *Evening News*, June 21, 1933, discusses their arrival.

88. *Boston Globe*, July 18, 1933.

89. *Daily Worker*, July 19, 1933.

90. *Salem* (Mass.) *Evening News*, July 18, 1933.

91. Ibid.

92. Ibid.; *Daily Worker*, July [19?], 1933.

93. *Salem* (Mass.) *Evening News*, July [20?], 1933. n.d.

94. Salem's workers were not the only ones to abandon the UTW during the Depression. Gerstle describes how the union's timidity provoked radical workers in Woonsocket, Rhode Island, to also secede from the International and form an independent union in 1931. See Gerstle, *Working-Class Americanism*, 103.

95. *Salem* (Mass.) *Evening News*, August 12, 1935.

96. Ibid. Though Smith does not mention where the mill machinery might be sold to, in fact Latin American textile factories were the purchasers of much used New England textile machinery in the 1930s. See chapter 3.

97. *Salem* (Mass.) *Evening News*, August 17, 1935. The complex of events and factors leading to the closure of Amoskeag in 1935 is described in Haraven and Langenbach, *Amoskeag*, 295–306. They note that many workers accepted the interpretation of the company treasurer who threatened during the 1922 strike that "grass will grow on the streets of Manchester unless the workers agree to the terms" (301); NSSC letter to union, reprinted in Salem (Mass.) *Evening News*, August 29, 1935.

98. Reprinted in *Salem* (Mass.) *Evening News*, August 26, 1935.

99. Ibid., September 20, 1935.

100. Reprinted ibid., August 30, 1935.

101. Ibid., October 5, 1935.

102. Ibid., October 11, October 21, 1935.

103. Ibid., June 16, 1933.

104. This was in fact typical of communist and, after 1928, NTWU involvement in textile strikes. Daniel describes communist activism in the 1926 Passaic strike, the 1928 New Bedford strike, and the 1929 Gastonia strike in strikingly similar terms. In New Bedford, for example, "While the UTW demanded only a rollback or reduction of the wage cut that sparked the strike as the price of labor peace in New Bedford cotton mills, the Communists skillfully played to their followers' anger and militancy by demanding large wage increases, equal pay for equal work, a forty-hour week, and an end to the speed-up. UTW leaders and other conservative elements cited the Communists' unrealistic demands as proof of their ulterior motives, but immigrant strikers without alternative sources of support embraced the Communists as the only allies available to them" (Daniel, *Culture of Misfortune*, 26).

105. Cited in the *Salem* (Mass.) *Evening News*, June 7, 1933.

106. Teter et al., "Textile Town Appendix," 315, 318.

107. The decision to close the Salem plant is detailed in reports in the *Salem* (Mass.) *Evening News*, August 14, August 17, August 19, August 20, 1953; and the *New York Times*, August 15, August 21, November 7, 1953. Quote is from the *New York Times*, August 20, 1953.

108. Little, *How to Lose $100,000,000*, 127–28, 129–130. See also Kiplinger, "Indian Head Remembered." Kiplinger notes that by the end of the 1960s Indian Head counted "18,700 employees, 60 plants [5 glass container companies, 5 metal and automotive companies, 12 specialty textile firms and the start of an information technology division] located in U.S., Canada and Netherlands."

109. Teter et al., "Textile Town Appendix," 318. In an ironic footnote, the Thomaston Mills in Thomaston, Georgia, which Naumkeag had contemplated buying years before, filed for bankruptcy and shut down in the same year. See Devin Steele, "Hanging by a Thread?" *STN Textile South Edition*, September 17, 2001, http://www.textilenews.com.

110. See "Spartan International Succumbs," *Textile News*, May 14, 2001, http://www.textilenews.com.

111. *Salem* (Mass.) *Evening News*, November 5, 1920.

112. Ibid.

113. Ibid., November 5, October 30, 1922.

114. Ibid., January 6, 1925.

115. Ibid., August 17, August 18, August 19, 1927. Callahan, who was acting chief of police in Peabody, was apparently angling for the position of police chief in Lynn, whose Mayor Bauer "hates the 'Reds.'" Ibid., August 20, 1927.

116. Ibid., August 20, August 23, 1927.

117. Ibid., August 23, 1927.

118. American Civil Liberties Union, "Blue Coats and Reds," 4, 10.

119. *Salem* (Mass.) *Evening News*, [April 22?, 1933].

120. See Ibid., May 8, 1933, for Bakeman's initial interest.

121. Robert A. Bakeman, letter to the editor, *Peabody* (Mass.) *Times*, June 9, 1933.

122. *Salem* (Mass.) *Evening News*, July 10, 1933.

123. Anne Burlak Timpson Papers, circa July 12.

124. Burlak autobiography ms., 12, Anne Burlak Timpson Papers.

125. Ibid., 19, 24, 29. On the Loray Mill strike, see Salmond, *Gastonia, 1929*. On the closing of the Rhode Island mills, see Gerstle, *Working-Class Americanism*, 56–57.

126. Burlak autobiography ms, 32, Anne Burlak Timpson Papers.

127. Trepp, "Union-Management Co-operation," 616–17.

128. Burlak, autobiography ms., 55, 57, 58, 60, 68, Anne Burlak Timpson Papers. At the 1932 AFL convention in Cincinnati, Green again took a position against federal unemployment insurance (81). Finally at the 1934 convention the organization reversed its position (89-A).

129. Ibid., 70, 71. In 1928 Fall River striking textile workers, backed by the American Civil Liberties Union, brought an injunction against Fall River police for interfering with their meetings in the Liberty Lot. See American Civil Liberties Union, "Blue Coats and Reds."

130. Burlak autobiography ms., 74, 91, 92, Anne Burlak Timpson Papers.

131. Ibid., 92.

132. Ibid., 96. Burlak does not mention the Royal Weaving Mill, but according to Lamphere, this mill was also involved in the strike. Both Royal Weaving and Weybosset closed in 1938. Lamphere, *From Working Daughters to Working Mothers*, 190–96, 206, 216.

133. Burlak, autobiography ms., 99, 98, Anne Burlak Timpson Papers.

134. Ibid., 77, 78.

135. Ibid., 78–79.

136. Ibid., 79.

137. Ibid.

138. Ibid., 73-A.

139. Ibid., 5.

140. *Salem* (Mass.) *Evening News*, May 8, June 7, 1933. The Protestant clergy of Salem, according to James Luther Adams, identified strongly with the mill owners and board who were among their parishioners. See J. L. Adams, *Not without Dust and Heat*, 133.

141. See J. L. Adams, *Not without Dust and Heat*.

142. J. L. Adams, "The Evolution of My Social Concern," 116.

143. *Salem* (Mass.) *Evening News*, July 17, 1933.

144. Ibid.

145. J. L. Adams, *Not without Dust and Heat*, 135.

3. Guns and Butter

1. In 2003, 24 percent of the company's revenues came from Bell and 23 percent from Cessna. Textron's industrial and fastening systems divisions were also military suppliers. See "Textron Businesses," http://www.textron.com. and *Textron 2005 Annual Report* (Providence, R.I.: Textron, Inc., 2006), 2.

2. By this statement I refer both to direct military occupations, as in Nicaragua (1912–33), Haiti (1915–34), and the Dominican Republic (1916–24), and the economic and political control exerted by major U.S. investors like the United Fruit Company (in Guatemala, Costa Rica, and Honduras). This argument has been developed in what is known as the revisionist school of U.S. diplomatic history, pioneered by William Appleman Williams in *The Tragedy of American Diplomacy*.

3. See Buhle, *Taking Care of Business*, and Lichtenstein, *State of the Union*, for critical assessments of the business unionism of the AFL and later AFL-CIO.

4. For a classic account, see Cardoso and Faletto, *Dependency and Development in Latin America*.

5. Hartford, *Where Is Our Responsibility?*, 44.

6. Margaret Parker, *Lowell: A Study of Industrial Development*, 159, found that the forty-eight-hour week (established in Massachusetts in 1920) and the "six o'clock law" (prohibiting women from working after 6 P.M.) contributed to plant closures in Lowell in the 1920s.

7. Hartford, *Where Is Our Responsibility?*, 95, describes how one New England "per-sister" supported TWUA efforts to raise the federal minimum wage, which would reduce the differential.

8. By 1948, eighteen of the forty-two largest textile companies in the South were controlled by northern capitalists. Hartford, *Where Is Our Responsibility?*, 91.

9. In addition to ibid., see especially Rosen, *Making Sweatshops*, who argues that U.S. government policies after World War II promoting the Japanese textile industry played a direct role in undermining the industry in the U.S. Lamphere makes the same argument in *From Working Daughters to Working Mothers*.

10. Rosen, *Making Sweatshops*, 78.

11. Hartford, *Where Is Our Responsibility?*, 91–92, 149–50, 157. Bluestone and Harrison emphasize the same phenomenon in *The Deindustrialization of America*.

12. As Cowie shows in *Capital Moves*, even some of the supposedly more stable mass production industries like electronics were more prone to capital flight than has generally been assumed.

13. Hartford, *Where Is Our Responsibility?*, 182. Collins, *Threads*, 10, notes that "more than half of all employers threatened to shut down operations during the period preceding the vote" in a 1998–99 sample. "In easily mobile industries such as apparel, threats occurred in 100 percent of cases." See Collins, *Threads*, 98 for a case study of the process at the Tultex knitting company in Virginia.

14. Willis, "Textile Town Pioneers," 15–16. The "Lowell of the South" brochure is reproduced in Teter, *Textile Town*, 37.

15. Rhode Island Historical Preservation and Heritage Commission, "Providence Industrial Sites," 7.

16. Hartford, *Where Is Our Responsibility?*, 52.

17. Eelman, "The English Manufacturing Company," 33; Racine, "Boom Time in Textile Town," 38. Waldrep, *Southern Workers and the Search for Community*, 14, writes that "most [of Spartanburg's mills] were either built outright by northern economic interests or ultimately controlled by northerners—especially the Milliken family and Boston's Lockwood-Greene engineering firm—under the guise of local management and incorporation." On Spartan Mills' board of directors sat, in addition to Seth Milliken, John W. Danielson of Providence, J. L. H. Cobb of Lewiston, Maine, and Stephen Greene of Newburyport, Massachusetts. Racine, "Boom Time in Textile Town," 41.

18. Gilman, *Human Relations in the Industrial Southeast*, 80. On New England machinery shops' interest in the south, see also Carlton and Coclanis, "Southern Textiles in Global Context," 10. Carlton, *Mill and Town in South Carolina*, 57, also points out that "northerners involved in commission sales, machinery, or engineering . . . were concerned comparatively little with the possible effects of southern competition with northern factories. On the other hand, as suppliers of capital goods and services to the textile industry, they were anxious to expand their southern trade."

19. Lockwood Greene website, http://www.lg.com.

20. Bridges, "Engineering the Mills," 72–73.

21. Lockwood Greene website, http://www.lg.com.

22. Hartford, *Where Is Our Responsibility?*, 170, discusses how the interpretation that union intransigence was at fault in the demise of the New England textile industry strengthened over time. Yet even in the face of extraordinary cooperation and concession from unions, stronger financial forces encouraged an accelerating process of buyouts and liquidations as the twentieth century progressed (179).

23. Ibid., 52.

24. Ibid., 104–5.

25. Ibid., 195.

26. Daniel, *Culture of Misfortune*, 134, 266.

27. Hartford, *Where Is Our Responsibility?*, 181, 187.

28. Daniel, *Culture of Misfortune*, 248–49.

29. Ibid., 19.

30. Hartford, *Where Is Our Responsibility?*, 79, 93–94. Gerstle, *Working-Class Americanism*, 322–23, suggests that as Woonsocket's manufacturers invested in new machinery in the 1940s, the reliance on skilled labor that tied them to the city diminished, making them even more likely to shift production to the South or abroad.

31. Hartford, *Where Is Our Responsibility?*, 92, cites Royal Little of Textron as the prime example of an interregionalist, "an inveterate empire builder who sometimes seemed more interested in acquiring new properties than in producing goods."

32. Ibid., 94. Gerstle, *Working-Class Americanism*, 106, describes an interesting counterpoint in Woonsocket, Rhode Island, where local owners proved more willing to accept the National Industrial Recovery Act and negotiate with unions in their plants, while (French) absentee owners were much more recalcitrant.

33. Gerstle, *Working-Class Americanism*, 327.

34. For examples of northern "persisters" supporting TWUA demands that a high minimum wage be set in the 1940s, see Hartford, *Where Is Our Responsibility?*, 83–84, 95.

35. Ibid., 114.

36. See "About Textron: Company History," http://www.textron.com; Rhode Island Historical Preservation and Heritage Commission, "Providence Industrial Sites," 30.

37. Hartford, *Where Is Our Responsibility?*, 119. The fact that capital gains taxes were lower than personal income taxes was another government incentive to sell profitable mills. See Lamphere, *From Working Daughters to Working Mothers*, 224.

38. Hartford, *Where Is Our Responsibility?*, 92.

39. Ibid., 178.

40. Little, *How to Lose $100,000,000*, 73; Hartford, *Where Is Our Responsibility?*, 179.

41. Hartford, *Where Is Our Responsibility?*, 180.

42. Little, *How to Lose $100,000,000*, 111. Indian Head closed the Cordova plant in 1962. See Kiplinger, "Indian Head Remembered."

43. Little, *How to Lose $100,000,000*, 119, 124, 126.

44. Ibid., 104–5. Interestingly, in 1950 Textron signed a groundbreaking pact with the TWUA—Hartford called it "the most lucrative pact in TWUA history"—providing, among other things, a guaranteed cost of living increase. It is possible that, in signing this agreement in its northern plants just as it was closing them down, Textron had found a way to increase the competitiveness of its new southern holdings. Hartford, *Where Is Our Responsibility?*, 131.

45. Little, *How to Lose $100,000,000*, 113, 186, 274.

46. Boris, "Needlewomen under the New Deal," 38, described Puerto Rico in the 1920s as "a nascent 'off-shore' production facility for the mainland industry." Analyses of Puerto Rico in the early part of the century tend to highlight this fact, although analyses of today's maquiladora industry tend not to recognize its historical antecedents in Puerto Rico.

47. Dietz, *Economic History of Puerto Rico*, 118.

48. Jones, "Sweatshops on the Spanish Main," 148.

49. Dietz, *Economic History of Puerto Rico*, 173.

50. Boris, "Needlewomen under the New Deal," 37.

51. "The Needlework Industry of Puerto Rico: Needlework, a $10,000,000 Industry," *Boletín Oficial de la Cámara de Comercio de Puerto Rico* (*Official Bulletin of the Chamber of Commerce of Puerto Rico*), 10, no. 6 (1934), posted on http://womhist.binghamton.edu. The report mentions D. E. Seicher and Weil and Weil as the first to operate their own manufacturing plants on the island, followed by Lande & Misken, Tiny Town Togs, Morris E. Storyk, Joseph Love, and Luis Tuttman.

52. For an in-depth study of how Liz Claiborne's business functioned, see Collins, *Threads*, 23, 104–25.

53. Gonález García, *Una puntada en el tiempo*, 32, 33 n. 1, 54, suggests all of these as contributing factors.

54. Ibid., 3, 20–22, 97, 20.

55. See G. L. García and Quintero Rivera, *Desafío y solidaridad*, 99.

56. Boris, "Needlewomen under the New Deal," 38; González García, *Una puntada en el tiempo*, 74. Kathleen Gladden, "Women in Industrial Development," 55, found a similar result in Colombia: the enactment of protective legislation for workers, including a comprehensive social security system, in Colombia in the 1930s, "encourages the use of subcontracting . . . and outworkers by the larger industries because these workers (small enterprise and outworkers) are unprotected by social security benefits and therefore provide a cheaper source of labor."

57. D. F. Ross, *The Long Uphill Path*, 17, 41–42. Ross worked for the Puerto Rican Economic Development Administration in the 1950s and was one of a group of staunch advocates of maintaining a low wage in order to attract industry. See Galvin, *The Organized Labor Movement in Puerto Rico*, 147.

58. Boris, "Needlewomen under the New Deal," 44.

59. Dietz, *Economic History of Puerto Rico*, 175, 177; D. F. Ross, *The Long Uphill Path*, 42.

60. Boris, "Needlewomen under the New Deal," 46. In the United States, unions argued for the abolition of homework, but Puerto Rican unions tended to argue for regulation rather than abolition.

61. Hernández Angueira, "El trabajo a domicilio femenino," 94. On the early history of the FLT and its affiliation with the AFL, see G. L. García and Quintero Rivera, *Desafío y solidaridad*, 36.

62. González García, *Una puntada en el tiempo*, 108.

63. G. L. García and Quintero Rivera, *Desafío y solidaridad*, 116.

64. D. F. Ross, *The Long Uphill Path*, 62, 64, 142.

65. Dietz, *Economic History of Puerto Rico*, 207.

66. D. F. Ross, *The Long Uphill Path*, 122.

67. Dietz, *Economic History of Puerto Rico*, 211. D. F. Ross, *The Long Uphill Path*, 120, notes that the Arthur D. Little firm was instrumental in both promoting textiles in Puerto Rico and in bringing Textron to the island. Little, *How to Lose $100,000,000*, xv, describes a very close family relationship; he lived with his uncle

during his high school years. His company contracted A. D. Little on numerous occasions for industry surveys (154, 226).

68. D. F. Ross, *The Long Uphill Path*, 121.

69. Little, *How to Lose $100,000,000*, 82–83. Little states that Textron put up $1 million; D. F. Ross, *The Long Uphill Path*, gives the $500,000 figure (121).

70. D. F. Ross, *The Long Uphill Path*, 121.

71. Little, *How to Lose $100,000,000*, 83.

72. The Ariguanabo mill had "more Draper looms than any other in Latin America." Draper Corporation, "Telares Draper en América Latina," in Draper Corporation, *Telares Draper*, section 4, 4, 11–13, 15.

73. D. F. Ross, *The Long Uphill Path*, 122.

74. Little, *How to Lose $100,000,000*, 83, says the price fell from 36 to 16 cents a yard; Ross, *The Long Uphill Path*, 123, gives the figures of 35 and 18 cents.

75. Little, *How to Lose $100,000,000*, 83.

76. Galvin, *Organized Labor in Puerto Rico*, 160, notes, "Many firms are housed in buildings leased from the Economic Development Administration and have minimal ties binding them to the island," thus they can easily resort to the threat of closing when confronted with union demands.

77. D. F. Ross, *The Long Uphill Path*, 122–23.

78. Ross notes that the plant was still operating in 1969 (ibid., 123). Joan Kiplinger mentions the 1961 sale in "Indian Head Remembered."

79. D. F. Ross, *The Long Uphill Path*, 123.

80. Galvin, *The Organized Labor Movement in Puerto Rico*, 157.

81. D. F. Ross, *The Long Uphill Path*, 149. "The formulation of wage policy is a perpetual problem for Puerto Rican politicians. The underlying justification for the entire program of economic development is that of creating employment at wage levels commensurate with a rapidly improving standard of living. Yet, the principal attraction for potential investors is the bait of relatively low wages and keeping them low." Galvin, *The Organized Labor Movement in Puerto Rico*, 132.

82. D. F. Ross, *The Long Uphill Path*, 150; Galvin, *The Organized Labor Movement in Puerto Rico*, 132, 146–49.

83. G. L. García and Quintero Rivera, *Desafío y solidaridad*, 133.

84. Galvin, *The Organized Labor Movement in Puerto Rico*, 136, 160.

85. On the ILGWU's wage restraint policy in Puerto Rico, see Rosado Marzán, "Successful Wage Restraint"; G. L. Garcia and Quintero Rivera, *Desafío y solidaridad*. On the ILGWU and Dubinsky's relationship with Muñoz Marín, see Galvin, *The Organized Labor Movement in Puerto Rico*, 157–59.

86. Richard L. Bolin, "What Puerto Rico Faced in Being First to Create EPZs [Export Processing Zones] in 1947," Flagstaff Institute, September 9, 2004, http://www.wepza.org. Similarly, in Mexico, offshore producers often chose to allow the official Mexican Confederación de Trabajadores de México (CTM) union into their plants because its presence would preclude radical worker organizing. See

Schmidt, *In Search of Decision*. Collins describes the Aguascalientes branch of the CTM (where Burlington and other textile producers located in the 1990s) as "committed to 'social peace' secured through collaboration between the union, management, and the state. . . . The Federación de Trabajadores de Aguascalientes' slogan was, 'For workers there is no worse company than one that closes.'" *Threads*, 129, quoting Eugenio Herrera Nuño, *Aguascalientes: Sociedad, economía, política y cultura* (Mexico City: Universidad Nacional Autónoma de México: Centro de Investigaciones Interdisciplinarias en Humanidades, 1989), 88.

87. D. Frank, *Buy American*, 148. The ILGWU took the same approach to domestic capital flight. In 1954, unable to enforce a union contract with a plant that had relocated to the South, the union negotiated a cash payment in lieu of a contract. In another case, the union itself purchased a plant in Virginia for a manufacturer who agreed to run it as a union operation. In yet another, the union pledged to refrain from trying to organize a runaway plant if the company agreed to pay slightly over minimum wage. While Rosen, *Making Sweatshops*, 101, terms all of these examples "creative labor strategies," they also served to reinforce the gap between the union's leadership and its members and to make the union a partner in the race to the bottom afflicting the garment industry.

88. G. L. García and Quintero Rivera, *Desafío y solidaridad*, 137, citing O. B. Server, "La degeneración del movimiento obrero en Puerto Rico," *Revista La Escalera* 2, no. 4 (summer 1967): 14. Collins, *Threads*, 129, describes the same procedure at offshore processing plants in Aguascalientes, Mexico.

89. Galvin, *The Organized Labor Movement in Puerto Rico*, 162.

90. "Supplemental Statement on Behalf of the International Ladies' Garment Workers' Union with Regard to the Provisions of S. 1861 Applicable to Puerto Rico," by Walter Mankoff, assistant director of research, ILGWU, before the Subcommittee on Labor and Public Welfare, U.S. Senate, July 19, 1971, mimeographed version, 1–2, quoted in Galvin, *The Organized Labor Movement in Puerto Rico*, 163.

91. International Labor Organisation Textiles Committee, "Recent Events," 97.

92. Dietz, *Economic History of Puerto Rico*, 247. Interestingly, as the textile industry grew in Puerto Rico, so did textile *imports* on the island. "In 1948, 80 percent of local textile demand was met by imports. By 1963, this had risen to 87 percent, despite the expansion of the textile industry. . . . Meanwhile, 72 percent of textile output was exported in 1948, and 91 percent in 1963" (272).

93. Ibid., 249, 263.

94. PRIDCO website, http://www.pridco.com.

95. See ibid. for a directory of current operations.

96. See "Government to Help Sara Lee's Laid Off Workers Find Jobs," *Puerto Rico Herald*, June 11, 2004. http://www.puertorico-herald.org; Associated Press, "Sara Lee to Cut 1,200 Jobs in Puerto Rico," February 25, 2003. http://www.puertorico-herald.org.

97. Rosen, *Making Sweatshops*, 37. Rosen (34) describes the formation of the Textile

Mission or Draper Commission. For William H. Draper Jr.'s relationship with Wickliffe Draper and the Draper Loom Corporation, see Probert, "Bright, White Folks." William H. Draper III went on to work as a fundraising cochair for George H. W. Bush's 1980 presidential campaign and also to serve as president of the Export-Import Bank under the Reagan and Bush administrations. Like others in the Draper clan, William Jr. was a strong advocate of population control, serving as honorary chair of the Population Crisis Committee, on the governing body of the International Planned Parenthood Federation, and as honorary vice chairman of Planned Parenthood in the United States, as well as representing the United States on the United Nations Population Commission. See Hess, "Oral History of Gen. William H. Draper, Jr."

98. D. Frank, *Buy American*, 123. George Meany of the AFL-CIO, however, endorsed the government's cold war free trade agenda (276 n. 58).

99. Rosen, *Making Sweatshops*, 49–50.

100. D. F. Ross, *The Long Uphill Path*, 134, 143, 175.

101. For a plethora of detail on the establishment of the zone, see Schmidt, *In Search of Decision*, especially the interview with Bolin.

102. Botero, "Arranca la gran industria."

103. Ibid.; Luis Fernando Molina, "Echavarría, Carlos J.," in *Gran Enciclopedia de Colombia en Círculo de Lectores*, tomo de biografías, http://www.lablaa.org. Carlos was the son of the Coltejer founder Alejandro Echavarría.

104. Farnsworth-Alvear, *Dulcinea in the Factory*, 49–52, 118.

105. Ibid., 151.

106. Glaessel-Brown, "Immigration Policy and Colombian Textile Workers," 109.

107. Botero, "Arranca la gran industria."

108. Farnsworth-Alvear, *Dulcinea in the Factory*, 151–52. Fabricato and Coltejer were actually both owned by an interlocking set of directors from the Echavarría family (51).

109. Ibid., 151, 269 n. 17.

110. Ibid., 57; Gladden, "Women in Industrial Development," 54; International Textile Group, http://www.burlington.com. According to Glaessel-Brown, "Immigration Policy and Colombian Textile Workers," 110, Burlington's interest was bought out by Colombian stockholders in 1958.

111. Gladden, "Women in Industrial Development," 54. On the Georgia strike, see Brattain, "Making Friends and Enemies," 91–92. Before being elected president of Colombia in 1970, Misael Pastrana served as president of Celanese from 1961 to 1965; Coltejer's Carlos Echavarría also sat on the board. Luz Stella Tocancipá, "Misael Pastrana Borrero," and Luis Fernando Molina, "Echavarria, Carlos J.," in *Gran Enciclopedia de Colombia en Círculo de Lectores*, tomo de biografías, http://www.lablaa.org. In 1981, Celanese announced the potential closure of three of its synthetic fiber factories in Colombia. *Wall Street Journal*, December 24, 1981.

112. For Burlington, see Wright, "The Aftermath of the General Textile Strike."
113. Farnsworth-Alvear, *Dulcinea in the Factory*, 210, 214.
114. Jaime, interviewed in Glaessel-Brown, "Immigration Policy and Colombian Textile Workers," 296.
115. Farnsworth-Alvear, *Dulcinea in the Factory*, 150–51.
116. Glaessel-Brown, "Immigration Policy and Colombian Textile Workers," 251–52. She is quoting Mariluz Cortés and José F. Escandón, "Use of Second-Hand Equipment in Colombia," unpublished paper, 1979.
117. Glaessel-Brown, "U.S. Immigration Policy and Colombian Textile Workers," 254, 383 n. 5.
118. "El Sitio Paisa: Fabricato," at http://www.lopaisa.com; Parsons, *Antioqueño Colonization*, 180.
119. "Informativo colombiano," at http://www.encolombia.com; Fabricato-Tejicóndor, "Filiales en el exterior," at www.fabricato.com.
120. Parsons, *Antioqueño Colonization*, 180–81.
121. Glaessel-Brown, "Immigration Policy and Colombian Textile Workers," 259. The Taxpayers Certificate of Allowance subsidized about 10 percent of export costs.
122. Ibid., 107–9.
123. Gladden, "Women in Industrial Development," 54, notes that the Barranquilla zone led to a decline in importance of Medellín's production as several new large plants located there.
124. "Colombia: Foreign Economic Relations," in Library of Congress, *Colombia: A Country Study*. Although this study gives the date for the Barranquilla EPZ as 1964, other sources agree on the 1958 date. See Richard L. Bolin and Robert C. Haywood, "WEPZA: Comments and Questions" (a response by the Flagstaff Institute to an ICFTU report entitled "Behind the Wire"), World Economic Processing Zones Association website, http://www.wepza.org; República de Colombia, Ministerio de Comercio, Industria y Turismo, "Zona Franca Industrial de Bienes y Servicios," Colombia Ministerio de Comercio, Industria y Turismo website, http://www.mincomercio.gov.co.
125. For 1991, see U.S. Department of State, "Country Reports on Human Rights Practices for 1991"; for 1999, see Intelligence Research Limited, "NAFTA Parity Comes before U.S. Senate: Regional Leaders Lobby as 'Maquilas' Move to Mexico," *Latin America Regional Reports: Caribbean and Central America*, September 28, 1999; for 2003, see United States, Office of the U.S. Trade Representative, "First Report to the Congress," 30.
126. U.S. Department of Agriculture, "World Cotton Situation." Other policies introduced as part of the economic liberalization of 1991 fostered exports, including a new export credit guarantee of $12 million, and the ending of domestic price guarantees and requirements that a portion of Colombian cotton be sold to domestic producers.

127. Tdctrade.com, "Colombia's (and Hong Kong's) Clothing Firms Cash In on U.S. Trade Deal," March 16, 2004, http://www.tdctrade.com.

128. It was in one of its Colombian plants that Liz Claiborne carried out a pilot program for its new "statistical process control" method—an updated version of the old speed-up. By 1998 the company had implemented the system in 98 out of its 250 suppliers. Collins, *Threads*, 121–22; see also photograph of a statistical processing control station at a Sara Lee factory producing on contract for Liz Claiborne in Colombia on 142.

129. Tdctrade.com, "Colombia's (and Hong Kong's) Clothing Firms Cash In on U.S. Trade Deal," March 16, 2004, http://www.tdctrade.com.

130. Edward Alden and James Wilson, "Bogota Jobs Plea to US: Trade Preferences Special Treatment for Caribbean May Penalise Colombia," *Financial Times*, September 21, 2000.

131. Ibid.

132. United States, Office of the U.S. Trade Representative, "First Report to the Congress," 12–13; United States, Office of the U.S. Trade Representative, "Second Report to the Congress," 9.

133. United States, Office of the U.S. Trade Representative, "Second Report to Congress," 5, 23, 7.

134. Ibid., 30.

135. United States, Office of the United States Trade Representative, "First Report to the Congress," 26.

136. Hugh Bronstein, "Medellín Leads Colombia's Push to Export Textiles," Reuters, August 29, 2004; Tdctrade.com, "Colombia's (and Hong Kong's) Clothing Firms Cash In on U.S. Trade Deal," March 16, 2004, http://www.tdctrade.com.

137. Tdctrade.com, "Colombia's (and Hong Kong's) Clothing Firms Cash In on U.S. Trade Deal," March 16, 2004, http://www.tdctrade.com.

138. Kelly Egan, "Thinking Locally, Shutting Globally," *Ottawa Citizen*, May 18, 2005.

139. Elizabeth Allen and Bonnie Pfister, "Ex-Levi Workers Start Job Retraining," *San Antonio Express-News*, May 18, 2004.

140. Cotton Council International Press Release, "Textile Mill Executives Seeking to Build Momentum for US COTTON in Latin America," January 29, 1999, http://www.cottonusa.org.

141. See Cotton Council International, "South American Events and Promotions," and archive of press releases regarding the council's activities mostly in Colombia, http://www.cottonusa.org.

142. United States, Office of the U.S. Trade Representative, "First Report to the Congress," 53–54.

143. Tdctrade.com, "Colombia's (and Hong Kong's) Clothing Firms Cash In on U.S. Trade Deal," March 16, 2004, http://www.tdctrade.com.

144. United States, Office of the U.S. Trade Representative, "First Report to the Congress," 55.

145. See the list of parties filing objections in United States, Office of the U.S. Trade Representative, "Second Report to Congress," 50–51.

146. Bert Lunan, "Legacy of Leadership: Roger Milliken," South Carolina Business Hall of Fame, http://www.myetv.org.

147. Melman, *The Permanent War Economy*; see also Melman's *Pentagon Capitalism* and *Profits without Production*.

148. Lamphere, *From Working Daughters to Working Mothers*, 172.

149. *Cotton Chats* 191, September 1918.

150. *Cotton Chats* 192, October 1918.

151. *Cotton Chats* 350, March 1942.

152. "Army Has a Big Job for Textiles," *Business Week*, October 19, 1940, 30–31, cited in Daniel, *Culture of Misfortune*, 132.

153. Minchin, *Don't Sleep with Stevens!*, 14.

154. Rhode Island Historical Preservation and Heritage Commission, "Providence Industrial Sites," 30; Richie, "Walter S. Montgomery, Sr.," 244.

155. Advertisements and editorial reproduced in Teter, *Textile Town*, 172, 173, 176.

156. John O'Connor, "New Gun Made in Hopedale Blazes Way for U.S. Victories," *Boston Herald*, August 29, 1943, reproduced in Draper Corporation, *Cotton Chats* 358, October 1943.

157. "History: Celanese, Building on a Strong Foundation," Celanese Corporation website, http://www.celanese.com. A 1946 advertisement for a Celanese rayon dress from *Semana* magazine is reproduced on Proyecto Diseño, "Historia del diseño del vestuario colombiano," http://www.proyectod.com.

158. Trepp, "Making Friends, Making Enemies," 135; Mary Otto, "The Hard Times Never Left: Forty Years after the War on Poverty, Western Maryland Still Hurts," *Washington Post*, May 20, 2004.

159. David Ignatius, "Our Weird Weapons Bazaar," *Washington Post*, June 26, 1988. He seems to be referring to Rick Atkinson and Fred Hiatt, "To Prepare for War, We Need a Revolution," *Washington Post*, December 15, 1985, C1.

160. Ted Larter, interviewed in Glaessel-Brown, "Immigration Policy and Colombian Textile Workers," 329.

161. See Little, *How to Lose $100,000,000*, 273, for an account of Textron's Bell purchase.

162. Stycos, "Torture Is the Issue."

163. John Berry, "Textron, Inc. Slush Fund Is Alleged," *Washington Post*, February 1, 1980.

164. Alexander Barnum, "Recent Agreements by International Lending and Financial Institutions," *Washington Post*, April 23, 1984.

165. Geov Parrish, "U.S. Arms Exporters: Textron," MoJo Wire, 2004, *Mother Jones* website, http://www.motherjones.com; Stycos, "Torture Is the Issue."

166. Keven McKiernan, "U.S. Should Block Copter Sale to Turkey," *The Gazette* (Montreal), March 7, 2000.

167. Dave Todd, "Canada to Sell Helicopters in Secret Deal," *Ottawa Citizen*, June 8, 1994.

168. Bell Helicopter Textron, press release, "Mexico Buys 24 Helicopters for Anti-Drug War," October 21, 1999, http://www.helis.com.

169. See Project Ploughshares and Amnesty International, Canada, "Concerns around the Sale of Helicopters to the Colombian Armed Forces," March 2001, Inter-Church Committee on Human Rights in Latin America website, http://www.web.net/icchrla/. For more on Textron's lobbying and weapons sales, see Stycos, "Torture Is the Issue."

170. Tim Golden, "Colombia and Copters and Clash over Choice," *New York Times*, March 6, 2000.

171. Stycos, "Torture Is the Issue."

172. George F. Kennan, "Review of Current Trends: U.S. Foreign Policy," PPS/23, February 24, 1938, *Foreign Relations of the United States* 1 (1948): 509–29.

173. A particularly ironic example of this occurred during the J. P. Stevens campaign, when the company repeatedly raised the specter of job loss due to cheaper imports if the union succeeded—when Stevens itself was already operating a plant in Mexico! See Minchin, *Don't Sleep with Stevens!*, 117, 137.

174. Teter, "Textile Town in Transition," 268–69.

175. D. Frank, *Buy American*, 189.

176. TWUA president Sol Stetin initiated talks for the merger in the 1970s in part to strengthen its position in the long-running battle against J. P. Stevens. Minchin, *Don't Sleep with Stevens!*, 87.

177. D. Frank, *Buy American*, 197, 198.

178. Peter M. Tirschwell, "U.S. Apparel Sector Takes 'Wait and See' Approach to NAFTA," *Journal of Commerce*, September 3, 1992; Susan Harte, "Textile Exec Seeks Allies against Free Trade Pact," *Atlanta Journal and Constitution*, September 24, 1992. Eight years later, Milliken resigned from the ATMI over its support for the Caribbean Basin Initiative. Collins, *Threads*, 53.

179. Greig Guthey, "Textile Mills Put Trust in Technology," *Journal of Commerce*, May 16, 1994.

180. Michael Fitzgerald, "Burlington's Future: Virtually Here," *Textile World*, March 2003 at http://www.textileworld.com. Burlington's Burlmex factory in Aguascalientes, which opened in 1999 and employed over one thousand workers, was contracted to produce blue jeans for Liz Claiborne, Calvin Klein, Levi Strauss, and Rocky Mountain. It used denim produced by its own mill in Yecapixtla, Morelos, and also precut fabric from the United States. Once sewn, the jeans were shipped to a Burlington-operated laundry in Chihuahua for bleaching. Burlington closed its Aguascalientes factory as part of a Chapter 11 bankruptcy reorganization in 2002. Collins, *Threads*, 127, 137–39.

181. Paula L. Green, "A Good Fit," *Journal of Commerce*, May 10, 1996.

182. Bert Lunan, "Legacy of Leadership: Roger Milliken," South Carolina Business Hall of Fame, http://www.myetv.org.

183. As Collins points out, "It is more accurate to think of the changes in the provenance of U.S. apparel in recent years as a result of the growth of global sourcing rather than the growth of imports" (*Threads*, 49; see also 103).

184. "Business Improved in 1992 for Textile Industry in U.S.," *Journal of Commerce*, January 5, 1993.

185. D. Frank, *Buy American*, 68–69, 77.

186. Ibid., 87–88.

187. Ibid., 103, 109, 110, 111, 273 n. 21.

188. Hartford, *Where Is Our Responsibility?*, 88, 111.

189. D. Frank, *Buy American*, 116–117, 127.

190. Ibid., 132–33.

191. Ibid., 138–43, 195–99.

192. AMTAC, "Labor Union UNITE Joins Textile/Fiber Coalition," September 3, 2003, http://www.amtacdc.org.

193. AMTAC, "2004 Issues," http://www.amtacdc.org.

194. AMTAC, "CAFTA Bad for U.S. Industry and Workers," press release, May 28, 2004, http://www.amtacdc.org.

195. Statement of Mark Levinson, chief economist, UNITE-HERE, before the Senate Finance Committee on the Dominican Republic—Central America Free Trade Agreement, April 13, 2005, http://www.unitehere.org.

196. "Labor Union UNITE Joins Textile/Fiber Coalition," September 3, 2003, AMTAC website, http://www.amtacdc.org.

197. Henry Frundt, "Cross-Border Organizing in the Apparel Industry."

198. United States Business and Industry Council, http://www.americaneconomic alert.org.

199. Valerie Bauerlien, "N.C. Businessmen Lobby for CAFTA: Trade Pact Would Bring Textile Growth, They Say," *News and Observer* (Raleigh, N.C.), April 14, 2005. See the list of clients in the Palmaseca zone at its website, http://www.zonafran cacolombia.com. For VF, see http://www.vfsolutions.com. Since a large portion of VF's production is outsourced to Asia already, the corporation would logically see China as more of an opportunity than a threat.

200. Cotton Council International, "CCI Launches Section 108 Program in Costa Rica," 2000, http://www.cottonusa.org.

201. Cotton Council International, "Sourcing CBI Moves Cotton in the Dominican Republic," http://www.cottonusa.org.

202. Cotton Council International, "CCI and Cotton Incorporated Team Up to Showcase U.S. Cotton," 2003, http://www.cottonusa.org.

203. Orçun Ünlüby, "State Businesses Lobby for CAFTA," *Duke Chronicle Online*, April 25, 2005, www.dukechronicle.com.

204. See Environmental Working Group, "What's the Plan? U.S. Farm Subsidies, 1995–2003," 2005, http://www.ewg.org. A list of Step 2 recipients can be found at the same site.

205. See Environmental Working Group, "Step 2 Cotton Plan Has Paid $2.16 Billion from 1995–2003," http://www.ewg.org. Brazil brought suit against the United States, arguing that the subsidies constituted unfair trading practices that harmed cotton producers outside the United States, and the WTO recently ruled in Brazil's favor.

206. Sewn Products Equipment Suppliers of the Americas Association website, http://www.spesa.org.

207. Devin Steele, "Hanging by a Thread?," *Southern Textile News* (Textile South Edition), September 17, 2001.

208. Collins, *Threads*, 41–42, 113–14.

209. Nutt, "Seth Milliken," 70–71.

210. D. Frank, *Buy American*, 193.

211. Daniel, *Culture of Misfortune*, 142, 159, 161.

212. Ibid., 161.

213. Ibid., 255.

214. DuPlessis, "Roger Milliken," 288.

215. Minchin, *Don't Sleep with Stevens!*, 38, 53. The company also did not hesitate to push the idea that "it was union wage demands that were responsible for the deindustrialization of the northern states" (130). The company did, in fact, close one southern plant where it was forced by the NLRB to recognize the union (54, 61, 145). Stevens had closed its last unionized plants in the North in 1951 rather than follow others in the industry in granting wage and cost-of-living increases in that year. Hartford, *Where Is Our Responsibility?*, 132. The brother of J. P. Stevens's founder Horace Nathaniel Stevens was also a textile magnate, founding the Ames Manufacturing Company of Lowell, discussed in chapter 4.

216. Minchin, *Don't Sleep with Stevens!*, 114, 162.

217. "Most northerners had witnessed how local firms had closed down plants and moved south in search of cheaper wages, just as Stevens had done. The company seemed to epitomize the 'runaway shops' that had turned large parts of the Northeast and Midwest into a declining 'rust belt.' " Ibid., 91; see also 100.

218. D. Frank, *Buy American*, 194.

219. Milliken closed a plant in Robbins, North Carolina, in 1990; two plants in Lockhart and Spartanburg, South Carolina, in 1994; and another in Spartanburg in 1995. See ibid., 196.

220. Carlton and Coclanis, "Southern Textiles in Global Context," 21.

221. "Fortune 100 Best Companies to Work for," *Fortune Magazine*, CNN website, http://money.cnn.com.

4. Invisible Workers

1. Dalzell, *Enterprising Elites*, 33–34.

2. Piore, *Birds of Passage*, 35.

3. This analysis summarizes Piore, *Birds of Passage*.

4. Piore documents the succession of recruitment processes ibid., 23–26.

5. The 2000 census counted 428,729 people of the "Hispanic or Latino" category in Massachusetts, up from 275,859 in 1990; 46.5 percent (in 2000) were Puerto Rican, 11.6 percent Dominican, 5.2 percent Mexican, and fewer than 5 percent each were Cuban, Salvadoran, Guatemalan, other Central American, Colombian, and other South American; 19.1 percent did not state a national origin or chose "other." U.S. Census, cited in Charles Jones, "Latinos in Massachusetts," Mauricio Gastón Institute, University of Massachusetts, Boston, April 2002, http://www.gaston.umb .edu. The cities of Boston (with a Latino population of 85,089 in 2000), Lawrence (43,019), Springfield (41,343), Worcester (26,155), and Chelsea (16,984) together accounted for almost half of the Latinos in the state. See Charles "Skuk" Jones, "Census Shows Growing, Changing Latino Population," Mauricio Gastón Institute, University of Massachusetts, Boston. Latinos constituted the highest proportion of the population in Lawrence (59.7 percent), followed by Chelsea (51.6 percent), Holyoke (41.4 percent), Springfield (27.2 percent), Lynn (18.4 percent), Fitchburg (16.0 percent), Worcester (15.1 percent), Boston (14.4 percent), Lowell (14.0 percent), Framingham (10.9 percent), and New Bedford (10.2 percent). Jim Campen, "New Census Figures Show Targeting of Latino Communities by Subprime Lenders," Gastón Institute *Report*, summer 2001, http://www.gaston.umb .edu.

   Rhode Island's Latino population almost doubled between 1990 and 2000, from 45,652 to 90,820. In 2000 over half (42,146) lived in Providence, with large numbers also in Pawtucket (10,141), Central Falls (9,041), Woonsocket (4,030), and Cranston (3,613). Latinos constituted the largest proportion of the population in Central Falls (47.8 percent), Providence (30.0 percent), Pawtucket (13.9 percent), and Woonsocket (9.3 percent). Uriarte and Jones, "Latinos in Rhode Island," 27.

6. The poverty rate for Latinos nationwide was 27.2 percent in the 1980s. Meléndez, "Latino Poverty and Economic Development in Massachusetts," 15.

7. On racial exclusions in U.S. immigration law see Haney López, *White By Law*, and Ngai, *Impossible Subjects*. On the "in between" status of southern and eastern European immigrants, legally and socially (neither fully white nor decisively nonwhite), see Roediger, *Working toward Whiteness*.

8. Numerous studies have shown that immigrants consistently pay more in taxes than they receive in social services. See Fix and Passel, *Immigration and Immigrants*.

9. Cannistraro and Meyer, "Italian American Radicalism, 2.

10. Vecoli, "The Making and Un-Making of the Italian American Working Class," 53. A similar argument has been made regarding the Irish in Ignatiev, *How the Irish Became White*.

11. Cannistraro and Meyer, "Italian American Radicalism," 1.

12. The best recent study of the phenomenon overall is Roediger, *Working toward Whiteness*.

13. Interview with Elizabeth Votta, June 2004.

14. The 2000 census counted 1,168 Latinos among Milford's 26,799 residents. Most of the town's 495 Brazilians probably did not classify themselves as Latinos. Of the 3,018 foreign-born residents in the town, over half were born in Europe and only 895 in Latin America. (Most of the 608 Puerto Ricans probably included themselves as "Latino" but not as "foreign-born.") These figures suggest that the degree of hysteria in the town is somewhat out of proportion to the actual number of immigrants, even given the probability of some undercounting. These figures are compiled from various census tables available at http://factfinder.census.gov.

15. Yvonne Abraham, "Towns Taking Own Action on Immigrants," *Boston Globe*, May 21, 2006.

16. In addition to the other sources cited in this section, Rosen describes the evolution of the culture of the ILGWU in *Making Sweatshops*, 96–103.

17. Zappia, "From Working-Class Radicalism to Cold War Anti-Communism," 151.

18. Guglielmo, "Donne Ribelli," 123.

19. Ibid., 125–26.

20. Zappia, "From Working-Class Radicalism to Cold War Anti-Communism," 153–54; Vecoli, "The Making and Un-Making of the Italian American Working Class," 58. Ortiz, "Puerto Rican Women in the Garment Industry," 65, describes the union's election process that prevented members from outside the preexisting power structures from attaining positions of power in the union.

21. Ortiz, "Puerto Rican Women in the Garment Industry," 58–59.

22. Guglielmo, "Donne Ribelli," 126.

23. Piore, *Birds of Passage*, 112.

24. Guglielmo, "Donne Ribelli," 126.

25. Ortiz, "Puerto Rican Women in the Garment Industry," 64–65, 71.

26. Ibid., 67, 71.

27. Sassen, "Why Migration?"; Piore, *Birds of Passage*; Meléndez, "Latino Poverty and Economic Development"; Borges-Méndez, "Latino Immigrant Labor"; Uriarte and Borges-Méndez, "Tales of Latinos in Three Small Cities," especially 7–10, 36.

28. Hartford, *Where Is Our Responsibility?*, 101, 163, 164.

29. Although he does not specifically draw the connection to military production, Gerstle, *Working-Class Americanism*, 332, 332 n. 25, mentions that better-paying opportunities in these industries led over a thousand of Woonsocket's workers to migrate out of that Rhode Island textile city between 1940 and 1944.

30. Glaessel-Brown, "Immigration Policy and Colombian Textile Workers," 114. The same process drew Puerto Rican immigrants into the garment industry in New York, as "the establishment of defense plants in the New York area . . . drew away white women workers, creating job openings in the garment factories." Ortiz, "Puerto Rican Women in the Garment Industry," 59.

31. Hartford, *Where Is Our Responsibility?*, 169, describes the poor quality of the jobs that replaced the mills, though he does not discuss immigrant workers.

32. Borges-Méndez, "Latino Immigrant Labor," 104–24.

33. The most comprehensive study is Glaessel-Brown, "Immigration Policy and Colombian Textile Workers." Glaessel-Brown published a portion of this work in "A Time of Transition." See also Beade, *The Wealth of Nations*, chap. 8; Lamphere, *From Working Daughters to Working Mothers*, chaps. 5–6.

34. Lowell Historical Society, "Lowell History Chronology," http://ecommunity.uml.edu.

35. Sylvie Pressman, quoted in Kathie Neff Ragsdale, "Dollar-an-Hour Jobs Beckoned First Latinos," *Lawrence* (Mass.) *Eagle-Tribune*, July 6, 2001.

36. Ibid.

37. See A. Chomsky and Holman, "The Hidden Maine."

38. On census undercounts of Latinos, see A. Chomsky, "Salem as a Global City," 230, 233; Rivera, "Diversity, Growth, and Geographic Distribution," 39–41. New England's smaller cities differ from the larger cities of the Northeast, which received large numbers of African American and Puerto Rican migrants in the 1940s and 1950s, prior to the new post-1965 immigration. Grosfoguel, "Puerto Rican Labor Migration." New England's smaller cities never attracted significant numbers of African American migrants. Puerto Ricans began to arrive in these smaller cities in the 1960s just as they were declining as a proportion of Caribbean immigrants; Dominicans followed a decade or two later.

39. Carlton, "Textile Town Settles In," 229–230.

40. "Carpet Industry," *New Georgia Encyclopedia*, http://www.georgiaencyclopedia.org. In Hampton, Virginia, a crab processor explained that immigrant workers saved his unstable business: "What's good about the Hispanics is they're here whenever I want them, and when I don't need them, they're in Mexico." Quoted in Jodi Snider, "Employers Praise Immigrants for Their Work Ethic, Attitude," *Hampton* (Va.) *Daily Press*, July 5, 2004, http://www.dailypress.com.

41. Héctor L., interviewed by Glaessel-Brown, "Immigration Policy and Colombian Textile Workers," 378.

42. Collins describes a similar effect of immigration restrictions on the garment industry in *Threads*, 34.

43. As Ted Larter recalled, when immigration authorities first threatened to deport undocumented Colombian workers at the Wannalancit Mills in the 1970s, his response was "O.K. Fine. You can have them. I'm going to give you something else. I'm going to give you the whole goddam thing. All the keys to the mill too. They're all yours too. If you take those fifty to sixty people out of here, mister, then you shut this mill down." Quoted in Glaessel-Brown, "A Time of Transition," 364. Continuing harassment by the Immigration and Naturalization Service was one of the factors that led to the mill's closure in 1980 (367).

44. Puerto Ricans constituted close to half of the Latino population in New England in the 2000 census and were the largest Latino group in all New England states except Maine, where Mexicans predominated. Martínez, "The Latinos of Rhode Island," 33–34.

45. Glasser, *Aquí me quedo*, 49 n. 11.

46. Mountain Lumber Company, "NECCO," http://www.mountainlumber.com. NECCO relocated to Revere, Massachusetts, in 2003. See "Our Story," http://www.necco.com. The Revere Sugar Refinery at 333 Medford Street in Charleston continued to process sugar until it closed in 1985; the facilities are now owned by MassPort. Ironically, the Mountain Lumber Company that recovered the lumber when NECCO's Cambridge plant was demolished also salvaged the lumber from Spartanburg's Spartan Mills complexes when they were closed in 2001. See www.mountainlumber.com.

47. Matos Rodríguez, "Puerto Rican Community in Boston."

48. Dietz, *Economic History of Puerto Rico*, 108–9, n. 80.

49. Martínez, "The Latinos of Rhode Island."

50. Glasser, *Aquí me quedo*, 55, 53–55.

51. Ibid., 49.

52. David Savona, "Made in the Shade," *Cigar Aficionado*, November–December 1999, http://www.cigaraficionado.com.

53. Glasser, *Aquí me quedo*, 75.

54. Piore, "Immigration, Work, and Market Structure," 113, 114.

55. Ibid., 119–20. The increase in social welfare programs and opportunities for African Americans in the 1960s, which paralleled the opening of opportunities for European immigrants in the 1930s and 1940s, may have also played a role in weakening their participation in the secondary labor market.

56. Martínez, "The Latinos of Rhode Island," 38.

57. Tatiana Pina, "Making Progress at Progreso," *Providence Journal-Bulletin*, April 11, 1996.

58. A. Chomsky, "Salem as a Global City," 232.

59. Glaessel-Brown, "A Time of Transition," 360.

60. The food stamp program was extended to Puerto Rico in 1974–75. In 1982 the Nutrition Assistance Grant program replaced the food coupons with cash. For a summary of transfer payments to Puerto Rico, see Santiago and Rivera-Batiz, *Island Paradox*, chap. 1, especially 14–17.

61. Sassen, "Why Migration?," 15.

62. Collins, *Threads*, 169. On the decision to locate maquiladoras in zones of out-migration, she cites Juárez Núñez, *Rebelión en el Greenfield*.

63. Daniel W. Vasquez, "Latinos in Lowell," Mauricio Gastón Institute, January 2003, http://www.gaston.umb.edu. See also Itzigsohn, "The Making of Latino Providence."

64. Lamphere, *From Working Daughters to Working Mothers*, 49, 177. Some of the silk producers, like Cadillac Silk, moved from Patterson, New Jersey, to escape radical worker organizing and union gains there. They spun and wove raw silk imported from China and Japan (176–77).

65. Lynn Arditi, "Elizabeth Webbing, a Long Goodbye," *Providence Journal-Bulletin*, June 3, 2001.

66. Lynn Arditi, "A Legacy Lost," *Providence Journal-Bulletin*, February 10, 2002. Four

hundred people were working there when the company closed, many of them Colombian immigrants. The local social service agency Progreso Latino helped to press for an appeal for trade adjustment assistance, a program extending unemployment benefits for workers who lose their jobs due to imports. Lynn Arditi, "Program May Extend Federal Benefits to Former Mill Workers in Central Falls, Rhode Island," *Providence Journal-Bulletin*, December 20, 2001.

67. William J. Donovan, "Pontiac Weaving Closes," *Providence Journal-Bulletin*, October 21, 1994.

68. "Obituaries: Samuel S. Schwartz," *Providence Journal-Bulletin*, October 19, 1994.

69. Kathleen Yanity, "Rhode Island Textile Firm Is an Old Company with New Leaders, Ideas," *Providence Journal-Bulletin*, October 19, 2000.

70. Parker, *Lowell*, 1.

71. The history of Ames and its relationship with Stevens is described in Glaessel-Brown, "Immigration Policy and Colombian Textile Workers," 89–93, 123 n. 6.

72. Ibid., 95.

73. See United States of America before the National Labor Relations Board, First Region, Case 1-RC-21687, NLRB website, http://www.nlrb.gov.

74. Collins and Aikman website, http://www.collinsaikman.com.

75. Glaessel-Brown, "Immigration Policy and Colombian Textile Workers," 98–99.

76. A 1963 survey showed that the Alliance for Progress had higher levels of recognition in Colombia than in any of the other six countries surveyed: 81 percent were aware of it, and most of them strongly approved. Report, USIA Research and Reference Service, "The Economic and Political Climate of Opinion in Latin America, and Attitudes towards the Alliance for Progress, June 1963," folder Alliance for Progress, 1/63–8/83, NSF Box 290A, John F. Kennedy Library, cited in Fajardo, "From the Alliance for Progress to Plan Colombia."

77. Glaessel-Brown, "Immigration Policy and Colombian Textile Workers," 111.

78. Hernández Angueira, "El trabajo a domicilio femenino," 86, 98, points out that the most modern industries in the United States sought the oldest forms of labor relations—home needlework—as part of their process of modernization.

79. Jaime, interviewed in Glaessel-Brown, "Immigration Policy and Colombian Textile Workers," 296.

80. Martínez, "The Latinos of Rhode Island," 41. This account is based on an interview with Giutarri done by Marta Martínez of the Rhode Island Historical Society. Although Martínez spells the name Guttiari, other variations appear in other accounts, including Guittari, Giutari, and Giuttari. I have chosen to use the most common spelling, Giutarri. An interview with Pedro Cano, who was recruited by Giutarri in Medellín in 1965, described him as the personnel manager for Lyons. Tatiana Pina, "Haciendo Historia: Making History, Hispanics in Rhode Island," *Providence Journal-Bulletin*, November 17, 1996.

81. This version is recounted in Lamphere, *From Working Daughters to Working Mothers*, 239–40. Both Martínez and Lamphere cite interviews with Jay Giutarri

as the source for their accounts. Glaessel-Brown, "A Time of Transition," 373 n. 30, confirms Lamphere's account, though in much less detail.

82. Lamphere, *From Working Daughters to Working Mothers*, 240–41.

83. Ibid., 241.

84. Martínez, "The Latinos of Rhode Island," 41.

85. Beade, *The Wealth of Nations*. Similarly, Clara Rodríguez concluded that Puerto Rican immigrants allowed New York's garment industry to survive through the 1960s and 1970s: "Without this source of cheap labor many more firms would have had to reduce their production. In this sense, New York's claim to be the garment capital of the world rests upon Puerto Rican shoulders." Rodríguez, "The Economic Factors Affecting Puerto Ricans in New York," 213, 229 n. 29, cited in Ortiz, "Puerto Rican Women in the Garment Industry," 80.

86. Martínez, "The Latinos of Rhode Island," 41, 42–43.

87. Glaessel-Brown, "A Time of Transition," 354.

88. Glaessel-Brown interviewed several of the men recruited in this "primer enganche" and included their testimonies in "Immigration Policy and Colombian Textile Workers," 129–34. My account is based on hers.

89. Ibid., 135.

90. Glaessel-Brown, "A Time of Transition," 357.

91. Glaessel-Brown, "Immigration Policy and Colombian Textile Workers," 133–34.

92. Ibid., 143–48, 158, 161, 165, 182, 227.

93. Ibid., 119.

94. *Latin America News Digest*, March 18, 2005.

95. For a description of the development of Colombia's social security system, see Gladden, "Women in Industrial Development." Glaessel-Brown describes the benefits provided by Medellín textile factories in "Immigration Policy and Colombian Textile Workers," 120.

96. Rubén, interviewed by Glaessel-Brown, "Immigration Policy and Colombian Textile Workers," 132.

97. For an excellent analysis of this phenomenon, see Folbre, *The Invisible Heart*, chap. 8. "Both immigration and capital mobility allow corporations to free-ride on the contributions of parents, friends and neighbors" (185). Even the very first generation of New England mill workers, young women from rural areas, fit this pattern. The costs of raising them were borne by the farm economy. "As daughters of 'respectable' farmers, few would have gone without the necessities of life had they remained at home. Rather, their hope was to save at least a portion of their wages, and many did so. The money was used for a variety of purposes; as a dowry, or a way of paying for a few terms at normal school, or sometimes for financing a brother's college education." Dalzell, *Enterprising Elite*, 33.

98. Humberto, quoted in Glaessel-Brown, "Immigration Policy and Colombian Textile Workers," 279.

99. Glaessel-Brown, "U.S. Immigration Policy and Colombian Textile Workers," 134–35.

100. Piore, *Birds of Passage*, 62.

101. Glaessel-Brown, "Immigration Policy and Colombian Textile Workers," 138, 294.

102. Héctor, interviewed ibid., 215.

103. Glaessel-Brown, "Immigration Policy and Colombian Textile Workers," 138–41, 142.

104. Briggs, "American Unionism and U.S. Immigration Policy."

105. David Bacon, "Employer Sanctions," *Z Magazine*, July 2001, http://www.zmag .org.

106. Union official interviewed in Glaessel-Brown, "Immigration Policy and Colombian Textile Workers," 298–99.

107. Piore, "Immigration, Work, and Market Structure," 117.

108. Briggs, "American Unionism and U.S. Immigration Policy." Leon Fink's *The Maya of Morganton*, chap. 5, gives an overview of the "new unionism" of the AFL-CIO and its relationship with Guatemalan and Mexican immigrant workers in the poultry industry.

109. David Bacon, "Labor Fights for Immigrants," *The Nation*, May 21, 2001.

110. Charles Bergquist's *Labor and the Course of American Democracy* summarizes the large literature on this topic. The links between U.S. imperialism and immigration are also the subject of much published analysis, made accessible to the general public in Juan González's *Harvest of Empire*.

111. "Interview Mr. S2, 4 April 1977," in Lamphere, Anzaldua, and Redondo, "Interviews for Central Falls NIMH Project."

5. The Cutting Edge of Globalization

A version of this chapter appeared in *International Labor and Working-Class History* 72 (November 2007).

1. Bucheli, *Bananas and Business*, 112. For a description of everyday life as the paramilitaries took over a town (not in Urabá), see Taussig, *Law in a Lawless Land*.

2. Tod Robberson, "Paramilitary Groups Gaining Strength in Colombia," *Dallas Morning News*, July 13, 1997.

3. While some aspects of today's neoliberal globalization are new to Latin America, much of it is familiar. An economy based on foreign investment and exports, a state committed to promoting the export sector through alliance with foreign capital and through creating financial structures that promote profits, and social and political structures that allow the harsh exploitation of labor are nothing new in Latin America. In fact, this pattern is characteristic of the colonial period, briefly upset in the mid-nineteenth century in the aftermath of the independence wars, but reconstituted in the period of liberal dictatorship throughout most of Latin America by the end of the century, to reign again until challenged by the Mexican Revolution of 1910 and the shift to state-sponsored industrialization and populism in the mid-twentieth century, only to swing back to the export economy after 1960.

4. F. U. Adams, *Conquest of the Tropics*, 15–16.

5. Wilson, *Empire and Green and Gold*, 207, 104.

6. F. U. Adams, *Conquest of the Tropics*, 9.

7. Wilson, *Empire in Green and Gold*, 70, 81.

8. Andrew Preston to Loren Baker, Boston, June 3, 1892, Lorenzo Dow Baker Papers, Box VI, Folder "A. W. Preston, 1892–1898," W. B. Nickerson Memorial Room, Cape Cod Community College, Barnstable, Massachusetts, cited in John Soluri, "Accounting for Taste," 390.

9. The most notorious example of this is the UFCO's involvement in promoting the 1954 military coup in Guatemala. For several different perspectives on the issue, see Schlesinger and Kinzer, *Bitter Fruit*; Immerman, *The CIA in Guatemala*; Handy, *Revolution in the Countryside*; Gleijeses, *Shattered Hope*.

10. *La violencia* refers to a decade-long period of bloodletting from the mid-1940s to the mid-1950s in Colombia. Historians have traditionally portrayed it as a partisan battle between Colombia's Liberal and Conservative parties, but recent research has looked more deeply at the many cross-cutting issues beneath the partisan divide. For a summary of the recent literature, see Roldán, *Blood and Fire*, introduction.

11. Martin and Steiner, "El destino de la frontera," 52; Roldán *Blood and Fire*, 171. Roldán focuses on the violence in Urabá in chap. 3; she describes the aftermath on 223–227.

12. Botero, *Urabá*, 25; Roldán, *Blood and Fire*, 173.

13. Farnsworth-Alvear, *Dulcinea in the Factory*, 60.

14. Roldán, *Blood and Fire*, 225, 226; Medina, "Violence and Economic Development," 162; Sandoval O., *Gloria Cuartas*, 151. Botero also mentions the displacement of Urabá's small dispersed communities by banana production in *Urabá*, 28, 39–40. In many cases, Chocoanos were contracted to clear the land, often losing it afterward to speculators (31).

15. Marcelo Bucheli documents an overall trend to pull out of direct production in the 1960s, due in part to the Guatemalan revolution of 1944–54 and the Cuban revolution of 1959. See Bucheli, "United Fruit Company in Latin America" and *Bananas and Business*. My own work on Costa Rica shows a decision there to rely on contract farmers by the beginning of the twentieth century. See A. Chomsky, *West Indian Workers and the United Fruit Company in Costa Rica*.

16. Botero, *Urabá*, 73–75; Bucheli, *Bananas and Business*, 171–73.

17. Carlos Echavarría, who ran Coltejer from 1940 to 1961 (and was the son of its founder), was one of the pioneers of Urabá's banana industry. Luis Fernando Molina, "Echavarría, Carlos J.," in *Gran Enciclopedia de Colombia en Círculo de Lectores*, tomo de biografías, http://www.lablaa.org. See also García, *Urabá*, 41, for a discussion of the role of the Echavarrías in the banana region.

18. Pearce, *Colombia*, 252.

19. Botero, *Urabá*, 76–77, 88–89.

20. Comisión Andina de Juristas, *Urabá*, 35.

21. Martin and Steiner, "El destino de la frontera," 52, say that from 1951 to 1964 the population grew 204 percent, to 149,850, and by 1985, to 249,239. Botero, *Urabá*, 81, cites a figure of 82,969 in 1964, saying this was five times the population in 1950.

22. Martin and Steiner, "El destino de la frontera," 64.

23. The country went from providing 4.5 percent of the world's banana production in 1974 to 11.5 percent in 1985. Pearce, *Colombia*, 250; Ramírez Tobón, *Los inciertos confines de una crisis*, 33.

24. Martin and Steiner, "El destino de la frontera," 71; Comisión Verificadora, "Informe de la Comisión," 14. The 4,400 figure is from 2004; John Nolan, "Chiquita's Admission Seen to Blunt Damage," *Boston Globe*, May 12, 2004.

25. Romero, "Los trabajadores bananeros de Urabá," 5–6, citing C. I. García, *Urabá*, 105; Sandoval O., *Gloria Cuartas*, 180; Pearce, *Colombia*, 251; Botero, *Urabá*, 81.

26. Botero Herrera and Sierra, *El mercado de fuerza de trabajo*, 93.

27. Martin and Steiner, "El destino de la frontera," 63.

28. Botero Herrera and Sierra, *El mercado de fuerza de trabajo*, 150; Comisión Andina de Juristas, *Urabá*, 44.

29. Botero, *Urabá*, 81.

30. Bergquist, *Labor in Latin America*.

31. Pearce, *Colombia*, 252; Botero, *Urabá*, 156, 161.

32. Romero, "Los trabajadores bananeros de Urabá," 6, citing C. I. García, *Urabá*, 112–15.

33. Botero, *Urabá*, 142.

34. Ibid., 163–65. In 1979, 46 percent of the region's farms had some kind of agreement governing labor relations, but the vast majority of these, 80 percent, were "collective pacts" between management and labor that excluded any union (Botero Herrera and Sierra, *El mercado de fuerza de trabajo*, 93; Botero, *Urabá*, 169).

35. Comisión Andina de Juristas, *Urabá*, 40.

36. Botero, *Urabá*, 156, 164.

37. Romero, "Los trabajadores bananeros de Urabá," 7. Botero, *Urabá*, 172, quotes conclusions of the EPL's 1980 Congress to the effect that "armed struggle should not be confined to marginal and agrarian zones, but rather linked decisively to the industrial and agricultural proletariat."

38. Some EPL members sought jobs on the plantations in order to organize among the workers there. See Bucheli, *Bananas and Business*, 146–47.

39. Botero, *Urabá*, 50–51. Apartadó was not electrified until 1980; electricity did not reach other Urabá urban centers until even later (67–68).

40. Comisión Andina de Juristas, *Urabá*, 39. Sandoval O., *Gloria Cuartas*, 181, cites a tax evasion rate of between 50 and 70 percent between 1977 and 1981.

41. Sandoval O., *Gloria Cuartas*, 179.

42. Ibid., 183.

43. The Comisión Andina, *Urabá*, 51–52, listed, in 1993, the Voltígeros Battalion and the Francisco de Paula Vélez Battalion in Carepa, an advance post of the Tenth

Brigade quartered in Carepa, a Mobile Brigade, a Cuyará Battalion military base in San Pedro de Urabá, the Nutibara Battalion of the Fourth Brigade and the Muiscas Counter-Guerrilla Battalion of the Second Division in Mututá, the Junín Battalion in Montería, and the police departments of Urabá and Sijín.

44. Ramírez Tobón, *Los inciertos confines de un a crisis*, 71–72. Infrastructure funding also came from the Alliance for Progress. García, *Urabá*, 37–38.

45. Comisión Andina de Juristas, *Urabá*, 160–61.

46. Many of these violations were documented in Gallagher and McWhirter, "Chiquita's Secrets Revealed." In 2001 Chiquita agreed to pay a $100,000 fine to the Securities and Exchange Commission, without admitting guilt, in the port bribery case. See SEC Release 44902, October 3, 2001, http://www.sec.gov. In 2003 the Organization of American States found Banadex guilty of participating in an illegal arms deal supplying the paramilitary AUC, but neglected to even mention that Banadex was a wholly owned subsidiary of Chiquita. Report of the General Secretariat of the Organization of American States on the Diversion of Nicaraguan Arms to the United Self Defense Forces of Colombia, January 6, 2003, Federation of American Scientists website, http://www.fas.org. In 2004, Chiquita publicly admitted to having made payments in 2003 to an unnamed illegal armed group in Urabá. Since the area was entirely under paramilitary control at this point, the AUC is the only plausible recipient. See John Nolan, "Chiquita's Admission Seen to Blunt Damage to Image," Associated Press Dispatch, May 12, 2004, available through LexisNexis.

47. Botero, *Urabá*, 144, 146.

48. Romero, "Los trabajadores bananeros de Urabá," 6.

49. Pearce, *Colombia*, 252–253, citing *Cien Días* (April–June 1988).

50. Luis Asdrúbal Jiménez Vaca, "Communication No. 859/1999" to the Office of the United Nations High Commissioner for Human Rights, Geneva, http://www.ohchr.org.

51. Comisión Andina de Juristas, *Urabá*, 52–53, 56–67.

52. Romero, "Los trabajadores bananeros de Urabá," 7. On the negotiations, accord, and creation of the UP, see Pearce, *Colombia*, 175.

53. Comisión Andina de Juristas, *Urabá*, 52–53, 56–67.

54. Romero, "Los trabajadores bananeros de Urabá," 7, citing Villarraga and Plazas, *Para reconstruir los sueños*, 205; Pearce, *Colombia*, 253.

55. Pearce, *Colombia*, 253, Comisión Andina de Juristas, *Urabá*, 58.

56. Botero, *Urabá*, 170.

57. He was killed on September 29, 1987. Comisión Andina de Juristas, *Urabá*, 103.

58. Ramírez Tobón, *Los inciertos confines de una crisis*, 130.

59. Botero, *Urabá*, 179; Comisión Andina de Juristas, *Urabá*, 57.

60. Botero, *Urabá*, 176–79.

61. Ramírez Tobón, *Los inciertos confines de una crisis*, 117, citing local interviews with union leaders.

62. Medina, "Violence and Economic Development," 162.

63. Romero, "Los trabajadores bananeros de Urabá," 8, 9, citing Botero, *Urabá*, 180–189; M. T. Uribe, Urabá, 251–56; Martin and Steiner, "El destino de la frontera," 76.

64. Romero, "Los trabajadores bananeros de Urabá," 8. Medina, "Violence and Economic Development," 162, says that seventeen were killed during this period.

65. *El Mundo*, June 4, 1987, quoted in Pearce, *Colombia*, 253.

66. Pearce, *Colombia*, 253, citing Amnesty International.

67. Comisión Andina de Juristas, *Urabá*, 104.

68. Ramírez Tobón, *Los inciertos confines de una crisis*, 127, citing "La contrarrevolución en Urabá," *Semana* (Bogotá), May 17, 1988.

69. Medina, "Violence and Economic Development," 162; Botero, *Urabá*, 154.

70. Botero, *Urabá*, 169. Pearce, *Colombia*, 253, gives even higher figures, citing 96 percent of workers unionized: 12,600 Sintagro members on 144 plantations, with Sintrabanano covering another 4,600 on 78 plantations.

71. Martin and Steiner, "El destino de la frontera," 67–68.

72. Dick Emanuelsson, "Los Mochacabezas se volvieron pacifistas?," *La Fogata*, November 2003, http://www.lafogata.org; Romero, "Los trabajadores bananeros de Urabá," 3.

73. Comisión Verificadora, "Informe de la Comisión," 17.

74. Pearce, *Colombia*, 254; "Colombia: Politics and Violence," *Latin American Weekly Report* 89, no. 45, November 16, 1989.

75. Mario Agudelo, interview in Villarraga and Plazas, *Para reconstruir los sueños*, 388.

76. *Revolución* 371 (April 3–9, 1989): 7, cited in Villarraga and Plazas, *Para reconstruir los sueños*, 389.

77. Villarraga and Plazas, *Para reconstruir los sueños*, 389.

78. "Colombia: Lower Growth Rates This Year and Next," *Latin America Weekly Report* 89, no. 45, November 23, 1989.

79. Stan Yarbro, Associated Press Dispatch, November 30, 1989. Available through LexisNexis.

80. "Banana Strike Is Over," *Latin America Weekly Report* 89, no. 49, December 14, 1989; Comisión Andina de Juristas, *Urabá*, 40–41.

81. Mario Agudelo, in Villarraga and Plazas, *Para reconstruir los sueños*, 390.

82. Human Rights Watch, *Colombia's Killer Networks*, part 5, "Impunity."

83. Mario Agudelo in Villarraga and Plazas, *Para reconstruir los sueños*, 390–392.

84. Human Rights Watch, *Guerra sin cuartel*, part 5, part 4; Comisión Andina de Juristas, *Urabá*, 119.

85. Ramírez Tobón, *Los inciertos confines de una crisis*, 139.

86. "Social Pact," *Latin America Weekly Report* 91, no. 16, May 2, 1991. To avoid confusion, I refer to the new political party as "Esperanza" and use the initials EPL only to refer to the Ejército Popular de Liberación.

87. "Pacto Social, Urabá, Colombia," Medellín, April 1991, cited in Ramírez Tobón, *Los inciertos confines de una crisis*, 65.

88. Ramírez Tobón, *Los inciertos confines de una crisis*, 64.

89. Romero, "Los trabajadores bananeros de Urabá."

90. Agudelo, in Villarraga and Plazas, *Para reconstruir los sueños*, 393.

91. Ibid. José Manuel Arias Carrizosa was minister of justice in the Barco administration (1986–90). He was forced to resign in September 1987 when faced with charges and later became the director of Augura.

92. Villarraga and Plazas, *Para reconstruir los sueños*, 473.

93. Comisión Andina de Juristas, *Urabá*, 109–110.

94. Uribe A., *Ni canto de gloria, ni canto fúnebre*, 49–50.

95. Romero, "Los trabajadores bananeros de Urabá," 9, citing Villarraga and Plazas, *Para reconstruir los sueños*, 389–90.

96. Romero, "Los trabajadores bananeros de Urabá," 9–10.

97. Ibid., 10, citing Villarraga and Plazas, *Para reconstruir los sueños*, 391.

98. Ramírez Tobón, *Los inciertos confines de una crisis*, 119.

99. Comisión Andina de Juristas, *Urabá*, 59.

100. Sandoval O., *Gloria Cuartas*, 173.

101. Human Rights Watch, *Guerra sin cuartel*, part 5.

102. Comisión Andina de Juristas, *Urabá*, 60–61; Comisión Verificadora, "Informe de la Comisión," 27.

103. Human Rights Watch, *Guerra sin cuartel*, part 5.

104. Martin and Steiner, "El destino de la frontera," 60, 63.

105. The Comisión Andina de Juristas, *Urabá*, 116, wrote that only 10 percent of reinserted EPL members got work in the banana sector, and that the 2 million pesos in social investment and 46 million pesos assigned to each municipio to support the reinsertion process never materialized.

106. Ibid., 63.

107. Agudelo, cited in Villarraga and Plazas, *Para reconstruir los sueños*, 486–87.

108. Alvaro Villarraga S., "Informe: Situación de derechos humanos del EPL al Defensor del Pueblo," responsable de Derechos Humanos del EPL, Bogotá, August 1992, cited in Villarraga and Plazas, *Para reconstruir los sueños*, 485.

109. Human Rights Watch, *Guerra sin cuartel*, n. 51, n. 98; Comisión Verificadora, "Informe de la Comisión," 26, 34; Martin and Steiner, "El destino de la frontera," 60.

110. Human Rights Watch, *Guerra sin cuartel*, part 5; Comisión Andina de Juristas, *Urabá*, 114.

111. Agudelo, cited in Villarraga and Plazas, *Para reconstruir los sueños*, 486.

112. Comisión Verificadora, "Informe de la Comisión," 34.

113. Comisión Andina de Juristas, *Urabá*, 61.

114. Comisión Verificadora, "Informe de la Comisión," 35.

115. Comisión Andina de Juristas, *Urabá*, 114–15.

116. Amnesty International, *Political Violence in Colombia*. Some sources accused the FARC of collaborating with this murder. Comisión Verificadora, "Informe de la Comisión," 25.

117. Comisión Andina de Juristas, *Urabá*, 115, 116, 123, 130.

118. Ibid., 175.

119. Ibid., 133–34.

120. Comisión Verificadora, "Informe de la Comisión," 32. The bishop of the Apartadó diocese first denounced the paramilitary presence in northern Urabá in September 1993. Sandoval O., *Gloria Cuartas*, 190.

121. Comisión Verificadora, "Informe de la Comisión," 32.

122. Sandoval O., *Gloria Cuartas*, 193.

123. Comisión Verificadora, "Informe de la Comisión," 32–33.

124. Amnesty International went on to explain, "Judicial investigations into human rights violations committed by paramilitaries operating with members of the XVII Brigade have implicated former general Rito Alejo del Río. The legal case against Rito Alejo del Rio was closed on 9 March 2004, despite strong prima facie evidence against him. At least one witness was killed during the criminal investigations and several prosecutors were forced to leave the country." Amnesty International, "Colombian NGO under Attack," May 28, 2004, http://news.amnesty.org.

125. Quoted in Romero, "Los trabajadores bananeros de Urabá," 11.

126. Comisión Verificadora, "Informe de la Comisión," 36, 39. By the middle of 1995 some one hundred demobilized EPL members had become DAS agents. Sandoval O., *Gloria Cuartas*, 189.

127. Romero, "Los trabajadores bananeros de Urabá," 4, citing Sandoval O., *Gloria Cuartas*.

128. Comisión Verificadora, "Informe de la Comisión," 19.

129. Patti Lane, "Colombian Banana Workers End Strike, Massacre of 17 Led to Walkout," *Journal of Commerce*, September 7, 1995.

130. Yadira Ferrer, "Colombia: Urgent Solutions Demanded after New Massacre," Inter Press Service, September 20, 1995.

131. Emanuelsson, "Los Mochacabezas se volvieron pacifistas?," *La Fogata* (November 2003), http://www.lafogata.org.

132. Sánchez G., "Problems of Violence," 26. This figure includes those killed in Córdoba and Urabá.

133. Ibid., 20–21. In ten cases, authorship of the massacres could not be determined.

134. Ibid., 20.

135. Sandoval O., *Gloria Cuartas*, 238–39.

136. Comisión Verificadora, "Informe de la Comisión," 30–31.

137. Sandoval O., *Gloria Cuartas*, 240.

138. Romero, "Los trabajadores bananeros de Urabá," 2.

139. Ramírez Tobón, *Los inciertos confines de una crisis*, 59–60.

140. Sandoval O., *Gloria Cuartas*, 241.

141. Romero, "Los trabajadores bananeros de Urabá," 11, 10, 13; IUF, "Huelga bananera en Urabá," May 19, 2004, http://www.rel-uita.org.

142. Emanuelsson, "¿Los Mochacabezas se volvieron pacifistas?," *La Fogata* (November 2003), http://www.lafogata.org.

143. Ibid.

144. Ibid. The declaration is reproduced on the Colombian government website. See Consejo Nacional Electoral (National Electoral Council), "Organizaciones sindicales de Antioquia invitan a votar el referendo," September 26, 2003, www.presidencia.gov.co.

145. Osvaldo Cuadrado Simanca and Luis Guillermo Peña Restrepo, "San José de Apartadó requiere una solución integral," press release, April 7, 2005, IUF website, http://www.rel-uita.org. See also the February 2005 press release categorically contradicting Gloria Cuartas's protest—based on the statements of witnesses—that the army was responsible for the massacre: http://www.rel-uita.org.

146. Romero, "Los trabajadores bananeros de Urabá," 4, 15.

147. Comisión Andina de Juristas, *Urabá*, 155. For a detailed description of the banana wars, see Raynolds, "The Global Banana Trade."

148. Sandoval O., *Gloria Cuartas*, 179.

149. Ramírez Tobón, *Urabá*, 59.

150. Comisión Andina de Juristas, *Urabá*, 62.

151. "Finalizó paro bananero en Urabá," *El Pais* (Cali, Colombia), May 23, 2002, http://elpais-cali.terra.com.co.

152. Correa quotes himself in a Powerpoint presentation for a May 2004 conference of the Centro Nacional de Productividad, available at http://www.cnp.org.co. The Centro is a nonprofit organization aimed at helping businesses increase productivity.

153. Frank, *Bananeras*, 63.

154. See Taylor and Scharlin, *Smart Alliance*, and "IUF/COLSIBA Agreement on Freedom of Association, Minimum Labor Standards and Employment in Latin American Banana Operations," June 2001. Available at http://www.usleap.org.

155. Lone Riisgaard, "The IUF/COLSIBA-Chiquita framework agreement: A case study" (Geneva: ILO Working Paper 94, n.d. [2003 or 2004]), http://www.ilo.org. Interestingly, this study evaluated the results of the agreement only in Central America, not Colombia. Its author does note that left-wing unions in Guatemala (UNISTRAGUA) maintained a comparable suspicion of the IUF because of its history of affiliating with the right, including employer-dominated "yellow" unions (16).

156. See http://www.bananalink.org.uk and http://www.usleap.org. BananaLink cites Colombian companies as having "one of the best records" in the world "for negotiating collective agreements with the workers" (www.bananalink.org.uk).

157. See Joint Press Release, "IUF, COLSIBA and Chiquita Sign Historic Agreement on Trade Union Rights for Banana Workers," June 14, 2001; US/LEAP, "Chiquita Tries High Road," at http://www.usleap.org.

158. Anne Claire Chambron, "Can Voluntary Standards Provide Solutions?" Inter-

national Banana Conference 2 Preparatory Papers, 104, 106, at http://www.ibc2 .org.

159. Romero, "Los trabajadores bananeros de Urabá."

160. Alistair Smith, "Growing in Unity: Union Peace Strategy Works in Urabá, Colombia, Banana Industry," *New Internationalist*, December 2001, 28–29.

161. John Bird, Bill Fairbairn, Carl Hetu, Rick Kitchen, Ken Luckhardt, David Onyalo, Don Schmidt, and Paul Smith, "Report of the Canadian Trade Union Delegation to Colombia," February 1998, Colombia Support Network website, http://www .colombiasupport.net; "Chiquita to Sell Colombia Banana Operations," Associated Press, June 11, 2004.

162. Taylor and Scharlin, *Smart Alliance*.

163. Juan Forero, "Colombia May Seek Chiquita Extraditions," *Washington Post*, March 21, 2007.

164. "Chiquita to Sell Colombia Banana Operations," Associated Press, June 11, 2004.

165. "Chiquita Brands International, Inc. Earnings Conference Call," August 5, 2004 (FDCHeMedia and CCBN Transcript 080504ac.749, available through LexisNexis).

166. Otis, "Critics question Chiquita's claim."

167. Reuters, "Colombia 'good model' for Afghan drug war, U.S. says," January 19, 2007.

168. Charlie Keys (Georgia State Federation of Labor), William S. McCarthy (Minneapolis Central Labor Council), and Jerry A. Acosta (AFL-CIO), "Colombia Work Plan," March 2, 2005. Copy in author's possession.

169. Thanks to Cecilia Zarate of the Colombia Support Network for providing a tape of the interview. Transcribed and translated by the author.

6. Taking Care of Business in Colombia

1. Buhle, *Taking Care of Business*, 15.

2. Ibid., 43.

3. Quoted in Foner, *U.S. Labor Movement and Latin America*, 28–29.

4. Carr recounts early twentieth-century cases of labor internationalism outside of the AFL in "Crossing Borders," 212–15.

5. Quoted in Trepp, "Union-Management Co-operation," 616–17, 614.

6. See Wehrle, "Guns, Butter, Leon Keyserling," 730–31.

7. Moody, "Global Capital and Economic Nationalism." In the words of Peter Rachleff, *Hard-Pressed in the Heartland*, 22, unions became " 'interest' groups, acting on behalf of their own members, but not on behalf of a larger *labor movement*, and certainly not on behalf of the working class." See also Fantasia and Voss, *Hard Work*, chap. 1.

8. See Moody, "Global Capital and Economic Nationalism."

9. Foner, *U.S. Labor Movement and Latin America*, 81–82.

10. Ibid., 84.

11. Rippy, *The Capitalists and Colombia*, 173; Villegas, *Petróleo, oligarquía e imperio*.

12. Díaz Callejas, *El 9 de abril 1948*, 54.

13. Torres Giraldo, *La huelga general en Medellín*, 86.

14. Díaz Callejas, *El 9 de abril 1948*, 67.

15. Urrutia, *Colombian Labor Movement*, chap. 7.

16. Díaz Callejas, *El 9 de abril 1948*, 63.

17. Ibid., 80, 86, 73–75.

18. See Pearce, "Beyond the Perimeter Fence."

19. Bergquist, *Labor in Latin America*, 335 n. 66, citing Restricted Memo, U.S. Department of State, September 13, 1948, USNA/DS 821.504/9–1348.

20. Willard L. Beaulac to Secretary of State, Bogotá, September 16, 1948, USNA/DS 821.504/9–1648, cited in Bergquist, *Labor in Latin America*, 358 n. 105.

21. Fulton Freeman, American Ambassador, "Memorandum of Conversation," December 5, 1962, Colombia General, Folder 10/62–2/63, JFK Library, Boston.

22. Embassy of Colombia in Washington, "Colombia's Energy Industry: Recent Developments and New Opportunities," n.d. [2005], http://www.coltrade.org.

23. Silvia Juliana Becerra Ostos and Camilo Rueda Navarro, "La huelga de USO y la política petrolera," Agencia Prensa Rural, June 18, 2004, http://www.prensarural.org.

24. Fred Hirsch, "Eyewitness to 'Terror': U.S. Links to Colombian Death Squads," *People's Weekly World*, March 9, 2002.

25. "Colombia: Foreign Economic Relations," in Library of Congress, *Colombia: A Country Study*.

26. Zamosc, *The Agrarian Question and the Peasant Movement in Colombia*, 123.

27. By the mid-1980s the United States accounted for two-thirds of the $2.7 billion in foreign capital invested in Colombia, and the country owed $3.8 billion to the World Bank and Inter-American Development Bank and $2.4 billion to USAID and the U.S. Export-Import Bank. "Colombia: Foreign Economic Relations," in Library of Congress, *Colombia: A Country Study*.

28. "Colombia Survey Report—Secret Supplement, 26 February 1962," cited in Rempe, "Guerrillas, Bandits, and Independent Republics," 311.

29. Quoted in McClintock, *Instruments of Statecraft*, 223.

30. Rempe, "Guerrillas, Bandits, and Independent Republics," 318.

31. Leal Buitrago, *El oficio de la guerra*, 54. See also Amnesty International, *Political Violence in Colombia*.

32. Dearborn (U.S. Embassy, Bogotá) to Secretary of State, Department of State, April 25, 1964, www.paulwolf.org.

33. Freeman to Secretary of State, August 17, 1962, Papers of Papers of President Kennedy, National Security Files, Countries—Series 1, Box 27, Folder Colombia General, 7/62–9/62, JFK Library, Boston.

34. "Report of the Colombia Survey Team, 4/60: Introduction," Colombia/Subjects/ Report of the Colombia Survey Team 4/60, Part II, Appendices I–III, Box 27, JFK Library, Boston.

35. See George Gedda, "U.S. Seeks to Protect Colombia Pipeline," Associated Press,

March 22, 2002; Javier Baena, "Colombian Rebels Condemn U.S. Plan to Expand Military Aid," Associated Press, February 6, 2002.

36. John Cumming, "Greystar Resumes Exploration at Angostura," *Northern Mining Journal* 89, no. 46 (January 5–11, 2004).

37. Sims, *Workers of the World Undermined*, 12. Throughout the 1960s and 1970s, the labor movement leadership also maintained strong support for the Vietnam War, even as public opinion turned against it.

38. Lichtenstein, *State of the Union*, 248.

39. In 1969 the AFL-CIO withdrew from the ICFTU, until 1982. The immediate spur was the ICFTU's rapprochement with the United Auto Workers, which had been expelled from the AFL-CIO in 1968 for its refusal to pay dues in protest of the federation's support for the Vietnam War. The larger context was the ICFTU's refusal to adhere to the extreme anticommunism of the AFL-CIO. The AFL-CIO's withdrawal helped to orient the ICFTU more toward the Social and Christian Democratic center. Despite this distancing, "ORIT has given the ICFTU a very bad name in Latin America." Hirsch and Muir, "A Plumber Gets Curious," 731. They are quoting Wedin, *International Trade Union Solidarity*, 32, 53, 69.

40. See Spalding, *Organized Labor in Latin America*, chap. 6, for a summary of AIFLD's efforts to undermine labor radicalism and governments that allowed it in Guatemala in the 1950s, Brazil, Guyana, and the Dominican Republic in the 1960s, and Chile in the 1970s.

41. Meany statement in United State Senate, "American Institute for Free Labor Development," 6. A list of corporations contributing to AIFLD is on 21–22.

42. Doherty's statement is quoted by Senator William Fulbright in United States Senate, "American Institute for Free Labor Development," 29.

43. See, for example, Compa, "Free Trade, Fair Trade," especially 318; Sims, *Workers of the World Undermined*; Barry and Preusch, *AIFLD in Central America*; Armstrong, Frundt, Spalding, and Sweeney, *Working Against Us*; Cantor and Schor, *Tunnel Vision*; Weinrub and Bollinger, *The AFL-CIO in Central America*; Forché and Wheaton, *History and Motivations of U.S. Involvement*; Levenson-Estrada, *Trade Unionists against Terror*, 29–39.

44. Shorrock, "Labor's Cold War."

45. Katherine Hoyt, "Concerns over Possible AFL-CIO Involvement in Venezuela Coup Led to February Picket," *Labor Notes* 278, May 2002, 5; David Corn, "Our Gang in Venezuela," *The Nation* 275 no. 5, August 5, 2002, 24–28.

46. Buchanan, "'Useful Fools' as Diplomatic Tools," quoting Lodge, *Spearheads of Democracy: Labor in Developing Countries*, 73–74.

47. Spalding, *Organized Labor in Latin America*, 265, 270, 274.

48. Richard Dudman in the *St. Louis Post Dispatch*, April 13 and 14, 1969; William Greider, "Unions Turn to AID after CIA Pullout," *Washington Post*, April 21, 1969. Both cited in United States Senate, "American Institute for Free Labor Development," 23–26, 77.

49. Urrutia, *Colombian Labor Movement*, 171–172, 185.

50. John C. Wiley to Secretary of State, February 28, 1945, USNA/DS 821.504/2–2846 and January 21, 1946, USNA/DS 821.504/1–2146, cited in Bergquist, *Labor in Latin America*, 358 n. 105.

51. Roldán, *Blood and Fire*, 68. Ospina also legalized the UTC, which, although not on its surface an antilabor measure, in fact served to weaken the CTC.

52. Romualdi, *Presidents and* Peons, 38–39. Chapter 2, entitled "Looking for Friends and Allies," describes this tour.

53. Ibid., 43, 66, 67, 111.

54. Urrutia, *Colombian Labor Movement*, 195.

55. Roldán, *Blood and Fire*, 80–81, 95, citing Archivo de la Secretaría de Gobierno de Antioquia, 1949, vol. 5, Sindicato Ferroviario de Antioquia to the Governor, October 11, 1949.

56. Roldán, *Blood and Fire*, 100.

57. Romualdi, *Presidents and Peons*, 112, approached the Liberal Party leader Carlos Lleras Restrepo on a visit to New York in 1950, and the latter agreed to exert pressure from his party on the CTC.

58. The vote at the Congress was 178 to withdraw from the CTAL, 141 to remain. Urrutia, *Colombian Labor Movement*, 196.

59. Ibid., 215; Vicente Andrade Valderrama, S.J., "Panorama del movimiento sindical en Colombia," January 1963, 1, RG 18–001, Series 4, 18/19, 2, George Meany Labor Archives (hereafter GMLA), Silver Spring, Maryland. Figures were available only for those years.

60. Romualdi, *Presidents and Peons*, 179, 405.

61. Buchanan, " 'Useful Fools' as Diplomatic Tools."

62. McLellan (Inter-American Representative) to Emilio Garza (AIFLD Director, Colombia), March 4, 1963, RG 18–001, Series 4, 18/19, GMLA.

63. O'Grady to McLellan, March 23, 1966, RG 18–001, Series 4, 18/20, GMLA.

64. S. Moskowitz, "Visit of Ambassador Moscoso with Colombian Trade Unions," Enclosure #11, Colombia, General, 10/62–2/63. JFK Library, Boston. The Barcelona-born Moscoso was president of PRIDCO from 1942 to 1950, then administrator to the Economic Development Administration in Puerto Rico from 1950 to 1961. He served briefly as ambassador to Venezuela before being named assistant administrator for Latin America to the Agency for International Development and Coordinator of the Alliance for Progress in 1962.

65. Osorio O., *Historia del sindicalismo antioqueño*, 77–78.

66. Valderrama, "Panorama del movimiento sindical," GMLA.

67. Osorio O., *Historia del sindicalismo antioqueño*, 77–78. Valle workers were actually in two separate federations: Festralva, which remained in the CTC, and Fedetav, which was expelled.

68. Valderrama, "Panorama del movimiento sindical," 1, GMLA.

69. Garza to McLellan, July 25, 1962, RG 18–001, Series 4, 18/18, GMLA.

70. Resolution 33, UTC 11th Plenary, September 3, 1962, RG 18–001, Series 4, 18/18, GMLA.

71. McLellan to Garza, August 1, 1962, RG 18–001, Series 4, 18/18, GMLA.

72. Garza to McLellan, February 28, 1963, RG 18–001, Series 4, 18/19, GMLA.

73. Valderrama, "Panorama del movimiento sindical," 3, GMLA. He claimed that the German Episcopado was providing "huge sums of money" to the CLASC.

74. Meany prepared statement in United States Senate, "American Institute for Free Labor Development," 16.

75. "La afiliación internacional de la U.T.C. y las actividades de la CLASC," attached to Valderrama, "Panorama del movimiento sindical," GMLA.

76. Jack O'Grady (Labor Attaché, U.S. Embassy, Bogotá) to McLellan, May 20, 1966, RG 18–001, Series 4, 18/20, GMLA.

77. Sidney Lens, "American Labor Abroad—Lovestone Diplomacy," *The Nation*, July 5, 1965, cited in United States Senate, "American Institute for Free Labor Development," 114–15.

78. McLellan to O'Grady, March 29, 1966, RG 18–001, Series 4, 18/20, GMLA.

79. O'Grady to McLellan, July 11, 1967, RG 18–001, Series 4, 18/22, GMLA.

80. McLellan to O'Grady, July 19, 1967, RG 18–001, Series 4, 18/22, GMLA. Mercado was kidnapped by the Colombian M-19 guerrilla movement in 1976 and assassinated in April of that year.

81. McLellan to O'Grady, July 19, 1967, RG 18–001, Series 4, 18/22, GMLA.

82. O'Grady to McLellan, March 23, 1966, RG 18–001, Series 4, 18/20, GMLA.

83. O'Grady to McLellan, September 17, 1966, RG 18–001, Series 4, 18/20, GMLA.

84. William Greider, "Unions Turn to AID after CIA Pullout," *Washington Post*, April 21, 1969, cited in United States Senate, "American Institute for Free Labor Development," 77.

85. United States Senate, Committee on Foreign Relations, "Survey of the Alliance for Progress," 15.

86. Brattain, "Making Friends and Enemies."

87. Zamosc, *The Agrarian Question and the Peasant Movement in Colombia*, 72–73.

88. Bagley, "The State and the Peasantry"; Zamosc, *The Agrarian Question and the Peasant Movement in Colombia*, 126–29. See also Americas Watch, *The Central Americanization of Colombia?*, 114–117.

89. Bagley, "The State and the Peasantry," n. 117.

90. George Meany statement in United States Senate, "American Institute for Free Labor Development," 9. The only other Latin American country where AIFLD ran campesino centers in the 1960s was Brazil, where radical peasant organizations provided key support for President João Goulart's land reform proposals before he was overthrown in an AIFLD-backed coup.

91. Bagley, "The State and the Peasantry," n. 166.

92. Carbonell Blanco and Erazo Coronado, *Hacia una central sindical unitaria*, 79.

93. Zamosc, *The Agrarian Question and the Peasant Movement in Colombia*, 123.

94. Pearce, *Colombia*, 139, 136–37, 141.

95. Ibid., 143–44. On the formation of the CUT, see also the confederation's own description: Carlos A. Rodríguez D. and Benjamín Rizzo Madrid, "Retrospectiva del Movimiento Sindical," http://www.cut.org.co; Carbonell Blanco and Erazo Coronado, *Hacia una central sindical unitaria*.

96. CUT, "Declaración de Principios," reproduced in Carbonell Blanco and Erazo Coronado, *Hacia una central sindical unitaria*, 253–54.

97. United States Department of Energy, Energy Information Administration, "Country Analysis Briefs: Colombia," July 2004, http://www.eia.doe.gov.

98. See Ramírez Cuellar, *The Profits of Extermination*, 42–64, for a discussion of foreign companies' and governments' involvement in the writing of the investor-friendly mining code of 2001.

99. Spalding, *Organized Labor in Latin America*, 273.

100. Hirsch and Muir, "A Plumber Gets Curious," 723. See below for further discussion of Hirsch's continued campaign thirty years later.

101. For a recent study of the National Labor Committee, see Battista, "Unions and Cold War Foreign Policy."

102. Buchanan, "'Useful Fools' as Diplomatic Tools."

103. Battista, "Unions and Cold War Foreign Policy," 450. For a comprehensive account of the New Voices, see Mort, *Not Your Father's Union*.

104. See Shailor, "A New Internationalism," for an official view of the changes.

105. "Labor Department Makes Grant to Train Unionists, Support Civil Society in Colombia," U.S. Newswire, April 11, 2001.

106. "AFL-CIO Statement on the Situation of Labor in Colombia and U.S. Policy," February 17, 2000, Central for International Policy website, http://ciponline.org.

107. See David Liscio, "Labor Activist Thanks Local Union," *Lynn* (Mass.) *Daily Item*, May 19, 2004; Héctor Giraldo, "In My Country, Privatization Is Enforced by Assassination," March 2003, Communication Workers of America website, http://www.cwa-union.org; Jeff Crosby, "Density, Democracy, and Transformation: We Need Them All," unpublished paper, March 17, 2005. Copy in author's possession.

108. Dorothee Benz, "Privatization through Assassination," CWA Local 1180 *Comunique*, May–June 2003, http://www.ilcaonline.org.

109. I translated Miguel's talks at Amherst College (October 2004) and at the Witness for Peace New England Annual Fall Retreat (November 2004), where he spoke eloquently against the neoliberal economic model being imposed on Colombia, against U.S. military aid, and in favor of the Stop Killer Coke campaign.

110. See Hank Frundt, "Has the AFL-CIO's Solidarity Center Turned Over a New Leaf?"; Shorrock, "Labor's Cold War"; Shorrock, "Toeing the Line?" Similar questions were being raised even before the 2002 Venezuela events. For earlier critiques, see Shorrock, "Creating a New Internationalism for Labor"; Rodberg, "The CIO without the CIA."

111. The various resolutions are summarized in Quaccia, "National Endowment for Death Squads?" For copies of the resolutions and an in-depth discussion of how they came about, see Scipes, "Building International Labor Solidarity," and Scipes, "It's Time to Come Clean."

112. Scipes, "AFL-CIO Foreign Policy."

113. Personal communications with Solidarity Center representatives and union leaders in Bogotá, August 2006.

114. Jeff Crosby, speech to the CUT Congress, Bogotá, August 23, 2006. Copy in author's possession.

115. "Coca Cola Boycott Launched after Killings at Colombian Plants," *The Guardian*, July 24, 2003.

116. The events are described in numerous articles and testimonies, including Leech, "Coca Cola Accused of Using Death Squads," and Bacon, "It's the Real Thing."

117. See, for example, "IUF Demands Protection for Threatened Sinaltrainal Leaders," April 7, 2005, IUF website, http://www.iuf.org.

118. "IUF Coca Cola Affiliates Reject Call for a Global Coca Cola Boycott," July 15, 2003, IUF website, http://www.iuf.org.

119. Canadian Labour Congress, "Subject: Does the CLC Support the Call to Boycott Coca-Cola Products Internationally?," April 30, 2004, CLC website, http://clc-ctc.ca.

120. A list of organizations supporting the boycott, with copies of their statements, is available at http://www.killercoke.org.

121. Terry Collingsworth, "Another 'Classic Coke' Move to Deny and Delay Accountability for Human Rights Violations in Colombia," *Worker Rights News* [International Labor Rights Fund] 8, no. 2 (spring 2006): 7, http://www.laborrights.org.

122. As Joe Drexler from the United Steelworkers suggested in a session on Exxon-Mobil. The conference was held at the Crowne Plaza Hotel on February 9–11, 2006.

7. Mining the Connections

1. U.S. Department of Energy, Energy Information Administration, *Coal Industry Annual*, 2000, http://www.eia.doe.gov.

2. *Wall Street Journal*, February 11, June 17, 1982; "Ex-Im Bank Clears $375 Million Loan for Coal Venture," *Wall Street Journal* August 13, 1982. European banks also contributed heavily to the project. See "Colombia Coal Authority Gets $50 Million Credit," *Wall Street Journal*, January 25, 1982.

3. Gil Klein, "Exxon Mine Project in Colombia Nettles U.S. Coal Community," *Christian Science Monitor*, June 14, 1985.

4. David Bacon, "Blood for Coal"; David Bacon, "U.S. Energy Plan Spells Danger for Colombian Labor."

5. U.S. Department of Energy, *Energy Overview of Colombia*, http://www.fossil.en

ergy.gov. Don Argus, BHP chairman, described the contract at a shareholders meeting in 2004, under challenge from human rights activists who also accused the mine of displacing local communities. See "BHP Facing Grilling over Colombia Claims," National Nine News, November 26, 2004.

6. Energy Information Administration, *Quarterly Coal Report*, December 2004, http://www.eia.doe.gov.

7. *Coal Americas* 45, June 14, 2004.

8. In protesting the Export-Import Bank support of the Cerrejón Zona Norte project, Senator Wendell H. Ford, a Democrat from Kentucky, said, "Our people are going down the drain while we're sending our money overseas to support other people." Senator Jay Rockefeller of West Virginia, also a Democrat, complained that the American goods and services purchased with the Export-Import Bank loans came from western and northeastern states: "California gets the money, and West Virginia loses the jobs. What's fair about that?" Gil Klein, "Exxon Mine Project in Colombia Nettles U.S. Coal Community," *Christian Science Monitor*, June 14, 1985.

9. Pacini Hernandez, "Resource Development and Indigenous People," 8–10. See also Aschmann, "The Persistent Guajiro," for a recounting of the history and culture of the Wayuu.

10. Cerrejón website, www.cerrejoncoal.com. In January 1999 Exxon received a twenty-five-year extension on its contract with Colombia. In October 2000, an international consortium consisting of the Anglo-Australian Billiton Company (later BHP Billiton), South Africa's Anglo American, and Switzerland's Glencore International AG purchased Carbocol's share of interest in the mine for about $384 million; in early 2002 the consortium purchased the remaining half from Exxon's Intercor. Glencore subsequently sold its share to Xstrata plc, in which Glencore is a major shareholder

11. Pacini Hernandez, "Resource Development and Indigenous People," 1; Andrew Wright, "El Cerrejón Moves Into the Market," *Coal Age*, October 1985. In the 1990s coal was transported to the port in two 120-car locomotive units making an average of four trips a day. See Cerrejón website, www.cerrejoncoal.com.

12. Pacini Hernandez, "Resource Development and Indigenous People," 13.

13. Ibid., 20–22. The sacred Cerro de la Teta mountain was included in one of the reservas earmarked for construction materials.

14. Fajardo Gómez, "Violación sistemática de los derechos humanos."

15. Pacini Hernandez, "Resource Development and Indigenous People," 27, 29, 31.

16. Paraphrased in Gedicks, "War on Subsistence."

17. Fajardo Gómez, "Violación sistemática de los derechos humanos."

18. Ibid.

19. Ministry of Health Resolución 02122 del 12 de febrero de 1991. The document cites both 1991 and 1992 as the date of this resolution; other documents cite the 1991 date.

20. The Superior Court in Riohacha and the Supreme Court denied his appeal (in February and April 1992), but the Sala de Revisión de Tutelas of the Corte Constitucional ruled in his favor in September, finding the Ministry of Health and the Ministry of Mines and Energy responsible for rectifying the "uninhabitable" and "high risk" character of the area due to pollutants from the mine within thirty days. Corte Constitucional de Colombia, Relatoría 11, Sentencia No. T-528, September 18, 1992, http://www.ideam.gov.co; Fajardo Gómez, "Violación sistemática de los derechos humanos," August 9, 2001.

21. Unpublished report by Andy Higginbottom, coordinator of the Colombia Solidarity Campaign in London. Copy in author's possession.

22. Armando Perez Araujo, et al, "The London Declaration," September 2001, Mines and Communities website, http://www.minesandcommunities.org. The London-based organization Partizans organized this meeting. Two other representatives of Yanama are also among the signatories.

23. Unpublished report by Andy Higginbottom.

24. Richard Solly and Roger Moody, "Background: Stripping the Guajira Bare," and "Indigenous and Farming Workers Targeted by Security Personnel at Colombian Coal Mine," unpublished papers, January 2001 and July 2001, Mines and Communities website, http://www.minesandcommunities.org; Richard Solly and Roger Moody, "Urgent Action," July 3, 2001, http://www.minesandcommunities.org. Mario Alberto Pérez was working "illegally" in the school, which had already been ordered closed.

25. *South American Business Information*, June 7, 2000 p. 1008158u3927, reported over 6,500 employees; Mining Technology put the workforce lower, at 4,600, http://www.mining-technology.com. The mine's own website claimed 4,000 direct employees and 4,000 subcontracted workers: http://www.cerrejoncoal.com.

26. Tom Boswell, "Exxon, Operator of a Mine That Colombian Indians Say Has Destroyed Their Homeland, Is Planning Another Venture in Wisconsin," emagazine.com 7, no. 4 (July/August 1996), http://www.emagazine.com. Gouyiru's testimony is cited in detail in Gedicks, "The Wolf River." See also Gedicks, *Resource Rebels*.

27. Zinn, "Labor Solidarity in the New World Order," 38.

28. See "ICEM Links Energy Unions in Latin America," *ICEM Info*. 2, no. 4 (1997), http://www.icem.org.

29. Zinn, "Labor Solidarity in the New World Order," 38.

30. Ibid.

31. "Carbocol Ships Despite Strike," *Coal Week International*, May 8, 1990.

32. "Industry Union Sets Strike Deadline for April 3 at El Cerrejón," *Coal Week International*, April 3, 1990. The following week the company denied that the slowdown had affected production. "Market Impact Minimized in Colombia Labor Pact Renewal," *Coal Week International*, April 10, 1990.

33. "Carbocol Ships Despite Strike," *Coal Week International*, May 8, 1990.

34. Zinn, "Labor Solidarity in the New World Order"; "Carbocol/Intercor El Cerrejón," *Coal Week International*, May 15, 1990.

35. "El Cerrejón Workers Return to Mines, Market Impact Minimized," *Coal Week International*, May 22, 1990.

36. Bacon, "Blood for Coal"; Bacon, "U.S. Energy Plan Spells Danger for Colombian Labor"; Zinn, "Labor Solidarity in the New World Order," 39.

37. ICEM, "Energy Industry in Upheaval, Energy Unions in Action" (conference documents), March 10, 1998, http://www.icem.org.

38. Ibid.

39. Zinn, "Labor Solidarity in the New World Order," 41–43.

40. Letters posted at ICEM website, http://www.icem.org; Cerrejón Press Release, December 20, 2006. Copy in author's possession.

41. Amnesty International, *AI Report, 1997* (New York: Amnesty International 1997); Amnesty International, " 'Just What Do We Have to Do to Stay Alive?' Colombia's Internally Displaced: Dispossessed and Exiled in Their Own Land," Amnesty International, October 1997, http://web.amnesty.org.

42. Roston, "It's the Real Thing."

43. Bacon, "The Colombian Connection"; Roston, "It's the Real Thing"; "Ejército frustra atentado de FARC contra multinacional Drummond en Colombia," Agence France-Presse, April 10, 2003.

44. Roston, "It's the Real Thing."

45. "Guerrilla Attacks May Cause Coal-mining Company to Suspend Operations," BBC Summary of World Broadcasts, December 9, 2000, available through Lexis-Nexis.

46. Roston, "It's the Real Thing."

47. Ibid.

48. See US/LEAP, "Violence against Colombian Trade Unions Bulletin," www.usleap.org.

49. El Observatorio para la Protección de los Defensores de los Derechos Humanos, "Colombia: Asesinato del Sr. Gustavo Soler Mora," October 11, 2001, World Organization against Torture website, http://www.omct.org.

50. Roston, "It's the Real Thing."

51. UMWA, "From Alabama to Colombia: Drummond's Trail of Tears."

52. Bacon, "The Colombian Connection."

53. Zinn, "Labor Solidarity in the New World Order," 36–37.

54. Bacon, "Blood for Coal"; Bacon, "U.S. Energy Plan Spells Danger for Colombian Labor."

55. See, for example, Human Rights Watch, Amnesty International, and the Washington Office on Latin America, "Colombia Human Rights Certification III," February 2002, http://www.hrw.org.

56. The Colombian Escuela Nacional Sindical has tallied 1,524 labor unionists murdered between 1991 and 2000, 299 of them union leaders. Between 1996 and 2000

another 1,597 have been victims of death threats, 141 illegally detained, 80 have survived attacks, 64 have been kidnapped, 49 have been "disappeared." Escuela Nacional Sindical, "Informe sobre los derechos humanos de los trabajadores colombianos: 2000," Escuela Nacional Sindical (National Union School), http://www.ens.org.co. According to Amnesty International in an April 2001 report, "112 trade unionists were killed in 2000 and 35 in the first three months of 2001 alone." Amnesty International, "Spike in Trade Unionist Deaths Proves Congress Must Stop Military Aid to Colombia, Says Amnesty International USA," news release, April 30, 2001, http://www.amnesty-usa.org. By the end of November 2001, 144 more had been killed, according to Colombia's CUT, giving Colombia the dubious distinction of being "the most dangerous country in the world to be a trade unionist." US/LEAP, *Violence against Colombian Trade Unions Bulletin*, no. 1 (December 2001), http://www.usleap.org.

57. ICEM Update 14/2001, March 15, 2001, http://www.icem.org.
58. "Steelworkers Condemn Murder of Colombian Trade Unionists," press release, USWA, March 16, 2001, http://www.uswa.org.
59. Bacon, "The Colombian Connection."
60. Quoted in Harry Kelber, "Death Lists in Colombia," *Labor Talk*, June 25, 2001, http://www.laboreducator.org.
61. Roston, "It's the Real Thing."
62. See Steve Greenhouse, "Alabama Coal Giant Sued over Three Killings in Colombia," *New York Times*, March 22, 2002.
63. Juan Forero, "Rights Groups Overseas Fight U.S. Concerns in U.S. Courts," *New York Times*, June 26, 2003.
64. Daniel M. Kovalik, assistant general counsel, United Steelworkers of America, personal communication, March 2005.
65. *Coal Americas* 45 (June 14, 2004).
66. Gary Band, "Cleanup, Buyer Needed for Salem Harbor Station," *Jewish Journal*, January 16–29, 2004.
67. Ibid.
68. Dave Gershman, "Politics and Promises," *Salem* (Mass.) *Evening News*, March 17, 2003.
69. Rafael Lewis, "Deal Is Cut on Salem Coal Plant," *Boston Globe*, June 14, 2003. Dominion, which purchased the plant in 2005, renegotiated the agreement but maintained the commitment to lowering emissions. See "Dominion Signs Environmental Agreement at Salem Harbor," Electric News Release, May 26, 2005, http://www.dom.com.
70. Dave Gershman, "Colombian Activist Brings Human Rights Fight to Area," *Salem* (Mass.) *Evening News*, October 28, 2002.
71. T. J. Costello, "Colombian 'Blood-Stained Coal,' Human Rights, and Donkin Mine Topics Raised During UCCB [University College of Cape Breton] Panel Discussion," *Cape Breton Post*, January 8, 2005.

72. Francisco Ramírez Cuellar to Edliberto Restrepo Caldera, April 17, 2005. Letter in author's possession.

73. See Ramírez Cuellar, *The Profits of Extermination*.

74. Edilberto Restrepo Caldera to Francisco Ramírez, March 29, 2005. The letter was pointedly copied to the president of El Cerrejón and to the general secretary of the ICEM. In April 2005 it was posted prominently on El Cerrejón's website, http://www.cerrejoncoal.com.

75. Sintracarbón, "Denuncia nacional e internacional sobre el impacto de la expansión minera del Cerrejón en las comunidades aledañas a la mina," November 9, 2006. Copy in author's possession.

76. Letter from Jairo Quiroz to the International Delegation, November 8, 2006. Copy in author's possession.

77. Sintracarbón, "Denuncia nacional e internacional."

78. Letter from Leo W. Gerard to the owners of the Cerrejón Mine, October 18, 2006; letter from Richard L. Trumka to León Teicher, president of Cerrejón, October 13, 2006; letter from John Gordon to León Teicher, October 24, 2006. These letters and others were delivered to Teicher at a meeting with the international delegation on October 31, 2006. Copies in author's possession.

79. This testimony was recorded by Sintraminercol in August 2004, and transcribed and translated by the author. A longer version was published as Barros Fince, "It Seems Impossible to Believe."

80. These are not nuclear families, but large extended families or matrilineal clans, the main units of Wayuu social organization.

81. Recorded, transcribed, and translated by the author.

Conclusion

1. Jane Collins describes some of the recent cross-border solidarity movements in *Threads*, 177–82. See also Armbruster-Sandoval, *Globalization and Cross-Border Labor Solidarity*; A. Ross, *No Sweat*.

2. See Jeff Crosby, "The Kids Are All Right . . . ," December 6, 1999. This essay is available on several websites, including http://www.zmag.org.

3. See Green, *On Strike at Hormel*; Rachleff, *Hard-Pressed in the Heartland*; Getman, *The Betrayal of Local 14*.

4. Getman, *The Betrayal of Local 14*, 90, 133.

5. Rachleff, *Hard-Pressed in the Heartland*, 4. See 55–56 for further discussion of the development of a "movement culture" in the local during the strike, and 61–74 on the role of solidarity from other unions and progressive organizations.

6. The impact of antisweatshop organizing and the campaigns that various labor rights organizations have launched against U.S. manufacturers like Kathie Lee Gifford and Phillips–Van Heusen can be seen in the individual companies' responses and in the larger movement on the part of outsourcers to find ways to

repair their images. A. Ross, *No Sweat* provides examples of the different popular and labor campaigns to expose abuses in the outsourcing system. Hartman, Arnold, and Wokutch, *Rising Above Sweatshops* brings together a large number of case studies from a corporate point of view, looking approvingly at codes of conduct and other industry responses.

7. Editorial, *Salem* (Mass.) *Evening News*, May 9, 1933.
8. Galvin, *The Organized Labor Movement in Puerto Rico*, 136.
9. Collins, *Threads*, 129.
10. Mario Agudelo in Villarraga and Plazas, *Para reconstruir los sueños*, 390–92.
11. Mintz, *Sweetness and Power*.
12. "Help Us Win Our Strike!," undated flyer [1933] from the strike committee, Anne Burlak Timpson Papers.

Adams, Frederick Upham. *Conquest of the Tropics: The Story of the Creative Enterprises Conducted by the United Fruit Company.* Garden City, N.Y.: Doubleday, Page, 1914.

Adams, James Luther. "The Evolution of My Social Concern." In *JLA: The Essential James Luther Adams: Selected Essays and Addresses,* ed. George Kimmich Beach. Boston: Skinner House Books, 1998.

——. *Not without Dust and Heat: A Memoir.* Chicago: Exploration Press, 1995.

American Civil Liberties Union. "Blue Coats and Reds." New York: n.p., 1929.

Americas Watch. *The Central Americanization of Colombia?* New York: Human Rights Watch, 1986.

Amnesty International. *Colombia. Political Violence: Myth and Reality.* New York: Amnesty International, 1994.

Armbruster-Sandoval, Ralph. *Globalization and Cross-Border Labor Solidarity in the Americas: The Anti-Sweatshop Movement and the Struggle for Social Justice.* New York: Routledge, 2005.

Armstrong, Robert, Hank Frundt, Hobart Spalding, and Sean Sweeney. *Working Against Us: The American Institute for Free Labor Development and the International Policy of the AFL-CIO.* New York: North American Congress on Latin America, n.d.

Aschmann, Homer. "The Persistent Guajiro." *AMNH/NH* (Natural History: American Museum of Natural History) 84, no. 3 (March 1975): 28–37.

Avrich, Paul. *Anarchist Voices.* Princeton: Princeton University Press, 1995.

——. *Sacco and Vanzetti: The Anarchist Background.* Princeton: Princeton University Press, 1991.

Bacon, David. "Blood for Coal." August 26, 2001. David Bacon's website, http://dbacon.igc.org.

——. "The Colombian Connection: U.S. Aid Fuels a Dirty War against Unions." *In These Times,* July 23, 2001, 11.

——. "It's the Real Thing: Murders at Coke." November 24, 2001. http://dbacon.igc .org.

——. "U.S. Energy Plan Spells Danger for Colombian Labor." Inter Press Service, September 11, 2001. http://www.globalexchange.org.

Baerga, María del Carmen, ed. *Género y trabajo: La industria de la aguja en Puerto Rico y el Caribe hispánico*. San Juan: Editorial de la Universidad de Puerto Rico, 1993.

Bagley, Bruce Michael. "The State and the Peasantry in Contemporary Colombia." *Latin American Issues* 6 n.d. http://webpub.allegheny.edu.

Barber, Benjamin R. *Jihad vs. McWorld*. New York: Times Books, 1995.

Barros Fince, Débora. "It Seems Impossible to Believe: A Survivor Describes the Massacre that Destroyed her Wayuu Community." Translated by Aviva Chomsky. *Cultural Survival Quarterly*, Winter 2005, 41–43.

Barry, Tom, and Deb Preusch. AIFLD *in Central America: Agents as Organizers*. Albuquerque, N.M.: Inter-Hemispheric Education Resource Center, 1986.

Battista, Andrew. "Unions and Cold War Foreign Policy in the 1980s: The National Labor Committee, the AFL-CIO, and Central America." *Diplomatic History* 26, no. 3 (summer 2002): 419–51.

Beade, Lisa Roseman. *The Wealth of Nations: A People's History of Rhode Island*. Montgomery, Ala.: Community Communications Incorporated, 1999.

Bergquist, Charles. *Labor and the Course of American Democracy: U.S. History in Latin American Perspective*. London and New York: Verso, 1996.

——. *Labor in Latin America: Comparative Essays on Chile, Argentina, Venezuela, and Colombia*. Stanford: Stanford University Press, 1986.

Bergquist, Charles, Ricardo Peñaranda, and Gonzalo Sánchez, eds. *Violence in Colombia: The Contemporary Crisis in Historical Perspective*. Wilmington, Del.: Scholarly Resources, 1992.

Bluestone, Barry, and Bennett Harrison. *The Deindustrialization of America: Plant Closings, Community Abandonment, and the Dismantling of Basic Industry*. New York: Basic Books, 1982.

Borges-Méndez, Ramón. "The Use of Latino Immigrant Labor in Massachusetts Manufacturing: Evidence from Lowell, Lawrence and Holyoke." In *Latino Poverty and Economic Development in Massachusetts*, ed. Edwin Meléndez and Miren Uriarte. Boston: Mauricio Gastón Institute for Latino Community Development and Public Policy, 1993.

Boris, Eileen. "Needlewomen under the New Deal in Puerto Rico, 1920–1945." In *Puerto Rican Women and Work: Bridges in Transnational Labor*, ed. Altagracia Ortiz. Philadelphia: Temple University Press, 1996.

Botero, Fernando. "Arranca la gran industria, Septiembre 19 de 1908: Tejiendo país." Colombialink website, http://www.colombialink.com.

——. *Urabá: Colonización, violencia, y crisis del Estado*. Medellín: Universidad de Antioquia, 1990.

Botero Herrera, Fernando, and Diego Sierra Botero. *El mercado de fuerza de trabajo en la zona bananera de Urabá*. Medellín: Universidad de Antioquia, 1981.

Brandis, R. Buford. *The Making of Textile Trade Policy, 1935–1981*.Washington, D.C.: American Textile Manufacturers Institute, 1982.

Brattain, Michelle. "Making Friends and Enemies: Textile Workers and Political Action in Post–World War II Georgia." *Journal of Southern History* 63, no. 1 (February 1997): 91–138.

Brecher, Jeremy, and Tim Costello. *Global Village or Global Pillage?* Boston: South End Press, 1994.

Bridges, Glenn. "The Draper Story: Rise and Fall of a Loom-Making Giant." In *Textile Town: Spartanburg County, South Carolina*, ed. Betsy Wakefield Teter. Spartanburg, S.C.: Hub City Writers Project, 2002.

——. "Engineering the Mills: Lockwood and Greene Come South." In *Textile Town: Spartanburg County, South Carolina*, ed. Betsy Wakefield Teter. Spartanburg, S.C.: Hub City Writers Project, 2002.

Briggs, V. M., Jr. "American Unionism and U.S. Immigration Policy." *Backgrounder, Center for Immigration Studies* August 2001. Ceenter for Immigration Studies website, www.cis.org.

Buchanan, Paul G. " 'Useful Fools' as Diplomatic Tools: Organized Labor as an Instrument of U.S. Foreign Policy in Latin America." Working Paper No. 136. Kellogg Institute. April 1990. http://www.nd.edu.

Bucheli, Marcelo. *Bananas and Business: The United Fruit Company in Colombia, 1899–2000*. New York: New York University Press, 2005.

——. "United Fruit Company in Latin America." In *Banana Wars: Power, Production, and History in the Americas*, ed. Steve Striffler and Mark Moberg. Durham: Duke University Press, 2003.

Buhle, Paul. *Taking Care of Business: Samuel Gompers, George Meany, Lane Kirkland, and the Tragedy of American Labor*. New York: Monthly Review Press, 1999.

Cameron, Ardis. *Radicals of the Worst Sort: Laboring Women in Lawrence, Massachusetts, 1860–1912*. Urbana: University of Illinois Press, 1995.

Cannistraro, Philip V., and Gerald Meyer. "Introduction: Italian American Radicalism: An Interpretive History." In *The Lost World of Italian American Radicalism: Politics, Labor, and Culture*, eds. Philip V. Cannistraro and Gerald Meyer. Westport, Conn.: Praeger, 2003.

Cannistraro, Philip V., and Gerald Meyer, eds. *The Lost World of Italian American Radicalism: Politics, Labor, and Culture*. Westport, Conn.: Praeger, 2003.

Cantor, Daniel, and Juliet Schor. *Tunnel Vision: Labor, the World Economy, and Central America*. Boston: South End Press, 1987.

Carbonell Blanco, Rafael, and Lucy Erazo Coronado. *Hacia una central sindical unitaria*. Bogotá: Pontífica Universidad Javeriana, 1987.

Carden, Maren Lockwood. *Oneida: Utopian Community to Modern Corporation.* Syracuse, N.Y.: Syracuse University Press, 1998.

Cardoso, Fernando Henrique, and Enzo Faletto. *Dependency and Development in Latin America.* Berkeley: University of California Press, 1979.

Carlton, David L. *Mill and Town in South Carolina, 1880–1920.* Baton Rouge: Louisiana State University Press, 1982.

——. "Textile Town Settles In." In *Textile Town: Spartanburg County, South Carolina,* ed. Betsy Wakefield Teter. Spartanburg, S.C.: Hub City Writers Project, 2002.

Carlton, David L., and Peter A. Coclanis. "Southern Textiles in Global Context," in *Global Perspectives on Industrial Transformation in the American South,* eds. Susanna Delfino and Michele Gillespie. Columbia: University of Missouri Press, 2005.

Carr, Barry. "Crossing Borders: Labor Internationalism in the Era of NAFTA." In *Neoliberalism Revisited: Economic Restructuring and Mexico's Political Future,* ed. Gerardo Otero. Boulder, Colo.: Westview Press, 1996.

Centro de Investigación y Educación Popular. *Urabá.* Bogotá: CINEP, 1995.

Chomsky, Aviva. "Salem as a Global City, 1850–2004." In *Salem: Place, Myth, and Memory,* ed. Dane Anthony Morrison and Nancy Lusignan Schultz. Boston: Northeastern University Press, 2004.

——. *West Indian Workers and the United Fruit Company in Costa Rica, 1870–1940.* Baton Rouge: Louisiana State University Press, 1996.

Chomsky, Aviva, and Claire Holman. "The Hidden Maine: Serfdom at DeCoster Egg Farm." *Maine Progressive* 6, no. 2 (December 1991): 1, 4–7.

Chomsky, Noam. *Turning the Tide: U.S. Intervention in Central America and the Struggle for Peace.* Boston: South End Press, 1985.

Coldwell, Joseph M. Papers. Rhode Island Historical Society. Providence.

Collins, Jane L. *Threads: Gender, Labor, and Power in the Global Apparel Industry.* Chicago: University of Chicago Press, 2003.

Comisión Andina de Juristas/Seccional Colombia. *Informes regionales de derechos humanos: Urabá.* Bogotá: Comisión Andina de Juristas, 1994.

Comisión Verificadora de los Actores Violentos en Urabá. "Informe de la Comisión Verificadora de los Actores Violentos en Urabá." In *Urabá,* ed. Centro de Investigación y Educación Popular. Bogotá: CINEP, 1995.

Compa, Lance. "Free Trade, Fair Trade, and the Battle for Labor Rights." in *Rekindling the Movement: Labor's Quest for Relevance in the Twenty-First Century,* ed. Lowell Turner, Harry C. Katz, and Richard W. Hurd. Ithaca: ILR Press/Cornell University Press, 2001.

Cooke, Morris L. Papers. Franklin D. Roosevelt Library, Hyde Park, N.Y.

Cowie, Jefferson. *Capital Moves: RCA's Seventy-Year Quest for Cheap Labor.* New York: New Press, 2001.

Dalzell, Robert F., Jr. *Enterprising Elite: The Boston Associates and the World They Made.* Cambridge, Mass.: Harvard University Press, 1987.

Daniel, Clete. *Culture of Misfortune: An Interpretive History of Textile Unionism in the United States.* Ithaca: ILR Press/Cornell University Press, 2001.

Danker, Anita Cardillo. "The Hopedale Strike of 1913: The Unmaking of an Industrial Utopia." In *New England's Disharmony: The Consequences of the Industrial Revolution,* eds. Doug Reynolds and Katheryn Viens. Kingston, R.I.: Rhode Island Labor History Society, 1993.

Deitz, James L. *An Economic History of Puerto Rico: Institutional Change and Capitalist Development.* Princeton: Princeton University Press, 1986.

Díaz Callejas, Apolinar. *El 9 de abril 1948 en Barrancabermeja: Diez días de poder popular.* Bogotá: El Labrador, 1988.

Draper Corporation. *Cotton Chats.* Hopedale, Mass. 1913–1945.

———. *Telares Draper.* Hopedale, Mass.: Draper Corporation Public Relations Department, 1946.

DuPlessis, Jim. "Roger Milliken: Legacy Crafted with Pride." In *Textile Town: Spartanburg County, South Carolina,* ed. Betsy Wakefield Teter. Spartanburg, S.C.: Hub City Writers Project, 2002.

Eelman, Bruce W. "The English Manufacturing Company: Early Interest from Abroad." In *Textile Town: Spartanburg County, South Carolina,* ed. Betsy Wakefield Teter. Spartanburg, S.C.: Hub City Writers Project, 2002.

Emmanuel, Arghiri. *Unequal Exchange: A Study of the Imperialism of Trade.* Trans. B. Pearce. New York: Monthly Review Press, 1972.

Fajardo, Luis Eduardo. "From the Alliance for Progress to Plan Colombia: A Retrospective Look at U.S. Aid to Colombia." Crisis States Program Working Paper No. 28. April 2003. http://www.crisisstates.com.

Fajardo Gómez, Remedios. "Violación sistemática de los derechos humanos de indígenas, negros y campesinos por parte de la multinacional minera Intercor, filial de la Exxon, en el departamento de La Guajira, Colombia." Unpublished manuscript. August 9, 2001. Copy in author's possession.

Fantasia, Rick, and Kim Voss. *Hard Work: Remaking the American Labor Movement.* Berkeley: University of California Press, 2004.

Farnsworth-Alvear, Ann. *Dulcinea in the Factory: Myths, Morals, Men, and Women in Colombia's Industrial Experiment, 1905–1960.* Durham: Duke University Press, 2000.

Fink, Leon. *The Maya of Morganton: Work and Community in the Nuevo New South.* Chapel Hill: University of North Carolina Press, 2003.

Fix, Michael E., and Jeffrey S. Passel. *Immigration and Immigrants: Setting the Record Straight.* Washington, D.C.: Urban Institute, 1994.

Folbre, Nancy. *The Invisible Heart: Economics and Family Values.* New York: New Press, 2002.

Foner, Philip S. *U.S. Labor Movement and Latin America,* Vol. 1, *1846–1919.* South Hadley, Mass.: Bergin and Garvey, 1988.

Forché, Carolyn, and Philip Wheaton. *History and Motivations of U.S. Involvement in* the Control of the Peasant Movement in El Salvador: The Role of AIFLD in the Agrarian Reform Process, 1970–1980. Washington, D.C.: EPICA, 1980.

Frank, Andre Gunder. Re-Orient: Global Economy in the Asian Age. Berkeley: University of California Press, 1998.

Frank, Dana. Bananeras: Women Transforming the Banana Unions of Latin America. Cambridge, Mass.: South End Press, 2005.

——. Buy American: The Untold Story of Economic Nationalism. Boston: Beacon Press, 1999.

Friedman, Thomas L. The World Is Flat: A Brief History of the Twentieth Century. New York: Farrar, Straus and Giroux, 2005.

Frundt, Hank. "Has the AFL-CIO's Solidarity Center Turned Over a New Leaf in Its Approach to Foreign Policy and Labor?" Resource Center for the Americas. July/August 2003. http://www.americas.org.

Frundt, Henry. "Cross-Border Organizing in the Apparel Industry: Lessons from Central America and the Caribbean?" Labor Studies Journal 24:1 (spring 1999), 89–106.

Galeano, Eduardo H. Open Veins of Latin America: Five Centuries of the Pillage of a Continent. Trans. Cedric Belfrage. Boston: Monthly Review Press, 1998.

Gallagher, Mike, and Cameron McWhirter. "Chiquita Secrets Revealed." Cincinnati Enquirer, May 3, 1998.

Galvin, Miles. The Organized Labor Movement in Puerto Rico. Cranbury, N.J.: Associated University Presses, 1979.

García, Clara Inés. Urabá: Región, actors y conflicto, 1960–1990. Bogotá: CEREC, 1996.

García, Gervasio L., and A. G. Quintero Rivera. Desafío y solidaridad: Breve historia del movimiento obrero puertorriqueño. Río Piedras, Puerto Rico: Ediciones Huracán, 1982.

Gedicks, Al. Resource Rebels: Native Challenges to Mining and Oil Corporations. Boston: South End Press, 2001.

——. "War on Subsistence: Exxon Minerals/Rio Algomm vs WATER." In Life and Death Matters: Human Rights and the Environment at the End of the Millennium, ed. Barbara Rose Johnston. Walnut Creek, Calif.: Alta Mira Press, 1997.

——. "The Wolf River: Ecology and Economics." In Life and Death Matters: Human Rights and the Environment at the End of the Millennium, ed. Barbara Rose Johnston. Walnut Creek, Calif.: Alta Mira Press, 1997.

Gerstle, Gary. Working-Class Americanism: The Politics of Labor in a Textile City, 1914–1960. Cambridge: Cambridge University Press, 1989.

Getman, Julius. The Betrayal of Local 14: Paperworkers, Politics, and Permanent Replacements. Ithaca: ILR Press, 1998.

Gilman, Glenn. Human Relations in the Industrial Southeast: A Study of the Textile Industry. Chapel Hill: University of North Carolina Press, 1956.

Gladden, Kathleen. "Women in Industrial Development: The Case of Medellín, Colombia." Journal of Popular Culture 22, no. 1 (summer 1998): 51–62.

Glaessel-Brown, Eleanor E. "Immigration Policy and Colombian Textile Workers in New England: A Case Study in Political Demography." PhD diss., MIT, 1984.

———. "A Time of Transition: Colombian Textile Workers in Lowell in the 1970s." In *The Continuing Revolution: A History of Lowell, Massachusetts*, ed. Robert Weible. Lowell, Mass.: Lowell Historical Society, 1991.

Glasser, Ruth. *Aquí Me Quedo: Puerto Ricans in Connecticut/Los puertorriqueños en Connecticut*. Middletown, Conn.: Connecticut Humanities Council, 1997.

Gleijeses, Piero. *Shattered Hope: The Guatemalan Revolution and the United States, 1944–1954*. Princeton: Princeton University Press, 1992.

Glick Schiller, Nina, Thaddeus C. Guldbrandsen, Ayse Caglar, and Evangelos Karagiannis. "Small-Scale City in Global Society: Non-ethnic Simultaneous Incorporation in Manchester, New Hampshire." Working paper, Brown University Sociology Department, 2004.

González, Juan. *Harvest of Empire: A History of Latinos in America*. New York: Penguin Press, 2001.

González García, Lydia Milagros. *Una puntada en el tiempo: La industria de la aguja en Puerto Rico (1900–1929)*. Santo Domingo, Dominican Republic: CEREP-CIPAF, 1990.

Gould, Stephen Jay. *The Mismeasure of Man*. Rev. ed. New York: Norton, 1996.

Green, Hardy. *On Strike at Hormel: The Struggle for a Democratic Labor Movement*. Philadelphia: Temple University Press, 1990.

Grosfoguel, Ramón. "Puerto Rican Labor Migration to the United States: Modes of Incorporation, Coloniality, and Identities." *Review: Fernand Braudel Center* 22, no. 4 (1999): 503–21.

Gross, Laurence. "The Game Is Played Out: The Closing Decades of the Boott Mills." in *The Continuing Revolution: A History of Lowell, Massachusetts*, ed. Robert Weible. Lowell, Mass.: Lowell Historical Society, 1991.

Guglielmo, Jennifer. "Donne Ribelli: Recovering the History of Italian Women's Radicalism in the United States." In *The Lost World of Italian-American Radicalism: Politics, Labor Culture*, eds. Philip V. Cannistraro and Gerald Meyer. Westport, Conn.: Praeger, 2003.

Handy, Jim. *Revolution in the Countryside: Rural Conflict and Agrarian Reform in Guatemala, 1944–1954*. Chapel Hill: University of North Carolina Press, 1994.

Haney López, Ian F. *White by Law: The Legal Construction of Race*. New York: New York University Press, 1998.

Haraven, Tamara K., and Randolph Langenbach. *Amoskeag: Life and Work in an American Factory-City*. New York: Pantheon Books, 1978.

Hartford, William F. *Where Is Our Responsibility? Unions and Economic Change in the New England Textile Industry, 1870–1960*. Amherst: University of Massachusetts Press, 1996.

Hartman, Laura P., Denis G. Arnold, and Richard E. Wokutch, eds. *Rising above*

Sweatshops: Innovative Approaches to Global Labor Challenges. Westport, Conn.: Praeger, 2003.

Hernández Angueira, Luisa. "El trabajo a domicilio femenino y la industria de la aguja en Puerto Rico, 1914–1940." In *Género y trabajo: La industria de la aguja en Puerto Rico y el Caribe Hispánico*, ed. María del Carmen Baerga. San Juan: Editorial de la Universidad de Puerto Rico, 1993.

Hess, Jerry N. "Oral History of Gen. William H. Draper, Jr." January 11, 1972. Truman Presidential Museum and Library, Washington D.C. http://www.trumanlibrary .org.

Hirsch, Fred, and Virginia Muir. "A Plumber Gets Curious about Exporting McCarthyism." In *The Cold War against Labor*, vol. 2, eds. Ann Fagan Ginger and David Christiano. Berkeley: Meiklejohn Civil Liberties Institute, 1987.

Human Rights Watch. *Colombia's Killer Networks.* New York: Human Rights Watch, 1996.

——. *Guerra sin cuartel: Colombia y el derecho internacional humanitario.* New York: Human Rights Watch, 1998.

Hutchinson, John G. *Managing a Fair Day's Work: An Analysis of Work Standards in Operation.* Ann Arbor: Bureau of Industrial Relations, University of Michigan, 1963.

Ignatiev, Noel. *How the Irish Became White.* New York: Routledge, 1996.

Immerman, Richard H. *The CIA in Guatemala.* Austin: University of Texas Press, 1983.

International Labor Organisation Textiles Committee. "Effects of Technological Developments on Wages and on Conditions and Level of Employment in the Textile Industry." Sixth Session, 1958. Geneva: ILO, 1958.

——. "General Report: Report Given to the Conclusions of the Previous Session." Sixth Session, 1958. Geneva: ILO, 1958.

International Labor Organization Textiles Committee. "General Report: Recent Events and Developments in the Textile Industry. Sixth Session, 1958." Geneva: ILO, 1958.

Itzigsohn, José. "The Making of Latino Providence." Unpublished manuscript. Brown University website, http://www.brown.edu.

Jakobsen, Kjeld A. "Rethinking the International Confederation of Free Trade Unions and Its Inter-American Regional Organization." *Antipode* 33, no. 3 (2001): 363–83.

Johnston, Barbara Rose. *Life and Death Matters: Human Rights and the Environment at the End of the Millennium.* Walnut City, Calif.: Alta Mira Press, 1997.

Jones, G. L. "Sweatshops on the Spanish Main." In *The Puerto Ricans: A Documentary History*, eds. Kal Wagenheim and Olga Jiménez de Wagenheim. Princeton: Markus Wiener, 1994.

Juárez Núñez, Huberto. *Rebelión en el Greenfield.* Puebla, Mexico: Benemérita Universidad Autónoma de Puebla and AFL-CIO, 2002.

Kiplinger, Joan. "Indian Head Remembered." *Vintage Fabrics* (March–April 2003). Copy in author's possession.

Kirk, Robin. *More Terrible Than Death: Massacres, Drugs, and America's War in Colombia*. New York: Public Affairs, 2003.

Lamphere, Louise. *From Working Daughters to Working Mothers: Immigrant Women in a New England Industrial Community*. Ithaca: Cornell University Press, 1987.

Lamphere, Louise, Ricardo Anzaldua, and Aida Redondo. "Interviews for Central Falls NIMH Project on Working Families." 1977. Interviews in the possession of Louise Lamphere.

Landes, David S. *The Unbound Prometheus: Technological Change and Industrial Development in Western Europe from 1750 to the Present*. 2nd ed. Cambridge: Cambridge University Press, 2003.

Leal Buitrago, Francisco. *El oficio de la guerra: La seguridad nacional en Colombia*. Bogotá: Tercer Mundo Editores, 1994.

Leech, Garry M. "Coca Cola Accused of Using Death Squads to Target Union Leaders." *Colombia Report*, July 23, 2001. Colombia Journal website, www.colombia journal.org.

LeGrand, Catherine. "The Colombian Crisis in Historical Perspective." *Canadian Journal of Latin America and Caribbean Studies* 28, no. 55/5 (2003): 165–209.

Levenson-Estrada, Deborah. *Trade Unionists against Terror: Guatemala City 1954–1985*. Chapel Hill: University of North Carolina Press, 1994.

Library of Congress. *Colombia: A Country Study*. Washington, D.C.: Library of Congress, 1988.

Lichtenstein, Nelson. *State of the Union: A Century of American Labor*. Princeton: Princeton University Press, 2003.

Little, Royal. *How to Lose $100,000,000 and Other Valuable Advice*. Boston: Little, Brown, 1979.

Lodge, George C. *Spearheads of Democracy: Labor in Developing Countries*. New York: Council on Foreign Relations, 1962.

Lyons, Eugene. *The Life and Death of Sacco and Vanzetti*. New York: International Publishers, 1927.

Mahler, Sarah. *American Dreaming: Immigrant Life on the Margins*. Princeton: Princeton University Press, 1995.

Malloy, Elaine, Daniel Malloy, and Alan J. Ryan. *Images of America: Hopedale*. Charleston, S.C.: Arcadia Publishing, 2002.

Martin, Gerard, and Claudia Steiner. "El destino de la frontera: Urabá en los años noventa." In *Urabá*, ed. Centro de Investigación y Educación Popular. Bogotá: CINEP, 1995.

Martínez, Marta. "The Latinos of Rhode Island." In *Rhode Island Latinos: A Scan of Issues Affecting the Latino Population of Rhode Island*, eds. Miren Uriarte et al. Providence, R.I.: Rhode Island Foundation, 2002.

Mass, William. "The Decline of a Technological Leader: Capability, Strategy, and Shuttleless Weaving, 1945–1974." *Business and Economic History* 18, 2nd ser. (1990): 234–44.

———. "Developing and Utilizing Technological Leadership: Industrial Research, Vertical Integration, and Business Strategy at the Draper Company, 1816–1930." *Business and Economic History* 18, 2nd ser. (1989): 129–39.

Matos Rodríguez, Félix V. "The Historical Development of the Puerto Rican Community in Boston." Unpublished manuscript in author's possession.

McClintock, Michael. *Instruments of Statecraft: U.S. Guerrilla Warfare, Counterinsurgency, and Counterterrorism, 1940–1990.* New York: Pantheon Books, 1992.

Medina, Medófilo. "Violence and Economic Development: 1945–50 and 1985–88." In *Violence in Colombia: The Contemporary Crisis in Historical Perspective*, ed. Charles Bergquist, Ricardo Peñaranda, and Gonzalo Sánchez. Wilmington, Del.: Scholarly Resources, 1992.

Meléndez, Edwin. "Latino Poverty and Economic Development in Massachusetts." In *Latino Poverty and Economic Development in Massachusetts*, eds. Edwin Meléndez and Miren Uriarte. Boston: Mauricio Gastón Institute for Latino Community Development and Public Policy, 1993.

Meléndez, Edwin, and Miren Uriarte, eds. *Latino Poverty and Economic Development in Massachusetts*. Boston: Mauricio Gastón Institute for Latino Community Development and Public Policy, 1993.

Melman, Seymour. *Pentagon Capitalism: The Management of the New Imperialism.* New York: McGraw Hill, 1970.

———. *The Permanent War Economy: American Capitalism in Decline.* New York: Simon and Schuster, 1974.

———. *Profits without Production.* Philadelphia: University of Pennsylvania Press, 1987.

Minchin, Timothy J. *"Don't Sleep with Stevens!" The J. P. Stevens Campaign and the Struggle to Organize the South, 1963–80.* Gainesville: University Press of Florida, 2005.

Mintz, Sidney W. *Sweetness and Power: The Place of Sugar in Modern History.* New York: Penguin Books, 1995.

Molano, Alfredo. "The Evolution of the FARC: A Guerrilla Group's Long History." *NACLA Report on the Americas*, September–October 2000.

Moody, Kim. "Global Capital and Economic Nationalism: Protectionism or Solidarity?" *Against the Current*, 87 (July/August 2000). Solidarity website, http://www.solidarity-us.org.

Mort, Jo-Ann, ed. *Not Your Father's Union Movement: Inside the AFL-CIO.* London and New York: Verso, 1998.

Naumkeag Steam Cotton Company Collection. Baker Library, Harvard Business School, Boston.

Ngai, Mae. *Impossible Subjects: Illegal Aliens and the Making of Modern America.* Princeton: Princeton University Press, 2005.

Nutt, Karen L. "Seth Milliken: The Money behind the Mills." In *Textile Town: Spartanburg County, South Carolina*, ed. Betsy Wakefield Teter. Spartanburg, S.C.: Hub City Writers Project, 2002.

Nyman, Richmond C., and Elliott Dunlap Smith. *Union-Management Cooperation in the "Stretch Out": Labor Extension at the Pequot Mills.* New Haven: Institute of Human Relations, Yale University Press, 1934.

Ortiz, Altagracia. *"'En la aguja y el pedal eché la hiel'*: Puerto Rican Women in the Garment Industry of New York City, 1920–1980." In *Puerto Rican Women and Work: Bridges in Transnational Labor,* ed. Altagracia Ortiz. Philadelphia: Temple University Press, 1996.

——, ed. *Puerto Rican Women and Work: Bridges in Transnational Labor.* Philadelphia: Temple University Press, 1996.

Osorio O., Iván Darío. *Historia del sindicalismo antioqueño, 1900–1986.* Medellín: Tipografía y Litografía Sigifredo, n.d.

Pacini Hernandez, Deborah. "Resource Development and Indigenous People: The El Cerrejón Project in Guajira, Colombia." Cultural Survival Occasional Paper 15. Cambridge, Mass.: Cultural Survival, December 1984.

Parker, Margaret. *Lowell: A Study of Industrial Development.* New York: Macmillan, 1940.

Parsons, James. *Antioqueño Colonization in Western Colombia.* 2nd ed. Berkeley: University of California Press, 1968.

Pearce, Jenny. "Beyond the Perimeter Fence: Oil and Armed Conflict in Casanare, Colombia." London School of Economics, Centre for the Study of Global Governance, Discussion Papers No. 32, June 2004.

——. *Colombia: Inside the Labyrinth.* London: Latin America Bureau, 1990.

Piore, Michael J. *Birds of Passage: Migrant Labor and Industrial Societies.* Cambridge: Cambridge University Press, 1979.

——. "Immigration, Work Expectations, and Labor Market Structure." In *The Diverse Society: Implications for Social Policy,* eds. Pastora San Juan Cafferty and Leon Chestang. Silver Spring, Md.: National Association of Social Workers, 1976.

Probert, Hywel. "Thumbs Up for the Bright, White Folks." *New Statesman* 131, no. 4583 (April 15, 2002): 32–33.

Quaccia, Jon. "National Endowment for Death Squads? The AFL-CIO and the NED." Unpublished manuscript. Copy in the author's possession.

Rachleff, Peter. *Hard-Pressed in the Heartland: The Hormel Strike and the Future of the Labor Movement.* Boston: South End Press, 1993.

Racine, Philip. "Boom Time in Textile Town, 1880–1909." In *Textile Town: Spartanburg County, South Carolina,* ed. Betsy Wakefield Teter. Spartanburg, S.C.: Hub City Writers Project, 2002.

Ramírez Cuellar, Francisco. *The Profits of Extermination: How U.S. Corporate Power Is Destroying Colombia.* Trans. Aviva Chomsky. Monroe, Me.: Common Courage Press, 2005.

Ramírez Tobón, William. *Urabá: Los inciertos confines de una crisis.* Bogotá: Planeta, 1997.

Raynolds, Laura T. "The Global Banana Trade." In *Banana Wars: Power, Production, and History in the Americas*, ed. Steve Striffler and Mark Moberg. Durham: Duke University Press, 2003.

Rempe, Dennis M. "Guerrillas, Bandits, and Independent Republics: U.S. Counterinsurgency Efforts in Colombia 1959–1965." *Small Wars and Insurgencies* 6, no. 3 (winter 1995): 304–27.

Rhode Island Historical Preservation and Heritage Commission. "Providence Industrial Sites." 1981. http://www.rihphc.state.ri.us.

Rippy, J. Fred. *The Capitalists and Colombia.* New York: Vanguard Press, 1931.

Ritchie, Lisa Caston. "Walter S. Montgomery, Sr. at Spartan's Helm for 67 Years." In *Textile Town: Spartanburg County, South Carolina*, ed. Betsy Wakefield Teter. Spartanburg, S.C.: Hub City Writers Project, 2002.

Rivera, Ralph. "Diversity, Growth, and Geographic Distribution: Latinos in Massachusetts." In *Latino Poverty and Economic Development in Massachusetts*, ed. Edwin Meléndez and Miren Uriarte. Boston: Mauricio Gastón Institute for Latino Community Development and Public Policy, 1993.

Rodberg, Simon. "The CIO without the CIA." *American Prospect* 12: 12 (July 2, 2001): 27–28.

Rodney, Walter. *How Europe Underdeveloped Africa.* Rev. ed. Washington, D.C.: Howard University Press, 1981.

Rodríguez, Clara. "The Economic Factors Affecting Puerto Ricans in New York." In *Labor Migration under Capitalism: The Puerto Rican Experience*, ed. Centro de Estudios Puertorriqueños, History Task Force. New York: Monthly Review Press, 1979.

Roediger, David R. *Working toward Whiteness: How America's Immigrants Became White. The Strange Road from Ellis Island to the Suburbs.* New York: Basic Books, 2005.

Roldán, Mary. *Blood and Fire:* La Violencia *in Antioquia, Colombia, 1946–1953.* Durham: Duke University Press, 2002.

Romero, Mauricio. "Los trabajadores bananeros de Urabá: De 'súbditos a ciudadanos'?" Draft. Centro de Estudos Sociais, Coimbra, Portugal, website, http://www .ces.fe.uc.pt.

Romualdi, Serafino. *Presidents and Peons: Recollections of a Labor Ambassador in Latin America.* New York: Funk and Wagnalls, 1967.

Rosado Marzán, César F. "Successful Wage Restraint: Trust and Labor Market Centralization in the Exercise of Wage Restraint in Sweden, Puerto Rico, and Kerala." Paper presented at the Princeton Institute for International and Regional Studies Graduate Student Conference, Princeton, April 2005.

Rosen, Ellen Israel. *Making Sweatshops: The Globalization of the U.S. Apparel Industry.* Berkeley: University of California Press, 2002.

Ross, Andrew, ed. *No Sweat: Fashion, Free Trade, and the Rights of Garment Workers.* London and New York: Verso, 1997.

Ross, David F. *The Long Uphill Path: A Historical Study of Puerto Rico's Program of Economic Development.* San Juan: Editorial Edil, 1969.

Roston, Aram. "It's the Real Thing: Murder." *The Nation* 237: 7 (September 3, 2001): 34–38.

Salmond, John A. *Gastonia, 1929: The Story of the Loray Mill Strike*. Chapel Hill: University of North Carolina Press, 1995.

Sánchez G., Gonzalo. "Introduction: Problems of Violence, Prospects for Peace." In *Violence in Colombia: The Contemporary Crisis in Historical Perspective*, ed. Charles Bergquist, Ricardo Peñaranda, and Gonzalo Sánchez. Wilmington, Del.: Scholarly Resources, 1992.

Sandoval O., Marbel. *Gloria Cuartas: Por qué no tiene miedo*. Bogota: Planeta Colombiana Editorial, 1997.

Santiago, Carlos E., and Francisco L. Rivera-Batiz. *Island Paradox: Puerto Rico in the 1990s*. New York: Russell Sage Foundation, 1998.

Sassen, Saskia. "Why Migration?" In NACLA *Report on the Americas* 26, no. 1 (July 1992): 14–19.

Savage, Charles H., Jr., and George F. F. Lombard. *Sons of the Machine: Case Studies of Social Change in the Workplace*. Cambridge, Mass.: MIT Press, 1986.

Schlesinger, Stephen C., and Stephen Kinzer. *Bitter Fruit: The Story of the American Coup in Guatemala*. Expanded ed. Cambridge, Mass.: Harvard University Press, 1999.

Schmidt, Samuel. *In Search of Decision: The Maquiladora Industry in Mexico*. Ciudad Juárez and Flagstaff: Universidad Autónoma de Ciudad Juárez and Flagstaff Institute, 2000.

Scipes, Kim. "AFL-CIO Foreign Policy: Final Report from the Convention." Znet, August 2, 2005. http://www.zmag.org.

———. "Building International Labor Solidarity: Escalating the Struggle within the AFL-CIO." Znet, 2000, http://www.zmag.org.

———. "It's Time to Come Clean: Open the AFL-CIO Archives on International Labor Operations." *Labor Studies Journal* 25, no. 2 (summer 2000): 4–25.

Shailor, Barbara. "A New Internationalism: Advancing Workers' Rights in a New Global Economy." In *Not Your Father's Union Movement: Inside the AFL-CIO*, ed. Jo-Ann Mort. London and New York: Verso, 1998.

Sharp, Jonathan Inman. "The Transformation of a Working-Class Neighborhood in Burlington, Vermont." *Proceedings of the New England–St. Lawrence Valley Geographical Society* 32 (2002): 9–22.

Shorrock, Tim. "Creating a New Internationalism for Labor." *Dollars and Sense* (September 1999): 36–41.

———. "Labor's Cold War." *The Nation* 276: 19 (May 19, 2003): 15–22.

———. "Toeing the Line? Sweeney and U.S. Foreign Policy." *New Labor Forum* 11 (fall/winter 2002): 9–19.

Sims, Beth. *Workers of the World Undermined: American Labor's Role in U.S. Foreign Policy*. Boston: South End Press, 1992.

Soluri, John. "Accounting for Taste: Export Bananas, Mass Markets, and Panama Disease." *Environmental History* 7: 3 (July 2002): 386–410.

Spalding, Hobart A., Jr. *Organized Labor in Latin America: Historical Case Studies of Urban Workers in Dependent Societies*. New York: Harper and Row, 1977.

Striffler, Steve, and Mark Moberg, eds. *Banana Wars: Power, Production, and History in the Americas*. Durham: Duke University Press, 2003.

Stycos, Steven. "Torture Is the Issue." [Portland] *Phoenix*, December 14–21, 2000.

Taussig, Michael. *Law in a Lawless Land: Diary of a Limpieza*. New York: New Press, 2003.

Taylor, J. Gary, and Patricia J. Scharlin. *Smart Alliance: How a Global Organization and Environmental Activists Transformed a Tarnished Brand*. New Haven: Yale University Press, 2004.

Teter, Betsy Wakefield. "Textile Town in Transition, 1975–2002." In *Textile Town: Spartanburg County, South Carolina*, ed. Betsy Wakefield Teter. Spartanburg, S.C.: Hub City Writers Project, 2002.

——, ed. *Textile Town: Spartanburg County, South Carolina*. Spartanburg, S.C.: Hub City Writers Project, 2002.

Teter, Betsy Wakefield, Karen Nutt, and Bill Lynch. "Textile Town Appendix." In *Textile Town: Spartanburg County, South Carolina*, ed. Betsy Wakefield Teter. Spartanburg, S.C.: Hub City Writers Project, 2002.

Timpson, Anne Burlak. Papers. Sophia Smith Collection, Smith College Library, Northampton, Mass.

Tonelson, Alan. *The Race to the Bottom: Why a Worldwide Worker Surplus and Uncontrolled Free Trade Are Sinking American Living Standards*. Boulder, Colo.: Westview Press, 2000.

Torres Giraldo, Ignacio. *La huelga general en Medellín*. Medellín: Editores Bedout, 1967.

Trepp, Jean Carol. "Union-Management Co-operation and the Southern Organizing Campaign." *Journal of Political Economy* 41: 5 (1933): 602–24.

Tucker, William H. *The Funding of Scientific Racism: Wickliffe Draper and the Pioneer Fund*. Urbana: University of Illinois Press, 2002.

United Mine Workers of America. "From Alabama to Colombia: Drummond's Trail of Tears." *United Mine Workers of America Journal* 112: 4 (July/August 2001). http://www.umwa.org.

United States. Department of Agriculture. *World Cotton Situation*. Washington, D.C.: U.S. Government Printing Office, March 1992.

United States. Department of State. *Country Reports on Human Rights Practices for 1991*. Washington, D.C.: United States Government Printing Office, February 1992.

United States. Office of the United States Trade Representative. "First Report to the Congress on the Operation of the Andean Trade Preference Act as Amended." April 30, 2003. http://www.ustr.gov.

——. Office of the United States Trade Representative. "Second Report to Congress on the Operation of the Andean Trade Preference Act as Amended." April 30, 2005. http://www.ustr.gov.

United States Senate. "American Institute for Free Labor Development." Hearing before the Committee on Foreign Relations, United States Senate, 91st Congress, First Session with George Meany, President, AFL-CIO. August 1, 1969. Washington, D.C.: U.S. Government Printing Office, 1969.

——. Committee on Foreign Relations. "Survey of the Alliance for Progress, Labor Policies and Programs." A Study Prepared at the Request of the Subcommittee on American Republics Affairs by the Staff of the Committee on Foreign Relations. United States Senate. Together with a Report of the Comptroller General. July 15, 1968. Washington, D.C.: U.S. Government Printing Office, 1968.

Uriarte, Miren, ed. *Rhode Island Latinos: A Scan of Issues Affecting the Latino Population of Rhode Island*. Providence: Rhode Island Foundation, 2002.

Uriarte, Miren, and Charles Jones. "Latinos in Rhode Island: Growth and Geographic Concentration." In *Rhode Island Latinos: A Scan of Issues Affecting the Latino Population of Rhode Island*, ed. Miren Uriarte. Providence: Rhode Island Foundation, 2002.

Uriarte, Miren, and Ramón Borges-Méndez, "Tales of Latinos in Three Small Cities: Latino Settlement and Incorporation in Lawrence and Holyoke, Massachusetts, and Providence, Rhode Island." Paper presented at Color Lines Conference: Segregation and Integration in America's Present and Future, Harvard University, August 30–September 1, 2003. http://www.cpcs.umb.edu.

Uribe A., María Victoria. *Ni canto de gloria, ni canto fúnebre: El regreso del EPL a la vida civil*. Bogotá: CINEP, 1994.

Uribe, María Teresa. *Urabá: región o territorio? Un análisis en el contexto de la política, la historia y la etnicidad*. Medellín: CORPOURABA-INER, 1992.

Urrutia, Miguel. *The Development of the Colombian Labor Movement*. New Haven: Yale University Press, 1969.

Vecoli, Rudolph J. "The Making and Un-Making of the Italian American Working Class." In *The Lost World of Italian American Radicalism: Politics, Labor, and Culture*, eds. Philip V. Cannistraro and Gerald Meyer. Westport, Conn.: Praeger, 2003.

Villarraga Sarmiento, Alvaro, and Nelson Roberto Plazas Niño. *Para reconstruir los sueños*. Bogotá: Fundación Cultura Democrática, 1994.

Villegas, Jorge. *Petróleo, oligarquía e imperio*. Bogotá: El Ancora, 1982.

Waldrep, G. C. III. *Southern Workers and the Search for Community: Spartanburg County, South Carolina*. Urbana: University of Illinois Press, 2000.

Ware, Norman. *The Industrial Worker, 1840–1860*. 1924; reprint, Chicago: Ivan R. Dee Publisher, 1990.

Wedin, Ake. *International Trade Union Solidarity: ICFTU 1957–1965*. Stockholm: Bokforlaget Prisma, 1973.

Wehrle, Edmund. "Guns, Butter, Leon Keyserling, the AFL-CIO and the Fate of Full-Employment Economics." *The Historian* 66, no. 4 (December 2004): 730–48.

Weinrub, Al, and William Bollinger. *The AFL-CIO in Central America*. Oakland, Calif.: Labor Network on Central America, 1987.

West, Dorothy. *The Living Is Easy*. New York: Arno Press and New York Times, 1969.

Wilkinson, Daniel. *Silence on the Mountain: Stories of Terror, Betrayal and Forgetting in Today's Guatemala*. New York: Houghton Mifflin, 2003.

Williams, Eric Eustace. *Capitalism and Slavery*. Chapel Hill: University of North Carolina Press, 1994.

Williams, William Appleman. *The Tragedy of American Diplomacy*. 2nd ed. New York: Norton, 1988.

Willis, Jeffrey. "Textile Town Pioneers, 1816–1879." In *Textile Town: Spartanburg County, South Carolina*, ed. Betsy Wakefield Teter. Spartanburg, S.C.: Hub City Writers Project, 2002.

Wilson, Charles Morrow. *Empire in Green and Gold: The Story of the American Banana Trade*. New York: Greenwood Press, 1968.

Winn, Peter. *Weavers of Revolution: The Yarur Workers and Chile's Road to Socialism*. New York: Oxford University Press, 1986.

Wolf, Eric R. *Europe and the People without History*. Berkeley: University of California Press, 1997.

Wright, Annette C. "The Aftermath of the General Textile Strike: Managers and the Workplace at Burlington Mills." *Journal of Southern History* 60, no. 1 (February 1994): 81–112.

Zamosc, Leon. *The Agrarian Question and the Peasant Movement in Colombia*. Cambridge: Cambridge University Press, 1986.

Zappia, Charles A. "From Working-Class Radicalism to Cold War Anti-Communism: The Case of the Italian Locals of the International Ladies' Garment Workers' Union." In *The Lost World of Italian-American Radicalism: Politics, Labor, and Culture*, eds. Philip V. Cannistraro and Gerald Meyer. Westport, Conn.: Praeger, 2003.

Zinn, Kenneth S. "Labor Solidarity in the New World Order: The UMWA Program in Colombia." *Labor Research Review* 23 (spring/summer 1995): 35–43.

Page numbers in italics refer to illustrations; acronyms are defined in the Abbreviations list, ix–xiii.

ACTWU, 131, 140, 169

Adams, James Luther, 89–92, *89*

AFL: anticommunism of, 84–85, 224, 238; anti-immigration position of, 22, 168; FLT and, 109; labor-management collaboration and, 85, 100, 129–30; Latin American labor movements and, 227, 233–34, 238–39; Naumkeag Steam Cotton Company strike and, 73; philosophy of, 222–23; on unemployment insurance, 85; war and conciliation and, 123. *See also* UTW

AFL-CIO: anticommunism of, 226, 233, 235, 239, 240, 241, 242, 301; on anti-immigrant legislation, 169, 170; ATPDEA and, 123; on "Buy American" campaigns, 133; Change to Win Coalition, 251–52; CIO, 95, 101–2; Colombian union movement and, 216, 251–52, 261–62; ICFTU and, 234, 346n39; Latin America and, 227, 233–36, 248, 251–52; membership dissent on Latin American policy, 248, 249, 251–52, 281; New Voices

movement, 225, 248, 297; Sweeney and, 248–49; U.S. government funding of, 129, 234, 244, 251. *See also* AIFLD; SEIU; Solidarity Center; Teamsters; UFCW; UNITE-HERE

African Americans: in American workforce, 21, 22, 36, 149, 150, 257, 306n17; exclusion of, from workforce, 22; migration of, to northern cities, 143, 332n38; Puerto Rican workers and, 157; support of, for U.S. foreign policies, 225

African palm cultivation, 191, 220

Afro-Colombians, 10–11, 188, 190, 269, 272, 284, 286

AFSCME, 236–37, 256

Agriculture, 152, 153, 155–57, *156*, *157*, 245, 302. *See also* Banana industry; Sintagro

Agudelo, Fabio, 164

Agudelo, Mario, 198, 199, 200, 201, 202–3, 205

Aguirre, Fernando, 215–16

AIFLD: affiliates' relations with, 243–44; American Center for International Labor Solidarity, 249; anticommunism promoted by, 226, 240, 241, 244; campesino centers of, 246, 348n90;

Bracero program (1942–64), 155

Brayton Point (Massachusetts) power plant, 266

Brazil, 157, 161, 235, 262, 329n205, 348n90

Bread and Roses strikers (Lawrence, Mass.), 24, 26, 45, 88, 147–48, 308n56

Brown, Geoffrey, 85

Buchanan, Pat, 134, 234

Bucheli, Marcelo, 337n15

Buhle, Paul, 222

Burke-Harte Act (1972), 134

Burlak, Anne, 86; arrests of, 85, 87; Atlanta Six and, 85; Communist Party and, 66, 84; as mayoral candidate in Pawtucket, 160; Naumkeag Strike and, 64, 65, 66, 67, 69–70, 72; NTWU and, 160; Polish workers and, 68; as Red Flame, 67, 73, 87; relief efforts and, 67, 70–71, *71*, 86–87; on return to work plan, 68–69; in Rhode Island, 86; on rights of unemployed, 85–86; strike leadership of, 69–70, 74, 84, 85–88; UTW southern campaign opposed by, 224

Burlington Mills, 118, 132, 327n180

Bush, George W., 121, 137, 216

"Buy American" campaigns, 130, 131, 133, 134, 135, 223

CAFTA, 132, 135, 303

Callahan, Edward D., 81, 315n115

Calvin Klein, 327n180

Calvo, Oscar William, 194

Calzone, Antonio, 44

Cameron, Ardis, 26

Campesino centers, 246, 348n90

Canada: auto workers in, 254; Export Development Bank in, 266–67; Nova Scotia Power Company in, 282, 283; Public Service Alliance of Canada in, 286

Canal Zone (Panama), 226–27

Caño Limon-Coveñas oil pipeline (Occidental Petroleum), 232–33

Capital mobility, 305n1; economic integration and, 304; radicalism of workforce and, 149; taxes and, 97; unions and, 101, 113, 134; U.S. government incentives for, 134

Caracolí, 272

Carbocol, 269, 270

Cardona, Diana, 198

Cardona, Luis Adolfo, 251

Carepa Coca Cola factory (Urabá, Colombia), 237, 251, 253

Caribbean Basin Initiative countries, 120–21

Castaño, Carlos, 199, 208

Castaño, Fidel, 195, 196, 198, 199

Castillo, Walter, 276

Castro, Fidel, 95, 245

Catholic Church: CLASC and, 242; coal mines and, 273; Peace Community of San José de Apartadó and, 209; strikes and, 88–89; on striking workers, 30–31, 308n56; support of, for Italian textile workers, 23, 30–31, 306n56; unions and, 191. *See also* UTC

CBI, 121, 136

Celanese Corporation of America. *See* American Celanese Corporation

Central America, 119, 136, 145–46, 212, 235, 248. *See also under names of specific nations*

Central American Free Trade Agreement, 132, 135, 303

Central Falls, Rhode Island: Colombian textile workers in, 159, 160, 163–64, 172, 295; General Fabrics strike in, 86–87; Joan Fabrics in, 162; Latino population of, 330n5; Lyons Fabric Company and, 163, 172; Puerto Ricans in, 159

Guajira province. *See* Cerrejón Zona
  Norte coal mine
Guatemala, 136, 212, 253, 343n155
Guerin Mills (Woonsocket, R.I.), 103,
  318n30, 319n32
Guerrilla organizations: Plan Lazo, 232;
  reinsertion process, 202, 203, 208,
  218, 341n105; United States–
  sponsored antiguerrilla training
  school, 231. *See also* ELN; EPL; FARC;
  Violence
Guest workers, 154, 155, 165
Guevara, Alirio, 204
Guglielmo, Jennifer, 150

Hartford, William F., 101, 305n1, 308n56
Haywood, "Big Bill," 26
HealthLink, 283
Hearst, William Randolph, 131, 132
Helicopters, 127–28, 128–29, 262, 295
Hirsch, Fred, 231, 248, 251
Home work, 107–9, 159, 163, 320n56
Honduras banana industry, 212
Hoover, Herbert, 132
Hopedale, Massachusetts, 19, 20, 22–23,
  34–35. *See also* Draper Loom
  Company
Hope Webbing, 160
Hormel, 297, 298
Housing: for banana workers, 190, 196,
  198, 200; for coal miners, 269; for
  Colombian workers, 167–68; for
  Draper workers, 20, 22–23, 32; evic-
  tion of strikers from, 32, 69; mill vil-
  lages, 53; racial segregation in, 36
H-2 guest worker program, 154, 155,
  165
Human rights organizations: Americas
  Watch, 266; Amnesty International,
  205, 209, 266, 277, 342n124, 353n56;
  on assassinations of Esperanza party
  activists, 201; on forced displace-

ments by Cerrejón Zona Norte coal
  mine, 350n5; on impact of guerrillas
  on social movements in Urabá, 194;
  on killings of trade unionists, 353n56;
  on military presence in Urabá region,
  193; on U.S. military aid to Colombia,
  266
Human rights violations: Alien Tort
  Claims Act and, 253; attacks on
  Esperanzados, 202; Colombian government and, 293; Comandos Populares and, 203–4; condemnation of,
  277; conditions of communities
  affected by coal mines and, 285; corporate responsibility for, 189; Intelligence and Counterintelligence Battalion, 232; killings of trade unionists,
  264, 279, 281, 353n56; by paramilitaries, 205–6, 264, 271–72, 277, 281,
  287–91, 291–93, 342n124, 353n56;
  Sintraminercol on, 284; by U.S. multinational corporations, 251, 281. *See
  also* Violence

ICEM, 268, 281, 284, 285
ICFTU, 234, 236, 237, 239, 240, 246
IFPCW, 236, 237, 244–45
ILGWU: "Buy American" campaigns and,
  133, 134; Hispanic workers and, 150–
  51; ICFTU, 234; Italian locals of, 149–
  50, 151; liquidated damages and, 113,
  322n87; male leadership of, 149; protectionist policies and, 133, 134; in
  Puerto Rico, 112–13; racial discrimination and, 150–51; wages and, 112–
  14
ILRF, 251, 252, 253, 281, 298
IMF, 2, 12, 95, 247, 249, 266, 267
Immigration: of agricultural labor, 152,
  153, 155–57, 245, 302; citizenship
  and, 22, 27, 31, 142, 146, 158, 177;
  costs of reproduction of the labor

Program, 116; efficiency studies of textile industry, 111; FAT, 260–61; free trade zones in, 116; helicopter sales to, 128; social reproduction in, 3, 299; textile industry in, 78, 126, 132, 159, 327n18o; wages in, 258; work environment in, 258

Meyer and Mendelsohn, 156

Milford, Massachusetts: anarchists in, 44, 45–46; funeral for murdered Italian textile worker in, 31–32; industry in, 23, 24, 29, 33–34; Italian settlement in, 23, 44, 307n2o; Latino immigrants in, 148, 331n14; nativism in, 148–49; Sacred Heart Parish, 23, 30–31; support of, for strikers, 31–32; utopian community of Hope Dale, 19

Military conscription, World War I, 46

Military contracts (U.S.), 94, 123–29, 135, 139, 161, 317n2

Military Keynesianism, 9, 224–25

Milliken, Roger, 21, 22, 123, 131, 132, 134

Milliken, Seth, 98, 186, 318n17

Milliken & Company: factory closings by, 139–40, 329n215; founding of, 138–39; protectionism and, 134, 141; unions opposed by, 139–40; U.S. government subsidies for, 136

Minercol, 284

Miners International Federation, 277

Mining industry in Colombia. *See* Cerrejón Zona Norte coal mine; Drummond Company; Sintercor; Sintracarbón; Sintramienergética; Sintraminercol; UMWA

Mintz, Sidney, 302

Mitchell, Mike, 215

Mobil Oil Company, 230

Mondragón, Hector, 262

Monsanto, 162

Morales, Evo, 262

More-looms-per-weaver movement, 37–40, 105

Morrill, Charles H., 28

Morris, John, 26, 34

Moscoso, Teodoro, 240, 347n64

Mountain Lumber Company, 333n46

Muerte a Revolucionarios del Nordeste, 195

Mullins, William, 65

Muñoz Marín, Luis, 112–13, 300

Murdock, Bill, 86

NAFTA, 132, 133

National Endowment for Democracy, 251

National Federation of Construction, Cement and Building Materials Workers, 241

National Industrial Recovery Act, 108, 319n32

National Labor Committee, 248, 252

National Labor Relations Board, 140, 329n215

National Peasant Association, 245–46

National Retail Association, 137

National Textile Workers Union. *See* Burlak, Anne; NTWU

Naumkeag Steam Cotton Company: coal as power source for, 295; contract negotiations and, 74–75; labor-management collaboration in, 9, 48, 51, 54–55; layoffs at, 56–57, 78; loan of, to Salem, 66, 69; reconstruction of New England factory, 37; relocation of, to U.S. South, 49, 53, 56, 78, 97; research plan of, 55–56, 58, 60, 62, 69, 72–73, 82–83; sale of, 105; stretch-outs, 56, 57, 64; union promotion of products of, 55, 131; wages at, 51, 58, 97; women employees of, 56–57, 83. *See also* Pequot Mills

Population Crisis Committee, 322n97

Ports for coal exports, 269, 270, 287–91

Power plants, U.S., 265, 266, 274, 282–84, 283–84, 295

Powers, Thomas, 15

PRD (Mexico), 261

Preston, Andrew W., 185, 186

PRIDCO, 109, 111, 112, 114

Primer enganche (contracting Colombian workers), 165, 166, 171

Progreso Latino, 333n66

Proletario, Il (newspaper), 24, 44–45

Protectionism: AFL-CIO on, 233–34; anti-immigrant politics and, 131, 134; "Buy American" campaigns and, 130, 131, 133, 134, 135, 223; CAFTA and, 135; Canadian coal industry and, 283; globalization and, 304; industry coalitions and, 135, 136–37; internationalism contrasted with, 135, 213; legislation for, 134; Milliken & Company support of, 139, 234; union support of, 130–31, 134; United States Business and Industry Council and, 135; World Trade Organization protests (Seattle, 1999) and, 226, 296

PTTI, 236, 244

Public employees unions, 250

Public relations campaigns, 140, 141

Public sector activism, 239

Public Service Alliance of Canada, 286

Public Services International, 237

Puerto Ricans: African Americans and, 157; on Connecticut tobacco farms, 156, 157; immigration of, to United States, 143, 152, 154–57; Italian locals (ILGWU) and, 150; population of, in New England, 144, 155, 330n5; racialized exclusion of, 150, 151; self-description of, as immigrants, 177; in textile industry, 149, 150–53, 155–

57, 159, 160, 170, 332n38; as U.S. citizens, 158, 177

Puerto Rico: contract labor and, 106–7, 320n51; Department of Labor and, 156; food stamp program in, 158, 333n60; imports from Drummond Coal mines, 267; incentives for factory relocation to, 98, 109–10, 111, 158, 321nn76, 81; Lockwood Greene & Company in, 99; as model for Point IV program, 115–16; New England investments in, 156; out-migration from, 158; PRIDCO, 109, 111, 112; social reproduction in, 299; state-supported industrialization in, 95; sugar production in, 155, 156, 333n46; textile industry in, 106, 107–8, 114, 158, 163, 322n92; tobacco processing in, 156; U.S. transfer payments to, 158, 333n60; wages in, 108, 110, 111, 113–14

Quiroz, Jairo, 285

"Race to the bottom," 11, 37, 211, 212, 268, 303

Rachleff, Peter, 344n7

Racism: Draper Loom Company strike and, 27–28; eugenics and, 17, 19, 20–21, 306n10; in housing for employees, 36; Pioneer Fund and, 8, 21, 131; protectionism and, 223; unions and, 150–51, 222, 245; upward mobility and, 145; whiteness and, 21, 28, 150, 223

Radicalism: accommodationism, 148–49; AIFLD opposition to, 234–35; American identity opposed to, 81–82, 223; of banana workers' labor movements, 191; of Italian workers, 44–45, 148, 149; in Naumkeag Steam Cotton Company strike (1933), 59,

97; strikes in, 84–85, 139; unionism in, 22; U.S. promotion of Japanese textile industry, 115; UTW southern campaign, 84–85, 224; worker recruitment, 105, 110. *See also* Milliken & Company

Soviet Union, 88, 237–38, 239

Spalding, Hobart, 248

Sparks, Ned, 65

Spartanburg, South Carolina: cotton industry in, 153; Draper Loom Company operations in, 17, 36–37, *37*, 43; Lockwood Greene & Company in, 99; Lowell, Mass., compared with, *99*; migration of New England textile industry to, 78; Milliken & Company in, 138–39; northern economic interests in, 98–99, 318n17; Rhode Island textile interests in, 98; synthetic textile manufacture in, 153; textile industry in, 17, 36–37, *37*; wartime contracts, 125–26; Whitney Mill, 78

Spartan Mills, 78, 123–24, 125

Speed-up, 38–40, 66, 73, 130, 295, 325n128

Standard Oil Company, 226, 228

"Stand Up for Steel," 223

State Board of Conciliation and Arbitration (Massachusetts), 50, 51

Step 2 program, 120, 136

Stevens, Robert Ten Broeck, 125

Stiglitz, Joseph, 259

Stretch-outs, 56, 57, 64

Strikes: alternate strategies to, 297, 298; American Celanese Corporation, 118, 245; Americanism and, 27, 28–30, 33, 34; Archer Rubber Company, 24; arrests of strikers, 31, 34, 85, 87; of banana workers, 193, 194, 197–98, 227, 228; Bread and Roses strike, 24, 26, 45, 88, 147–48; Draper Loom Company, 17, 24–27; firings as

retaliation for, 245; formation of new unions by, 73; Gaffney Manufacturing Company, 139; General Fabrics, 86; Hormel, UFCW Local P-9 protests against, 297, 298; legal action against, 276; local opposition to, 61, 63, 65, 66–67; mediation of, 51, 72–73, 551; military intervention, 193, 276; Milliken & Company, 139; NTWU, 160; in paper industry, 297–98; in petroleum industry in Colombia, 228, 229; police actions and, 31–32, 32–33, 35, 139, 298; relief efforts and, 67, 70–72, *71*, 86–87; Royal Weaving and General Fabric mills, 160; Santa Marta strike, 228; seniority system and, 56–57, 60, 62; support for, 229, 244, 297–98; Wagner Act and, 74. *See also* Factory closings; Naumkeag Steam Cotton Company strike; UFCO

Students United Against Sweatshops, 298

Sugar production, 155, 156, 333n46

Sweatshops, 152, 187, 298, 355n6

Sweeney, John, 248–49

Swift, Morrison, 28–29, 30

Synthetic textile manufacture, 126, 153, 161–62, 166

Tabaco (village), 264, 269, 273–74

Tanton, John, 306n16

Taxes: factory liquidations, 97, 104; federal income tax exemption in Puerto Rico, 158; as incentives for relocation, 97–98, 114; location of textile mills and, 53, 192; protectionist legislation and, 106; reform initiatives in, 101

Teachers' unions, 247, 250, 260

Teamsters, 251

Tejidos El Cóndor (Tejicóndor), 117, 165, 229

Aviva Chomsky is professor of history at Salem State College. She is the author of *West Indian Workers and the United Fruit Company in Costa Rica, 1870–1940* (1996) and *They Take Our Jobs! And Twenty Other Myths about Immigration* (2007), and the coeditor of *Identity and Struggle at the Margins of the Nation-State: The Laboring Peoples of Central America and the Hispanic Caribbean* (Duke, 1998) and *The Cuba Reader: History, Culture, Politics* (Duke, 2003).

Library of Congress Cataloging-in-Publication Data
Chomsky, Aviva
Linked labor histories : New England, Colombia, and the making of a global working class / Aviva Chomsky.
p. cm. — (American encounters/global interactions)
Includes bibliographical references and index.
ISBN-13: 978-0-8223-4173-4 (cloth : alk. paper)
ISBN-13: 978-0-8223-4190-1 (pbk. : alk. paper)
1. Industrial relations—New England—Case studies. 2. Industrial relations—Colombia—Case studies. 3. Globalization—Economic aspects. 4. Working class. 5. Labor unions. 6. Neoliberalism. I. Title.
HD8083.N34C56 2008
331.0974—dc22   2007043862